(continued from front page)

" I am writing to congratulate you on preparing an exceptional study guide. In five years of teaching this course I have never encountered a more thorough, comprehensive, concise and realistic preparation for this examination. "
Teacher, Davie, FL

" I have found your publications, *The Best Test Preparation ...,* to be exactly that. "
Teacher, Aptos, CA

" I used your *CLEP Introductory Sociology* book and rank it 99% — thank you! " *Student, Jerusalem, Israel*

" Your *GMAT* book greatly helped me on the test. Thank you. "
Student, Oxford, OH

" I recently got the *French SAT II* Exam book from REA. I congratulate you on first-rate French practice tests. "
Instructor, Los Angeles, CA

" Your *AP English Literature and Composition* book is most impressive. "
Student, Montgomery, AL

" The REA *LSAT* Test Preparation guide is a winner! "
Instructor, Spartanburg, SC

" Your *GMAT* book greatly helped me on the test. Thank you. "
Student, Oxford, OH

The Best Test Preparation for the

AP
French
Language Exam

2nd Edition

Ellen Valtri Knauer, M.A.
Instructor of French and Italian
West Chester Area School District, West Chester, PA

Research & Education Association
Visit our website at
www.rea.com

Research & Education Association
61 Ethel Road West
Piscataway, New Jersey 08854
E-mail: info@rea.com

The Best Test Preparation for the
AP FRENCH LANGUAGE EXAM

Printed in the United States of America

Library of Congress Control Number 2007940517

ISBN-13: 978-0-7386-0426-8
ISBN-10: 0-7386-0426-7

TABLE OF CONTENTS

Reading

Writing

Speaking

Detailed Explanations of Answers

Practice Test 1 393

Practice Test 2 445

Practice Test 3 497

Appendix—Audio CD Transcripts 549

FOREWORD

AVIS AU LECTEUR

It is my sincere hope that you will enjoy using this book as much as I have enjoyed writing it. The study of the French language has been my raison d'être for more than forty years.

I am pleased that I can provide you with a new, thorough, and user-friendly study aid to guide you in your preparation for the AP French Language exam. The drills were designed to allow you to concentrate on specific focus areas. The pre-exam exercises and three full-length practice tests provide the best opportunity to prepare for the actual exam. All answers are explained for you in detail. Complete transcripts are provided for everything you will hear on the CDs. All of the exchanges and dialogues were recorded by native speakers who model authentic accents, pronunciation, and intonation.

Work with this book on a regular basis; pace yourself as the exam approaches. If you have a question, you can reach me at this address: *EAKnauer@aol.com.*

Bon courage!
Ellen Valtri Knauer

AUTHOR ACKNOWLEDGMENTS

The author gratefully acknowledges the invaluable expertise of the following dedicated, veteran teachers, my colleagues and dear friends:

Pamela Bastings, AP French, East High School WCASD
Louise Classen, French and Spanish, Fugett Middle School WCASD
Susan Ostien, French and German, Great Valley High School GVSD
Gloria Schwenk, French 4 and 5, Henderson High School WCASD

and my *jusqu'au-boutiste*,

Carol Scott, AP French, Henderson High School WCASD

The author would also like to extend special thanks to:

David Sanderson, age 14, for the excellent sketches with which he brought to light the little scénarios of my mind's eye; Susan Shapot, Fugett Middle School WCASD and Keith Patton, Stetson Middle School WCASD, for their expertise and advice regarding computer issues; and Danielle Josset, *mon atout*, who wrote the student essay samples and who spent endless hours proofreading, advising, and corralling wayward accent marks.

ABOUT OUR AUTHOR

Ellen Knauer earned her B.A. in French Literature at Pennsylvania State University in State College, Pennsylvania. She also studied as an exchange student at the Université de Strasbourg, in Strasbourg, France. She was awarded the Copeland-Andelot Fellowship for graduate study at the University of Delaware, where she earned her M.A. in French Literature. Subsequent coursework at Immaculata College, Saint Joseph's College, West Chester University, and Temple University led to the completion of Pennsylvania teaching certificates in French, German, and Italian. Mrs. Knauer still enjoys taking courses and has accumulated more than 60 post-M.A. graduate credits. She has also published a series of animated lessons for the foreign language classroom in French, German, Italian, and Spanish. She currently teaches French and Italian for the West Chester Area School District, in West Chester, Pennsylvania.

ABOUT RESEARCH & EDUCATION ASSOCIATION

Founded in 1959, Research & Education Association (REA) is dedicated to publishing the finest and most effective educational materials—including software, study guides, and test preps—for students in middle school, high school, college, graduate school, and beyond. REA's test preparation series includes books and software for all academic levels in almost all disciplines. REA publishes test preps for students who have not yet entered high school, as well as high school students preparing to enter college. We invite you to visit us at *www.rea.com* to find out how "REA is making the world smarter."

ACKNOWLEDGMENTS

In addition to our author, we would like to thank Larry B. Kling, Vice President, Editorial, for his overall guidance; Pam Weston, Vice President, Publishing, for setting the quality standards for production integrity and managing the publication to completion; Diane Goldschmidt, Senior Editor, for coordinating revisions to this edition; Christine Saul, Senior Graphic Artist, for designing our cover; and Jeff LoBalbo, Senior Graphic Artist, for post-production file mapping.

We also extend our thanks to Publication Services for typesetting this edition.

CHAPTER 1
Excelling on the AP French Language Exam

EXCELLING ON THE AP FRENCH LANGUAGE EXAM

ABOUT THIS BOOK

This book provides a thorough review for the Advanced Placement French Language Examination written in a way that high school students will readily grasp and appreciate. REA's mission is to explain the subject matter in terms the student can understand and benefit from.

The full-length practice exams included in this book help you get ready for the actual exam. Use them, along with the detailed explanations of answers, to help determine your strengths and weaknesses, and to prepare yourself to score well on exam day.

ABOUT THE ADVANCED PLACEMENT PROGRAM

The Advanced Placement program is designed to provide high school students with the opportunity to pursue college-level studies. The program consists of two components: an AP course and and AP exam.

Students are expected to gain college-level skills and acquire college-level knowledge of French through the AP course. Upon completion of the course, students take the AP exam in French Language. Test results are used to grant course credit and/or determine placement level in the subject when entering college.

AP exams are offered every May. For more information contact the College Board at:

AP Services
P.O. Box 6671
Princeton, NJ 08541-6671
Phone: (609) 771-7300 or (888) 225-5427
Fax: (609) 530-0482
E-mail: *apexams@info.collegeboard.org*
Web site: *www.collegeboard.com*

ABOUT THE EXAM

The AP French Language Exam is approximately two and a half hours long. It tests your ability to understand both written and spoken French. It also tests the ease and fluency with which you can respond in speaking and in writing. No dictionaries or reference materials are permitted during the exam.

The test is divided into four sections. Each one represents a targeted skill area: listening comprehension, reading comprehension, writing ability, and speaking ability. Each of the four sections has the same value and therefore represents one-fourth of your total score.

Multiple-Choice Test Sections

Listening and reading skills are tested with multiple-choice questions. You will be expected to choose the correct answer from a field of four different possibilities for each multiple-choice question. You will mark your choice as A, B, C, or D on an answer grid that is provided in your test booklet.

In the listening portion of the exam, you will hear a series of short exchanges between speakers. Each exchange is heard twice. While you listen, you will have four possible rejoinders in front of you. You are expected to pick the remark most likely to follow if the conversation were to continue.

The listening section then goes on to present a series of longer dialogues. After each dialogue you will hear four or five questions. Each question is heard twice. You will answer the questions by choosing the best response among the four choices provided. You have about 25 minutes to complete the listening portion of the exam.

You will then have approximately one hour to complete the reading segment of the test. The passages vary in length and subject matter. They usually come from French literature (mostly prose), newspaper or magazine articles, or virtually any nontechnical, nonfiction text.

Each passage is followed by a series of questions for which you are given four possible answers. Again, you mark your choice by blackening the corresponding letter on the answer sheet in your text booklet. The writing and speaking segments of the test are not multiple-choice. They are both free response.

Writing Test Sections

There are <u>three</u> writing exercises. First you will be given a passage that has <u>single words</u> missing here and there. The missing words are represented by numbered blanks. You are expected to <u>write out</u> the missing word in a column of blanks to the right of the text. None of the answers in this first fill-in segment will be verbs.

Next, you will have a similar passage devoted entirely to verbs. This time, the blank indicates the infinitive form of the verb you are to use. You must provide the correct tense. The verb could also be a command form, or you may have to determine whether to use the indicative or the subjunctive. The verb you supply must match its subject. If the verb is reflexive, you will need to include the reflexive pronoun that matches it. If the verb is in a compound tense, you will need the correct auxiliary verb, the correct past participle, and possibly agreement.

The final writing segment is the essay. There is no choice of topic. Only one essay question is given. You are expected to write a coherent and well-organized essay in French in response to the given question. Your answer should showcase your mastery of verbs and grammatical structures. Your vocabulary should be varied, well-chosen, and as idiomatic as possible. That means you should <u>not think in English</u> and then try to translate into French. Being idiomatic means thinking like a French person, or at least asking yourself how a French person would say what you mean. Plan to write a minimum of three paragraphs and at least 200 words. You will have one hour and five minutes to complete the writing section of the test.

Allot at least 40 minutes for the essay; use the rest of the time for the fill-ins. Always read over what you have written, checking your spelling, accent marks, and agreement. Don't be nervous about the essay; the questions are always very open-ended and generally require your thoughtful opinion rather than specific facts. You will definitely be able to think of an answer; your challenge will be to express it as best you can.

Speaking Test Sections

You will be recording your own voice in the speaking segment of the exam. It is entirely free-response—that is, you may say whatever you think best answers the question. You will have approximately 15 minutes for this segment of the exam.

You will have 90 seconds to look over some drawings. You will then answer three questions based on what takes place in the sketches. You have exactly 60 seconds to record <u>each</u> answer. The first question asks you to tell what takes place in the sketch or series of sketches. The second and third questions use the drawings as a point of departure for a more general discussion.

There will be two sets of sketches on which you must comment. The first set is generally a series of five events that take place in sequence. The second set will have only two pictures, which you are usually asked to compare or contrast. Sometimes the second set has only one sketch with a split-screen effect. Look over the sketches carefully and jot down details as you note them and ideas as they come. The sketches invariably depict a typical life experience, and in that respect, they are not difficult at all.

It is imperative that you make an effort to familiarize yourself with whatever recording equipment you will be expected to use. Ask about this well in advance. If your testing location is your own school, ask to see exactly what you will be using. Get permission to practice using the device well before the exam. This will help you so much! If you are experienced in using the equipment, you will be <u>calm</u>. You will be able to concentrate on what you are going to say, rather than worrying whether the volume is adequate or whether you're close enough to the microphone. Work out all of those details <u>before</u> the exam, and practice over and over until using the equipment is a cinch for you. Some schools allow students to use their own tape recorders. This is ideal. Buy your recorder well ahead of time and get comfortable using it.

TOOLS TO HELP YOU PREPARE FOR THE EXAM

Read and study this book thoroughly and do all of the drills provided. Keep a little notebook in which you can compile all of your written answers. Keep track of what you have completed and what you have yet to cover. Make notes on things you've mastered. Identify your weaknesses and devote extra effort to those areas. <u>Take your time</u>. Work no more than two or three hours at a sitting. Come back to it later when you are fresh. You will have the best possible results from a <u>steady series of two-hour sessions spread over a long period of time</u>. The first and most important answer to the question "What will you need?" is <u>time</u>! Schedule time to work with this book on a regular basis, just as you might schedule a regular workout or run. When you have completed the drills, try your hand at the pre-exam exercises, and then move on to the three practice tests. Explanations are provided for every answer! Go over them carefully.

You should invest in the best and most complete French-English dictionary you can afford. There are many good ones available. *Le Robert* and *Oxford-Hachette* are both excellent choices. My personal all-time favorite dictionary is *Harrap's*. It is the best French-English dictionary I have come upon in over 40 years of studying French. There is one caveat: *Harrap's* is written for British speakers of English, and you may consider that a drawback. Definitions may include terms that are not readily familiar to American speakers of English.

If you have the inclination, it is also very useful to have access to an all-French dictionary, such as the inimitable *Petit Larousse*. This is a wise investment, especially if you will be continuing with your study of French in college. Looking up a word in an all-French dictionary allows you to study <u>the way</u> the word is explained, as well as its meaning. It exposes you to authentic expression. You glimpse the actual choreography of the words in use. The more you delve into this all-French milieu, the easier it is to come away with a truly Gallic turn of phrase.

You should acquire a tape recorder with which to record your voice or use your voice mail or answering machine to practice speaking French. Call yourself up and leave a message in French! Do it every day. The more you do it, the easier it becomes. Recording your voice allows you to hear how you actually sound. You can then evaluate what you hear. Is your accent authentic? Are your vowels pure? Are your nasal sounds accurate? Is your pronunciation correct?

Once you have your recording device, tape yourself reading a passage aloud, reciting a poem, or singing a song in French. This is the best kind of activity for working on your accent and correct pronunciation. Ad-lib into your microphone; describe your room or your current state of mind. Mute the television set and do your own voice-over in French.

STUDYING FOR THE EXAM

Ideally, you should begin your preparation for the exam six months ahead of your testing date. This deluxe approach produces the best possible result. Look at your calendar, and map out your plan. Set aside time to work regularly with this book. Schedule time to watch French films, to read French novels and periodicals, and to listen to French singers. Pencil in some time each week to explore French chat rooms and various French language sites on the Internet. Team up with other friends who are also preparing for the test. Vow to speak to one another in French on a regular basis. Send each other instant messages and e-mails in French.

Starting four months ahead of your test date will still give you enough time to do an adequate job of preparing. This would be a "good" plan for success, provided that you remain faithful to a regular regimen of review, study, reading, writing, speaking, and listening.

Planning a calendar, no matter which plan you adopt, gives you an excellent overview of just how much time you have at your disposal. You can schedule what you'd like to have accomplished by a certain date. It's also a good idea to record how much time you've actually spent working. Time will slip by quickly. Suddenly you may notice that it's been two weeks since you last worked. Not good!

The bare-bones approach gives you only two months to prepare for this behemoth of an exam. That is really not much time at all; yet, with unswerving dedication, you could probably finish this book, possibly catch a few films, and do some reading, writing, and speaking.

What to Read

Try to read at least two short French novels a month. That comes out to a dozen books in six months, eight books in four months, or four books on the bare-bones plan of two months. You will find some excellent titles to choose from on the list provided in this chapter. The books were selected for their ease in reading, their relatively short length, and the pleasure that you will undoubtedly experience while reading them.

How do you get your hands on these books? They are all available in paperback. One of the best sources of these little *livres de poche* is your own French teacher. There are a few undeniable and universal truths about French teachers. First, they always cut up calendars at the end of the year. The pictures thus obtained are then filed away for possible future classroom use. It is very stressful for them if two good pictures are back to back and cutting out one destroys the other. Secondly, they save cheese boxes, cancelled *Métro* tickets, and little round candy tins. Thirdly, and happily for you, most of them have a considerable personal library of paperbacks, which they are willing to lend to responsible students.

You can also scrounge French paperbacks wherever good used books congregate. If you live near a college or university, the student bookstore will have different titles at different times of the year, depending on the courses offered. Once you've found a good title, share it with a friend.

In addition to the novels in the list on the next page, make an effort to read as many French newspapers and magazines as possible. All French publications now have websites where you can read articles daily. Simply go to your search engine and type in *Le Monde*, *Le Figaro*, *Paris-Match*, *L'Express*, *Salut les Copains*, *Elle*, or *Marie-Claire*. Read only what interests you. There is a huge variety of specialty magazines as well. *Jazzman* and *Le Monde de la Musique* are just a few examples. Read about your own interests. There are French magazines about cycling, skiing, cars, soccer, tennis, and fashion. There are also gossipy movie-star magazines, if that's what you like. Make an effort on your search engine and you will be amazed at the possibilities you will find. Family members and friends who fly often should be pressed into service, as well. French language magazines are often available during a flight and in airport lounges, usually without cost. Air France provides a huge selection of free reading material for its passengers.

Once you have begun your preparation for the AP exam, you should be reading in French <u>daily</u>.

Here is a list of some very enjoyable French paperbacks. None of them are very long or very hard to read. This is by no means a complete list. It is rather just a starting point.

The list is alphabetical by author.

Alain-Fournier, Henri	*Le grand Meaulnes*
Aymé, Marcel	*Le passe-muraille*
Balzac, Honoré de	*Le Père Goriot*
Barratier, Christophe	*Les Choristes: Le journal de Clément Mathieu*
Begag, Azouz	*Le Gone du Chaâba*
Camus, Albert	*La Peste***
Colette	*Gigi*
Colette, Sidonie-Gabrielle	*Claudine à l'École*
Colette, Sidonie-Gabrielle	*La Chatte*
Dumas, Alexandre *père*	*Le Comte de Monte-Cristo*
Flaubert, Gustave	*Un cœur simple*
Garcin, Christian	*Le vol du pigeon voyageur*
Gavalda, Anna	*Je voudrais que quelqu'un m'attende quelque part*
Gavalda, Anna	*Je l'aimais*
Gide, André	*La Symphonie pastorale*
Léger, Diane Carmel	*La butte à Pétard* (http://www.boutondoracadie.com)
MacDonald, Patricia*	*La double mort de Linda*
MacDonald, Patricia	*La fille sans visage*
MacDonald, Patricia	*Une femme sous surveillance*
Maupassant, Guy de	*Boule de Suif*
Maupassant, Guy de	*La Parure*
Montherlant, Henri de	*Les Bestiaires*
Orsenna, Erik	*Les Chevaliers du Subjonctif*
Orsenna, Erik	*La grammaire est une chanson douce*
Pagnol, Marcel	*Jean de Florette*
Pagnol, Marcel	*Manon des sources*
Pagnol, Marcel	*Le Château de ma mère*
Pagnol, Marcel	*La Gloire de mon père*
Pagnol, Marcel	*Topaze*
Perrault, Charles	*Contes*
Queneau, Raymond	*Exercices de Style*
Queneau, Raymond	*Zazie dans le métro*
Sagan, Françoise	*Bonjour tristesse*
Saint-Exupéry, Antoine de	*Le Petit Prince*

Saint-Exupéry, Antoine de	*Vol de Nuit*
Sartre, Jean-Paul	*Huis-Clos*
Sempé, René Goscinny	*Le petit Nicholas a des ennuis*
Sempé, René Goscinny	*Les vacances du petit Nicholas*
Simenon, Georges	*L'amie de Madame Maigret*
Simenon, Georges	*Touriste de bananes*
Verne, Jules	*L'Île mystérieuse*
Zola, Émile	*Germinal***

* Patricia MacDonald is an American writer whose books are widely popular in France. She lives in Cape May, NJ.

** *La Peste* and *Germinal* are longer and perhaps somewhat harder to read than the other titles, but they are worth the time and effort.

Just a few pointers on how to approach this kind of reading:

(1) Remember that you are not writing essays or book reports on these novels. Try to read them the way you would read any book for pleasure. The secret lies in finding one that you will enjoy. Try a few pages, and if it's just not going to hold your attention, stop.

(2) It is not a crime if you don't understand every single word on a page. Dive in. If you've read the whole page and have a pretty good idea about what's going on, that's good enough. As you read further, things will become clearer and you will discover that you can learn new words just by context. Sometimes you will have a hunch about what a word means. Don't run right to the dictionary. Be patient. You may find that you were right all along. Once you get the hang of this kind of reading, your comfort level will increase and your vocabulary will quadruple.

(3) Don't allow yourself to go to the dictionary more than once per page. Trust me here. If you have only one ticket (for a trip to the dictionary) per page, you will slowly begin to analyze which word you should spend it on. Which word is most crucial to your understanding of this passage? The more conscientious the student, the harder this is to learn. Go with the flow, and guess if you can. The point is not to get bogged down with too many stops and starts. Just try it. The dictionary is a great tool, but here you are trying to wean yourself from it just long enough to develop confidence in your ability to figure out what's going on.

What to Watch

While preparing for the exam, try to watch as many movies in French as you can. Try to work in a film at least once a week. If you're not in the mood to study the subjunctive one evening, pop in a video or DVD. Many French films are available at your local video rental. Short of visiting France or Canada, this is the absolute best way to prepare yourself for the listening portion of your test. Films provide an ideal opportunity to hear spoken French, and <u>that is what you need</u>! Think of the generations of French students before you who did not have DVDs such as we have today. Finding a film in French was almost impossible in the old days. Take full advantage of this excellent resource at your fingertips!

What follows is a list of wonderful films for you to enjoy:

- *Adèle H.*
- *Un Air de Famille*
- *Amélie (Le Fabuleux destin d'Amélie Poulain)*
- *L'Argent de Poche*
- *Les Apprentis*
- *L'Auberge espagnole*
- *Au revoir les enfants*
- *Le Battement d'ailes du papillon*
- *Boudu sauvé*
- *La Bûche*
- *Camille Claudel*
- *Le Château de ma mère*
- *Les Choristes*
- *Le Colonel Chabert*
- *Cousin, Cousine*
- *Cyrano de Bergérac*
- *Les Demoiselles de Rochefort*
- *Le Dernier métro*
- *Être et Avoir*
- *La Gloire de mon père*
- *Trois Hommes et un couffin*
- *Un Homme et une femme*
- *Jean de Florette*
- *Un Long dimanche de fiançailles*
- *Manon des sources*
- *Le Retour de Martin Guerre*

- *Les Parapluies de Cherbourg*
- *Mon Oncle d'Amérique*
- *Peau d'Âne*
- *Place Vendôme*
- *Touchez Pas au Grisbi*
- *Vatel*

Don't forget that American DVDs frequently feature foreign-language soundtracks or subtitles as options. If your family has a DVD collection, be sure to look through your titles to see whether you can listen to any of them in French. Being familiar with the story enhances your ability to understand what you hear. You may already have a French soundtrack that you weren't aware of in your collection of films at home.

What to Listen To

Try to obtain some CDs with French lyrics. Whenever you're doing a chore at home, or just relaxing, French can be on in the background. When you drive a long distance, listen to French. Read French magazines for teenagers, such as *Salut*, to find out who is currently popular. There are French rappers and hip-hop artists. The artist doesn't really have to be hip and new for you to benefit from listening, though. Old smoothies like Charles Aznavour, Jacques Brel, Yves Duteil, or Yves Montand will do just as well.

Record your own voice and listen to it. You don't have to sing, just read aloud. There are wonderful audio programs you can subscribe to as well. *Champs-Élysées* sends a monthly CD or audiocassette with an interesting and authentic radio broadcast format. All the speakers are native, and a magazine that allows you to follow the script verbatim is also available. Notations for study are included.

You may be able to get a Canadian radio program if you live close enough to receive the broadcast signal (or if you can find it on the internet). I was surprised to discover just such a program late one night as I fiddled with the channel dial in southern Pennsylvania! I was able to find the same French broadcast channel many times over, from about 11 PM on. Check your TV schedule for French films or French programming.

Don't dismiss listening to French songs. Your goal should be to increase your exposure to spoken French as much as possible. Listening to songs is a legitimate and effective way to do this. The musical format is also an ideal conduit for learning and remembering. It's a painless way to stay in contact with French. Another unexpected bonus is that the music and words don't have to be your primary focus for you to benefit from them. Do your nails, clean out a drawer, or wash the car while you listen. Let the words seep into your consciousness on a secondary level, just as the words of any other song would. It's this very relaxing and indirect route that allows music to leave its impression on us so effortlessly.

What to Write

If your French teacher does not already require you to write on a regular basis, you need to begin doing so now. The simplest and easiest thing to do is to keep a diary, or *journal intime*. Place a little notebook and pencil by your bed. Write a few paragraphs each night as you settle in. Try to capture a few thoughts, maybe what you did today, or what you hope to accomplish tomorrow. Students often enjoy this little routine and relish the privacy afforded them by writing in French instead of English. They are able to collect themselves and reflect a bit. Many find themselves writing at length. Of course you can always try your hand at poetry. You can also concoct a story to which you add a chapter each evening. Make your heroine suffer the consequences if you've had a bad day. The more you write, the easier it becomes. As you step up your reading and listening exposure to French, your writing skills will improve in tandem.

Where to Go

If you should have the good fortune to travel to France or Canada on a school trip or with your family, make every effort to use your language skills. Don't make the mistake so many students do—staying together en masse and maintaining their English idiom just as though they were back in the United States. If you've traveled that far, be brave enough to wean yourself from the group long enough to make a purchase all by yourself, to exchange pleasantries with the gentleman at the front desk of your hotel, or to strike up a little conversation with the person riding in the elevator with you. Each little success begets another.

For those who aren't traveling to France, the Internet is the next best thing. There are French chat rooms, forums on film, politics, and cheese. You can make a virtual visit to the Louvre, to the Eiffel tower, or to any region you so desire. For the AP French Language student, the Internet provides a dizzying array of current and interesting articles to read, as well as the opportunity to interact with other French speakers. There are audio dictionaries that pronounce words for you. You can listen to speeches by Charles de Gaulle. You can hear Colette read her own work aloud.

Avail yourself of these wonderful resources. They will help you keep your commitment to your goal of preparing fully and well for the AP French Language Exam.

Thinking in French!

If you immerse yourself in French for an extended period of time you may very well discover yourself thinking in the language. It is very exciting the first time you realize that this has happened to you. The immersion must be extended, let's say a full day, and you must have been actively using the language, speaking or writing at length. Suddenly it will dawn on you that you are thinking in French.

It is a very gratifying moment. Many people remember when it first happened to them. Of course, the more often you use the language exclusively, the more frequently it will happen, and over time, just becomes routine. When you begin to think spontaneously in French, it is your mind's way of telling you that it is quite comfortable using it.

It is possible to experiment with thinking in French before it comes to you spontaneously. Try making a deliberate effort to think in French and see how you fare. It is best to try this when you are alone so that no one interrupts your thoughts. Just do whatever you would normally do but make a conscious effort to think about each step in French. It's fun to try. You don't need a pencil or any equipment to do it, and it's excellent training. You will give yourself a chance to think in French when there is no pressure to perform, and therein lies its beauty. When you've used French all day long and then drift off to sleep after having written in your journal or read in your novel for a while, who's to say that you won't dream in French, too?

CHAPTER 2
AP French Review

AP FRENCH REVIEW

ALPHABET AND PRONUNCIATION

The French Alphabet

Letter	French Name	Sample Word	English Approximation
a	*a (ah)*	*ma, âge*	Mama, at
b	*bé*	*beau*	boy
c	*cé*	*ce, carte*	cell, car[1]
d	*dé*	*deux*	day
e	*e (euh)*	*été, très*	bay, bet
f	*effe*	*Fifi*	free
g	*gé*	*Gigi, garçon*	pleasure, go[2]
h	*hache*	silent or aspirated	
i	*i (ee)*	*Mimi*	bee
j	*ji*	*je*	pleasure
k	*ka*	*képi*	keep
l	*elle*	*lait*	low
m	*emme*	*maman*	my
n	*enne*	*ne*	no
o	*o (oh)*	*sot, sotte*	ho ho, hut
p	*pé*	*pépin*	peep[3]
q	*ku*	*qui*	key (no *w!*)
r	*erre*	*rire*	rear
s	*esse*	*son*	sea
t	*té*	*tante*	tea
u	*u* [y]	*eu*	(no equivalent)

v	*vé*	*voir*	veal
w	*double vé*	*WC*	veal[4]
x	*ixe*	*fixe*	so**ck**s
y	*i grec*	*yaourt*	**y**es
z	*zède*	*zéro*	**z**oo

1. [s] vs [k]: The [s] sound (as in **c**ell) occurs if **c** has a **cedilla** attached to it (**ç**), or if **c** appears in front of **i**, **e**, or **y**. The sound of **c** is hard [k] (as in **c**ar) if it appears next to any other letter, or if it is sounded in final position (as in ave**c**).

2. [ʒ] vs [g]: Similarly, **g** is soft (**G**i**g**i) in front of **i**, **e**, or **y**, and hard (**g**o) any other time.

3. The French **p** does not produce the little puff of air that escapes when **p** is pronounced in English. The same is true for the sound of **t**.

4. **W** is always pronounced as though it were a **v**.

The French alphabet uses the same 26 letters we have in the English alphabet. The pronunciation attributed to each letter is quite different, of course, in French. Study the charts provided here and give special attention to the French vowels and nasal sounds.

Mastering the <u>International Phonetic Alphabet</u> (IPA) symbols used in French is well worth your time. All good dictionaries provide pronunciation via IPA symbols. The IPA provides a foolproof guide to good pronunciation because there is only one symbol for each sound.

Below is a useful guide to correct French pronunciation:

The International Phonetic Alphabet Symbols Used in French

Symbol	Sound	Sample Words to Say Aloud (*Prononcez ces mots à haute voix*)
Consonants		
p	*pas*	*papa, poupée, pépin, peu, pure, près, crêpe, point, pain, pont*
b	*bas*	*baba, bébé, beau, belle, bout, but, bien, bonbon*
m	*ma*	*mes, mou, mot, molle, mur, ment, mon, maman*
t	*ta*	*tes, tout, tôt, tel, te, tu, toi, tiens, tant, tonton*
d	*doux*	*dit, des, de, date, dur, dans, dindon*
n	*nous*	*ni, né, ne, net, nœud, nounou, nain, non*

Symbol	Sound	Sample Words to Say Aloud (*Prononcez ces mots à haute voix*)
ɲ	*ligne*	*cygne, gagne, mignon, montagne, campagne, compagnon*
k	*car*	*carte, clair, crayon, avec, cure, conte, képi, klaxon, qui, quoi*
g	*gare*	*gui, gaz, gai, gauche, goût, aigu, gras, gant, gain*
f	*fou*	*faux, fixe, fée, fête, feu, flou, franc, fois, fin, font, enfant, photo*
v	*vous*	*vie, va, vaut, vol, veut, vu, viens, voie, vin, vont, WC, wagon*
s	*sot*	*ça, ce, ici, si, sa, seau, sotte, seul, sur, sans, son, singe, basse, passion, nation, calvitie, démocratie, six, dix, soixante*
z	*zoo*	*zède, zéro, zut, aise, oiseau, présent, maison, raison, voisin*
ʃ	*chaud*	*chichi, chat, chaise, chou, chut, échelle, fiche, flèche, franche*
ʒ	*je*	*jaune, jeune, joli, jupe, nage, neige, givre, gentil, gèle, Égypte*
r	*rit*	*rive, rat, rétro, rêve, parure, parent, ronron*
l	*lit*	*libellule, lilas, les, le, leur, loup, lotte, lin, lent*

Semi-Vowels

Symbol	Sound	Sample Words to Say Aloud
j	*hier*	*janvier, pied, piano, radio, rions, Lyon;* also *œil, fille*
w	*moi*	*oui, ouate, vouer, voyage, poids, soi, toi, trois, mois, moins*
ɥ	*huit*	*cuivre, suis, nuit, fuit, puis, bruit, fruit, pluie*

Vowels[1]

Symbol	Sound	Sample Words to Say Aloud
i	*Mimi*	*chimie, difficile, fini, midi, rigide, vite, cygne, rythmique*
u	*fou*	*doux, douze, joue, sous, route, toujours, troupe, vous*
y	*sur*	*bu, butte, cure, cru, du, juge, mur, sur, pur, vu, menu*

Symbol	Sound	Sample Words to Say Aloud (*Prononcez ces mots à haute voix*)
e	*été*	*aîné, bébé, ces, chez, léger, les, mes, préférer, répéter*
ɛ	*très*	*bergère, bête, cher, chèvre, près, sept, seize, tête, zède*
ə	*le*	*je, ne, me, le, te, de, ce, se, que, reçu, harceler, revoir*
o	*beau*	*chaud, drôle, eau, flot, mot, maux, pot, peau, sot, seau*
ɔ	*botte*	*donne, bonne, bord, brosse, fort, prof, sort, sommes*
ø	*peu*	*aveu, deux, émeut, feu, jeudi, œufs, pleut, vieux*
œ	*peur*	*beurre, heure, œuf, leur, meurt, seul, sœur, veulent*
a	*ma*	*cage, la, pas, quoi, rage, sa, sac, sage, ta, tabac*
ɑ	*fâche*	*âge, âme, blâme, Jacques, Jeanne, pâte, ras, tâche*

Nasals[2]

Symbol	Sound	Sample Words to Say Aloud
ã	*enfant*	*an, ambre, blanc, cent, chant, grand, en, paon, semble, temps, tremblant*
ɛ̃	*vin*	*bain, crin, main, mince, pain, pince, plein, rein, sein, thym, vingt*
ɔ̃	*mon*	*bon, conte, compte, dont, font, mont, nom, ombre, pont, plomb, rond, ronron, son, sont, tromper, vont*
œ̃	*un*	*brun, chacun, défunt, humble, lundi, opportun, parfum, chacun, défunt, humble, lundi, opportun, parfum*

1. Learn how to distinguish an open syllable (it ends in a vowel sound) from a closed syllable (it ends in a consonant sound). The word *sot* [so] is an open syllable. In the word *sotte*, the syllable [sɔt] is closed by the consonant [t]. The vowels [o] and [e] appear exclusively in open syllables, whereas [ɔ] and [ɛ] appear in closed syllables.

2. <u>Never</u> pronounce the *n* or *m* that follows a nasal vowel. The *n* (or *m*) only signals to make the vowel nasal; it is <u>silent</u>!

Accent Marks Used In French

There are five accent marks used in French. An accent mark most often signals how a vowel should be pronounced. In some cases the accent merely marks the site of a letter that is no longer in the word. Sometimes the accent is applied to distinguish one short word from another.

1. *L'accent aigu* (**acute accent**) appears on the letter *e* (*é*) when it must be pronounced [*e*] as in *été*.

2. *L'accent grave* (**grave accent**) appears on the letter *e* (*è*) when it must be pronounced [ɛ] as in *très*. In the word *voilà*, the accent indicates stress. It can also be used to avoid confusion in short, similar words. Compare: *a* (**has**) versus *à* (**at, to**), *ou* (**or**) versus *où* (**where**), *la* (**the**) versus *là* (**there**).

3. *L'accent circonflexe* (**circumflex accent**) is often placed over a vowel to mark the loss of a consonant in an earlier version of the word, usually an *s*. By reinserting the *s* in *hâte*, for example, we can see how the French word was once more like the English word **haste**. Try these: *arrêt, forêt, hôte, intérêt*.

   Use the sound [ɛ] when the circumflex appears over *e*, and the sound [ɑ] when it appears over *a*. When the circumflex appears over *o*, it could be pronounced [o] as in *drôle*, or [ɔ] as in *rôti*.

4. *Le tréma* (called the **diaeresis** in English) appears on the second of two adjacent vowels to separate them into two different syllables. *Noël*, therefore, is pronounced with two syllables, as are *haïr*, *iämbe*, *maïs*, and *naïf*. In proper names like *Saint-Saëns*, the *tréma* serves to silence the letter under it.

5. *La cédille* (called the **cedilla** in English) is attached under the letter *c* when it should be pronounced [s] as in *français* or *François*.

Drill 1: French Pronunciation

Complete the statement by writing an IPA symbol in the blank:

1. When the letter combination **gn** appears in a French word, the resulting sound will always be _____.

2. The vowel **o** becomes nasal when followed by an **n** or an **m** in the same syllable. Therefore both **on** and **om** result in the nasal sound _____. (Note: If the letter **e** follows the **n** or **m**, <u>the nasal will not occur</u>, as in *téléphone* or *tome*.)

3. The cedilla (*garçon*) always produces the sound of _____.

4. A single **s** in between two vowels (*raisin*) always results in the sound _____.

5. The combination of **un** or **um** (without the presence of an **e** as in *une*) always produces the nasal sound _____.

6. All of the following combinations: **an**, **am**, **en**, **em**, and **aon** (without an **e** as in *âme*) produce the nasal sound _____.

7. In the combinations of **tion** or **tie**, the letter **t** produces the sound of _____.

8. The combinations **ain**, **ein**, **in**, **im**, **yn**, and **ym** (without an **e** as in *fine*) produce the nasal sound _____.

9. When an *accent grave è*, or an *accent circonflèxe ê* is applied, or if the letter **e** shares its syllable with a following consonantal sound, as in *cher*, it is pronounced _____. This type of syllable (which ends in a consonant) is called a "closed syllable."

10. When an *accent aigu é* is applied, or if **e** appears in an open syllable, as in *mes* (ending in the vowel sound alone), it is always pronounced _____.

11. When the letter *o* appears in a closed syllable as in *école*, it is pronounced _____.

12. When *u* + *i* appear together in the same syllable, as in the word *suis*, they create the semi-vowel _____. When *o* + *i* combine in the same syllable, as in *moins*, they create the semi-vowel _____.

13. This vowel sound does not exist in English and occurs in French whenever the letter *u* appears alone, that is, not in combination with another vowel. It is pronounced _____.

14. When the vowels *eu* share their syllable with a following consonantal sound as in *peur*, the combination is noted as _____.

15. When the vowels *eu* end in an open syllable, as in *peu*, the combination is noted as _____.

16. Sometimes the vowel *e* is not really essential for comprehension. Compare *je* versus *j'ai*, *ne* versus *n'ai*, *le* versus *l'*. If this optional *e* sound is pronounced, it is transcribed by the symbol _____.

17. The letters *au*, *eau*, *o*, and *ô* produce the sound _____.

18. When this vowel is not nasalized by an *n* or an *m*, its sound is <u>always</u> _____, regardless of the type of syllable it appears in.

19. The letter *y* produces the same sound as _____.

20. The letter *a* is pronounced _____ in open syllables and _____ in closed syllables.

21. The letter *x* can be pronounced [**ks**] as in *Aix*, *excellent*, *Mexique*; however, in the numbers *six*, *dix*, and *soixante*, it is pronounced _____.

22. When the vowel *i* ends the syllable, and the next syllable begins with another vowel (as in *piano* or *janvier*), the syllable containing the *i* will produce the semi-vowel _____. (Note: This semi-vowel can also arise after <u>vowel</u> + *il*, as in *œil*, or <u>vowel</u> + *ill*, as in *famille* and *feuille*.)

23. The letter **g**, in front of an **i**, **e**, or **y**, as well as the letter **j**, produces the sound _____.

24. The combination of **c + h** is usually pronounced _____.

25. The letter **w** is always pronounced _____.

Transcribe these words into phonetic symbols:

26. *chaud* (two sounds, two symbols needed for this word) _____

27. *bref* (four sounds, four symbols needed) _____

28. *meurt* (three sounds, three symbols needed) _____

29. *ont* (only one sound, one symbol) _____

30. *pain* (two sounds heard, two symbols needed) _____

Drill 1—Answers and Explanations

1. ɲ   This is always true. Here are more sample words: *champagne*, *cocagne*, *Allemagne*, *Espagne*.

2. ɔ̃   A very common nasal, this is the one that appears in words like *mon*, *ton*, and *son*, or *ombre* and *sombre*.

3. s   This is always true. More sample words: *ça, déçu, façon, reçu, soupçon*.

4. z   This is always true and worth remembering. More sample words: *choisir, framboise, française, obèse, osier, usé*.

5. œ̃   This is the least common of the four nasal sounds, yet it is heard constantly in the masculine article *un*.

6. ã   This is the nasal heard in *décembre, faon, flan, lampe, manger, menthe, pendant,* and *sans*.

7. s   More examples: *natation, autocratie*.

8. ɛ̃   A very common nasal heard in *fin, frein, lin, olympique, saint, simple, syndicat, sympathique, Reims*.

9. ɛ   Here are more examples: *être, fer, fête, guerre, mère, mètre, Michel, père*. Note: the same sound can arise from the combination *ei* in closed syllables as in *neige, seize, reine,* and *treize*.

10. e   Always heard in open syllables, such as *danser, dansé, Élysée,* and *ses*. Note that *accent aigu é* is always pronounced [e], whereas *accent grave è* and *accent circonflèxe ê* are pronounced [ɛ].

11. ɔ   Other examples: *folle, notre, homme, port*.

12. ɥ / w   Other examples of [ɥ]: fuir, huile, huître, suivre. Other examples of [w]: *fois, quoi, soi*. Note: *o + u* and *o + y* also produce the [w], as in *louer, Louis, voyons*.

13. y   More examples: *cruel, su, super, tu*.

14. **œ**

15. **ø**

16. **ə**

17. **o**   More examples: *au*, *aux*, *épaule*, *faux*, *fléau*, *joli*, *hôtel*. Exception: *Paul* is pronounced [pɔl].

18. **i**

19. **i**

20. **a / ɑ**

21. **s**

22. **j**

23. **ʒ**

24. **ʃ**   There are exceptions, such as *chœur*, *chorale*, *chorégraphie*, *orchestre*, and *orchidée*, in which *c + h* produces the hard sound [k].

25. **v**

26. **ʃo**

27. **brɛf**

28. **mœr**

29. **ɔ̃**

30. **pɛ̃**

CARDINAL AND ORDINAL NUMBERS

A cardinal number is invariable when it appears as an adjective in front of a noun, except for *un*, which has a feminine form, *une*.

Beginning with the number 17, *dix-sept*, and up to the number 99, *quatre-vingt-dix-neuf*, use a hyphen in all compound numbers except for those formed with *et*: 21, *vingt et un*; 31, *trente et un*; 41, *quarante et un*; and so on.

The hyphenated compounds continue in the same manner after 100, *cent*, and 1000, *mille*, but <u>do not attach</u> to either *cent* or *mille*. Thus:

135	*cent trente-cinq*
827	*huit cent vingt-sept*
5.278	*cinq mille deux cent soixante-dix-huit*

The number 80 is *quatre-vingts*. The number 81 is *quatre-vingt-un*. The final *s*, which appears in *quatre-vingts*, drops out in the hyphenated forms. Similarly, we write 300 *trois cents*, but 360 is *trois cent soixante*. *Mille* is invariable and never takes an *s*. Neither *cent* nor *mille* may ever be preceded by the word *un*. Simply say *cent* to mean **one hundred** and *mille* to mean **one thousand**. We do say *un million* (**one million**) and *un milliard* (**one billion**).

French uses a period where we would use a comma.

> 5.591 (French) versus 5,591 (English)

French uses a comma where we would use a period. The comma is called *la* (*une*) *virgule*.

> 7,50 € (French) versus $7.50 (English)

Lastly, you will hear *septante* for 70 in Belgium and Switzerland instead of *soixante-dix*. They also replace *quatre-vingts*. The Belgians say *octante* for 80 and the Swiss use *huitante*. Both use *nonante* for 90.

Ordinal numbers are created by adding the suffix *-ième* to the cardinal number. *Premier* and *second* for **first** and **second** are exceptions. Both show agreement with the nouns they modify:

> *la **première** fois, les **premiers** venus*
> *la **seconde** saison, les **seconds** venus*

There are two other small exceptions to note: *cinq + u + ième* and *neuf = neuve + ième* produce *cinquième* and *neuvième*.

Writing abbreviations for ordinal numbers (1st, 2nd, 3rd, 4th, and so on) is easy in French. For all numbers except ***premier***, simply place the letter *e* in superscript:

2e, 3e, 5e, 16e, 20e, 79e, 100^e
1st = 1er *premier*, 1^{ière} *première*

It is also possible to write 3eme or 3ième.

Une huitaine is often used to mean **about a week**, and *une quinzaine* to mean **about two weeks**.

Drill 2: Cardinal and Ordinal Numbers

Spell the following numbers in French:

1. 79   _____

2. 103   _____

3. 51   _____

4. 80   _____

5. 83   _____

6. 600   _____

7. 613   _____

8. 2.000   _____

9. 15.718   _____

10. 1.000.000.000   _____

Drill 2–Answers and Explanations

1. **79**   *soixante-dix-neuf*
   Hyphenate compound numbers from 17 to 99 (except for those with *et*).

2. **103**   *cent trois*
   Cent does not take an *s* when another number follows it.

3. **51**   *cinquante et un*
   This is an example of a compound number using *et*.

4. **80**   *quatre-vingts*
   The *s* appears if no other number follows.

5. **83**   *quatre-vingt-trois*
   The *s* drops when another number follows.

6. **600**   *six cents*
   Cent takes the *s* when it is last.

7. **613**   *six cent treize*
   There is no *s* because 600 is followed by 13.

8. **2.000**   *deux mille*
   Mille is invariable and never takes an *s*.

9. **15.718**   *quinze mille sept cent dix-huit*
   No hyphens appear until you reach the compound, 18.

10. **1.000.000.000**   *un milliard, un billion*
    Million, *milliard*, and *billion* all use *un*.

THE INDEFINITE ARTICLE

The indefinite article exists in three forms in French. *Un* is used in front of all masculine singular nouns, whereas *une* is for all feminine singular nouns. They are the equivalent of **a** or **an** in English. The third form, **des**, is for all plural nouns and is translated as **some** or **any**.

Use and Omission of the Indefinite Article

1. The indefinite article must be used after *c'est* or *ce sont*.

   *C'est **un** livre intéressant.*
   It's an interesting book.

   *Ce sont **des** fraises.*
   They're strawberries.

   *C'est **un** gentil garçon.*
   He's a nice boy.

   *C'est **une** jolie fille.*
   She's a pretty girl.

2. When a <u>pronoun</u>, <u>noun</u>, or <u>name</u> precedes *être*, the indefinite article is not used with the noun that follows. The article drops out because the noun takes on the role of an adjective.

   Caroline est étudiante.
   Caroline is a student.

   This construction is frequently encountered when expressing one's occupation or profession. Study the following examples:

   Il est avocat.
   He's a lawyer.

   Mon père est comptable.
   My father is an accountant.

   Anne est professeur.
   Anne is a teacher.

   The indefinite article will reappear if the profession is modified.

   C'est un bon avocat.
   He's a good lawyer.

   (Note the switch from *il* back to *c'est*.)

Mon père est un comptable experimenté.
　My father is an experienced accountant.

Anne est un professeur remarquable.
　Anne is a remarkable teacher.

3. The indefinite article is never used in exclamations with *quel*.

Quel dommage!
　What a shame!

Quelle surprise!
　What a surprise!

4. The indefinite article drops out in <u>apposition</u>, after *sans* and after *avec* (if the noun is abstract) just like the definite article.

Monsieur Richard, coiffeur des vedettes
　Mr. Richard, hairdresser to the stars

Je suis sorti sans parapluie.
　I went out without an umbrella.

Je vous aiderai avec plaisir.
　I'll gladly help you. (**with pleasure** = abstract noun)

Elle délaie la pâte avec de l'eau.
　She thins the dough with water. (concrete noun)

5. The plural of *un autre* and *une autre* is always *d'autres*.

J'ai demandé un autre tissu.
　I asked for another fabric.

Il m'en a envoyé d'autres.
　He sent me others.

6. The indefinite article is replaced by *de* (or *d'*) in a partitive negation.

Elle a une sœur.
Elle n'a pas de sœur.
Tu as un stylo.
Tu n'as pas de stylo.

But:

Ce n'est pas un homme honnête.
　He's not an honest (*decent, respectable*) man.

Drill 3: The Indefinite Article

Supply the correct form of the indefinite article if it is necessary. If there is no article required, place an **X** on the blank.

1. Mon père est _____ médecin.

2. C'est _____ bon chirurgien.

3. Ce sont _____ amis.

4. Quel _____ chaton mignon!

5. Il est _____ charpentier.

6. "_____ poire pour la soif."

7. Ravaillac a assassiné Henri IV, _____ roi de France.

8. Il a réussi sans _____ problème.

9. "_____ oiseau dans la main vaut deux tu l'auras."

10. Grand-mère marche avec _____ difficulté.

Drill 3–Explanations and Answers

1. **X**
    My father is a doctor. French omits the definite article with profession and trades. (Use and Omission of the Indefinite Article, Rule 2)

2. *un*
    He's a good surgeon. The indefinite article is required if the profession is modified. The indefinite article is also required after *c'est*. (Rule 1)

3. *des*
    They're friends. The indefinite article is required after *ce sont*. (Rule 1)

4. **X**
    What a cute kitten! The indefinite article is never used after *quel*. (Rule 3)

5. **X**
    He's a carpenter. French omits the definite article with profession and trades. (Rule 2)

6. *Une*
    (Save) a pear for thirst. In this old saying, the French equivalent of a "penny for a rainy day," we see the basic use of the indefinite article as it is used in both French and English.

7. **X**
    Ravaillac assassinated Henri the Fourth, (the) King of France. The article is omitted when the noun is placed in apposition. (Rule 4)

8. **X**
    He succeeded without a problem. The article is routinely omitted after *sans*. (Rule 4)

9. *Un*
    A bird in the hand is worth two in the bush. This is another illustration of the basic use of the indefinite article.

10. **X**
    Grandmother walks with difficulty. This is an example of omission of the article after *avec* with an abstract noun. (Rule 4)

THE DEFINITE ARTICLE

The English definite article **the** has four possible forms in French. Each is based on the gender, number, or sound of the noun that follows.

1. *Le* is used in front of singular masculine nouns.

    le chien   *le garçon*   *le livre*

2. *La* is used in front of singular feminine nouns.

    la chaise   *la fille*   *la souris*

3. *L'* is required before all singular nouns beginning with a vowel or silent *h*, regardless of gender.

    l'ami   *l'amie*   *l'été*   *l'île*   *l'outil*   *l'utopie*
    l'heure   *l'homme*   *l'hôtel*   *l'hiver*

    It should be noted that aspirate *h* is treated like a regular consonant.

    le haricot   *le héros*   *le houx*   *le huit*
    la haine   *la hanche* *la honte* *la huche*

4. *Les* is used for <u>all</u> plurals. The final *s* of *les* will produce the phonetic sound [z] in front a vowel or silent *h*. This is called <u>liaison</u>.

    les amis, les enfants, les idées, les ordures, les usines, les hommes

    The final *s* of *les* is <u>never</u> pronounced in front of <u>aspirate *h*</u>! It is silent, just as it is in front of any other consonant.

    les / halles   *les / héros*   *les / homards*

Special Uses of the Definite Article Particular to French

1. Unlike English, French requires the definite article when the noun is used in <u>general</u>. Study these examples:

    *Les cigarettes sont mauvaises pour **la** santé.*
    Cigarettes are bad for your health.

    *Le gras est mauvais pour **le** cœur.*
    Fat is bad for the heart.

This use extends to <u>liking</u> or <u>disliking</u> something.

> *Aimez-vous **le** vin rouge?*
> Do you like red wine?

> *Non, je préfère **le** vin blanc.*
> No, I prefer white wine.

> *Je déteste **le** lait.*
> I hate milk.

> *J'adore **le** chocolat.*
> I love chocolate.

2. The definite article is required in front of <u>geographical names</u>—of continents, countries, regions, mountains, lakes, and rivers.

l'Europe	*la France*	*l'Alsace*
les Alpes	*le Léman*	*la Seine*

3. The definite article is used with the names of the <u>seasons</u>.

l'été	*l'automne*	*l'hiver*	*le printemps*

    But definite articles are <u>omitted</u> after *en*:

en été	*en automne*	*en hiver*	*au printemps*

4. The definite article is used in expressing the <u>date</u>.

    > *Aujourd'hui, c'est **le** 3 septembre.*
    > Today is September 3rd.

    If the definite article is used with the name of a weekday, it indicates a <u>repetition</u> of that day of the week.

    > *Je n'aime pas travailler **le** samedi.*
    > I don't like to work on Saturdays.

5. French uses the definite article with <u>body parts</u>.

    > *J'ai **les** yeux marron.*
    > My eyes are brown.

    > *Elle a **les** cheveux longs.*
    > Her hair is long.

    > *J'ai **le** nez camus.*
    > I have a pug nose.

6. The definite article is used with <u>quantities</u> and <u>prices</u>.

    Ces pommes coûtent 1 euro le kilo.
        These apples cost 1 euro per kilo.

    Cette eau minérale-ci coûte moins le litre.
        This mineral water costs less by the liter.

7. The definite article is used with <u>the names of languages</u> and with <u>subjects of study</u>.

    L'espagnol et l'italien se ressemblent beaucoup.
        Spanish and Italian are very similar.

    La chimie est intéressante.
        Chemistry is interesting.

    Qui enseigne les maths cette année?
        Who's teaching math this year?

Omission of the Definite Article

1. The definite article is omitted when the name of a language follows the verb *parler*. Compare:

    J'étudie le français.   *with*   *Je parle français.*
        I study French.   I speak French.

    If *parler* is modified, the article is retained.

    Je parle bien le français.
        I speak French well.

2. Omit the article if the language is preceded by the preposition *en*.

    Je lui ai écrit en français.
        I wrote to him in French.

    The same omission occurs with geographical names preceded by *en*.

    Nous allons en France.
        We're going to France.

    Elle va en Provence.
        She goes to Provence.

3. The article is also omitted after *de* with the names of <u>feminine countries</u>:

    > *Elle vient d'Allemagne.*
    >   She comes from Germany.

4. The definite article is often omitted after *de* when one noun modifies another. Here are some examples:

    > *J'aime le pain d'épices.*
    >   I like gingerbread.

    > *Jason cherchait la toison d'or.*
    >   Jason went in search of the Golden Fleece.

    > *SNCF veut dire la Société Nationale des Chemins de Fer.*
    >   SNCF stands for The National Railroad.

    > *Henri IV, roi de France*   but   *le lion, roi des animaux*
    >   Henry IV, King of France   the lion, king of beasts

    Note also that the article is retained after *président*:

    > *De Gaulle, premier Président de la 5ième République*
    >   De Gaulle, first president of the 5th Republic

    > *Le Président des États-Unis*
    >   the president of the United States

4a. The definite article is omitted after *de* when the noun that follows is used adverbially.

    > *Je pleure de joie.*
    >   I'm crying for joy. (tells <u>how</u> I'm crying)

    > *Je crève de faim.*
    >   I'm dying of hunger.

    > *Le seau est rempli d'eau.*
    >   The pail is filled with water.

4b. The definite article is omitted after verbs that require *de*.

    > *On dirait une princesse, **vêtue de** soie.*
    >   She looked like a princess dressed in silk.

    > *Mes élèves sont **surchargés de** travail.*
    >   My pupils are overloaded with work.

*J'aime voir les arbres **couverts de** neige.*
I like to see the trees covered with snow.

*Elle a les yeux **étincelants de** vie.*
Her eyes sparkle with life.

The definite article is also omitted after *à* and *en* when one noun modifies another. This is a very common usage. Study these examples:

une brosse à cheveux
a hair brush

un sac en cuir
a leather bag

5. The definite article is omitted after the preposition *sans* if the noun that follows is unmodified.

    Il a réussi sans aide.
    He succeeded without help.

    Nous l'avons trouvé sans problème.
    We found it without a problem.

    But:

    J'ai commencé sans la moindre idée de ce que je faisais.
    I began without the slightest idea of what I was doing.

6. The definite article is omitted after the preposition *avec* if the noun that follows is abstract rather than concrete. Compare:

    Je le ferai avec plaisir.
    I'll do it with pleasure.

    Je le ferai avec l'argent que tu m'as donné.
    I'll do it with the money you gave me.

7. The definite article is omitted after *à* in many set expressions. Here are some common examples:

à bicyclette	*à pied*
à bras ouverts	*à rebours*
à cheval	*à reculons*
à fond	*à table*
à genoux	*à volonté*
à peine	

8. The definite article is omitted in <u>all idiomatic expressions</u> based on the verb *avoir*. Here are some examples:

> *avoir chaud*   *avoir faim*   *avoir peur*   *avoir raison*
> *avoir froid*   *avoir soif*   *avoir pitié*   *avoir tort*

9. The definite article is omitted if the descriptive noun is used in apposition to the first noun. <u>Apposition</u> means that the second noun has the same value or status as the first noun. Here's an example:

> *Gérard Depardieu, acteur inimitable, a reçu le César.*
>   Gérard Depardieu, the inimitiable actor, received the French Oscar.

10. The definite article is omitted in an exclamation.

> *"Ô temps, suspends ton vol."*
>   Lamartine, *Le Lac*

> *"Je suis belle, ô mortels! comme un rêve de pierre."*
>   Baudelaire, *La Beauté*

11. In enumeration the definite article may be omitted or retained.

> *"Vieillards, hommes, femmes, enfants,"*
>   Montesquieu, *Lettres persanes*

> *"La sottise, l'erreur, le péché, la lésine,"*
>   Baudelaire, *Au Lecteur*

12. The definite article is usually omitted after *ni*.

> *Il n'a ni frère ni sœur.*
>   He has neither brother nor sister.

It is retained with *l'un . . . l'autre*:

> *Ni l'un ni l'autre n'a répondu.*
>   Neither one nor the other answered.

Drill 4: The Definite Article

Supply the correct form of the definite article if it is necessary. If there is no article required, place an **X** on the blank.

1. Elle aime lire _____ bandes dessinées.

2. Ils vont faire du camping dans _____ Jura.

3. Son copain parle _____ espagnol.

4. _____ bleu te convient.

5. Nous passons _____ été à la plage.

6. Tu as _____ joues hâlées.

7. Elle a juré sans _____ honte.

8. J'ai _____ hâte de partir.

9. Elle étudie _____ biologie.

10. Claude de France, _____ femme de François I, est enterrée ici.

Drill 4–Answers and Explanations

1. *les*

   She likes to read the comics. The article accompanies the noun in French and is required when expressing general likes and dislikes. (Special Uses of the Definite Article, Rule 1)

2. *le*

   They're going camping in the Jura. The article is required with geographical expressions, in this case the Jura mountains. (Special Uses of the Definite Article, Rule 2)

3. **X**

   Her friend speaks Spanish. The article is omitted when the name of a language appears after the verb *parler*. (Omission of the Definite Article, Rule 1)

4. *Le*

   Blue suits you. The article is required with the noun used in general here. (Special Uses of the Definite Article, Rule 1)

5. *l'*

   We spend the summer at the beach. The article is required with the names of the seasons. (Special Uses of the Definite Article, Rule 3)

6. *les*

   Your cheeks are sun tanned. French generally uses the definite article with body parts, avoiding the possessive used in English. (Special Uses of the Definite Article, Rule 5)

7. **X**

   She swore without shame. The definite article is routinely omitted after the preposition *sans*. (Omission of the Definite Article, Rule 5)

8. **X**

   I'm in a hurry to leave. The article is omitted with all idioms based on the verb *avoir*. (Omission of the Definite Article, Rule 8)

9. *la*

   She's studying biology. The definite article is required with subjects of study. (Special Uses of the Definite Article, Rule 7)

10. **X**

    Claude de France, wife of Francis I, is buried here. The article is omitted here as the wife of Francis I has been placed in apposition by the commas. (Omission of the Definite Article, Rule 9)

THE PARTITIVE ARTICLE

Partitive articles are made by combining the <u>definite article</u> with the preposition *de* as follows:

*de + le = **du***   *de + la = **de la***
*de + l' = **de l'***   *de + les = **des***

The partitive is used in front of the noun to express a part or a portion of that noun. Partitive articles stand for **some** in the affirmative and **some** or **any** in the interrogative. The use of the partitive in French and English is the same, but in English we may leave out the article, while in French we cannot. Here are some examples:

Je dois acheter du beurre.
   I have to buy butter.

Elle boit du café.
   She's drinking coffee.

Je voudrais de la crème.
   I'd like some cream.

Tu veux de l'eau?
   Do you want some water?

Y a-t-il des fraises?
   Are there any strawberries?

Tu as des frères?
   Do you have any brothers?

Omission of the Definite Article from the Partitive

1.   The partitive article is reduced to *de* or *d'* when negated. Let's look at the same example sentences, but this time in the negative:

Je n'achète pas de beurre.
   I'm not buying (any) butter.

Elle ne boit pas de café.
   She doesn't drink coffee.

Je ne veux pas de crème.
   I don't want any cream.

Tu ne veux pas d'eau?
   Don't you want any water?

N'y a-t-il pas de fraises?
Aren't there any strawberries?

2. Don't mistake *ne . . . que* for a negation. It just restricts or limits the noun that follows it; it doesn't negate. You must retain the full partitive after *ne . . . que*:

*Elle **ne** mange **que des** fruits et **des** légumes.*
She only eats fruits and vegetables.

Ne . . . que is a synonym for *seulement* (**only**).

3. The partitive article is reduced to *de* or *d'* after most <u>adverbs of quantity</u>:

*Tu as **assez d'**argent.*
You have enough money.

*Maman a **beaucoup de** recettes.*
Mom has many recipes.

***Combien de** fois?*
How many times?

*Elle a très **peu de** patience.*
She has very little patience.

*J'ai **moins de** 20 cousins.*
I have fewer than 20 cousins.

*J'ai **plus de** 20 cousins.*
I have more than 20 cousins.

*Il y a **tant de** choix.*
There are so many choices.

*Tu as mis **trop de** sel.*
You put in too much salt.

The only exceptions to this rule are *bien* and *la plupart*, which are followed by the complete partitive article:

*J'ai visité le Louvre **bien des** fois.*
I've visited the Louvre lots of times.

*J'ai aimé **la plupart du** film.*
I liked most of the film.

4. The partitive article is reduced to *de* or *d'* after nouns of quantity:

> *une **boîte de** chocolats*
> a box of chocolates

> *une **bouchée de** vin*
> a mouthful of wine

> *un **bouquet de** fleurs*
> a bouquet of flowers

> *une **bouteille d'** eau minérale*
> a bottle of mineral water

> *un **bout de** pain*
> an end slice of bread

> *une **cuillerée de** sucre*
> a spoonful of sugar

> *une **douzaine d'** œufs*
> a dozen eggs

> *une **goutte de** cognac*
> a drop of cognac

> *un **kilo de** viande*
> a kilo of meat

> *un **litre de** lait*
> a litre of milk

> *une **livre de** pommes*
> a pound of apples

> *un **morceau de** craie*
> a piece of chalk

> *un **paquet de** cigarettes*
> a pack of cigarettes

> *un **panier de** serviettes*
> a basket of towels (or napkins)

> *une **pincée de** sel*
> a pinch of salt

> *une **poignée de** farine*
> a fistful of flour

> *un **sac de** bonbons*
> a bag of candies
>
> *une **tasse de** thé*
> a cup of tea
>
> *un **verre de** jus d'orange*
> a glass of orange juice

5. The partitive article is reduced to *de* or *d'* in front of plural nouns modified by preceding adjectives:

> *J'ai **de belles fleurs** dans mon jardin.*
> I have (some) beautiful flowers in my garden.
>
> *Il y a **de beaux tableaux** dans ce musée.*
> There are (some) beautiful paintings in this museum.

Exceptions to this rule include those nouns whose very meaning is partly derived from the preceding adjective. The adjective and noun combination is thought of as one.

> *des faux pas*
> missteps, blunders
>
> *des jeunes filles*
> girls, before adulthood
>
> *des petits pois*
> peas
>
> *des jeunes gens*
> young people
>
> *des vieilles filles*
> old maids

Drill 5: The Partitive Article

Complete the sentence with one of the following answers: *du, de la, de l',
des, de, d'.*

1. Elle ne mange pas _____ viande.

2. J'ai chipé un morceau _____ chocolat.

3. Nous avons trop _____ devoirs.

4. Il y a _____ fromage dans le frigo.

5. Tu veux _____ bonbons ?

6. Il veut _____ crème pour son café.

7. Elle ne lit que _____ romans policiers.

8. Si vous n'aimez pas ces modèles, nous en avons _____ autres.

9. Veux-tu _____ bonnes notes ?

10. Veux-tu _____ petits pois ?

11. La plupart _____ femmes mariées ont voté pour le président.

12. On finira le repas avec _____ glace.

13. J'ai vu ce film bien _____ fois.

14. Je n'ai pas _____ argent.

15. Je n'ai pas beaucoup _____ patience.

16. Ce sont _____ frères.

17. Il y a tant _____ étoiles visibles ce soir.

18. J'ai mis une cuillerée _____ moutarde dans ma vinaigrette.

19. Voulez-vous _____ pain ?

20. Elle a tant _____ amis.

Drill 5–Answers and Explanations

1. **de**

   She doesn't eat meat. The definite article is routinely omitted from the partitive with <u>negated</u> **some** or **any**. (Omission of the Definite Article from the Partitive, Rule 1)

2. **de**

   I snitched a piece of chocolate. The definite article is always omitted from the partitive construction after a noun of quantity. (Omission of the Definite Article from the Partitive, Rule 4)

3. **de**

   We have too much homework. The definite article is generally omitted from the partitive formula after adverbs of quantity. (Omission of the Definite Article from the Partitive, Rule 3)

4. **du**

   There's cheese in the fridge. This is the basic use of the complete partitive article to express a part or portion of the noun.

5. **des**

   Do you want (some, any) candy? This is another example of the basic use of the partitive article before the noun to express a part or portion of that noun.

6. **de la**

   He wants cream for his coffee. He wants **some** cream for his coffee, not all the cream in the world, just enough (a portion) for his cup. This is basic use of the complete partitive article.

7. **des**

   She only reads detective novels. *Ne . . . que* is not a real negation; therefore the full partitive article follows it. (Omission of the Definite Article from the Partitive, Rule 2)

8. **d'**

   If you don't like these styles, we have others. The plural *autres* is always preceded by *d'*. (Omission of the Definite Article from the Partitive, Rule 5)

9. **de**

   Do you get good grades? This is a plural noun preceded by a plural adjective, in which case the partitive article is reduced to *de* or *d'*. (Omission of the Definite Article from the Partitive, Rule 5)

10. ***des***

Do you want (some, any) peas? *Petits pois* is treated as though it were one word; therefore it takes the complete partitive article. (See exceptions to Omission of the Definite Article from the Partitive, Rule 5)

11. ***des***

Most married women voted for the president. *La plupart* is one of two exceptions to the rule that adverbs of quantity are followed by *de* or *d'*. The other exception is *bien*. (See exceptions to Omission of the Definite Article from the Partitive, Rule 3)

12. ***de la***

We'll finish the meal with ice cream. This is basic use of the complete partitive to express a part of the whole.

13. ***des***

I've seen that film many times. Like *la plupart, bien* requires the full partitive article. (See exceptions to Omission of the Definite Article from the Partitive, Rule 3)

14. ***d'***

I don't have any money. The article is reduced to *de* when the partitive noun is negated. (Omission of the Definite Article from the Partitive, Rule 1)

15. ***de***

I don't have a lot of patience. *Beaucoup* is an adverb of quantity typically followed by *de* or *d'*. (Omission of the Definite Article from the Partitive, Rule 3)

16. ***des***

They're brothers. The full partitive is required after *ce sont*. (Use and Omission of the Indefinite Article, Rule 1)

17. ***d'***

There are so many stars visible tonight. Omit the definite article from the partitive formula after *tant*, an adverb of quantity. (Omission of the Definite Article from the Partitive, Rule 3)

18. ***de***

I put a spoonful of mustard in my salad dressing. *Cuillerée* is a noun of quantity, all of which take just *de* or *d'*. (Omission of the Definite Article from the Partitive, Rule 4)

19. **du**

Do you want any bread? This is basic use of the the complete partitive article to express a part or portion of the whole.

20. **d'**

She has so many friends. Like *beaucoup*, *tant* is an adverb of quantity, most of which take just *de* or *d'*. (Omission of the Definite Article from the Partitive, Rule 3)

Drill 6: The Partitive versus the Definite Article

Explain the presence or the absence of the definite article in the following sentences by assigning to each sentence one of these five reasons:

A— omission of the definite article from the partitive formula after an adverb of quantity

B— omission of the definite article from the partitive formula after a noun of quantity

C— use of the complete partitive to express **some** or **any**

D— omission of the definite article from the partitive formula to express a **negated some** or **any**

E— use of the definite article to express general preference or dislike

		Choose A–E
1.	Il a choisi une bouteille de vin rouge.	1. _____
2.	Voulez-vous du vin maintenant?	2. _____
3.	Elle n'aime pas le vin.	3. _____
4.	Elle ne boit pas de vin.	4. _____
5.	Achète du vin pour ce soir.	5. _____
6.	Il reste encore un peu de vin.	6. _____
7.	Il a bu trop de vin.	7. _____
8.	Elle déteste le vin.	8. _____
9.	Elle aime beaucoup le vin.	9. _____
10.	Je prendrai volontiers une goutte de vin.	10. _____

Drill 6–Answers and Explanations

1. **(B)** *Bouteille* is a noun of quantity, therefore we omit the definite article portion of the partitive.

2. **(C)** We use the complete partitive to express **some wine, any wine**.

3. **(E)** We retain the definite article to express general preference.

4. **(D)** The definite article is routinely omitted from the partitive to express a negated quantity as in **She doesn't drink (any) wine**.

5. **(C)** The complete partitive is required here to express **some wine**.

6. **(A)** *Un peu* is an adverb of quantity, therefore the definite article drops out of the partitive formula.

7. **(A)** *Trop* is also an adverb of quantity. Drop the definite article.

8. **(E)** Retain the definite article to express general like or dislike.

9. **(E)** This is a tricky one. Here *beaucoup* simply tells us how much she likes wine. This is an expression of preference. Retain the definite article.

10. **(B)** *Goutte*, like *bouteille*, is a noun expressing quantity, so the definite article drops.

THE GENDER OF NOUNS

All French nouns are either masculine or feminine. Knowing the gender of nouns is essential in French! The gender of the noun determines the formation of the adjective, as well as how the article assigned to the noun will contract.

Here are a few tips worth remembering:

1. The **days** of the week, the **months** of the year, the **seasons**, and all **colors** used as nouns are <u>masculine</u>.

2. All **languages** are <u>masculine</u>.

3. The names of all **metals** and all **elements** are <u>masculine</u>. For example:

    l'argent massif, *le* *cuivre,* *le* *fer,* *l'or pur,* *le cobalt,* *le soufre*

4. Nouns ending in *-a*, *-age*, *-as*, *-emme*, *-gramme*, *-ier*, *-in*, *-isme*, *-logue*, *-oir*, *-ours*, and *-scope* are <u>masculine</u>.

    Notable exceptions: *l'image,* *la page,* *la rage,* *la* *crème*

5. **Adjectives**, **verbs**, and **adverbs** used as nouns are always <u>masculine</u>. For example:

    le beau, le réel
    le savoir, le toucher
    le bien, le mal

6. Nouns ending in *-eur* can be masculine or feminine. If the meaning is concrete, it is usually masculine. If it is more abstract, it is generally feminine. Compare:

le professeur	*la douceur*
le facteur	*la peur*
le tailleur	*la langueur*

6a. Although the above rule is fairly reliable, there are some exceptions:

    le bonheur, le malheur, la lueur, la fleur, la couleur

7. Nouns ending in *-is* are usually <u>masculine</u>. For example:

    l'avis, le mépris, le paradis, le radis

    Notable exceptions: *la brebis, la souris*

8. Nouns ending in *-ade*, *-ance*, *-ande*, *-aille*, *-aison*, *-ence*, *-euse*, *-ique*, *-ise*, *-ison*, *-nne*, *-ose*, *-sse*, *-tié*, *-tte*, *-trice*, *-ude*, and *-ure* are <u>feminine</u>.

9. The names of most **sciences** are <u>feminine</u>. For example:

   la botanique, *la* chimie, *la* physique, *la* biologie, *l'*informatique

   All words ending in *-tion* are also <u>feminine</u>.

   la nation, *la* satisfaction, *la* station

10. The names of many **fruits** are <u>feminine</u>. The names of most **trees** are <u>masculine</u>. Compare:

la pomme	*le* pommier
la poire	*le* poirier
la cerise	*le* cerisier

    Notable exceptions: some masculine fruits, such as the following:

    le citron, *le* pamplemousse, *le* raisin, *le* melon

10a. The distinction between fruits and the trees they come from exists for **nuts** as well. Compare:

la noix	*le* noyer
la noisette	*le* noisetier

11. Some nouns can be either masculine or feminine without changing in form:

    un enfant, *une* enfant
    a male child, a female child

    un élève, *une* élève
    a male pupil, a female pupil

12. There are some nouns which change meaning through gender. Compare:

le livre (book)	*la* livre (pound)
le tour (turn, spin, ride, stroll)	*la* tour (tower)
Le Tour de France	*La* Tour Eiffel
le vase (vase for flowers)	*la* vase (mud, sludge, ooze)

Drill 7: The Gender of Nouns

Decide whether the word is masculine or feminine. Mark **M** or **F** one the line and then check your answers:

1. ___ baguette

2. ___ coloris

3. ___ sottise

4. ___ fleur

5. ___ comptoir

6. ___ janvier

7. ___ calculatrice

8. ___ velours

9. ___ bleu

10. ___ moitié

11. ___ caisse

12. ___ programme

13. ___ acteur

14. ___ expérience

15. ___ platine

16. ___ oxygène

17. ___ carotte

18. ___ daltonisme

19. ___ magnétoscope

20. ___ sociologue

21. ___ dimanche

22. ___ automne

23. ___ allemand

24. ___ froideur

25. ___ camarade

Drill 7–Answers and Explanations

1. **F**   *-tte* is a common feminine suffix. (See tip 8)

2. **M**   *-is* is a masculine suffix. (See tip 6)

3. **F**   *Sottise* is F. *-ise* is a common feminine suffix. (See tip 8)

4. **F**   *Fleur* is an exception to tip 6. It is an *-eur* noun with a concrete meaning, yet it is feminine. (See tip 6a)

5. **M**   *-oir* is a common masculine suffix. (See tip 4)

6. **M**   It is the name of a **month**. See tip 1. *-ier* is also a common masculine suffix. (See tip 4)

7. **F**   *-trice* is a common feminine suffix. (See tip 8)

8. **M**   *-ours* is a common masculine suffix. (See tip 4)

9. **M**   It is a **color** used as a noun, all of which are masculine. (See tip 1)

10. **F**   *-tié* is a common feminine suffix. (See tip 8)

11. **F**   *-sse* is a common feminine suffix. (See tip 8)

12. **M**   *-gramme* is a common masculine suffix. (See tip 4)

13. **M**   It ends in *-eur* with a literal, concrete meaning. (See tip 6)

14. **F**   *-ence* is a common feminine suffix. (See tip 8)

15. **M**   Platinum is a metal, and all **metals** are masculine. (See tip 3)

16. **M**   Oxygen is a **chemical element**, all of which are masculine. (See tip 3)

17. **F**   *-tte* is a common feminine suffix. (See tip 8)

18. **M**   *-isme* is a common masculine suffix. (See tip 4)

19. **M**   *-scope* is a common masculine suffix. (See tip 4)

20. **M**   *-logue* is a common masculine suffix. (See tip 4)

21. **M**   The name of a **day of the week** is always masculine. (See tip 1)

22. **M**   The name of a **season of the year** is always masculine. (See tip 1)

23. **M**   The name of a **language** is always masculine. (See tip 2)

24. **F**   *Froideur* (ending in *-eur*) is feminine because it is often used figuratively. (See tip 6)

25. **M** or **F**   *Camarade* can be either, like *enfant*. (See tip 11)

THE PLURAL OF NOUNS

Most French nouns are made plural by adding an *s* to the singular form of the noun, just as in English:

le chat	*les chats*
la chatte	*les chattes*

Titles such as **Monsieur**, **Madame**, and **Mademoiselle** are made plural in the following manner:

Messieurs, Mesdames, Mesdemoiselles

Family names are invariable in French; they do not take an *s*.

Les LeBlanc, Les Pelletier, Les Smith

Some nouns change in meaning from singular to plural:

le ciseau (chisel)	*les ciseaux* (scissors)
la lunette (telescope)	*les lunettes* (eyeglasses)

Here are some common <u>irregular</u> plurals.

1. Nouns ending in *-eau* take an *x* instead of the regular *s*.

cadeau	*cadeaux*
bateau	*bateaux*
couteau	*couteaux*

2. Words ending in *-eu* also usually take an *x* instead of the *s*.

feu	*feux*
jeu	*jeux*

    Exceptions include:

bleu, bleus	*pneu, pneus*

3. Most nouns ending in *-al* form their plural in *-aux*.

animal	*animaux*
cheval	*chevaux*
journal	*journaux*

3a. Exceptions to the above rule include *bal, carnaval, chacal, festival,* and *regal,* all of which take the *s*.

4. Most nouns ending in **-ou** take the regular *s* in the plural.

clou	*clous*
sou	*sous*
trou	*trous*

4a. Exceptions to Rule 4: these seven words all take the **x** ending; remember them!

bijou	*bijoux*
caillou	*cailloux*
chou	*choux*
genou	*genoux*
hibou	*hiboux*
joujou	*joujoux*
pou	*poux*

5. Most nouns ending in **-ail** take the *s* ending.

chandail	*chandails*
éventail	*éventails*
portail	*portails*

5a. The following nouns ending in **-ail** use the **-aux** ending, like the nouns in Rule 3:

bail	*baux*
corail	*coraux*
émail	*émaux*
fermail	*fermaux*
soupirail	*soupiraux*
travail	*travaux*
vantail	*vantaux*
vitrail	*vitraux*

6. Nouns ending in *s*, *x*, or *z* in the singular <u>do not change</u> in the plural.

le fils	*les fils*
la croix	*les croix*
le nez	*les nez*

7. There are irregular plurals for *œil, ciel*.

l'œil	*les yeux*
le ciel	*les cieux* (heavens)
le ciel	*les ciels* (skies)

7a. *Bœuf*, *œuf*, and *os* make their written plurals regularly but undergo an audible change in pronunciation! In the singular, the final consonants *f* and *s* are heard, but in the plural they are silent! The vowel sounds also change from [œ] to [ø] in *bœuf* and *œuf*, and from [ɔ] to [o] in *os*.

Drill 8: Making Nouns Plural

Change these singular nouns to plural:

1. le singe   les _____

2. le manteau   les _____

3. le mal   les _____

4. le creux   les _____

5. le livre   les _____

6. le travail   les _____

7. l'enjeu   les _____

8. le bal   les _____

9. le genou   les _____

10. le tribunal   les _____

11. la nounou   les _____

12. la règle   les _____

13. le crystal   les _____

14. le détail   les _____

15. le troupeau   les _____

Drill 8–Answers and Explanations

1. *les singes*
    Le singe is an <u>ordinary noun</u>; it follows the general rule of making plurals by adding an *s*.

2. *les manteaux*
    Le manteau ends in *-eau*; therefore it makes its plural with an *x*. (Rule 2)

3. *les maux*
    Le mal ends in *-al*, the plural of which is usually *-aux*. (Rule 3)

4. *les creux*
    Le creux ends in the letter *x* in the singular; therefore it does not change in the plural. (Rule 6)

5. *les livres*
    Le livre is an ordinary noun that follows the general rule of adding an *s* for plural.

6. *les travaux*
    Le travail is an exception to the general rule for *-ail*; its plural is *-aux*. (Rule 5a)

7. *les enjeux*
    L'enjeu follows Rule 2; because it ends in *-eu*, it takes the *x* plural.

8. *les bals*
    Le bal is an exception to Rule 3; it takes an *s* instead of *-aux*. (Rule 3a)

9. *les genoux*
    Le genou is one of the seven words that do not follow Rule 4. (Rule 4a)

10. *les tribunaux*
    Le tribunal follows Rule 3; its plural is *-aux*.

11. *les nounous*
    La nounou follows Rule 4; it takes an *s*.

12. *les règles*
    La règle is an ordinary noun that follows the general rule of adding an *s* for plural.

13. *les crystaux*
    Le crystal follows Rule 3; its plural ends in *-aux*.

14. **les détails**

   Le détail follows Rule 5; it takes an *s*.

15. **les troupeaux**

   Le troupeau is like *cadeau* and *bateau* in Rule 2. Nouns in **-eau** take *x* for plural.

THE PLURAL OF COMPOUND NOUNS

There are eight types of compound nouns in French. Rules for making these compounds plural vary based on which parts of speech are combined to make the noun. This is actually easier than it sounds.

Remember that only <u>nouns</u> and <u>adjectives</u> can accept the addition of an *s* or an *x*. <u>Verbs</u>, <u>adverbs</u>, and <u>prepositions</u> never change their form. They are always invariable in the compound noun.

1. **Noun with noun**—If both words on either side of the hyphen are are <u>nouns</u>, each one is made <u>plural</u>:

    le bateau-mouche = les bateaux-mouches
    le chef-lieu = les chefs-lieux
    le loup-garou = les loups-garous
    l'oiseau-mouche = les oiseaux-mouches

1a. Exception to Rule 1:

    des timbres-poste: only the first noun changes to plural.

2. **Noun with adjective or adjective with noun**—Both parts of speech can accept the plural (*s*, *z*, and so on) so <u>both words</u> are made <u>plural</u>.

    le papier-filtre = les papiers-filtres
    le grand-parent = les grands-parents

2a. Special notes to Rule 2: Traditionally **la grand-mère** has been an exception to Rule 2, the plural being *les grand-mères*. It is interesting to note, however, that Larousse now lists the plural as *les grand*[*s*]*-mères*. The gradual acceptance of the two-*s* version would bring *grand-mère* into alignment with **arrière-grand-mère**, which now requires both *s*'s.

    les arrière-grands-mères

    This can also be said for:

    les grand[*s*]*-tantes*
    les arrière-grands-tantes

    The adjectives *demi-* and *semi-* remain invariable when combined with nouns; thus:

    *un **demi**-frère, deux **demi**-frères*
    *une **demi**-heure, trois **demi**-heures*
    *une **semi**-voyelle, des **semi**-voyelles*

3. **Adjective with adjective**—<u>Both words</u> are generally <u>plural</u>.

> *le sourd-muet = les sourds-muets*
> *le clair-obscur = les clairs-obscurs*

An exception is *le nouveau-né = les nouveau-nés*.

4. **Verb with noun**—Only the <u>noun</u> becomes <u>plural</u>; the verb remains unchanged.

> *l'essuie-glace = les essuie-glaces*
> *le chasse-mouche = les chasse-mouches*
> *le tire-bouchon = les tire-bouchons*
> *le croque-mitaine = les croque-mitaines*

4a. A special exception to Rule 4: Neither the verb nor the noun changes in:

> *le gratte-ciel = **les gratte-ciel***

Within *les gratte-ciel* (**skyscrapers**) the plural element, **scrapers**, becomes the invariable verb *gratte*. Because the sky is thought of as singular in both French and English, there is no need to make *ciel* plural.

5. and 6. **Verb with verb or verb with adverb**—Neither word is changed; both remain invariable.

> *le laissez-passer = les laissez-passer*
> *le laisser-aller = les laisser-aller*
> *le va-et-vient = les va-et-vient*
> *le passe-partout = les passe-partout*

7. **Noun or adjective with adverb**—Only the <u>noun</u> (or <u>adjective</u>) becomes <u>plural</u>; the adverb stays the same:

> *le haut-parleur = les haut-parleurs*
> *le bien-aimé = les bien-aimés*

7a. **Noun and preposition**—Only the <u>noun</u> becomes <u>plural</u>; the preposition stays the same:

> *l'arrière-pensée = les arrière-pensées*
> *l'avant-cour = les avant-cours*
> *le sans-culotte = les sans-culottes*

8. **Two nouns separated by a preposition**—Generally only the <u>first</u> <u>noun</u> is made <u>plural</u>.

> *la pomme de terre = les pommes de terre*
> *le chef-d'œuvre = les chefs-d'œuvre*
> *la fleur de lis = les fleurs de lis*
> *l'arc-en-ciel = les arcs-en-ciel*

8a. There are exceptions to Rule 8, such as:

> *le tête-à-tete = les tête-à-tete*
> *le pied-à-terre = les pied-à-terre*

Common Invariable Compound Nouns

Here are some frequently used compound nouns that <u>never</u> change in the plural:

> *abat-jour, brise-vent, cache-cou, cache-pot, casse-cou, casse-croûte, casse-tête, chasse-neige, crève-cœur, gratte-ciel* (which we have analyzed), *mange-tout, porte-monnaie, rabat-joie, trompe-l'œil, sans-abri, sans-cœur, sans-emploi, sans-souci*

Drill 9: The Plural of Compound Nouns

Which part or parts of the compound noun change in the plural?

A — Both parts?

B — Just the first word?

C — Just the second word?

D — Neither word?

Choose A–D

1. ___ la femme de ménage

2. ___ le cul-de-sac

3. ___ le pèse-personne

4. ___ le mal de tête

5. ___ le mal-logé

6. ___ le libre-service

7. ___ le tire-bouchon

8. ___ l'arrière-goût

9. ___ la belle-sœur

10. ___ le nom de plume

11. ___ le porte-monnaie

12. ___ le casse-croûte

13. ___ le laisser-aller

14. ___ le saint-père

15. ___ l'avant-bras

Drill 9–Answers and Explanations

1. **(B)**   *les femmes de ménage*
When two nouns are separated by a preposition, only the first noun is made plural. (Rule 8)

2. **(B)**   *les culs-de-sac*
Again two nouns are separated by a preposition, so only the first noun is made plural. (Rule 8)

3. **(C)**   *les pèse-personnes*
Pèse, a verb, is invariable; only the noun *personne* can accept the *s*. (Rule 4)

4. **(B)**   *les maux de tête*
Two nouns are separated by a preposition, so only the first noun becomes plural. (Rule 8)

5. **(C)**   *les mal-logés*
In the preceding problem *mal* is a noun; here it is an adverb and therefore is invariable. Only the adjective *logé* can accept the *s*. (Rule 7)

6. **(A)**   *les libres-services*
Both the adjective and the noun accept the plural *s*. (Rule 2)

7. **(C)**   *les tire-bouchons*
The verb form is invariable; the noun takes the *s*. (Rule 4)

8. **(C)**   *les arrière-goûts*
In preposition and noun combinations, only the noun takes the *s*. (Rule 7a)

9. **(A)**   *les belles-sœurs*
Both the adjective and the noun accept the plural *s*. (Rule 2)

10. **(B)**   *les noms de plume*
Noun, preposition, noun—only the first noun reflects the plural *s*, as explained in Rule 8.

11. **(D)**   *les porte-monnaie*
This is a common invariable compound; no change.

12. **(C)**   *les casse-croûtes*
This is a verb and noun combination. Only the noun takes the *s*. (Rule 4)

13. **(D)** *les laisser-aller*
Two verbs in combination—neither changes. (Rule 5)

14. **(A)** *les saints-pères*
Two nouns in combination—both accept *s*. (Rule 1)

15. **(D)** *les avant-bras*
Preposition and noun combination (Rule 7a)—the preposition is invariable. The noun *bras* already ends in the letter *s*, therefore it will not change. (See Rule 6 under "The Plural of Nouns.")

ADJECTIVE FORMATION—MAKING FEMININE FORMS

Adjectives must match the gender and number of the nouns or pronouns they describe. Here are the rules for making an adjective feminine:

1. We generally just add an *e* to the masculine adjective to create the feminine form:

    petit = petite
    clair = claire
    joli = jolie
    fané = fanée

    If the masculine adjective already ends in an unaccented *e*, there is no change in the feminine form. Compare:

    le drapeau russe   *la famille russe*

2. These feminine adjective forms double the last consonant of the masculine adjective before the addition of *e*:

ancien = ancienne	(*ien* to *ienne*)
bon = bonne	(*on* to *onne*)
paysan = paysanne	(*an* to *anne*)
cruel = cruelle	(*el* to *elle*)
gentil = gentille	(*il* to *ille*)
nul = nulle	(*ul* to *ulle*)
pareil = pareille	(*eil* to *eille*)
bas = basse	(*as* to *asse*)
épais = épaisse	(*ais* to *aisse*)
gros = grosse	(*os* to *osse*)
muet = muette	(*et* to *ette*, but see Rule 2a)
sot = sotte	(*ot = otte*)*

    * Many exceptions such as: *dévot = dévote, idiot = idiote, manchot = manchote*

    2a. Adjectives that end in *-et* in the masculine also take on the accent **grave**, and then the *e finale*:

    complet, incomplet, concret, désuet, discret, indiscret, inquiet, replet, secret

    Examples: *complet = complète, secret = secrète*

3. Adjectives that end in **-er** in the masculine also take on the **accent grave**, and then the *e finale*:

> *dernier = dernière*
> *premier = première*

Adjectives that end in *c, f, g* (or *gu*), *x*, *-eur*, or *-teur* in the masculine undergo special changes in the feminine.

4. The *c* ending is generally replaced by **-que** to make the feminine:

> *public = publique*
> *turc = turque*

Note that *grec* retains the *c* before adding **-que**.

> *grec = grecque*

4a. Some masculine adjectives ending in *c* will become **-che** in the feminine:

> *blanc = blanche*
> *sec = sèche*

Note that *franc* becomes *franche* to mean **open, frank, candid**, and *franc* becomes *franque* to mean **Frankish**.

5. The *f* ending of the masculine adjective becomes **-ve** in the feminine:

> *naïf = naïve*
> *sportif = sportive*

6. The *g* ending of the masculine adjective becomes **-gue** in the feminine:

> *long = longue*

6a. If the masculine adjective ends in **-gu**, then a *tréma* will appear over the last *e* as follows:

> *aigu = aiguë*   *ambigu = ambiguë*

7. Most adjectives ending in *x* in the masculine become **-se** in the feminine.

> *curieux = curieuse*
> *heureux = heureuse*
> *jaloux = jalouse*

7a. Notable exceptions:

> *doux = douce*
> *faux = fausse*

8. The masculine ending **-eur** generally becomes **-euse** in the feminine:

> *trompeur = trompeuse*
> *voleur = voleuse*

8a. There are 10 common adjectives that become **-eure** instead of **-euse**. They are all adjectives of comparison or relativity. Remember them:

> *antérieur, extérieur, inférieur, intérieur, majeur, meilleur, mineur, postérieur, supérieur, ultérieur*

8b. A few adjectives in **-eur** become **-eresse** in the feminine:

> *chasseur = chasseresse* (poetic) versus *chasseuse*
> *pécheur = pécheresse*
> *vengeur = vengeresse*

9. The masculine suffix **-teur** generally becomes **-trice** in the feminine:

> *acteur = actrice*
> *lecteur = lectrice*
> *protecteur = protectrice*

9a. If the **-teur** adjective is built on a verb form rather than a noun, its feminine form will be **-euse** like the group in Rule 10:

> *menteur = menteuse*
> *prêteur = prêteuse*

10. There are 10 adjectives that change radically from masculine to feminine and that have not already been noted as exceptions. They must be learned by heart:

> *beau = belle* *frais = fraîche*
> *béni = bénite* *malin = maligne*
> *bénin = bénigne* *rigolo = rigolote*
> *fou = folle* (also *mou = molle*) *tiers = tierce*
> *favori = favorite* *vieux = vieille*

Drill 10: Making Adjectives Feminine

Make the following adjectives feminine:

1. créateur = _____

2. actif = _____

3. chanteur = _____

4. paresseux = _____

5. aveugle = _____

6. fier = _____

7. tel = _____

8. meilleur = _____

9. net = _____

10. laïc = _____

11. canadien = _____

12. inquiet = _____

13. exigu = _____

14. dévot = _____

15. favori = _____

Drill 10–Answers and Explanations

1. *créatrice*
   Typical change of the suffix *-teur* to *-trice* as explained in Rule 9.

2. *active*
   Actif works like *naïf* and *sportif* in Rule 5, *f* ending becomes *-ve*.

3. *chanteuse*
   This *-teur* ending comes from the verb form *chanter*, therefore it takes *-euse* in the feminine like *menteuse* in Rule 9a.

4. *paresseuse*
   One of the many adjectives that change from *x* to *-se*. (Rule 7)

5. *aveugle*
   There is no change from masculine to feminine because *aveugle* already ends in an unaccented *e* in the masculine. (Rule 1)

6. *fière*
   This *-er* ending requires an *accent grave* and a final *e*, like *dernier* = *dernière*, in Rule 3.

7. *telle*
   Telle is an example of <u>doubling the consonant</u> before adding the final *e* in the feminine form. It is like *cruel* = *cruelle* in Rule 2.

8. *meilleure*
   This *-eur* adjective of comparison becomes *-eure* as in Rule 8a.

9. *nette*
   Nette doubles the consonant and gets an *e*. (Rule 2)

10. *laïque*
    The *c* ending in *laic* is replaced by *-que* in the feminine form. (Rule 4)

11. *canadienne*
    The <u>consonant is doubled</u> and the *e* is added. This is a common variant of Rule 2; *parisien* and *italien* work the same way.

12. *inquiète*
    This adjective in *-et* takes an *accent grave* instead of doubling the consonant before the final *e*. (Rule 2a)

13. **exiguë**

An adjective ending in **-gu** picks up a *tréma* over the final *e* in the feminine. (Rule 6a)

14. **dévote**

This is an exception to Rule 3. The consonant does not double. Instead, it works like *idiot = idiote*.

15. **favorite**

This is an irregular form that must be memorized. (Rule 10)

ADJECTIVE AGREEMENT—MAKING PLURALS

Most French adjectives are made plural by adding an *s* to the singular form, just as with nouns:

une fleur jaune = des fleurs jaunes

There are some irregular plurals similar to those we encountered with nouns. <u>Notice how the same rules that govern nouns also apply to adjectives!</u>

1. Masculine adjectives ending in *-eau* take *x* instead of *s* in the plural.

    beau = beaux
    nouveau = nouveaux

    The feminine plural is regular: *belle = belles*; *nouvelle = nouvelles*

2. Most masculine adjectives ending in *-al* become *-aux* in the plural:

    amical = amicaux
    loyal = loyaux
    spécial = spéciaux

    The feminine plural is regular: *amicale = amicales*

2a. There are four adjectives in *-al* that do not change to *-aux*. They become plural with the regular *s* ending instead. Remember them: *bancal*, *fatal*, *natal*, *naval*. The adjectives *final*, *idéal*, *glacial*, and *jovial* also used to require *s* instead of *-aux*, but current dictionaries now show either plural as acceptable.

3. Just as with nouns, adjectives that already end in *s* or *x* in the singular do not change in the plural:

    un fait divers = des faits divers
    un gâteau délicieux = des gâteaux délicieux

4. The plural of some colors is invariable. If the adjective of color also exists as the name of a **fruit**, a **nut**, a **food**, or a **precious stone**, it remains invariable as an adjective. Here are some examples:

cerise	*olive*
chocolat	*orange*
marron	*carmin* (**crimson**) is also invariable
noisette	

    All other colors show regular agreement.

5. All **numbers** (except *cent* and *vingt*) are also **invariable** as adjectives:

> *les **cinq** frères*
> *les **sept** nains*
> ***trois mille** soldats*

5a. *Cent* will take an *s* in the plural if it is not followed by another number. Compare *trois cents* and *trois cent cinquante*.

5b. *Vingt* will take an *s* as part of the number *quatre-vingts* if it is not followed by another number. Compare *quatre-vingts* and *quatre-vingt-trois*.

6. When one adjective refers back to more than one noun, that adjective will be <u>masculine plural</u> in form unless all of the nouns are feminine.

> ***Le** lion et **la** panthère sont dangéreux.*
> ***Sa** mère et **son** père sont charmants.*
> ***Sa** mère et **sa** grand-mère sont charmantes.*

The Plural of Compound Adjectives

1. Compounds of color are always invariable:

> *les yeux bleu-vert*
> *les cheveux châtain clair*
> *les cheveux blond foncé*

2. When compounds combine nouns, adjectives, or past participles, those elements become plural:

> *des fins douces-amères*
> *des enfants petits-choux*

3. If the compound contains an adverb, it will remain invariable, just as it does in compound nouns.

> *mes enfants bien-aimés*

Drill 11: Making Adjectives Plural

Make the adjectives plural:

1. un garçon français   des garçons _____

2. un truc génial   des trucs _____

3. un foulard café au lait   des foulards _____

4. un accident fatal   des accidents _____

5. un mur gris-vert   des murs _____

6. un chien mal-traité   des chiens _____

7. un homme nerveux   des hommes _____

8. une recette provençale   des recettes _____

9. un gant noir   des gants _____

10. une dent éclatante   des dents _____

Is an *s* necessary? If not, leave the space blank.

11. quatre-vingt____-dix-huit

12. les douze____ jours de Noël

13. cinq cent____ soldats

14. les yeux noisette____

15. les yeux bleu____

Drill 11–Answers and Explanations

1. *des garçons **français***
No change in spelling because the adjective *français* already ends in an *s*. (Rule 3)

2. *des trucs **géniaux***
Typical change of a masculine adjective in *-al* to *-aux*. (Rule 2)

3. *des foulards **café au lait***
No change in spelling. The color exists as a food name and is therefore invariable as an adjective. (Rule 4)

4. *des accidents **fatals***
One of the four exceptions to the *-al* to *-aux*. (Rule 2a)

5. *des murs **gris-vert***
No spelling change permitted; compounds of color are invariable. (Compounds, Rule 1)

6. *des chiens **mal-traités***
The adverb remains invariable while the participle takes an *s*. (Compounds, Rule 3)

7. *des hommes **nerveux***
An adjective ending in an *x* cannot accept another letter; it remains the same in the plural. (Rule 3)

8. *des recettes **provençales***
This is a standard feminine plural from Rule 2.

9. *des gants **noirs***
Use the standard masculine plural from the basic rule of adding an *s* to the singular adjective.

10. *des dents **éclatantes***
This is a standard feminine plural; add an *s* to the singular adjective.

11. **(blank)**
Quatre-vingt does not take an *s* when followed by another number. (Rule 5b)

12. **(blank)**
All numbers (except *cent* and *vingt*) are invariable as adjectives. (Rule 5)

13. *cinq cents soldats*

Cent <u>does</u> need an *s* here because it is not followed by another number. (Rule 5b)

14. **(blank)**

The color *noisette* is invariable as an adjective because it is also the name of a nut (**hazlenut**). (Rule 4)

15. *les yeux bleus*

A <u>single</u> color shows agreement unless it is also the name of a fruit, etc., as explained in Rule 4. Compound colors are invariable.

THE POSITION OF ADJECTIVES RELATIVE TO THE NOUN

Most French adjectives <u>follow </u>the noun they modify. There is a small group of common adjectives that precede the noun, and there are adjectives that change in meaning depending on their placement.

English speakers generally learn the preceding adjectives with ease because this is the position they are familiar with in their native language. The most common student error is <u>not remembering to place the majority of French adjectives after the noun</u>.

Adjectives that precede the noun in French include:

- All <u>interrogative</u>, <u>demonstrative</u>, and <u>possessive</u> adjectives:

    Quels livres?   *Ces livres.*   *Mes livres.*

- All <u>cardinal</u> and <u>ordinal</u> numbers:

    trois livres   *mon premier livre*

- The following adjectives (BANGS):
B = Beauty	*beau* and *joli*
A = Age	*jeune*, *vieux* (not *âgé!*), and *nouveau*
N = Number	*aucun*, *autre*, *chaque*, *certain*,* *maint*, *même*, *plusieurs*, *quelque*, *tel*, *tout*, *different*, *divers*, and *nouveau***
G = Goodness	*bon* and *mauvais*
S = Size	only *petit*, *grand*, and *gros****

    *   When *certain* appears after the noun, its meaning is **assured.**

    **   Appears in both positions with slight changes in meaning.

    ***   Other adjectives of size follow!

Adjectives that <u>follow</u> the noun in French include:

- All adjectives of **color**
- All adjectives expressing **nationality**, **origin**, or **religion**
- All adjectives denoting **shape** or **texture**
- Adjectives denoting **position** or **office**
- Most adjectives descriptive of **physical** or **mental state**

Study these examples. Observe the position of the adjectives and then try the drill.

> *C'est une petite fille mince.*
> She's a slim little girl.

> *C'est un jeune homme français.*
> He's a young Frenchman.

> *J'ai choisi un grand cadre carré.*
> I chose a large square frame.

> *Voici un tissu souple.*
> Here is a soft fabric.

> *J'ai mis mes sandales blanches.*
> I wore (put on) my white sandals.

> *Le vieil homme a grondé le jeune chiot.*
> The old man scolded the young puppy.

> *Ma meilleure amie a acheté une nouvelle voiture japonaise.*
> My best friend bought a new Japanese car.

> *Le crocodile pleure de grosses larmes.*
> The crocodile cries big (fat) tears.

> *C'est une fille écervelée.*
> She's a scatterbrain.

Drill 12: Position of Adjectives

Choose the correct position for the adjective—**in front of** or **after** the noun:

1. un _____ garçon _____ (mauvais)

2. un _____ garçon _____ (américain)

3. un _____ garçon _____ (amusant)

4. un _____ garçon _____ (grand)

5. un _____ garçon _____ (insupportable)

6. une _____ femme_____ (âgée)

7. une _____ femme _____ (blonde)

8. une _____ femme _____ (norvégienne)

9. une _____ sœur _____ (jumelle)

10. une _____ sœur _____ (cadette)

11. une _____ soupe _____ (bonne)

12. une _____ soupe _____ (chaude)

13. une _____ soupe _____ (appétissante)

14. des _____ chaussures _____ (bleu marine)

15. des _____ parents _____ (indulgents)

Drill 12–Answers and Explanations

1. *un **mauvais** garçon*
   Bon and *mauvais*, two degrees of goodness, always precede.

2. *un garçon **américain***
   Adjectives of nationality always follow.

3. *un garçon **amusant***
   Like *amusant*, the majority of French adjectives follow.

4. *un grand **garçon***
   Petit, *grand*, and *gros* are the only adjectives of size that precede.

5. *un garçon **insupportable***
   Normal adjective placement following the noun.

6. *une femme **âgée***
   Âgée follows as an ordinary adjective descriptive of state. *Jeune* and *vieux* are the BANGS adjectives that precede.

7. *une femme **blonde***
   Typical adjective placement for *blonde*.

8. *une femme **norvégienne***
   All nationalities follow.

9. *une sœur **jumelle***
   Like most French adjectives, *jumelle* follows the noun.

10. *une sœur **cadette***
    Another common adjective, *cadette* follows the noun.

11. *une **bonne** soupe*
    Like *mauvais*, *bonne* precedes the noun (BANGS).

12. *une soupe **chaude***
    Common adjective descriptive of state, *chaude* follows.

13. *une soupe **appétissante***
    Usual placement of the adjective after the noun.

14. *des chaussures **bleu marine***
    Colors always follow. Note the absence of agreement.

15. *des parents **indulgents***
    Another example of an adjective in its usual position.

Adjectives that Change in Meaning According to Placement

This is a very interesting feature of French adjectives. Adjectives tend to be <u>figurative</u> in meaning when placed in front of the noun. When they follow the noun the meaning is usually more <u>literal</u> or concrete. Here are some examples worth remembering:

*une **chère** amie*	*versus*	*une robe **chère***
a dear friend		an expensive dress

*mon **pauvre** enfant!*	*des gens **pauvres***
my poor, unfortunate child!	poor people (destitute, without money)

*ma **propre** maison*	*ma maison **propre***
my own house	my clean house
	also *le mot **propre***
	the correct, exact word

*un **ancien** élève*	*une civilisation **ancienne***
a former student	an ancient civilization

*le **même** jour*	*le jour **même***
the same day	the very day

*de **différentes** solutions*	*une solution **différente***
several, various solutions	an alternative solution

*C'est la **dernière** fois!*	*samedi **dernier***
That's the last (final) time!	last (in a series) Saturday

The speaker can inject subjectivity with the placement he chooses:

*une **triste** nouvelle*	*une nouvelle **triste***
subjective (he feels sad about the news)	more objective (factual)

*un **long** discours*	*des cheveux **longs***
a long (and probably boring) lecture	long hair

Drill 13: Adjectives That Change Meaning

Place the adjective in order to convey the meaning desired:

1. une _____ fille _____   Place *maigre* to mean **very thin, skinny**.

2. une _____ existence _____   Place *maigre* to mean **meager**.

3. mes _____ draps _____   Place *propres* to mean **clean, fresh**.

4. mes _____ draps _____   Place *propres* to mean **my own**.

5. un _____ restaurant _____   Place *cher* to mean **pricey, expensive**.

6. mon _____ collègue _____   Place *ancien* to mean **former**.

7. un _____ pays _____   Place *pauvre* to mean **financially poor**.

8. le _____ chapeau _____   Place *même* to mean **same, identical**.

9. une _____ chose _____   Place *certaine* to mean **sure, definite**.

10. une _____ chose _____   Place *certaine* to mean **some indefinite thing**.

Drill 13–Answers and Explanations

1. *une fille **maigre***
   The literal meaning **thin** is conveyed by placing *maigre* after the noun.

2. *une **maigre** existence*
   Positioned in front of the noun, *maigre* is no longer concrete. Here it suggests a **meager**, **bare-bones** existence.

3. *mes draps **propres***
   Here, *propres* means **clean**.

4. *mes **propres** draps*
   In front of the noun, *propres* translates as **own**.

5. *un restaurant **cher***
   After the noun, *cher* has the literal meaning **expensive**.

6. *mon **ancien** collègue*
   Preceding the noun, *ancien* means **former**.

7. *un pays **pauvre***
   The literal meaning of **poor**, **without money**, is expressed when *pauvre* follows the noun.

8. *le **même** chapeau*
   In front of the noun, *même* means **same**.

9. *une chose **certaine***
   After the noun *certaine* is concrete. Here it means **sure**, **definite**.

10. *une **certaine** chose*
    In front of the noun, *certaine* becomes imprecise. Here it conveys an **indefinable something**.

INDEFINITE ADJECTIVES

Indefinite adjectives may determine nouns in place of an article. Like any other adjective, they agree in gender and number with the nouns they modify. Later, we will see that many of these adjectives also function as indefinite pronouns.

Aucun

Aucun is not generally seen in the plural, as its meaning is intrinsically singular: **not one**, **not any**, **no**. It can also be translated as . . . **a single**, . . . **one single**, . . . **any**. *Aucune* is the feminine form.

    Aucun is frequently used in combination with *ne*:

> *Je n'ai **aucune** idée.*
> I have no idea.

> ***Aucun** de ces poissons **n'**est assez frais.*
> Not one of these fish is fresh.

> ***Aucun** oiseau **n'**est venu.*
> Not a single bird came.

It can also appear without *ne*:

> *Je l'aime plus qu'**aucun** acteur américain.*
> I like him better than any American actor.

> ***Aucun** repos pour Maman.*
> No rest for Mom.

Autre

Study the slight differences in these translations of *autre*:

> *Tu veux un **autre** café?*
> Do you want **another** coffee? (**a second one**)

> *Pourriez-vous me montrer une **autre** couleur?*
> Could you show me **another** color? (**a different one**)

> *Nous **autres**, nous restons.*
> **As for us**, we're staying.

Certain

> ***Certains** étudiants amènent leur portable en classe.*
> **Some** students bring their cell phones to class.

> Un **certain** enfant devrait se laver les mains!
> A **certain** child had better wash his hands!

Note that *certain* loses its indefinite quality when it appears after the noun; there it means **certain** in the sense of **sure**:

> Ce film est un navet **certain**.
> That film is a dud (a flop) **for sure**.

Chaque

Use *chaque* to convey **each** or **every** when you wish to stress the singularity of the thing. Use a form of *tout + article* when you want to stress the plurality of the thing. Compare:

> Elle choisit **chaque** cerise avec soin.
> She picks **each** cherry carefully.

> Je cours **chaque** après-midi.
> I run **each** afternoon.

But also:

> Je cours **tous** les matins.
> I run **every** morning.

Différent, Divers

Différent and *divers* both mean **various**. *Divers* has the additional meaning of **miscellaneous**, whereas *différent* also means **unlike** and **unusual**:

> Elle porte un chapeau **différent**.
> She's wearing an **unusual** hat.

> Il y a un choix **divers**.
> There's a **variety** of (there are many) choices.

Maint

> Maintes fois.
> Many a time.

This expression is much too stilted to use in every day French. You may encounter it in a formal text. Use **bien des**, **de nombreux**, or **plusieurs** to mean **many** instead.

Même

Même means **same** when it precedes the noun and **very** if it follows. If it is attached by a hyphen, it means **self**.

> *Grand-père raconte toujours les **mêmes** histoires.*
> Grandfather always tells the **same** stories.

> *Elle a perdu son parapluie le matin mais l'a récupéré le soir **même**.*
> She lost her umbrella in the morning but got it back that **very** evening.

> *Je l'ai fait moi-**même**.*
> I made it **myself**. (emphatic pronoun)

Here *même* is best translated as **even, including**:

> *Tout le monde est invité, **même** les gosses.*
> Everyone is invited, **even** the kids.

Nul

Nul precedes the noun it modifies. Its feminine is *nulle*. Because it means *not one*, it generally appears only in the singular. When nouns have no singular form at all, such as *noces* or *funérailles*, it can be made plural to match them.

Nul is often encountered as part of a negation with *ne*:

> *Nulle femme ne pourra plaire à sa mère.*
> His mother won't like any woman (he might bring home).

It can also be used as a descriptive adjective meaning **null**, **worthless**, or **void**:

> *Que je suis nul en maths!*
> I am so worthless in math!

Plusieurs

Plusieurs exists in one form only. It means **many** and always precedes the noun it modifies. Its use is very common:

> *Il y a plusieurs bons restaurants dans ce quartier.*
> There are many good restaurants in this neighborhood.

Quelconque

Quelconque has only two forms, singular and plural. It means **any one at all**. It may appear in front of or after the noun:

> *Ça m'est égal! Mets une cravate **quelconque**!*
> I don't care (which one you choose)! Put on **any** tie.

> *Elle te quittera pour un **quelconque** individu.*
> She'll leave you for **the first guy** she meets.

Quelconque takes on the meaning of **ordinary** or **poor** when combined with a negative or an adverb:

> *Ce n'est pas un professeur quelconque!*
> He's no ordinary teacher!

> *Ce restaurant-là est très quelconque.*
> That restaurant is second-rate (very poor).

Quelque

Quelque suggests **an indefinite amount** when it precedes the noun. It agrees with the noun and is usually translated as **some**, **a little**, or **a few**. It is **invariable** if it precedes a number; there it means **approximately**, **around**, or **about**:

> *Il y a juste quelques bagages à monter.*
> There are just a few suitcases to bring up.

> *Il faudra quelque sept heures pour le vol à Paris.*
> It will take about seven hours for the flight to Paris.

The subordinating conjunctions *quel + être + que* and *quelque . . . que* are explained under "The Subjunctive."

Tel

Tel can precede a noun with no other determiner to mean **like** or **such**:

> *Tel père, tel fils.*
> Like father, like son.

When preceded by *un*, *une*, or *de*, it still means **such**, **like**, or **similar**:

> *Je n'ai jamais vue de telles dents blanches.*
> I never saw such white teeth.

> *C'est un tel menteur!*
> He's such a liar!

If *tel* follows the noun, *que* generally comes after it:

> *J'admire un homme tel que Jean-Paul II.*
> I admire a man such as John Paul II.

The *que* is sometimes absent:

> *J'adore les fleurs odorantes, tels les oeillets.*
> I love fragrant flowers, such as carnations.

Note: *Tel* may agree with either the noun in the clause that precedes it, or the noun in its own clause.

Tel + quel are used to mean **just as they are**, **as is**:

> *Je te les donne, tels quels.*
> You can have them, as is.

Tout

Tout may appear in front of a noun with no other determiner. This usage is reserved for universal truths or widely accepted generalities:

> *Toute casserole a son couvercle.*
> Every pot has its lid.

Tout may be followed by a variety of other determiners to express **all** or **the whole**:

> *toute la nuit* (definite article)
> all night long

> *toute une semaine* (indefinite article)
> a whole week

> *tout ce mois* (demonstrative adjective)
> this whole month, all this month

> *toutes celles-ci* (demonstrative pronoun)
> all of these

> *tous mes amis* (possessive adjective)
> all my friends

> *tous les siens* (possessive pronoun)
> all of his

Tout can also refer to a noun or pronoun <u>via a verb</u>. It appears <u>after</u> the verb in simple tenses and between auxiliary and participle in compounds:

> *Nous venons **tous**.*
>> We're all coming.

> *Je vous invite **toutes**.*
>> I'm inviting all of you (girls).

> *La glace? Les enfants l'ont **toute** mangée.*
>> The ice cream? The children ate all of it.

> *Les coupables ont **tous** été punis.*
>> The guilty were all punished.

Whenever *tous* appears in this post-noun, post-pronoun position, its final *s* is distinctly pronounced. Compare:

> *Nous avons invité **tous** les garçons.* [**tu**]
>> We invited all the boys.

> *Les garçons vont **tous** venir.* [**tus**]
>> The boys are all coming.

Tout can also function as an adverb meaning **completely**:

> *Il est rentré **tout** mouillé.*
>> He came home completely soaked.

Oddly enough this adverb <u>will agree</u> with a feminine adjective beginning in a consonant or an aspirate *h*! Compare:

> *Tu as les mains **toutes** sales.*
>> Your hands are completely filthy.

> *Elles étaient **toutes** honteuses . . .*
>> They were completely ashamed . . . (They were all ashamed . . .)

But:

> *Elles étaient tout étonnées . . .*
>> They were completely surprised . . .

Drill 14: Indefinite Adjectives

Supply the French equivalent for the English cue. Use an indefinite adjective as part of each answer.

1. On a les _____.
   (same eyeglasses)

2. À cause d'une allergie, _____ noix ne lui est permise.
   (not one, not any)

3. Ils arrivent à ce _____.
   (very moment)

4. J'ai coupé ces fleurs ce matin et je les ai _____ mises dans un vase.   **(all)**

5. Où sont _____?
   (all the boys)

6. On se voit _____.
   (everyday)

7. Elle pose _____ avec soin.
   (each glass)

8. Prenez toutes ces boîtes _____, _____ celles sans couvercle.   **(as is)**   **(even)**

9. J'irai en France pour _____.
   (a whole year)

10. Les filles sont arrivées _____ essoufflées.
    (completely)

11. Sandrine, sais-tu faire la cuisine? Mais non! J'y suis _____!
    (worthless)

12. Il fait _____ chaleur!
    (such a)

13. Elle descendra dans _____ minutes.
    (a few)

14. Elle a essayé _____ robes avant de choisir celle-ci.
    (many)

15. Nous avons ce modèle dans toutes les tailles et en _____
    couleurs.   **(various)**

Drill 14–Answers and Explanations

1.   *mêmes lunettes*
We've got the same glasses. *Même* precedes the noun to mean **same**. It is plural to match *lunettes*.

2.   *aucune*
Because of his allergy, he's not allowed to have any nuts. This is a typical use of *aucun* + *ne* to mean **not one, not any**. Notice that it is <u>feminine</u> to match *noix*.

3.   *moment même*
They're arriving at this very moment. Position *même* after the noun to mean **very**.

4.   *toutes*
I cut these flowers this morning and I put them all in a vase. Here *toutes* refers to **them** (**the flowers**) via the verb *mettre*. It appears in between the auxiliary and the participle and reflects the feminine, plural nature of the flowers.

5.   *tous les garçons*
Where are all the boys? This is an example of *tout* + **definite article** to mean **all the**. The final *s* on *tous* is silent.

6.   *tous les jours*
We see each other everyday. *Tous les jours* is the best way to express **everyday**. It stresses the <u>multiple</u> or <u>plural</u> nature of these get togethers.

7.   *chaque verre*
She places each glass with care. Using *chaque* puts emphasis on **each single** glass.

8.   *telles quelles / même*
Take all of these boxes just as they are, even the ones without lids. Use *tel* + *quel* to mean **as is, unchanged**. Use *même* to mean **even, including**.

9.   *toute une année*
I will go to France for a whole year. Use *tout* + **indefinite article** to express **a whole, an entire year**.

10. *tout*

The girls arrived completely out of breath. *Tout* functions as an adverb here. It means **completely** or **entirely**. If the adjective had not begun with a vowel, *tout* would have agreed with it! *Les filles sont arrivées **toutes** rafraîchies* (**completely refreshed**).

11. *nulle*

Sandrine, do you know how to cook? Not at all, I'm hopeless (in the kitchen)! *Nul* is used here to mean **useless** or **worthless**. Notice that it is feminine because the speaker is a woman.

12. *une telle*

It's so hot! (Literally, **such a heat!**)

13. *quelques*

She'll be down in a few minutes. Use *quelque* to express the indefinite amount **a few**. Note the agreement.

14. *plusieurs*

She tried on many dresses before choosing this one. Always plural, *plusieurs* is placed in front of a noun to mean **many**.

15. *diverses*

We have this style in every size and a variety of colors. The adjective *différentes* would also be possible here.

INDEFINITE PRONOUNS

Many of the indefinite adjectives we discussed earlier also exist as pronouns. They stand on their own, in place of nouns. These include *aucun* and *aucune*; *autre*; all four forms of *certain*; *chacun* and *chacune*, which are the pronoun versions of *chaque*, *plusieurs*, *quelque chose*, and *quelqu'un*; the pronouns that correspond to the adjective *quelque*; *tel*; and all the forms of *tout*.

Here are examples of each:

>*Elle n'a lu **aucun** de ses livres.*
>> She has read none of his books.

>*J'ai gâché cette feuille, Madame, puis-je en avoir une **autre**?*
>> I messed up this paper, Madame; may I have another one?

>***Certains** sont très osés.*
>> Some of them are very daring.

>*J'ai aimé **chacun** de ses films.*
>> I liked each one of his films.

>*Choisis un bonbon. Il y en a **plusieurs**.*
>> Choose a candy. There are many.

>*Tu veux **quelque chose** à boire?*
>> Do you want something to drink?

>*Il y a **quelqu'un** à la porte.*
>> There's someone at the door.

>***Tel** dansait, **tel** regardait.*
>> Some danced; some watched.

>***Tout** est prêt maintenant.*
>> Everything is ready now.

Drill 15: Indefinite Pronouns

Supply the French equivalent for the English cue. Use an indefinite pronoun for each answer.

1.   Maman, on réclame _____ à manger !
        (something)

2.   As-tu vu les photos ? _____ sont vraiment bonnes.
        (some of them)

3.   _____ causait, _____ dormait.
        (some)   **(some, others)**

4.   Tu as lu _____ de mes lettres !
        (each one)

5.   Ils sont _____ partis en guerre.
          (all)

6.   As-tu trouvé une belle robe pour la fête ? Non, _____ !
                                        (not one)

7.   Lequel est allé en Californie, Arthur ou André ? Ils y sont allés

     _____.

   (both of them, i.e., **all)**

8.   Pourquoi Antoine n'y est-il pas allé aussi ? Il avait d'_____
     choses à faire.   **(other)**

9.   Il y a _____ à l'appareil pour Carlos. Je crois que c'est Dani-
     elle.   **(someone)**

10. Combien de sucettes nous reste-t-il ? Il nous en reste _____.
                                              (several)

Drill 15–Answers and Explanations

1. *quelque chose*
Mom, they're asking for something to eat. *Quelque chose* literally means **something**.

2. *Certaines*
Have you seen the photos? Some of them are really good. The indefinite pronoun standing in for *les photos* must be feminine and plural, hence *certaines*.

3. *Tel / tel*
Some were chatting; others slept. As a pronoun *tel* is invariable. It can be translated as **one, some,** or **other.** It often appears in proverbs and sayings such as *Tel qui rit vendredi, en pleurera dimanche.* (**Laugh today, cry tomorrow.**)

4. *chacune*
You read each one of my letters! The indefinite pronoun stands for a feminine noun, thus *chacune*.

5. *tous*
They've all gone off to war. In a compound tense, the indefinite pronoun *tous* appears in between the helping verb and the participle. The final *s* of *tous* is sounded in this position.

6. *aucune*
Did you find a nice dress for the party? No, not one! The indefinite pronoun reflects that the noun it stands for is feminine.

7. *tous les deux*
Which one went to California, Arthur or Andy? They both went. *Tous les* + **number** is the same as *tous les* + **noun.** It means **all of them,** in this case, **both,** because there are only two.

8. *d'autres*
Why didn't Tony go too? He had other things to do. The indefinite pronoun is plural here to match *choses*.

9. *quelqu'un*
There's someone on the phone for Carlos. I think it's Danielle. Use the indefinite pronoun *quelqu'un* for an **unknown person**.

10. *plusieurs*
How many lollipops do we have left? We have several left. The indefinite pronoun *plusieurs* means **several** or **many**.

ADVERBS

Adverbs modify verbs, adjectives, and other adverbs. All adverbs are invariable. The following are groups of common adverbs that you should know:

Adverbs of Time (*répondent à la question quand?*)

alors, then
après, afterwards
aujourd'hui, today
auparavant, before
autrefois, formerly
aussitôt, immediately
bientôt, soon
cependant, (as) meanwhile
d'abord, first
déjà, already
demain, tomorrow
encore, again, still, yet
enfin, at last

ensuite, then, next
hier, yesterday
lontemps, a long time
maintenant, now
parfois, sometimes
puis, then
quelquefois, sometimes
rarement, seldom
souvent, often
tard, late
tôt, early
toujours, always
tout de suite, immediately

Adverbs of Place (*répondent à la question où?*)

ailleurs, elsewhere
dedans, inside
dehors, outside
devant, in front
derrière, behind
dessous, underneath

dessus, on top, on it
ici, here
là, there
loin, far
partout, everywhere
près, near

Adverbs of Manner (*répondent à la question comment?*)

ainsi, thus, like so
bien, well, very
ensemble, together
exprès, on purpose

fort, very
mal, badly
vite, quickly
volontiers, willingly

Adverbs of Quantity *(répondent à la question combien?)*

assez, enough, quite
autant, as much
beaucoup, much
davantage, more
moins, less

peu, little, few
plus, more
tant, so much, so many
tellement, so much, so many
trop, too much, too

Adverbs of Relative Degree *(clarifient les degrés de signification)*

aussi, also, too
à peine, hardly
cependant, however
comme, as
environ, about, approximately
même, even
peut-être, maybe, perhaps

plutôt, rather
presque, almost
seulement, only
si, so
surtout, especially
très, very

ADVERB FORMATION

Rule 1

Adverbs are generally made from adjectives by adding **-ment** to singular adjective forms that end in a <u>vowel</u>. Because the masculine singular adjective generally ends in a consonant, we most often use the <u>feminine singular adjective</u> as our base. This form provides the <u>required vowel</u> we need before we can add -*ment*:

affreux	*affreuse*	*affreusement*
bon	*bonne*	*bonnement*
doux	*douce*	*doucement*
franc	*franche*	*franchement*
gentil	*gentille*	*gentiment*
premier	*première*	*premièrement*
seul	*seule*	*seulement*
vif	*vive*	*vivement*

Adding *-ment* directly to a masculine singular adjective is possible if it already ends in a vowel:

autre = autrement   *facile = facilement*   *joli = joliment*
poli = poliment   *résolu = résolument*   *vrai = vraiment*

Only three masculine adjectives ending in vowels don't comply:

> *Gai* uses its feminine form to create the adverb *gaiement*.
> *Fou* is replaced by folle to create the adjective *follement*.
> *Nouveau* is also replaced by its feminine form to make *nouvellement*.

Rule 2

Sometimes the silent *e* of the adjective will become <u>accented</u> in the adverb form. This may happen to break up <u>three consonantal sounds in a row</u>. Here are some examples:

> *aveugle = aveuglément*
> *énorme = énormément*
> *expresse = expressément*
> *profonde = profondément*

This also occurs to separate a strong consonantal sound such as [z] from the *-ment*:

> *confuse = confusément*
> *précise = précisément*
> *profuse = profusément*

Rule 3

Adjectives that end in *-ant* and *-ent* in the masculine singular are made into adverbs by first removing the *-nt*, which exposes the vowel. We then attach *-mment* (notice the doubled *m*) to create the adverb.

> *constant = constamment*
> *puissant = puissamment*
> *évident = évidemment*
> *récent = récemment*

Exceptions to Rule 3 (the *-nt* is retained):

> *lent = lentement*
> *présent = présentement*

Rule 4

These irregular forms are quite commonly used and should be learned by heart:

bon, good	*bien*, well
bref, brief	*brièvement*, briefly
gentil, kind	*gentiment*, kindly
mauvais, bad	*mal*, badly
meilleur, better	*mieux*, better

Rule 5

There are many adjectives with no corresponding adverbial form. In this case we use a prepositional phrase that retains the adjective. Here are some examples:

charmant	*Elle nous a accueillis **d'un ton** charmant.*
content	*Elle a souri **d'une manière** contente.*
givré	*Il m'a répondu **d'un air** givré.*
répugnant	*Il mange **de façon** répugnante.*

Drill 16: Adverb Formation

Make adverbs from the following adjectives:

1.   amical = _____

2.   absolu = _____

3.   méchant = _____

4.   intense = _____

5.   bref = _____

6.   concis = _____

7.   suffisant = _____

8.   conscient = _____

9.   infini = _____

10.   uniforme = _____

11.   impulsif = _____

12.   long = _____

13.   éperdu = _____

14.   patient = _____

15.   moyen = _____

Drill 16–Answers and Explanations

1. *amicalement*
   Because *amical* ends in a consonant, we add *-ment* to the feminine form instead. (Rule 1)

2. *absolument*
   Absolu ends in a vowel, so it can take *-ment* directly. (Rule 1)

3. *méchamment*
   Méchant loses *-nt*, and then takes *-mment*. (Rule 3)

4. *intensément*
   The silent *e* of *intense* becomes <u>accented</u> in the adverb form. This prevents three consonant sounds from coming together. (Rule 2)

5. *brièvement*
   This is an irregularity that must be remembered. (Rule 4)

6. *concisément*
   The feminine *concise* will trigger the accented *e* in the adverb to set off the strong consonant sound of [z].(Rule 2)

7. *suffisamment*
   Suffisant drops *-nt* and takes *-mment* to form the adverb. (Rule 3)

8. *consciemment*
   Conscient also drops *-nt* and takes *-mment* to form the adverb. (Rule 3)

9. *infiniment*
   Ending in a vowel allows *infini* to take *-ment* directly. (Rule 1)

10. *uniformément*
    Like *intense* in question 4, *uniforme* needs the accented *e* to separate three consonant sounds. (Rule 2)

11. *impulsivement*
    Like the majority of masculine adjectives, *impulsif* ends in a consonant, so the adverb is based on the feminine *impulsive* instead. (Rule 1)

12. *longuement*
    Long is replaced by its feminine form *longue* before accepting *-ment*. This is the most common type of adverb formation. (Rule 1)

13. *éperdument*

Éperdu ends in a vowel and accepts *-ment* directly. (Rule 1)

14. *patiemment*

Like most adjectives in *-ent* and *-ant*, *patient* drops *-nt* and takes *-mment*. (Rule 2)

15. *moyennement*

We use the feminine form *moyenne* as a base for *-ment*. (Rule 1)

ADVERB POSITION

French adverbs come as close to the words they modify as possible.

Rule 1

The adverb must come directly in front of the adjective or adverb it modifies.

> *J'ai **si** chaud.*
> *Ce tissu est **moins** épais.*
> *Elle parle **trop** vite.*
> *Je l'ai embrassé **très** fort.*

Rule 2

The adverb must come directly <u>after</u> the simple verb it modifies. (A simple verb has just one part.)

> *Elle travaille **assidûment**.*
> *J'aime dormir **tard**.*

Notice that this common adverb position in English is to be avoided in French:

He **often** drinks wine.	*Il boit **souvent** du vin.*
He **always** orders fish.	*Il prend **toujours** du poisson.*
He **never** orders meat.	*Il ne prend **jamais** de viande.*
He **already** knows.	*Il le sait **déjà**.*

Rule 3

In compound tenses <u>short adverbs</u> are placed <u>between</u> the auxiliary verb and the past participle.

*Il a **bien** réussi.*	*Le film m'a **beaucoup** plu.*
*Nous avons **déjà** dîné.*	*Je ne me suis pas **encore** habillée.*
*J'ai **mal** compris.*	*Il m'a **souvent** aidé.*
*J'ai **presque** fini.*	*Je l'ai **toujours** aimé.*
*Il a **trop** bu.*	*J'ai **vite** compris.*

Rule 4

In compound tenses, longer adverbs and those ending in *-ment* are placed <u>after</u> the past participle.

> *Elle m'a salué **chaleureusement**.*
> *On s'est écrit **fidèlement**.*

Exceptions: ***certainement***, ***complètement***, and ***probablement*** are placed between the auxiliary and the participle:

> *J'ai **complètement** oublié.*

Rule 5

In compound tenses, adverbs of **time** and **place** are also positioned after the past participle, even the short ones.

> *Je l'ai vu **hier**.*
> *Je me suis levé **tôt**.*
> *J'ai les ai laissés **dehors**.*

Drill 17: Position of Adverbs in Compound Tenses

Place the adverb correctly. Does it come between the auxiliary and past participle, or after the past participle?

1. Il a _____ répondu_____. (brusquement)

2. Je me suis _____ couché _____. (tard)

3. Il est _____ arrivé _____. (aujourd'hui)

4. Tu es _____resté _____. (dehors)

5. J'ai _____vu _____ ce film. (déjà)

6. Il m'a _____énervé _____. (constamment)

7. Nous avons _____ appris _____. (beaucoup)

8. Il m'a _____ convaincue _____. (petit à petit)

9. Ils ont _____fini _____ leurs devoirs. (vite)

10. Est-ce que tu as _____ mangé _____? (trop)

11. Ils sont _____ partis _____ ce matin. (tôt)

12. J'ai _____ cherché _____. (ailleurs)

13. Mémé nous a _____ attendus _____.
    (patiemment)

14. Gaston est _____ allé _____ de chez lui. (loin)

15. Il m'a _____ invitée _____. (souvent)

Drill 17–Answers and Explanations

1. *Il a répondu **brusquement**.*
   He answered abruptly. Adverbs ending in *-ment* come after the participle. (Rule 4)

2. *Je me suis couché **tard**.*
   I went to bed late. Adverbs of <u>time</u> come after the participle. (Rule 5)

3. *Il est arrivé **aujourd'hui**.*
   He arrived today. Adverbs of <u>time</u> come after the participle. (Rule 5)

4. *Tu es resté **dehors**.*
   You stayed outside. Adverbs of <u>place</u> come after the participle. (Rule 5)

5. *J'ai **déjà** vu ce film.*
   I already saw that film. <u>Short</u> adverbs come <u>between</u> the auxiliary and the participle. (Rule 3)

6. *Il m'a énervé **constamment**.*
   He irritated me constantly. Adverbs ending in *-ment* come after the participle. (Rule 4)

7. *Nous avons **beaucoup** appris.*
   We learned a lot. *Beaucoup*, with only two syllables, comes <u>between</u> the auxiliary and the participle. (Rule 3)

8. *Il m'a convaincue **petit à petit**.*
   He convinced me little by little. <u>Long</u> adverbs come <u>after</u> the participle. (Rule 4)

9. *Ils ont **vite** fini leurs devoirs.*
   They finished their homework quickly. <u>Short</u> adverbs come <u>between</u> the auxiliary and the participle. (Rule 3)

10. *Est-ce que tu as **trop** mangé?*
    Did you eat too much? Short adverbs come between the auxiliary and the participle. (Rule 3)

11. *Ils sont partis **tôt** ce matin.*
    They left early this morning. Adverbs of <u>time</u> come after the participle. (Rule 5)

12. *J'ai cherché **ailleurs**.*
    I looked elsewhere. Adverbs of <u>place</u> come after the participle. (Rule 5)

13. *Mémé nous a attendus **patiemment**.*

  Granny waited for us patiently. Adverbs ending in **-ment** come after the participle. (Rule 4)

14. *Gaston est allé **loin** de chez lui.*

  Gaston went a long way from home. Adverbs of <u>place</u> come after the participle. (Rule 5)

15. *Il m'a **souvent** invitée.*

  He invited me often. *Souvent*, with only two syllables, comes <u>between</u> the auxiliary and the participle. (Rule 3)

ADJECTIVES USED AS ADVERBS

There are quite a few adjectives used as adverbs in some fixed expressions. The <u>adjective</u> always remains <u>masculine and singular</u> to indicate its adverbial role.

Here are some common examples:

> *Les œillets **sentent bon***.
> Carnations smell good.

> *Les ordures **sentent mauvais***.
> Garbage smells bad.

> *Je **chante faux***.
> I sing off key.

> *Ma sœur **chante juste***.
> My sister sings in tune.

> *Elle s'est **arrêtée court***.
> She stopped short.

> *Il s'est fait **couper ras** les cheveux*.
> He had his hair cut very short.

> *Elle **parle bas***.
> She speaks softly.

> *Elle doit **parler** plus **fort**, plus **haut***.
> She should speak louder.

> *Elle est **fort** jolie*.
> She's very pretty.

> *Les filles modernes **s'habillent court***.
> Modern girls wear their skirts short.

> *Nous **travaillons dur***.
> We work hard.

> ***Marchez droit** devant vous*.
> Walk straight ahead.

> *Je lui dirai **clair** et **net** ce que je pense*.
> I will tell him clearly what I think.

> ***Haut** les mains!   **Bas** les mains!*
> Hands up!   Hands down!

*Je voudrais conforter la petite fille **tout** en pleurs.*
 I would like to comfort the little girl all in tears.

*Il a **refusé net**.*
 He flatly refused.

*Je ne **vois** pas **clair**, allume!*
 I can't see well; turn on the light.

Drill 18: Adjectives Used as Adverbs

Complete the little sentences in French. Each one contains an adjective in an adverbial role:

1. Travaillez _____ pour réussir dans la vie.

2. Quand va-t-on manger ? Le dîner sent si _____ !

3. Allume ta torche électrique et tu y verras plus _____.

4. Arrête de chanter comme ça ! Tu chantes _____ !

5. C'est la police ! Posez vos armes ! _____ les mains !

6. Je dois laver le chien cet après-midi. Il sent _____ !

7. Je vous entends à peine. Parlez plus _____ !

8. Il a dit non, tout _____ !

9. Regardez _____ devant vous !

10. Il m'a chuchoté tout _____.

Drill 18–Answers and Explanations

1. *dur*
   Work hard to succeed in life. Like all adjectives used in this manner, *dur* is invariable.

2. *bon*
   When are we going to eat? Dinner smells so good! This expression parallels English verbatim.

3. *clair*
   Turn on your flashlight and you will see better. *Voir clair* is a fixed expression meaning **to see well, adequately**.

4. *faux*
   Stop singing like that! You're singing off key! The opposite of this idiom is *chanter juste*, **to sing in tune**.

5. *Haut*
   It's the police! Put down your weapons! Hands up! Notice the position of *haut*, <u>in front of</u> *les mains*. Similarly, **hands down!** is *bas les mains!*

6. *mauvais*
   I must wash the dog this afternoon. He smells bad! This expression is just like its English counterpart, word for word.

7. *fort* (or *haut*)
   I can hardly hear you. Speak up! (Speak louder!) Use either *fort* or *haut* for **louder**.

8. *court* (or *net*)
   He said no, flat out! Straight out! *Tout court* means **abruptly, right away**. *Net* is **flatly**.

9. *droit*
   Look straight ahead! *Droit* means **straight**. Likewise, **sit up straight** is *asseyez-vous droit*.

10. *bas*
    He whispered to me quietly, softly. Literally *bas* means **low**.

COMPARISON OF ADJECTIVES

The Comparative

French cannot alter the spelling of an adjective for comparison the way we do by adding **-er** or **-est** in English. French relies on the placement of an <u>adverb</u> in front of the adjective to be compared.

Here are the comparative adverbs:

plus (**more, -er**)	*Tu es plus grand que moi.*
moins (**less, fewer**)	*Tu es **moins** grand **que** Papa.*
aussi (**as**)	*Tu es **aussi** grand **que** Jean.*
si (**not as, not so**)	*Tu n'es pas **si** grand **que** ça.*

The remainder of the comparative is introduced by *que*, unless a countable quantity or number is involved, in which case we use *de*. Both words are translated as **than** or **as**:

> *Cette jupe-ci est **moins** chère **que** celle-là.*
> This skirt is **less** expensive **than** that one.

> *Ils ont trouvé **plus de** 100 euros.*
> They found **more than** a hundred euros.

> *Il fait **aussi** froid en janvier **qu'**en février.*
> It's **as** cold in January **as** (it is) in February.

> *J'ai **moins de** cinq pages à finir.*
> I have **fewer than** five pages to finish.

> *Je ne suis pas **si** vieux **que** ça !*
> I'm **not as** old **as** that! I'm **not that** old!

> *Il nous en reste **plus d'**une douzaine.*
> We have **more than** a dozen (of them) left.

Use *plus de* (also *moins de*) with a countable noun <u>but</u> use *plus que* (or *moins que*) with a quantity that doesn't divide into smaller parts:

> *Il nous reste **plus que** la moitié.*
> We have **more than** half left.

The Superlative

To make the superlative of adjectives (except for those that are irregular in comparison), we place a form of *le plus* or *le moins* directly in front of the adjective in question:

> *Pépé, c'est le plus vieux membre de notre famille.*
> Grand-Pop is the oldest member of our family.

> *Sandrine est la jeune fille la plus sportive que je connaisse.*
> Sandrine is the most athletic girl I know.

> *Monsieur Clayton est mon professeur le plus intéressant.*
> Mr. Clayton is my most interesting teacher.

> *Ce repas était le moins cher de notre voyage.*
> That meal was the least expensive of our trip.

> *Ce sont les livres les moins intéressants que j'aie lus.*
> Those are the least interesting books that I read.

> *Tu es le plus beau garçon du monde.*
> You are the most handsome boy in the world.

Looking over the examples, we can make the following observations about the superlative construction:

1. If the adjective <u>follows</u> the noun, the definitive article appears twice: once in front of the noun, and once in front of the adjective. The position of the adjective relative to the noun is the same as usual; most follow, but BANGS adjectives precede.

2. The article <u>agrees</u> with the noun it refers to.

3. The superlative may use a <u>possessive adjective</u> instead of an article.

4. The English word **in** is expressed by *de* or a contraction of *de* + **article**. Do not use *dans*!

5. Verbs following the superlative are subjunctive, unless an actual fact is being related.

Irregular Comparatives and Superlatives

A few adjectives have irregular forms of comparison. It is interesting to note that they are also irregular in English:

bon	*meilleur*	*le meilleur*
good	better	the best
mauvais	*pire; plus mauvais*	*le pire; le plus mauvais*
bad	worse	the worst
petit	*plus petit*	*le plus petit*
small	smaller	the smallest (for size)
	moindre	*le moindre*
	lesser, slighter	the least, the slightest (for importance)

Here are some examples of irregular comparatives and superlatives in context:

*Je n'ai pas **la moindre** idée **de** ce que je vais faire.*
I haven't the slightest idea what I'm going to do.

*Tu es **ma meilleure** amie.*
You are my best friend.

*C'est **la pire** note **de** ma vie !*
It's the worst grade of my life!

*Nous voulons **les meilleurs** qui soient !*
We want the best ones there are!

*C'est **le pire** soufflé **de** ma carrière; il est si plat qu'on dirait une crêpe !*
It's the worst soufflé of my career; it's so flat it looks like a pancake!

Drill 19: Comparative and Superlative of Adjectives

Write these sentences in French. Observe the rules of placement and agreement. Know when to use an irregular form. Use the subjunctive where needed. Know when to use *de* versus *que*. Translate **in** correctly.

1. He's the smartest boy in the class.

2. It's the least of my problems.

3. She is younger than I.

4. This box is less heavy than yours.

5. You ate less than half of your dessert.

6. Your mother is the most patient woman I know.

7. These are the warmest socks.

8. I worked more than five hours.

9. French is my strongest subject.

10. He is taller than your brother.

Drill 19–Answers and Explanations

1. *C'est le garçon le plus intelligent de la classe.*
    This is a regular superlative formation. The article appears twice because *intelligent* follows the noun. **In the class** is translated by the prepositional phrase *de la classe.*

2. *C'est le moindre de mes problèmes.*
    This is an irregular superlative based on *petit,* the **smallest** in the sense of the **least** or the **slightest**.

3. *Elle est plus jeune que moi.*
    This is a regular comparative using *plus que*. Note the disjunctive pronoun after *que.*

4. *Cette boîte est moins lourde que la tienne (la vôtre).*
    This is a regular comparative using *moins que.*

5. *Tu as mangé moins que la moitié de ton dessert. (Vous avez mangé moins que la moitié de votre dessert.)*
    Regular comparative **less than**. We use *que* because the quantity cannot be divided into smaller parts (and still be half).

6. *Ta mère est la femme la plus patiente que je connaisse.*
    This regular superlative is followed by the subjunctive to reflect the opinion of the speaker.

7. *Ce sont les chaussettes les plus chaudes.*
    The article appears twice in this regular superlative—once in front of **socks**, and once in front of *plus* + **adjective**. This repetition occurs whenever the adjective follows the noun, which is most of the time. Note how the articles match the noun to which they refer.

8. *J'ai travaillé plus de cinq heures.*
    Because the second part of the comparison involves a countable number, we use *de* instead of *que* to introduce it.

9. *Le français est ma plus forte matière.*
    This sentence uses a possessive adjective in the superlative construction. Note the placement of the adjective in front of the noun here; it is figurative as opposed to concrete.

10. *Il est plus grand que ton frère.*
    This is a regular comparative using *plus que.*

THE COMPARISON OF ADVERBS

To make the comparative of adverbs we rely on the same combinations we learned for the comparative of adjectives:

plus (**more**, **-er**)	*Tu cours plus vite que moi.*
moins (**less**)	*Tu voyages moins fréquemment que Papa.*
aussi (**as**)	*Tu chantes aussi follement que Jean.*
si (**not as**, **not so**)	*Tu ne réponds pas si souvent que ça.*

The Superlative of Adverbs

To make the superlative of adverbs (except for those that are irregular in comparison) we place a form of *le plus* or *le moins* directly in front of the adverb in question. Because adverbs always remain invariable, the masculine singular article is the only one used:

> *Elle parle **le plus vite** de toutes mes amies.*
> Of all my girl friends, she talks the fastest.

> *C'est le plus faible de la portée et il a grandi **le moins**.*
> He's the runt of the litter and he grew the least.

Irregular Comparatives and Superlatives

A few adverbs have irregular forms of comparison:

beaucoup a lot, much	*plus* more	*le plus* the most
bien well	*mieux* better	*le mieux* the best
mal badly	*plus mal*, *pire* worse	*le plus mal*, *le pire* the worst
peu little	*moins* less	*le moins* the least

Students often confuse adjective and adverb forms. Never try to modify a verb form with *meilleur*, for example. This is a common mistake because both the <u>adjective</u> *meilleur* and the <u>adverb</u> *mieux* have the same English translation: **better**. In English we can use **better** in either case without giving it a thought. In French we must distinguish between the need for an adjective (to modify a noun) and the need for adverb (to modify a verb or an adjective). No wonder students often report that they understand English grammar better through their study of French.

Study these examples:

C'est une meilleure chanson et tu la chantes mieux que moi.
It's a better song and you sing it better than I do.

Voici un meilleur tailleur que tu portes mieux que moi.
Here's a better suit that you wear better than I do.

Drill 20: Comparative and Superlative of Adverbs

Supply the needed adverb:

1. Je chante _____. (**badly**)

2. Elle chante _____. (**well**)

3. Tu manges _____ que moi. (**faster**)

4. Je cours _____ que toi. (**less fast**)

5. Vous travaillez _____ que nous (**as hard**)

6. Papa danse _____ que Maman. (**better**)

7. Elle mange très _____. (**little**)

8. Je les vois _____ maintenant. (**more often**)

9. Tu manges _____ que moi. (**less**)

10. Elle prononce _____ de tous. (**the best**)

Drill 20–Answers and Explanations

1. *mal*
   I sing badly. *Mal* is the adverb meaning **badly**.

2. *bien*
   She sings well. *Bien* means **well**. Its other comparative forms are irregular: *mieux* and *le mieux*.

3. *plus vite*
   You eat faster than I. This is a standard comparative using *plus* + adverb to mean **more**.

4. *moins vite*
   I run less quickly/less fast than you. This is a standard comparative using *moins* + adverb to mean **less**.

5. *aussi dur*
   You work as hard as we do. Another basic comparative, this one uses *aussi* + adverb to mean **as**.

6. *mieux*
   Dad dances better than Mom. This is the irregular comparative of *bien*.

7. *peu*
   She eats very little. *Peu* means **little**. Its other comparative forms are irregular: *moins* and *le moins*.

8. *plus souvent*
   I see them more often now. This is a standard comparative using *plus* + adverb to mean **more**.

9. *moins*
   You eat less than I. This is a standard comparative using *moins* + adverb to mean **less**.

10. *le mieux*
    She pronounces the best of all. Notice the masculine article in this irregular superlative form of *bien*.

THE DEMONSTRATIVE

Demonstrative Adjectives

Like their English counterparts, French demonstrative adjectives refer to nouns that are at hand, are in full view, or are being discussed. They always precede the nouns they modify and match them in gender and number. Because they are bound to <u>agree with the noun</u>, French demonstrative adjectives cannot distinguish between **this** and **that**, as they do in English. **These** and **those** are also indistinguishable.

ce	**this** or **that** for a singular masculine noun
cet	**this** or **that** for a singular masculine noun/vowel, silent *h*
cette	**this** or **that** for a singular feminine noun
ces	**these** or **those** for all plural nouns

Ce garçon est mon neveu.
   This (that) boy is my nephew.

Cet ordinateur est tombé en panne.
   This (that) computer crashed.

Qui est cet homme?
   Who is **this (that)** man?

Cette chemise est trop chère.
   This (that) shirt is too expensive.

J'ai reçu ces pantoufles comme cadeau d'anniversaire.
   I got **these (those)** slippers as a birthday present.

If two things are very similar and you wish to make a contrast, French does allow the attachment of *-ci* (**here**) and *-là* (**there**) to the end of the nouns in question.

Ce fromage-ci est français, ce fromage-là est hollandais.
   This cheese (here) is French; that cheese (there) is Dutch.

Demonstrative Pronouns

A demonstrative pronoun takes the place of a demonstrative adjective + noun. They agree in gender and number with the nouns they replace and provide the equivalent of **the one** or **the ones** in English.

celui	masculine singular	**the one**
celle	feminine singular	**the one**
ceux	masculine plural	**the ones**, also **these**, **those**
celles	feminine plural	**the ones**, also **these**, **those**

> *Ce stylo bave, je vais chercher **celui** dans mon tiroir.*
> This pen leaks; I'm going to get **the one** in my drawer.

> *Cette jupe est trop longue, mets **celle** de vendredi soir.*
> That skirt is too long, put on **the one** (you wore) Friday night.

> *Voici tes devoirs, **ceux** que tu repassais pour l'examen.*
> Here are your assignments, **the ones** you were reviewing for the test.

> *As-tu vu mes lunettes, **celles** en strass?*
> Have you seen my glasses, **the ones** with the rhinestones?

> *J'ai trouvé une bague sensationnelle, **celle** dont je rêvais toujours.*
> I found a great ring, **the one** I've always dreamed of.

The attachment of *-ci* or *-là* directly to the demonstrative pronoun creates contrast or emphasis, just as it does with a noun and adjective combination. Study these examples:

> *Elle n'aime pas ce vélo-**ci**, elle préfère **celui-là**.*
> She doesn't like **this** bike; she prefers **that one**.

> *Ces fleurs-**ci** sont des marguerites, **celles-là** des anémones.*
> **These** flowers are daisies; **those** are anemones.

If you look back over all of the examples we have used for demonstrative pronouns, you will notice that they never stand alone, but are generally supported by a <u>preposition</u>, a <u>relative pronoun</u> (*qui*, *que*, or *dont*), or the attachment of *-ci* or *-là*.

Ceci, Cela, and *Ça*

Ceci (**this**) and *cela* (**that**) never relate to a noun that has already been mentioned. They refer, instead, to something that has not yet been named. *Ceci* is becoming uncommon, with *cela* serving more and more as both **this** and **that**. In everyday speech *cela* is frequently shortened to *ça*.

> *Ne fais pas **ça**!*
>> Don't do that!

> *Et **ça** sert à quoi, **cela**?*
>> And what's that for?

> *Prenez **ceci**, je vous le donne.*
>> Take this; I'm giving it to you.

The pronoun *ce* (*c'*) is used as the subject of the verb *être* to convey **this** or **that is**, **these** or **those are**. The same combination can also be translated as **he**, **she**, or **it is**, or **they are**. Here are some examples.

C'est le mien.	This is mine.	That is mine.
Ce sont les miens.	These are mine.	Those are mine.
C'est mon frère.	It's my brother. He's my brother.	This is (that is) my brother.
Ce sont mes frères.	These (those) are my brothers.	They're my brothers.

Ce qui, ce que, and *ce dont* are relative pronouns and are discussed under that topic.

Drill 21: Demonstrative Adjectives and Pronouns

Supply the demonstrative adjective or pronoun suggested by the English clue:

1. J'admire _____ qui sont bilingues.
    (those)

2. Qui est _____ homme masqué?
    (that)

3. Donnez-moi _____, s'il vous plaît.
    (that)

4. Où as-tu eu _____ livres?
    (those)

5. _____ est trop épaisse. Prends _____; elle est plus mince.
    (That one)   **(this one)**

6. Je ne comprends pas_____.
    (that)

7. J'ai fait _____ exercices _____, mais pas _____.
    (these)   **(those)**

8. _____ me fatigue beaucoup.
    (This)

9. Laquelle est Mme Aubry? _____ aux cheveux courts.
    (The one)

10. Puis-je m'asseoir sur _____ chaise?
    (this)

11. Ce pull-ci me va bien; _____ est trop serré.
    (that one)

12. Expliquez-lui _____.
    (this)

13. Je vais prendre ces robes-là, tu peux prendre _____.
    (these)

14. Où a-t-elle trouvé _____ vin pétillant?
    (this)

15. Ce contrôle est facile, mais _____ de l'autre jour était beaucoup
    plus difficile.   **(the one)**

16. Qu'est-ce que tu fais _____ week-end?
    (this)

17. _____ était en 1946.
    (That)

18. _____ ne sont pas mes livres.
    (These)

19. Je ne crois pas que _____ soit vrai.
    (that)

20. _____ est un beau pays.
    (That)

21. _____ ne se dit pas.
    (That)

22. Confortez _____ qui sont tristes, et aidez _____ qui sont pauvres.
    (those)   **(those)**

23. _____ se trouve dans tous les grands magasins.
    (That)

24. Mon portable est dans mon sac; _____ est-il le tien?
    (this one)

25. Pourrais-tu déposer _____ colis à la poste?
    (these)

Drill 21–Answers and Explanations

1. *ceux*

   I admire those who are bilingual. With no noun present, use the demonstrative pronoun *ceux* to convey **those**. Notice the supporting relative pronoun *qui*, a clue that you need to supply a pronoun, not an adjective.

2. *cet*

   Who is that masked man? *Cet* is the adjective form needed in front of this masculine noun beginning a silent *h*.

3. *cela*

   Give me that, please. No noun has yet been mentioned; therefore we chose *cela* to convey **that**.

4. *ces*

   Where did you get those books? *Ces* is needed here; it is the only plural form of the demonstrative adjective.

5. *Celle-là / celle-ci*

   That one is too thick. Take this one; it's thinner. The adjective *épaisse* and the pronoun *elle* are clues that a distinction is being made between two unnamed nouns that are both feminine and singular.

6. *cela*

   I don't understand that. The pronoun *cela* stands for an as-yet-unmentioned noun.

7. *ces / -ci / ceux-là*

   I did these exercises but not those. We can distinguish between two very similar nouns, one named, and one unnamed, by attaching *-ci* to *exercices* and *-là* to *ceux*.

8. *Ceci*

   This is very tiring for me. The nonspecific pronoun *ceci* is used when no noun has yet been named.

9. *celle*

   Which one is Mrs. Aubry? The one with the short hair. The feminine singular demonstrative adjective *celle* refers to the woman in question. The supporting preposition *aux* is a giveaway clue that a pronoun is needed.

10. *cette*

May I sit on this chair? The noun *chaise* requires a feminine singular demonstrative adjective to modify it.

11. *celui-là*

This sweater fits me well; that one is too tight. We attach *-ci* to **this sweater** and *-là* to **that one** to distinguish between two similar nouns, one named and one unnamed.

12. *ceci*

Explain this to him. Choose the nonspecific pronoun *ceci* when no noun has yet been named.

13. *celles-ci*

I'm going to take those dresses; you can take these. We know that the pronoun stands for **dresses**, so we chose the feminine plural form and attach *-ci* for contrast.

14. *ce*

Where did she find this (that) sparkling wine? *Ce* is the masculine singular adjective form needed to modify *vin*.

15. *celui*

This quiz is easy, but the one the other day was much more difficult. We know the pronoun refers to **quiz**, so we chose the masculine singular form of the pronoun to stand for *contrôle*.

16. *ce*

What are you doing this weekend? **Week-end** requires the masculine singular form of the adjective, *ce*.

17. *C'*

That was in 1946. The nonspecific pronoun *ce* commonly provides the subject of *être*.

18. *Ce*

These are not my books. This is an example of the pronoun *ce* serving as the subject of a form of the verb *être*.

19. *ce*

I don't think that's true. The pronoun *ce* is again the subject of *être*, in this case *soit*.

20. *C'*

That's (it's) a beautiful country. The nonspecific pronoun *ce* again provides the subject of *être*.

21. *Cela*

   That is not said. The pronoun *cela* stands for an as-yet-unmentioned noun.

22. *ceux / ceux*

   Comfort those who are sad and help those who are poor. The presence of the relative pronoun *qui* indicates that a pronoun is needed. We choose a plural form to convey **those**, and when no gender is specified, we always chose the masculine, thus *ceux*.

23. *Cela*

   That can be found in all the big department stores. The pronoun *cela* stands for the unmentioned noun.

24. *celui-ci*

   My cell phone is in my purse; is this one yours? We are distinguishing between two similar masculine singular nouns. One has been named, and the other is being shown. The pronoun, therefore, must also be masculine and singular, and *-ci* is added for contrast.

25. *ces*

   Could you drop off these packages at the post office? *Ces* is required here because it is the only <u>plural</u> form of the adjective.

INTERROGATIVE ADJECTIVES AND PRONOUNS

The adjective *quel* means **which** or **what**. It exists in four forms so it can agree in gender and number with the noun it modifies:

masculine singular: *Quel âge as-tu?*
feminine singular: *Quelle heure est-il?*
masculine plural: *Quels livres veux-tu emprunter?*
feminine plural: *Quelles chaussures dois-je mettre?*

The adjective asks a direct question in the preceding examples, but may also be used in indirect questions like these:

Je ne sais pas quel âge tu as.
Je voudrais savoir quelle heure il est.
Tu n'as pas dit quels livres tu veux prendre.
Je me demande quelles chaussures choisir.

The same adjective forms are also used in exclamations. Note the absence of the article in the French exclamation:

Quelle chance!
Quels beaux enfants!
Quel temps de chien!

Interrogative Pronouns: *Qui, Que,* and *Quoi*

There are two ways to ask questions with *qui* and *que*. The long construction is easy to learn. Think of it as a barbell: the central hand bar is always *est-ce*. The weight on the <u>left</u> signals **person** (*qui*) or **thing** (*qu'*). The weight on the <u>right</u> signals **subject** (*qui*) or **object** (*que, qu'*):

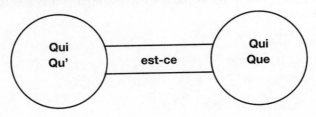

Que becomes *qu'* in front of a vowel or silent *h*. *Qui* never contracts. Study these examples of the long form question:

Qui est-ce qui parle?   person/subject
Qui est-ce que tu aimes?   person/object
Qui est-ce qu'il voit?   person/object

Qu'est-ce qui se passe?	thing/subject
Qu'est-ce que tu manges?	thing/object
Qu'est-ce qu'elle boit?	thing/object

The long form question is always followed by normal word order. In the <u>short</u> form question, the hand bar and the right weight are eliminated. Only the left side remains (*qui* = person; *que* = thing). Thus *qui parle?* is less cumbersome than *qui est-ce qui parle?* The remaining short form questions must be followed by an inverted verb and subject:

> *Qui aimes-tu?*
> *Qui voit-il?*
> *Que se passe-t-il?*
> *Que manges-tu?*
> *Que boit-elle?*

When the interrogative pronoun *qui* is the subject of the verb, use the 3rd person singular form of that verb. If the verb in question is *être*, any one of its forms may appear:

> *Qui parle?*
> Who is speaking?

> *Qui êtes-vous?*
> Who are you?

Qui may appear as the object of a preposition, in which case it is translated as **whom**. Study these examples:

Avec qui sort-elle?	short form with inversion
Avec qui est-ce qu'elle sort?	long form, regular word order

Que can <u>never</u> be the object of a preposition. The interrogative pronoun *quoi* takes its place when the object of the preposition is a thing. It is translated as **what**:

> *Avec quoi écrit-il?*
> *De quoi as-tu besoin?*
> *À quoi pensez-vous?*

Quoi can also express surprise:

> *Quoi? Ils sont partis sans nous!*

If you have not heard something clearly, it is considered bad manners to use *Quoi?* for **What?** It is preferable to ask instead, *Comment?* You will, however, hear both in modern usage.

Drill 22: Interrogative Adjectives and Pronouns

Complete the question or exclamation, incorporating the English cue.

1. _____ est-ce _____ tu veux ? (**what**)

2. _____ veux-tu ? (**what**)

3. _____ est-ce _____ arrive ? (**who**)

4. _____ arrive ? (**who**)

5. _____ est-ce _____ arrive ? (**what**)

6. _____ arrive-t-il ? (**what**)

7. _____ est-ce _____ te plaît ? (**what**)

8. _____ faites-vous ? (**what**)

9. _____ surprise ! (**what a . . .**)

10. _____ jumeaux mignons ! (**what . . .**)

11. _____ jeune homme va-t-elle inviter ? (**which**)

12. Sais-tu _____ boisson servir ? (**which**)

13. De _____ a-t-on besoin ? (**whom**)

14. De _____ avez-vous peur ? (**what**)

15. Dis-moi _____ vol tu prendras. (**which**)

Drill 22–Answers and Explanations

1. *Qu' est-ce **que** tu veux ?*
   What do you want? The left side of the barbell states <u>thing</u>, and the right side states <u>object</u> of *tu veux*.

2. ***Que** veux-tu ?*
   What do you want? *Que* states <u>thing</u>, followed by inversion.

3. *Qui est-ce **qui** arrive ?*
   Who's arriving? The left side of the barbell states <u>person</u>, and the right side states <u>subject</u> of *arriver*.

4. *Qui arrive ?*
   Who's arriving? Here *qui* states <u>person</u> and acts as the <u>subject</u> of *arriver*.

5. *Qu'est-ce **qui** arrive ?*
   What's happening? The left side of the barbell states <u>thing</u>, and the right side states <u>subject</u> of *arriver*.

6. *Qu'arrive-t-il ?*
   What's happening? *Qu'* states <u>thing</u>, followed by inversion.

7. *Qu'est-ce **qui** te plaît ?*
   What do you like? (What pleases you?) The left side of the barbell states <u>thing</u>, and the right side states <u>subject</u> of *plaire*.

8. *Que faites-vous ?*
   What are you doing? *Que* states <u>thing</u>, followed by inversion.

9. *Quelle surprise !*
   What a surprise! The feminine singular form of *quel* matches the noun in this exclamation.

10. *Quels jumeaux mignons !*
    What cute twins! The adjective form must be masculine and plural here.

11. *Quel jeune homme va-t-elle inviter ?*
    Which young man is she going to invite? The masculine singular adjective matches *jeune homme*.

12. *Sais-tu **quelle** boisson servir ?*

Do you know which drink to serve? The feminine singular adjective matches *boisson* in this indirect question.

13. *De **qui** a-t-on besoin ?*

Whom do we need? *Qui* is the human object of the preposition *de*.

14. *De **quoi** avez-vous peur ?*

What do you fear? *Quoi* is the inanimate object of the preposition *de*.

15. *Dis-moi **quel** vol tu prendras.*

Tell me which (what) flight you'll take. The masculine singular adjective matches *vol* in this indirect question.

POSSESSIVE ADJECTIVES

Possessive adjectives always precede the noun. They match the nouns they modify in gender and number. Here are the various forms of the possessive adjectives:

mon, ma, mes	**my**
ton, ta, tes	familiar **your**
son, sa, ses	**his**, **her**, **its**, **one's**
notre, nos	**our**
votre, vos	polite **your**, plural **your**
leur, leurs	**their**

Observe that the first three persons have separate forms for masculine and feminine singular nouns. The forms corresponding to *nous*, *vous*, *ils*, and *elles* do not. Plural forms don't distinguish masculine from feminine either. They should be thought of as all-purpose because they can be applied to all plural nouns regardless of gender.

Use of Possessive Adjectives

1. The possessive adjective must be repeated in French for each noun included in the possession. This is not necessary in English:

    Mon frère et ma sœur sont jumeaux.
    My brother and sister are twins.

    Ma tante et mon oncle ne sont pas encore arrivés.
    My aunt and uncle have not yet arrived.

2. ***Mon***, ***ton***, and ***son*** replace *ma*, *ta*, and *sa* if the following word begins with a <u>vowel</u> or <u>silent *h*</u>. This makes pronunciation simpler and smoother. Study these examples:

    Mon amie Gisèle est alsacienne.
    My friend Gisèle is Alsatian.

    Ton haleine sent le chocolat.
    Your breath smells like chocolate.

    Son ancienne collègue est morte.
    His/her former coworker died.

3. Avoid the common error of trying to match the gender of the owner instead of the gender of the thing owned. This is a difficult concept for English speakers to grasp. We are so used to giving the gender of

the owner with **his** and **her** in English, that we can lose sight of the basic tenet of possession in French, that is, we <u>always</u> identify the gender of the thing possessed, and <u>never</u> the gender of the owner. Thus *son*, *sa*, and *ses*, translate as either **his** or **her** as follows:

her father = *son père*	his father = *son père*
his mother = *sa mère*	her mother = *sa mère*
her pencil = *son crayon*	his pencil = *son crayon*
his eraser = *sa gomme*	her eraser = *sa gomme*

If you are left wondering how French distinguishes between **his** and **her**, the answer is simple: it doesn't! Remember that the English possessors **my**, **your**, **our**, and **their** don't reveal the gender of the owner either, and it never mattered to you. In French the same is true with **his** and **her**.

4. Be careful to respect which form of **you** the sentence requires before selecting *ton*, *ta*, *tes*, *votre*, or *vos*:

> *Madame, **vous** avez laissé **votre** paquet!*
> **You** left **your** package, Ma'am.

> *Dédé, **tu** as laissé **ton** paquet!*
> Andy, **you** left **your** package!

5. Always choose *son*, *sa*, or *ses* to match indefinite subjects such as *qui*, *on*, *personne*, or *tout le monde*. This makes good sense because they also use the 3rd person form of the verb:

> *Qui a oublié son billet?*
> Who forgot his ticket?

> *Est-ce que tout le monde a son billet?*
> Does everyone have his ticket?

> *Personne ne veut perdre son billet.*
> No one wants to lose his ticket.

> *On fait son choix dans la vie.*
> We make our own choices in life.

6. ***Chacun*** can also use *son*, *sa*, and *ses* as its possessors:

> *Chacun a son billet.*
> Each one has his ticket.

If *chacun* relates back to another pronoun, however, use the possessor that matches that pronoun:

> *Nous avons chacun notre billet.*
> We each have our ticket.

> *Vous avez chacun votre billet?*
> Do you each have your ticket?

If *chacun* refers back to the 3rd person plural (*ils*, *elles*, or a plural noun), it is common to see *son*, *sa*, and *ses*, as well as *leur* and *leurs*:

> *Ils étaient, chacun à sa place.*
> They were, each one in his place.

> *Elles se sont assises, chacune de son côté.*
> They sat down, each one on her side.

> *Elles se sont couchées, chacune dans leur chambre.*
> They went to sleep, each in their rooms.

7. Choose *son*, *sa*, and *ses* to match an inanimate object, just as you would in English:

> *le nuage et ses larmes . . .*
> the cloud and its tears . . .

> *l'hiver dans son étreinte glacée*
> winter in its icy embrace . . .

If the inanimate object and the noun it possesses are not in the same clause, we may use the possessive adjective, or <u>more commonly</u>, *en* and the <u>definite article</u>, like this:

> *La porte était fermée et je n'en avais pas la clé.*
> The door was locked and I didn't have **its** key.

> *J'aime bien ton sac; le cuir en est si souple.*
> I really like your bag; **its** leather is so soft.

8. Remember that French generally avoids the use of the possessive adjective with parts of the body.

> *Il a les yeux bleus.*
> His eyes are blue.

> *J'ai mal aux pieds.*
> My feet hurt.

9. When each member of a group possesses one thing, we generally use a plural noun and a corresponding plural possessor in English. This is not the case in French, which emphasizes that each single member of the group has **one**. Compare the use of the plural versus the singular in French and English in the following sentences:

> *Les enfants ont ôté leur chapeau et leur manteau.*
> The children took off their hats and coats.

> *Les oiseaux font leur nid dans les hautes branches.*
> Birds make their nests in the upper branches.

Drill 23: Possessive Adjectives

Supply the possessive adjective that matches the <u>subject of the verb</u>. Look for one problem in which you must substitute the definite article for the possessive adjective.

1. Cherchez _____ livre.

2. Est-ce que tu as _____ livre?

3. Thierry est parti avec _____ amie Claire.

4. Je crois que _____ père et _____ mère vont venir aussi.

5. On aide _____ enfants.

6. Sylvie veut ramasser _____ courrier.

7. Martin doit déposer _____ mère chez le médecin.

8. Les enfants qui regardaient passer le défilé ont agité _____ petit drapeau.

9. Nous préférons chacun _____ propre oreiller.

10. Chacun veut que _____ enfant réussisse.

11. Ils sont rentrés chacun dans _____ maison. (**two correct answers**)

12. Ton pull me plaît; _____ laine _____ est si fine.

13. Ma vieille bagnole et _____ ronronnement particulier me plaisent.

14. Tout le monde a _____ problèmes.

15. Il a _____ cheveux châtain clair.

Drill 23–Answers and Explanations

1. *votre*
   Get your book. The verb form ending in *-ez* narrows the choice to a *vous* form possessor. (Rule 4)

2. *ton*
   Do you have your book? A *tu* form is required to match the 2nd person subject and verb. (Rule 4)

3. *son*
   Thierry left with his friend Claire. *Son* is required in front of a feminine noun beginning in a vowel sound. (Rule 2)

4. *mon / ma*
   I think my father and mother are going to come too. French repeats the possessor in its appropriate form for each member included in the possession. (Rule 1)

5. *ses*
   On, an indefinite pronoun, uses a 3rd person possessor here. (Rule 5)

6. *son*
   Sylvie wants to pick up her mail. The masculine possessor is required to match the masculine noun *courrier*. (Rule 3)

7. *sa*
   Martin has to drop off his mother at the doctor's. *Mère*, a feminine singular noun, requires a feminine singular possessor. (Rule 3)

8. *leur*
   The children who were watching the parade pass waved their little flags. Each child in the group possesses one flag; consequently French uses the singular noun and possessor, whereas English uses the plural. (Rule 9)

9. *notre*
   We each prefer our own pillow. Because *chacun* refers back to *nous*, the possessor matches *nous*. (Rule 6)

10. *son*
    Everyone wants his child to succeed. *Chacun* uses the 3rd person possessor here, because it does not refer back to another pronoun. (Rule 6)

11. *sa* (or *leur*)

They went home, each to his own (each to their own) house. When the possessor refers back to a 3rd person plural subject, both **his** and **their** are acceptable, just as in English. (Rule 6)

12. *la / en*

I like your sweater; its wool is so fine. Because **sweater** and **its wool** are in different clauses, we use the definite article in front of the possessed noun, and follow with *en*. (Rule 7)

13. *son*

I like my old jalopy and its quirky noises. Match a 3rd person possessor to an inanimate object, just as in English. (Rule 7)

14. *ses*

Everyone has his problems. Use a 3rd person possessor to match the indefinite pronoun *tout le monde*. (Rule 5)

15. *les*

He has light brown hair. French avoids possessive adjectives with body parts by using the definite article instead. (Rule 8)

POSSESSIVE PRONOUNS

Possessive pronouns replace the combination of a possessive adjective plus a noun. They match the noun they replace in gender and number, and as with possessive adjectives, show the gender of the thing possessed, rather than the gender of the possessor.

Here are the possessive pronouns:

le mien, la mienne, les miens, les miennes	**mine**
le tien, la tienne, les tiens, les tiennes	familiar **yours**
le sien, la sienne, les siens, les siennes	**his, hers, its, one's**
le nôtre, la nôtre, les nôtres	**ours**
le vôtre, la vôtre, les vôtres	polite **yours**, plural **yours**
le leur, la leur, les leurs	**theirs**

Special Uses and Omission of the Possessive Pronoun

1. The masculine plural of the possessive pronoun may be used to convey the meaning of one's closest friends, relatives, followers, or supporters:

    Joyeux Noël à toi et aux tiens.
      Merry Christmas to you and yours.

    Invitez tous les vôtres !
      Invite all of your friends and family!

    Il a voulu vivre parmi les siens.
      He wanted to live among his own (kind).

    Est-ce que vous êtes des nôtres ?
      Are you one of us?

2. To express ownership with the verb *être*, we use a disjunctive pronoun with the preposition *à*, rather than the possessive pronoun construction common in English. Compare:

    Ces livres-ci sont à moi.
      These books are **mine**.

    Ces livres-là sont à toi.
      Those books are **yours**.

3. The definite article portion of the possessive pronoun will combine with the prepositions *à* and *de*, just as they would if they were freestanding.

> *Je parle **au** prof.*
> I'm speaking to the teacher.

> *Je parle **au** mien.*
> I'm speaking to mine.

> *Je parle **des** profs.*
> I'm talking about the teachers.

> *Je parle **des** miens.*
> I'm talking about mine.

Drill 24: Possessive Pronouns

Supply the possessive pronoun that best translates the English clue.

1. Ta chaise est plus commode que _____.
    (mine)

2. Votre maison est aussi grande que _____.
    (ours)

3. Notre voiture est vieille, mais chez les voisins, dis donc, _____
    est toute neuve. **(theirs)**

4. Je ne trouve pas mes gants, est-ce que je peux emprunter _____ ?
    (yours)

5. Si ton ordinateur est en panne, demande-lui si _____ est
    disponible. **(his)**

6. Notre professeur de français est canadien; _____ est belge.
    (theirs)

7. Mon jardin n'est pas encore fleuri mais _____ s'épanouit.
    (yours)

8. Vos enfants sont toujours petits; _____ sont déjà à
    l'université. **(ours)**

9. Nos meilleurs vœux à toi et _____.
    (to yours)

10. Il n'a pas de crayon; peux-tu lui prêter un _____.
    (of yours)

Drill 24—Answers and Explanations

1. *la mienne*
   Your chair is more comfortable than mine. Select the feminine singular pronoun to represent the unnamed **chair**.

2. *la nôtre*
   Your house is as big as ours. Here the feminine singular pronoun represents the unnamed **house**.

3. *la leur*
   Our car is old, but at the neighbors, don'tcha know, theirs is brand new. The feminine singular pronoun is needed to represent the **neighbors' car**.

4. *les tiens*
   I can't find my gloves; may I borrow yours? Here the masculine plural pronoun stands for the needed **gloves**.

5. *le sien*
   If your computer is down, ask him if his is available. The masculine singular pronoun represents **his computer**.

6. *le leur*
   Our French teacher is Canadian; theirs is Belgian. **Their teacher** is represented by the masculine singular pronoun.

7. *le vôtre*
   My garden hasn't blossomed yet, but yours is in full bloom. Here the masculine singular pronoun stands for **your garden**.

8. *les nôtres*
   Your children are still little; ours are already in college. We convey **our children** with the masculine plural pronoun.

9. *aux tiens*
   Our best wishes to you and to yours. Here the masculine plural pronoun combines with the preposition *à* and means **to your closest family and friends**.

10. *des tiens*
    He doesn't have a pencil; can you lend him one of yours? Now the masculine plural pronoun combines with the preposition *de* to mean **one of your pencils**.

SUBJECT PRONOUNS

je	I	*nous*	we
tu	you	*vous*	you
il	he, it	*ils*	they
elle	she, it	*elles*	they
on	one, we, they		

Je becomes *j'* in front of any verb beginning in a vowel or silent *h*.

Tu is familiar. It is only used with intimate friends, relatives, small children and animals. Students commonly use the *tu* form when speaking to their classmates.

Vous is the polite or formal counterpart to *tu*. It is always used with strangers, superiors, or anyone to whom you wish to show respect. *Vous* is also the only plural form of **you**.

Il and *elle* and *ils* and *elles* refer to inanimate things and animals as well as people. When referring back to nouns with different genders, use *ils* to summarize them as follows:

> *Où sont ta montre, ton portefeuille, et tes lunettes?*
> Where are your watch, wallet, and glasses?

> *Je crois qu'ils sont sur la table.*
> I think they're on the table.

On is very commonly used as a subject in French, and it can convey a variety of English meanings—**one**, **you**, **they**, **someone**, **somebody**, **people**, and even **we**, because it frequently replaces *nous* in spoken French. Study these examples:

> *On ne sait jamais.*
> One never knows. (You never know.)

> *On te l'enverra.*
> Someone will send it to you. (It will be sent to you.)

> *En France on boit du vin avec son repas.*
> In France they (people) drink wine with their meal.

> *On y va?*
> Shall we go?

> *Qu'est-ce qu'on mange ce soir?*
> What are we having to eat tonight?

OBJECT PRONOUNS

Object pronouns replace <u>direct</u> and <u>indirect</u> objects. *Y* replaces an <u>inanimate</u> noun introduced by the preposition *à*, and *en* replaces a noun introduced by the preposition *de*. Here are all of the object pronouns. Observe that they appear in the order in which they combine in a sentence.

me (**me, to me**)	*le* (**him, it**)	*lui* (**to him/her, for him/her**)	*y* (**there**)	*en* (**some**)
te (**you, to you**)	*la* (**her, it**)	*leur* (**to them, for them**)		
nous (**us, to us**)	*les* (**them**)			
vous (**you, to you**)				

Me, *te*, *le*, and *la* become *m'*, *t'*, and *l'* before a vowel or silent *h*.

Position of Object Pronouns

An object pronoun is usually positioned directly in front of the verb that governs it. If the verb is in a compound tense such as the *passé composé*, the object pronoun appears directly in front of the auxiliary verb. In the <u>affirmative</u> command, the pronoun object will <u>follow</u> the verb and will <u>attach</u> to that verb with a hyphen. In this affirmative command construction *me* and *te* become *moi* and *toi*, <u>unless</u> in combination with *y* or *en*, in which case they take an apostrophe. Study these examples of position:

Je la vois.
I see her.

Je l'ai vue.
I saw her.

Je leur parle.
I speak to them.

Je leur ai parlé.
I spoke to them.

Tu me parles?
Are you speaking to me?

Donne-moi la main.
> Give me your hand.

Donne-m'en!
> Give me some!

Special attention should be given to distinguishing between the 3rd person direct object forms (*le*, *la*, and *les*) and the 3rd person indirect object forms (*lui* and *leur*). *Me*, *te*, *nous*, and *vous* forms are fairly user-friendly because their direct and indirect objects forms are identical. This is <u>not</u> the case with 3rd person object pronouns, and so we must select them with great care. You should always ask yourself whether the French verb requires a direct object or an indirect object before choosing your answer. This is complicated by the fact that a verb that requires a direct object in English may require an indirect object in French. The reverse is also true! Furthermore it is very common to place the indirect object in an English sentence in such a way that it seems like a direct object. Study these examples:

Je lui ai donné mon crayon.
> I gave him my pencil. (I gave my pencil to him.)

Je lui ai vendu mon vélo.
> I sold him my bike. (I sold my bike to him.)

Nous leur avons envoyé les cadeaux.
> We sent them the gifts. (We sent the gifts to them.)

Tu lui ressembles.
> You look like him. (*ressembler à*)

Tu lui téléphones.
> You call her (him). (*téléphoner à*)

Demande-lui.
> Ask him. (*demander à*)

Écoute-la!
> Listen to her! (*Écouter* does not use a preposition in French.)

Attends-la!
> Wait for her! (*Attendre* does not use a preposition in French.)

The Pronoun Y

Y can be translated loosely as **there**, but it also functions as the indirect object of a verb that requires *à* before the noun. It is not difficult to master, but you must remember that it can't replace a person. For people, French will use a disjunctive pronoun (which we will review) after the preposition. *Y* has a variety of other translations in English. Study these examples:

*Ta sœur, joue-t-elle **au tennis**?* Does your sister play **tennis**?	*Oui, elle **y** joue bien.* Yes, she plays **it** well.
*Je pense **à mes devoirs**.* I'm thinking about **my homework**.	*N'**y** pense pas!* Don't think about **it**!
*As-tu jamais été **à Philadelphie**?* Have you ever been **to Philadelphia**?	*Oui, j'**y** ai été plusieurs fois.* Yes, I've been **there** many times.
*Elle s'intéresse **aux langues**.* She's interested **in languages**.	*Elle s'**y** intéresse.* She's interested **in them**.
*Je songe **à l'été**.* I'm dreaming **about summer**.	*J'**y** songe souvent. (**songer à**, **to think about**, **dream of**, **daydream**)* I think **about it** often.
*Je m'habitue **au régime**.* I'm getting used **to the diet**.	*Je m'**y** habitue.* I'm getting used **to it**.

Y can also replace inanimate nouns introduced by *en*, *dans*, or *sur*.

*Nous allons **en Italie** le mois prochain.* We're going **to Italy** next month.	*Nous **y** allons le mois prochain.* We're going **there** next month.
*Elle a mis ses clés **dans son sac**.* She put her keys **in her bag**.	*Elle **y** a mis ses clés.* She put her key **in it**.
*Elle a jeté ses clés **sur la table**.* She threw her keys **on the table**.	*Elle **y** a jeté ses clés.* She threw her keys **there** (**on it**).

Y is commonly used with the verb *aller* (**to go**) when the destination is not mentioned.

> *Allez-y! (Vas-y!)*
> Go! (Go on!)
>
> *Allons-y!*
> Let's go!
>
> *On y va?*
> Shall we go?

The Pronoun *En*

En is generally translated as **some** or **any**, but it also replaces an inanimate noun introduced by the preposition *de*. Like *y*, it has many possible translations when used this way. Here are some examples:

*Veux-tu **de la glace**?* Do you want **some ice cream**?	*Bien sûr, j'**en** veux!* Of course, I want **some**.
*Est-ce qu'on achète **des croissants**?* Shall we buy **some croissants**?	*D'accord, on n'**en** a pas à la maison.* Okay, we don't have **any** at home.
*Tu as combien **de timbres**?* How many **stamps** do you have?	*J'**en** ai trois.* I have three **of them**.
*Il **en** a assez?* Does he have enough? (**of them**)	*Non, il n'**en** a qu'un.* No, he only has one. (**of them**)
*Es-tu content **de ton cadeau**?* Are you happy **with your gift**?	*Oui, j'**en** suis très content.* Yes, I'm very happy **with it**.
*Je n'ai pas besoin **de cette pelle**.* I don't need that shovel.	*N'**en** as-tu pas besoin?* Don't you need it?
*Est-ce qu'elle parle **de ses problèmes**?* Does she talk **about her problems**?	*Oui, elle **en** parle.* Yes, she does. (Yes, she talks about them.)
*On n'a plus **de vin**.* We don't have any more **wine**.	*J'**en** achèterai une bouteille demain.* I'll buy a bottle (**of it**) tomorrow.

En is reserved for use with inanimate nouns unless a <u>number</u> is involved. Only then may it replace a person. Study these examples:

*Je parle **de mon travail**.*	*J'**en** parle.*
I talk **about my work**.	I talk **about it**. (inanimate noun)

*Je parle **de mes frères**.*	*Je parle **d'eux**.*
I talk **about my brothers**.	I talk **about them**.

French generally uses a disjunctive pronoun after *de* with people that are not being counted. Note the use of *en* in the following cases:

***Combien de frères** as-tu?*	*J'**en** ai deux.*
How many brothers do you have?	I have two **of them**.

En refers to **the brothers** with the <u>number</u> **two**.

Drill 25: Object Pronouns

Rewrite the sentence by replacing the underlined words with an appropriate pronoun.

1. J'écris <u>à mes parents</u>.

2. Je parle <u>au professeur</u>.

3. Nous voyons souvent <u>Grand-mère</u>.

4. Veux-tu goûter <u>du vin rouge</u>?

5. Ils vont <u>en Alsace</u> cet été.

6. Donne cette lettre <u>à Sylvie</u>.

7. Donne <u>ce vase</u> à Maman.

8. Coupons <u>la pizza</u> pendant qu'elle est chaude.

9. Je ne vois pas <u>les assiettes</u>.

10. Je vais mettre les bonbons <u>dans ce sac</u>.

Drill 25–Answers and Explanations

1. *Je **leur** écris.*
   I write to them. Use an indirect object pronoun with *écrire à*.

2. *Je **lui** parle.*
   I speak to him. *Parler à* also needs an indirect object pronoun.

3. *Nous **la** voyons souvent.*
   We see her often. *Voir* requires a direct object pronoun.

4. *Veux-tu **en** goûter ?*
   Do you want to taste some? *Du vin rouge* is replaced by *en*.

5. *Ils **y** vont cet été.*
   They're going there this summer. *Y* replaces *en Alsace*.

6. *Donne-**lui** cette lettre.*
   Give her this letter. The letter is the direct object. We give it **to her**, indirect.

7. *Donne-**le** à Maman.*
   Give it to Mom. The vase is a direct object.

8. *Coupons-**la** pendant qu'elle est chaude.*
   Let's cut it while it's hot. The pizza is the direct object of the verb *couper*.

9. *Je ne **les** vois pas.*
   I don't see them. *Voir* uses a direct object pronoun.

10. *Je vais **y** mettre les bonbons.*
    I'm going to put the candies in here. *Y* replaces the prepositional phrase *dans le sac*.

Combining Object Pronouns with One Verb

It is common for one verb to have two objects (one direct and one indirect) in both French and English. If you place two objects with a single verb, that <u>pair</u> of objects will be positioned exactly as we learned to place them separately. The difficulty lies in knowing which one to place first. Here are four simple rules to guide you in placing two objects in the right order—they apply to all types of sentences <u>except</u> the affirmative command:

1. ***En*** is the caboose. No matter what other object you combine with it, ***en*** will always be last.

2. ***Y*** is always the last of two objects, unless it is combined with ***en***.

3. If ***y*** and ***en*** are not present, then the pronoun beginning with the letter *l* is last.

4. If both pronouns begin with the letter ***l***, place them in alphabetical order!

These four little rules will never fail; just remember them! Here are some examples. Observe how the pronouns combine according to the little rules.

*Il **nous en** a donné.*
　He gave us some.

*Je **les y** ai mis.*
　I put them there.

*Il n'**y en** a pas.*
　There isn't any (there).

*Je **te les** donne.*
　I'm giving them to you.

*Il **me l**'explique.*
　He explains it to me.

*Je **vous la** montre.*
　I show it to you.

*Tu **le lui** renvoies.*
　You send it (him) back to her (him).

*Je **la leur** enverrai.*
　I will send it (her) to them.

Combining Object Pronouns in the Affirmative Command

When placing a pair of pronouns in the affirmative command, attach them to the rear of the verb with a hyphen, and to each other with another hyphen. Follow these rules for placement:

1. *En* is <u>always</u> last; *y* is last, unless *en* is present.

2. If *y* and *en* are not present, place the direct object <u>before</u> the indirect object.

Observe how the pronouns combine according to these two simple rules:

> *Donne-**le-moi**!*
> Give it to me!
>
> *Expliquez-**la-leur**!*
> Explain it to them!
>
> *Donne-**m'en**!*
> Give me some!

Drill 26: Combining Object Pronouns

Each sentence already contains one pronoun object. Replace the underlined words with <u>another object pronoun</u> and combine it with the one that is already present. Example:

*Je vous donne **ma parole**.*   *Je **vous la** donne.*
   I give you my word.   **I give it to you.**

1.   Il *m'*envoie <u>de l'argent</u>.

2.   Nous *te* montrons <u>notre nouvelle maison</u>.

3.   Mets-*les* <u>sur la chaise</u>.

4.   Donne-*moi* <u>la main</u>.

5.   Raconte-*nous* <u>l'histoire</u>.

6.   Donnez-*leur* <u>les clés</u>.

7.   Ne *lui* dis pas <u>le secret</u>.

8.   Il *nous* raconte <u>ses aventures</u>.

9.   Je *lui* promets <u>la plus grande tranche</u>.

10.   Maman *nous* prépare trois <u>boissons</u>.

Drill 26–Answers and Explanations

1. *Il m'en envoie.*
    He sends me some. *En* is always last in combination.

2. *Nous te la montrons.*
    We show it to you. The pronoun beginning with *l* is last.

3. *Mets-les-y.*
    Put them there. *Y* is last, unless in combination with *en*.

4. *Donne-la-moi.*
    Give it to me. In the affirmative command, place direct before indirect.

5. *Raconte-la-nous.*
    Tell it to us. In the affirmative command, place direct before indirect.

6. *Donnez-les-leur.*
    Give them to them. In the affirmative command, place direct before indirect.

7. *Ne le lui dis pas.*
    Don't tell it to him. Place both pronouns beginning with *l* in alphabetical order.

8. *Il nous les raconte.*
    He tells them to us. The pronoun beginning with *l* is last.

9. *Je la lui promets.*
    I promise it to him. Place both pronouns beginning with *l* in alphabetical order.

10. *Maman nous en prépare trois.*
    Mom prepares three of them for us. *En* is last; here it conveys **of them**.

Drill 27: Combining Object Pronouns

Rewrite the sentence, replacing the underlined words with two object pronouns. Example:

*J'explique **la leçon aux élèves**.*   *Je **la leur** explique.*
  I explain the lesson to the pupils.   **I explain it to them.**

1.   Je lis <u>l'histoire aux enfants</u>.

2.   Je mets <u>les lettres à la poste</u>.

3.   Nous envoyons <u>le cadeau aux grand-parents</u>.

4.   Je donne <u>la sucette au petit garçon</u>.

5.   Envoyez <u>les fleurs à vos parents</u>.

6.   Tu verses <u>de l'eau dans le verre</u>.

7.   Vous montrez <u>la photo à Magalie</u>.

8.   Je prête <u>mon stylo à mon ami</u>.

9.   Tu dis <u>la vérité à tes parents</u>.

10. J'ai envoyé <u>des madeleines à André</u>.

11. Ne dis pas <u>le secret à Maman</u>.

12. Posez <u>votre veste sur la chaise</u>.

13. Ne mettez pas <u>les coudes sur la table</u>.

14. Il emprunte <u>le livre à son professeur</u>.

15. Elles cueillent <u>des fleurs pour leur mère</u>.

Drill 27–Answers and Explanations

1. *Je **la leur** lis.*
    I read it to them. Alphabetical order!

2. *Je **les y** mets.*
    I mail them there. *Y* is last with every pronoun except *en*.

3. *Nous **le leur** envoyons.*
    We send it to them. Alphabetical order!

4. *Je **la lui** donne.*
    I give it to him. Alphabetical order!

5. *Envoyez-**les-leur**.*
    Send them to them. Attach the pronouns to the end of the verb and to each other with hyphens, and place the direct object in front of the indirect object.

6. *Tu **y en** verses.*
    You pour some in. *En* is always last.

7. *Vous **la lui** montrez.*
    You show it to her. Alphabetical order!

8. *Je **le lui** prête.*
    I lend it to him. Alphabetical order!

9. *Tu **la leur** dis.*
    You tell it to them. Alphabetical order!

10. *Je **lui en** ai envoyé.*
    I sent him some. *En* is always last.

11. *Dis-**le-lui**.*
    Tell it to her. In the affirmative command place direct before indirect.

12. *Posez-**l'y**.*
    Put it there. *Y* is last with every pronoun except *en*.

13. *Ne **les y** mettez pas.*
    Don't put them there. *Y* is last with every pronoun except *en*.

14. *Il **le lui** emprunte.*
    He borrows it from him. Alphabetical order!

15. *Elles **lui en** cueillent.*
    They pick some for her. *En* is always last.

RELATIVE PRONOUNS

Qui, Que, and *Dont*

Qui refers back to a noun that functions as the <u>subject</u> of the verb. The subject noun may be a <u>person</u> or a <u>thing</u>. When it refers back to a <u>person</u>, *qui* is translated as **who** or **that**. When it refers to a <u>thing</u>, it is translated as **which** or **that**:

> *Comment s'appelle la femme **qui** parle au prêtre?*
> What's the name of the woman **who's** talking to the priest?

> *Voici le colis **qui** est arrivé hier.*
> Here is the parcel **that** arrived yesterday.

Que refers back to a noun functioning as the <u>direct object</u> of the verb. The direct object may be a <u>person</u> or a <u>thing</u>. When referring to a <u>person</u>, *que* means **whom** or **that** in English. When referring back to a <u>thing</u>, it means **which** or **that**:

> *C'est une femme **que** je ne connais pas.*
> It's (she's) a woman **whom** I don't know.

> *C'est le colis **que** j'attendais.*
> It's the package **that** I was waiting for.

In English the relative pronoun is often left out of the sentence entirely. In French the relative pronoun may <u>never</u> be omitted. Compare:

> *Est-ce le livre **que** tu voulais?*
> Is this the book _____ you wanted?

> *Regarde la fille **qui** bâille à gauche!*
> Look at the girl _____ yawning on the left!

Dont replaces *qui* or *que* when the noun object is introduced by the preposition *de* or one of its forms. That object may be a <u>person</u> or a <u>thing</u>. The English translation is **about**, **of**, or **whose**.

> *J'ai rencontré le voisin dont tu m'as parlé.*
> I met the neighbor you told me about.

> *Voilà le chien dont j'ai peur.*
> There's the dog I'm afraid of.

> *Je ne trouve pas les lunettes dont j'ai besoin.*
> I can't find the glasses I need. (of which I have need)

C'est un fromage dont se servent les Suisses.
   It's a cheese used by the Swiss.

Note the inversion of subject and verb in the last example. This is an occasional variant of the usual word order after ***dont***.

When ***dont*** means **whose**, it is always followed, <u>in this order</u>, by <u>subject</u>, <u>verb</u>, and <u>object</u>. If the subject or object is a noun, it must be preceded by *le*, *la*, *l'*, or *les*. This word order is quite different from English. Compare:

On va chez Mireille, dont tu connais les parents.
   We're going to Mireille's, whose parents you know.

Je vous présente mon collègue dont la fille part pour la France.
   This is my coworker whose daughter is leaving for France.

Ce qui, Ce que, Ce dont, and Ce à quoi

Ce qui and *ce que* mean **what** or **that which**. These pronouns never refer to people, only to <u>things</u>. They may also refer to a <u>whole phrase</u> or <u>idea</u>. They replace *qui* and *que* when no noun object is present. Compare:

La pizza que tu manges a l'air délicieux.	*Ce que tu manges a l'air délicieux.*
The pizza you're eating looks delicious.	What you're eating looks delicious.
Le dessert qui va venir sera inoubliable.	*Ce qui va venir sera inoubliable.*
The dessert that is coming will be unforgettable.	What's coming will be unforgettable.
Il ne veut pas travailler pour réussir . . .	*ce qui est dommage.*
He doesn't want to work to succeed . . .	which is a shame.

Ce dont replaces *ce que* if the unnamed object is introduced by the preposition *de*. Like *ce que*, it can only refer to a **thing** or an **idea**. Compare:

*C'est **ce que** je voulais.*
   It's **what** I wanted.

*C'est **ce dont** je rêvais.*
   It's **what** I was dreaming **of**.

Ce à quoi replaces *ce que* if the unnamed object is introduced by the preposition *à*. It can only refer to a **thing** or an **idea**, not people. Compare:

Dis-moi ce que tu penses.
Tell me **what** you think.

Dis-moi ce à quoi tu penses.
Tell me **what** you're thinking **about**.

Drill 28: *Qui, Que, Dont*

Supply the needed pronoun.

1. La robe _____ tu portes est mignonne.

2. Où sont les crayons _____ j'ai taillés ?

3. La jeune fille _____ pleure est très malheureuse.

4. Voici la médaille _____ je suis si fier.

5. Il a mis la cravate _____ me plaît.

6. Les devoirs _____ nous devons faire sont longs.

7. Le chien _____ aboie toute la nuit m'énerve.

8. Philippe choisit un livre _____ lui semble intéressant.

9. J'ai découpé en chiffons la vieille chemise _____ tu as perdu tous les boutons.

10. Elle a biffé la note _____ elle avait honte.

Drill 28–Answers and Explanations

1. *que*
The dress (that) you're wearing is cute. Note that the verb *porter* already has a subject (*tu*); therefore *la robe* is the object of the verb *porter*, and it needs *que*.

2. *que*
Where are the pencils (that) I sharpened? *Les crayons* are the object of the verb *tailler*; use *que*.

3. *qui*
The girl who's crying is very unhappy. *La jeune fille* is the subject of the verb pleurer; use *qui*.

4. *dont*
Here's the medal I'm so proud of. *La medaille* is the object of the verb phrase *être fier de*. Because the noun is introduced by *de*, we use *dont* instead of *que*.

5. *qui*
He put on the tie I like. (He put on the tie that pleases me.) *La cravate* is the subject of the verb *plaire*, so it takes *qui*.

6. *que*
The assignments (that) we must do are long. *Les devoirs* are the object of the verb *faire*; use *que*.

7. *qui*
The dog that barks all night really irritates me. *Le chien* is the subject of the verb *aboyer*; it requires *qui*.

8. *qui*
Phillip chooses a book that seems interesting to him. *Le livre* is the subject of the verb *sembler*; it requires *qui*.

9. *dont*
I cut up for rags the old shirt whose buttons you lost. Here the subject-verb-object word order after the blank suggests *dont*, meaning **whose**.

10. *dont*
She crossed out the grade she was ashamed of. *La note* is the object of the verb phrase *avoir honte de*. **Dont** replaces *que*.

Drill 29: *Ce qui, Ce que, Ce dont, Ce à quoi*

Supply the needed pronoun.

1. _____ tu veux n'est pas possible !

2. Dis-moi _____ te plaît.

3. Voici _____ nous avons besoin.

4. C'est _____ je réussis.

5. Montre-moi _____ tu as dans la main.

6. Raconte-moi _____ te trouble.

7. Dites-leur _____ vous voulez.

8. Dites-leur _____ vous avez envie.

9. Je vois _____ tu veux dire.

10. Je veux savoir _____ l'inquiète.

Drill 29–Answers and Explanations

1.   *ce que*
   What you want isn't possible. The unnamed object of the verb *vouloir* is represented by *ce que*.

2.   *ce qui*
   Tell me what you like. (Tell me what pleases you.) The unnamed subject of the verb *plaire* requires *ce qui*.

3.   *ce dont*
   Here is what we need. The unnamed object of *avoir besoin de* is expressed by *ce dont*.

4.   *ce à quoi*
   It's what I'm good at. We need *ce à quoi* to express the unnamed object of the verb *réussir à*.

5.   *ce que*
   Show me what you have in your hand. We use *ce que* to stand for the unnamed object of the verb *avoir*.

6.   *ce qui*
   Tell me what is troubling you. *Ce qui* stands for the unnamed subject of the verb *troubler*.

7.   *ce que*
   Tell them what you want. *Ce que* represents the unnamed object of *vouloir*.

8.   *ce dont*
   Tell them what you want. *Ce dont* is required to convey the unnamed object of the verb phrase *avoir envie de*.

9.   *ce que*
   I see what you mean. The unnamed object of the verb phrase *vouloir dire* is represented by *ce que*.

10.   *ce qui*
   I want to know what's worrying him (her). The verb *inquiéter* is governed here by an unnamed subject.

Lequel

Lequel and its variations are relative pronouns that generally refer to non-human objects of a preposition. There are four forms that must match the nouns to which they refer: *lequel*, *laquelle*, *lesquels*, and *lesquelles*.

If the preposition in question is *à* or *de*, the pronouns will contract just as the definite article does in combination with these prepositions, producing the forms *auquel*, *à laquelle*, *auxquels*, and *auxquelles*, and *duquel*, *de laquelle*, *desquels*, and *desquelles*.

Lequel may only be used to refer to a **person** after the prepositions *entre* (**between**) or *parmi* (**among**). After any other preposition, use *qui* for a human object and *lequel* for everything else. Study these examples:

*C'est un ordinateur **sur lequel** tu peux compter.*
It's a computer you can depend on.

*Voici les crayons **avec lesquels** j'ai fait le dessin.*
Here are the pencils I made the sketch with.

*J'avais bouclé ma ceinture de sécurité, **sans laquelle** j'aurai péri.*
I had buckled my safety belt, without which I would have perished.

*Il y a deux hebdos **auxquels** je m'abonne.*
There are two weeklies to which I subscribe.

*J'ai plusieurs cousines, **parmi lesquelles** Carole est ma favorite.*
I have many cousins, among whom Carole is my favorite.

*Elle est amoureuse de deux garçons, **entre lesquels** elle ne peut pas choisir.*
She's in love with two boys she can't choose between.

*C'est le monsieur **pour qui** je travaille.*
That's the gentleman I work for. (Use *qui* for people after all prepositions other than *entre* or *parmi*.)

Dont generally replaces *de qui*, *duquel*, and its forms:

*C'est un homme **dont** je me méfie.*
He's a man I don't trust.

*C'est la breloque **dont** j'ai envie pour mon bracelet.*
It's the charm I want for my bracelet.

Lequel can also be used as an interrogative, meaning **which one** or **which ones**:

> *Comme parfum, il y a vanille, chocolat, ou fraise. **Lequel** prends-tu ?*
>> The flavors are vanilla, chocolate, or strawberry. Which one are you having?

> *Je dois choisir des chaussures. **Lesquelles** me conseilles-tu ?*
>> I have to choose some shoes. Which ones do you think I should wear?

Où

Où means **where** and can be used to replace the combination of a preposition with *lequel*, like this:

C'est la maison dans laquelle je suis né. It's the house in which I was born.	*C'est la maison où je suis né.* It's the house where I was born.
C'est une région dans laquelle je voyage souvent. It's a region in which I travel often.	*C'est une région où je voyage souvent.* It's a region where I travel often.

Où can also mean **when** in expressions such as the following:

> *le jour où je suis né*
>> the day (when) I was born

> *l'année où on s'est connu*
>> the year (when) we met

Drill 30: *Lequel, Dont, Qui, Où*

Supply the needed pronoun.

1. Je te présente mon ami Benoît, avec _____ je travaille.

2. Voici la recette avec _____ je prépare ma quiche.

3. C'est le dictionnaire (à) _____ je me fie le plus.

4. C'est le dictionnaire (de)_____ je me sers le plus souvent.

5. Ce sont des souvenirs (à)_____ je pense de temps en temps.

6. Il y avait beaucoup d'étudiants, parmi _____ je t'ai reconnu.

7. C'est le petit village (dans) _____ nous vivions.

8. _____ de ces sucettes veux-tu ?

9. C'est le médecin chez _____ nous allons.

10. Je connais deux jumeaux entre _____ je ne peux pas distinguer.

Drill 30—Answers and Explanations

1. *qui*
   This is my friend Benoît, with whom I work. Use *qui* for the human object of all prepositions except *entre* and *parmi*.

2. *laquelle*
   Here's the recipe with which I make my quiche. Use the feminine singular form of *lequel* for the inanimate object of the preposition *avec*.

3. *auquel*
   It's the dictionary I trust the most. Here the preposition from the verb *se fier à* contracts with *lequel*.

4. *duquel (dont)*
   It's the dictionary I use most often. The preposition from *se servir de* can contract with *lequel*, or it can be replaced with the shorter, smoother *dont*.

5. *auxquels*
   They're memories I think of from time to time. The preposition from *penser à* contracts with *lesquels*.

6. *lesquels*
   There were many students, among whom I recognized you. Like *entre*, *parmi* uses a *lequel* form with the human object of a preposition. All other prepositions require *qui* with people.

7. *dans lequel (où)*
   It's the little village in which (where) we used to live. Match *lequel* to *le village* for use after *dans*, or opt for the shorter *où*.

8. *laquelle*
   Which one of these lollipops do you want? Choose the feminine singular form of *lequel* to represent the *sucette* governed by the preposition *de*.

9. *qui*
   He's the doctor we go to (to whom we go). You must use *qui* because *le médecin* is the human direct object of the preposition *chez*.

10. *lesquels*
    I know twins I can't tell apart (between whom I cannot distinguish). Like *parmi*, *entre* accepts a form of *lequel* for its human object.

DISJUNCTIVE PRONOUNS

moi	me	*nous*	us
toi	you	*vous*	you
lui	him	*eux*	them
elle	her	*elles*	them
soi	oneself		

Disjunctive or <u>stressed</u> pronouns can only refer to people. They replace object pronouns in the following circumstances:

1. After prepositions, a disjunctive pronoun is required if the object of the preposition is human, as in these examples:

   > *Voici une lettre **pour elle**.*
   > Here's a letter for her.

   > *Nous allons dîner **chez moi** ce soir.*
   > We're going to eat at my house this evening.

   > *Regarde **devant toi** !*
   > Look in front of you!

   > *J'habite près **d'eux**.*
   > I live near them.

2. To emphasize:

   > *J'ai fini, **moi** !*
   > **I'm** finished.

   > *Il parle **à toi** !*
   > He's speaking **to you**.

3. When used alone, or when there is no verb:

   > *Qui est là ? **Moi** !*
   > Who's there? **Me!**

   > *Qui l'aidera ? **Pas moi** !*
   > Who will help him (her)? **Not me!** (Not I!)

   > *Je vais bien, merci, **et toi** ?*
   > I'm fine, thanks, **and you**?

4. After *c'est* or *ce sont*:

> *C'est **lui**!*
> That's **him**!

> *C'était **moi**!*
> That was **me**.

> ***Ce sont** eux qui manquent.*
> **They're** the ones who are missing.

5. In a comparison:

> *Je suis plus nerveuse que toi.*
> I'm more nervous than you.

> *Vous êtes plus fortunés qu'eux.*
> You are wealthier than they are.

6. With multiple subjects or objects:

> *Toi et moi, on s'entend bien.*
> You and I get along well.

> *Tu les vois, elle et lui?*
> Do you see him and her?

7. With *-même*, *aussi*, and *seul*:

> *Je l'ai fait moi-même.*
> I made it myself.

> *Lui aussi, il veut venir.*
> He wants to come too.

> *Il t'aime, toi seul.*
> He loves only you.

8. As a synonym for a possessive pronoun:

> *C'est le tien, ce livre? Il est à toi, ce livre?*
> It's yours, this book? (This book is yours?)

9. In front of a relative pronoun:

> *C'est toi qui es fâché.*
> You're the one who's angry.

> *Tu vas l'inviter, lui que tu n'aimes pas?*
> You're going to invite him, the one you don't like?

10. The pronoun *soi* refers back to an indefinite subject or object, such as *chacun*, *tout le monde*, *personne*, or *on*:

> *On doit être confortable chez soi.*
>> One should be comfortable at home.

> *Cela va de soi.*
>> That goes without saying.

Drill 31: Disjunctive Pronouns

Supply the necessary pronoun to convey the English meaning:

1. C'est _____ qui es en retard, pas _____.
   You're the one who's late, not I.

2. Chacun pour _____!
   Each man for himself!

3. Tu as préparé le repas _____-même?
   Did you prepare the meal by yourself?

4. Tu laisses traîner tes affaires partout! Mais Maman, elles ne sont pas à _____!
   You leave your things lying around everywhere! But Mom, they're not mine!

5. _____ et _____ on se connaît depuis trois ans.
   He and I have known each other for three years.

6. Tu es plus chanceux que _____.
   You are luckier than he is.

7. Tu as fini, _____?
   Have you finished?

8. Tu m'accuses, _____ qui suis innocent!
   You accuse me, (I) who am innocent!

9. Voici un brin de muguet pour _____.
   Here is a sprig of lily of the valley for you.

10. Je me suis assis à côté d'_____.
    I sat down next to them.

Drill 31–Answers and Explanations

1. **toi / moi**
Here we use the disjunctive pronoun **toi** after *c'est*, and **moi** because it stands alone, without a verb.

2. **soi**
Soi refers back to the indefinite subject *chacun*.

3. **toi**
Disjunctive pronouns are required with *même*, *aussi*, and *seul*.

4. **moi**
This means *Ce ne sont pas les miennes!* (Rule 8)

5. **lui / moi**
This is a multiple subject. (Rule 6)

6. **lui**
Disjunctives are always used in comparisons. (Rule 5)

7. **toi**
The disjunctive pronoun is added for emphasis here.

8. **moi**
Here the disjunctive pronoun comes in front of a relative pronoun.

9. **toi** (or **vous**)
The human object of a preposition must be disjunctive.

10. **eux** (or **elles**)
This is another human object of a preposition.

PREPOSITIONS

A preposition may be a single word or an expression of two or three words in French. French prepositions can be followed by nouns, pronouns, or infinitives. Choosing the right preposition will be crucial in your writing sample. Because each one may have several meanings, learning to master prepositions can feel like walking through a minefield. One needs to go slowly and pay attention!

What follows is a study of the most useful common prepositions. They are presented in small groups that juxtapose similar prepositions that are frequently confused. With some earnest study, you will be able to avoid the errors that commonly plague student writing.

Pour, *Pendant*, and *Depuis*

Avoid the error of using the preposition *pour* (**for**) with the verbs *attendre*, *chercher*, *demander*, and *payer*. The preposition is already built into the verb. Thus we say:

> *J'attends mes amis.*
>> I wait for my friends.

> *Je cherche mes lunettes.*
>> I'm looking for my glasses.

> *Je demande les clés de la voiture.*
>> I ask for the car keys.

> *Je paie la pizza.*
>> I pay for the pizza.

Use *pour* to convey <u>intent</u> or <u>destination</u>.

> *Pour faire une omelette, il faut des œufs.*
>> To make an omelet, you need eggs.

> *J'utilise ces ciseaux pour couper l'étoffe.*
>> I use these scissors to cut fabric.

> *Il est parti pour la France.*
>> He left for France.

Use *pour* with the verbs like *aller*, *venir*, *voyager*, *partir* and *sortir* to indicate an imprecise period of time or a period of time that has not been completed.

> *Ma copine française est venue pour Noël.*
>> My French girlfriend came for Christmas.

> *Cet été j'espère aller en France pour un mois.*
> This summer I hope to go to France for a month.

Use *pendant* to express a completed period of time:

> *L'an dernier j'ai voyagé en Europe pendant un mois.*
> Last year I traveled in Europe for a month.

Pendant can also mean **during** or **all through**. See how it changes the meaning slightly in the sentence about the girl coming for Christmas.

> *Ma copine française est venue pendant Noël.*
> My French girlfriend came for Christmas. (She stayed for all of the festivities.)

> *Elle ne met pas de chaussures pendant l'été.*
> She doesn't wear shoes during the summer.

Depuis is needed to express **for** if the period of time began in the past and continues into the present.

> *J'étudie le français depuis cinq ans.*
> I have been studying French for five years.

Notice the use of the <u>present tense</u> in the French construction, which is much simpler than the clumsy "I have been studying" of the English sentence. If the action began in the past and continued to a point also in the past, you use the <u>imperfect tense</u> with *depuis*.

> *J'étudiais le français depuis cinq ans quand j'ai eu la bourse.*
> I had been studying French for five years when I got the scholarship.

Thus we have two very simple constructions:

> present tense verb + *depuis* + time element (**have been**)
> imperfect verb + *depuis* + time element (**had been**)

Depuis can also mean **since** when referring to a point in time. If you want to express **since** meaning **because**, you must use the preposition *puisque*. Compare:

> *Je n'ai pas mangé depuis ce matin. J'ai faim.*
> I haven't eaten since this morning. I'm hungry.

> *Tu devras aller seul puisque je ne peux pas venir.*
> You'll have to go alone since I can't come.

Dans, En, Sur, and Sous

Use *dans* when **in** means **inside**.

> *Elle est dans sa chambre.*
> She's in her room.

> *Qu'est-ce que tu as dans la bouche?*
> What's in your mouth?

> *Il habite dans Manhattan même.*
> He lives right in Manhattan.

> *J'ai mis la lettre dans l'enveloppe.*
> I put the letter in the envelope.

Because *dans* means **inside**, it is the preposition of choice for air and train travel. The French see themselves **inside** the plane and **inside** the train. Therefore you must use *dans l'avion* and *dans le train* when you mean **on the plane** or **on the train**. Using *sur l'avion* will elicit chuckles because that means **on top of the plane**! To express getting into (inside) a car, a train, a plane, or a bus, use the verb *dans* with the verb *monter*:

> *On monte dans la voiture.*

Dans is also used rather than *sur* when referring to a street location with *rue*:

> *Elle habite dans la rue Poissonnière.*
> She lives on rue Poissonnière.

We do, however, use *sur* with *la route* and *le boulevard*.

Dans is used when **in** refers to a period of time that has not yet taken place.

> *Ils vont partir dans une heure.*
> They're going to leave in an hour.

> *La nouvelle succursale ouvrira dans un mois.*
> The new branch will open in a month.

Looking back over the examples of *dans*, you will note that it is always followed by an article or possessive adjective. When no such article is present, use *en* to mean **in** or **by**.

> *Les étudiants font attention en classe.*
> The students pay attention in class.

> *J'aime voyager en avion.*
> I like to travel by plane.

Followed by an element of time, *en* conveys how much time is or was spent doing something.

> *J'ai lu le roman en trois heures.*
> I read the novel in three hours.

> *Il a fait ses devoirs en dix minutes.*
> He did his homework in ten minutes.

En expresses **in** or **to** in front of all feminine countries and provinces.

> *Je l'ai connue en Allemagne.*
> I met her in Germany.

> *J'ai passé deux semaines en Dordogne.*
> *J'ai passé deux semaines dans le Périgord.*
> I spent two weeks in Périgord. (two ways to refer to the same region—one feminine and one masculine)

En can also mean **in** as in **made of**.

> *Je cherche un sac en cuir.*
> I'm looking for a leather purse.

En can be followed by the present participle, in which case it is translated as **by** or **while**.

> *Elle tricote en écoutant les informations.*
> She knits while listening to the news.

> *C'est en forgeant qu'on devient forgeron.*
> It's by blacksmithing that one becomes a blacksmith. (This is an old proverb, the French equivalent of "practice makes perfect.")

The use of *sur* to mean **on** is limited to being physically on the surface of something. We sing *Sur le pont d'Avignon* because we are **on** the bridge. The French also see themselves as *sur la photo*, whereas English speakers generally say that they are **in** a picture. With numbers *sur* means **out of**, as in *un garçon sur trois*.

Sur does not translate the many idiomatic uses of **on** in English. There are so many that you should make an effort to memorize those that you encounter. Here are some examples:

on foot: *à pied*
on the right: *à droite*
on the floor: *par terre*
on purpose: *exprès*
on fire: *en feu*

Sous is translated as **under**. It can be physical as well as historical.

> *On ne peut pas respirer sous l'eau.*
> One cannot breathe under water.

> *Les arts ont fleuri sous François Premier.*
> The arts flourished under Francis the First.

> *Il a disparu sous les yeux.*
> He disappeared in plain sight.

French uses *sous* to express the idea of **in the rain**.

> *Aimes-tu marcher sous la pluie?*
> Do you like to walk in the rain?

Avant, Après, Devant, and Derrière

Avant and *devant* both mean **before**. *Avant* is used exclusively for <u>time</u>, and *devant* is for <u>physical placement</u> (**in front of**). *Avant* requires the preposition *de* when it appears if front of an infinitive. *Avant que* must be followed by the subjunctive.

> *Cendrillon devait rentrer avant minuit.*
> Cinderella was supposed to come home before midnight.

> *Avant de me coucher, j'étends ce que je vais porter le lendemain.*
> Before going to bed, I lay out what I'm going to wear the next day.

> *Étudiez avant qu'il ne soit trop tard !*
> Study before it's too late!

> *J'ai vu ton sac devant la porte.*
> I saw your bag in front of the door.

Derrière (**behind**), like *devant*, is only for physical placement.

> *La fillette s'est cachée derrière le chêne.*
> The little girl hid behind the oak tree.

Derrière is <u>not</u> suitable for time expressions.

> *Je suis en retard dans mon courrier.*
> I'm behind in my letter writing.

> *L'avion est en retard (sur l'horaire).*
> The plane is behind schedule.

> *Je vais laisser cette valise. Je la ramasserai plus tard.*
> I'm going to leave this suitcase behind. I'll pick it up later.

Après (**after**) is the opposite of *avant* (**before**).

> *On va partir après le petit déjeuner.*
> We're going to leave after breakfast.

To create the equivalent of the English after + present participle construction, French requires *après* + infinitive + past participle:

> *Après avoir rangé ma chambre, je suis sorti.*
> After straightening my room, I went out.

> *Après avoir gagné à la loterie, ils ont construit une nouvelle maison.*
> After winning the lottery, they built a new house.

> *Après s'être maquillée, elle a mis sa robe.*
> After putting on her makeup, she put on her dress.

À cause de and Parce que

À cause de (**because of**) is always followed by a noun group or a pronoun. *Parce que* (**because**) is needed in front of a whole clause with a subject, a verb, and possibly an object. Compare:

> *Nous avons manqué l'avion à cause de toi!*
> We missed the plane because of you!

> *Nous avons manqué l'avion parce que tu étais en retard.*
> We missed the plane because you were late.

Malgré and En dépit de

Both prepositions translate as **in spite of** or **despite**.

> *Il a échoué malgré ses efforts de dernière minute.*

> *Il a échoué en dépit de ses efforts de dernière minute.*
> He failed in spite of his last-minute efforts.

Sauf, Excepté, and Hormis

All three prepositions are translated as **except** or **but**. They may be used interchangeably, but *sauf* is most commonly heard.

> *J'ai fait tous les exercices sauf le numéro 17.*
> *J'ai fait tous les exercices excepté le numéro 17.*
> *J'ai fait tous les exercices hormis le numéro 17.*
> I did all of the exercises except for number 17.

Entre and *Parmi*

Entre means **between** and is used much as it is in English.

> *L'enfant s'est assis entre nous.*
>> The child sat down between us.

> *Il y a un choix entre la viande et le poisson.*
>> There's a choice between meat and fish.

> *Il y a une grande différence entre vouloir et pouvoir.*
>> There's a big difference between wanting to and being able to.

In the expression *entre-temps*, it conveys **meanwhile** or **in the meantime**.

> *Je t'attendrai ici, entre-temps je lirai.*
>> I'll wait for you here; I'll read in the meantime.

Parmi means **among** or **amongst**.

> *Ils vont choisir parmi nous.*
>> They're going to choose amongst us.

> *Attention ! Il y a un voleur parmi nous.*
>> Be careful! There is a thief in our midst.

Vers and *Envers*

Vers and *envers* mean **toward** or **towards**. *Envers* is used for feelings or emotions **toward** <u>people</u>, whereas *vers* conveys <u>direction</u> in <u>movement</u> or <u>time</u>. Compare:

> *Le tournesol se tourne vers le soleil.*
>> The sunflower turns toward the sun.

> *Les cours reprennent vers avril.*
>> Courses start again around (toward) April.

> *Elle est toujours gentille envers moi.*
>> She's always very nice toward me.

> *Le bébé marche d'un petit pas vers moi.*
>> The baby takes a little step toward me.

Avec and *Sans*

Avec and *sans* are discussed under "Omission of the Definite Article" for use with nouns. *Sans* may also be followed by the infinitive:

> *J'ai répondu sans réfléchir.*
> I answered without thinking.

Selon, D'après, and *Quant à*

Selon and *d'après* mean **according to** or **in the opinion of**. *Quant à* means **as for**:

> *Quelle sera la mode cet hiver, selon vous?*
> *Quelle sera la mode cet hiver, d'après vous?*
>> What, in your opinion, according to you, will be in fashion this winter?

> *Quant à moi, je mettrai les mêmes habits que je portais l'année dernière.*
>> As for me, I'll wear the same outfits I wore last year.

Chez

Chez is a very handy preposition that means **at the home of** or **at the place of business of**. It can also mean **in the work of**. It has no real equivalent in English. Here is how to use it:

> *Ils ne sont pas chez eux.*
>> They're not home.

> *Je vais chez le dentiste après les cours.*
>> I'm going to the dentist's office after classes.

> *Chez Ingres on voit souvent une élongation des bras, du cou et du torse.*
>> We often see an elongation of the arms, the neck, and the torso in the paintings of Ingres.

À

The preposition *à* has a myriad of different meanings. It is often translated as **to**, **at**, **in**, **on**, **by**, or **with**. It is featured in a variety of idioms that give rise to many other translations as well. As you study the following examples, observe the different nuances in the English translations, all of which use *à* in French:

> *Ils vont à la plage.*
> They're going **to** the beach.

> *Il fait beau à la plage.*
> It's nice **at** the beach.

> *Il pleut au mois d'avril.*
> It rains **in** the month of April.

> *C'est elle à gauche.*
> She's **on** the left.

> *Nous viendrons à pied.*
> We'll come **on** foot.

> *On l'a reconnu à ses lunettes en écaille.*
> We recognized him **by** his horn-rimmed glasses.

> *Le voilà, le monsieur à la serviette.*
> There he is, the gentleman **with** the briefcase.

> *C'est toi, le gosse aux cheveux blonds sur la photo?*
> Is that you, the kid **with** the blond hair in the photo?

> *Nous habitons à cinq kilomètres de Paris.*
> We live five kilometers **away** from Paris.

À can also express possession or style:

> *Ce verre est à moi.*
> This glass belongs to me.

> *C'est une omelette à la française.*
> It's a French-style omelet.

Sometimes the preposition is entirely lost in the English translation, as follows:

> *Quelle jolie tasse à thé!*
> What a pretty tea cup!

> *À la prochaine fois!*
> (See you) next time!

À can be followed by a pronoun or an infinitive:

> *C'est à toi (de jouer).*
> It's your turn.

> *Ce n'est pas facile à faire.*
> It's not easy to do.

You will also find that many verbs require *à* before the infinitive, while others take *de*. See "Est-Ce À ou De?"

De

De also has multiple uses. It can be translated as **from**, **of**, **to**, **with**, **in**, or **than**:

> *Elle vient de Philadelphie.*
> She comes from Philadelphia.

> *Danielle sera en France du 30 juin jusqu'au 15 juillet.*
> Danielle will be in France from June 30th to July 15th.

> *Je prendrais volontiers une tasse de café.*
> I'd love to have a cup of coffee.

> *Je suis enchanté de vous connaître.*
> I'm delighted to meet you.

> *N'entre pas! Tes chaussures sont couvertes de boue !*
> Don't come in! Your shoes are covered **with** (**in**) mud. (This is a common construction, that is, a past participle used as an adjective + *de* + noun.)

> *J'ai bu plus de deux tasses.*
> I drank more **than** two cups.

De has other translations, as in these expressions:

> *Ne perds pas les enfants de vue.*
> Don't let the children **out of** your sight.

> *Je suis tombé de fatigue.*
> I collapsed **with** exhaustion.

De can express possession, too.

> *J'ai mis le foulard de ma sœur.*
> I wore my sister's scarf.

Drill 32: Prepositions

Supply the preposition suggested by the English cue:

1. Qu'est-ce qu'il y a d'important dans la vie, _____ toi ?
   (according to, in your opinion)

2. J'ai lu ce livre _____ ton conseil.
   (because of)

3. J'ai lu ce livre _____ tu me l'as conseillé.
   (because)

4. Elle a hérité la bague _____ sa grand-mère.
   (belonging to)

5. Il a trouvé son vieux nounours _____ les jouets au grenier.
   (among)

6. _____ quelle région venez-vous ?
   (From)

7. Elle aime porter des vêtements _____ la mode.
   (in)

8. On est resté en Auvergne _____ un mois.
   (for)

9. On ira en Auvergne _____ un mois.
   (for)

10. On est en Auvergne _____ un mois.
    (for)

11. Attends-moi _____ le cinéma.
    (in front of)

12. Peux-tu me déposer _____ centre commercial ?
    (at the)

13. Qu'est qu'il y a _____ frigo ?
    (in the)

14.   Il aime la fille _____ taches de rousseur.
        (with the)

15.   Ils se sont connus _____ l'avion.
        (on)

16.   Téléphone-leur _____ 17 heures.
        (before)

17.   Téléphone-leur _____ 17 heures.
        (toward)

18.   Il faut que nous soyons gentils _____ nos anciens.
        (toward)

19.   Il nous invite _____ lui.
        (to his home)

20.   _____ moi, je monte au lit.
  (As for)

Drill 32–Answers and Explanations

1. ***d'après*** (or ***selon***)
Because they are synonymous, either preposition works here.

2. ***à cause de***
Because we follow with a noun group, *ton conseil*, we must use *à cause de* to express **because**.

3. ***parce que***
This time we have a clause (subject and verb) following **because**. In this case we must use *parce que*.

4. ***de***
Here *de* can mean **from**, which is one of its primary meanings, as well as **belonging to**.

5. ***parmi***
There is only once choice for **among** or **amongst**: *parmi*.

6. ***De***
Another basic example of *de* meaning **from**.

7. ***à***
An idiomatic use of *à*, to mean **in** fashion.

8. ***pendant***
Because the month was spent **in the past**, choose *pendant* to translate **for**.

9. ***pour***
Because the month has <u>not yet taken place</u>, choose *pour* to translate **for**.

10. ***depuis***
Because the month<u> began in the past</u> and is still <u>continuing into the present</u>, use *depuis* to translate **for**.

11. ***devant***
Here we want **in front of** (position), so we use *devant* instead of *avant* (time).

12. ***au***
À combines with *le* to produce **at the**.

13. ***au***

    Here we make the same contraction, but now it means **in the**.

14. ***aux***

    Common idiomatic use of *à* for the girl **with** the freckles.

15. ***dans***

    Always use ***dans*** to translate **in** a vehicle of transportation.

16. ***avant***

    To express **before** in the sense of time, we choose ***avant***.

17. ***vers***

    To express **toward** in the sense of time, we need ***vers***.

18. ***envers***

    Here we relate an <u>emotion toward people</u>. We must choose ***envers***.

19. ***chez***

    Chez expresses **at his home** succinctly and neatly.

20. ***Quant à***

    This is the only translation possible to mean **as for**.

CONJUNCTIONS

There are two types of conjunctions. Coordinating conjunctions simply <u>link</u> two words or phrases. <u>Subordinating</u> conjunctions connect a <u>dependent</u> clause to a <u>main clause</u>.

Coordinating Conjunctions

Many coordinating conjunctions express sequence, such as *d'abord* (**first**), *enfin* (**finally**), and *ensuite* and *puis* (**then**). Others, like *et* (**and**), *d'ailleurs* (**besides**), and *en plus* (**in addition**), simply <u>add</u> or <u>enhance</u>. Still others, such as *ou* (**or**), *mais* (**but**), *pourtant* (**yet**), *cependant* and *toutefois* (**however**), and *néanmoins* (**nevertheless**), provide <u>opposition</u> or <u>contrast</u>.

There is also a group of coordinating conjunctions that conveys consequence. Examples include *donc* (**therefore**) and *par conséquent* (**consequently**). *Alors* can fit into either category because it may mean **then** sequentially, as well as **then** or **so** consequentially.

A few conjunctions require <u>repetition</u>, like this:

> *Soit tu restes, soit tu t'en vas.*
>> Either you stay or you go.

> *Je vais mettre ou mes espadrilles ou mes escarpins.*
>> I'm going to wear either my espadrilles or my pumps.

> *Elle n'avait ni le caractère ni la patience pour être mère.*
>> She had neither the temperament nor the patience to be a mother.

> *Veux-tu prendre et ta valise et la mienne.*
>> Would you take both your suitcase and mine.

The conjunction *aussi* differs from its adverbial meaning of **also**. As a conjunction, *aussi* means **so** or **consequently** and appears <u>in front of an</u> <u>inverted verb and subject</u>. Compare:

> *Elle chante aussi.* (<u>adverb</u> placed after the verb)
>> She also sings. (She sings too, as well.)

> *Ils la suppliaient constamment de chanter pour eux.*
>> They begged her constantly to sing for them.

> *Aussi a-t-elle enfin chanté.* (<u>conjunction</u> followed by inversion)
>> Therefore (so) she finally sang.

Study the following examples and you will see that French coordinating conjunctions work much like their English counterparts:

*J'ai mis du sel **et** du poivre.*
I added salt **and** pepper.

*Tu veux quelque chose à manger **ou** à boire?*
Do you want something to eat **or** to drink?

*Elle aimerait bien y aller **mais** elle ne peut pas.*
She would like to go **but** she can't.

*Je te laisserai cette vaisselle **car** tu l'aimes tant.*
I'll leave you this china **because** you like it so much.

*Il faisait froid hier soir, **alors** je ne suis pas sorti.*
It was cold last night **so** I didn't go out.

*Je n'ai pas étudié du tout, **donc**, j'ai échoué.*
I didn't study at all, **so** (therefore) I flunked.

*Il a **enfin** donné sa permission.*
He **finally** gave his permission.

*Je n'ai pas très faim. **En plus** je suis au régime.*
I'm not very hungry. **Besides**, I'm on a diet.

*Son mari est mort jeune. **Aussi** devait-elle soutenir ses enfants toute seule.*
Her husband died young. **Therefore** she had to support her children all by herself.

***D'abord**, il faut étendre la nappe.*
First, you must spread the tablecloth.

***Ensuite**, tu mets les couverts.*
Next (then) you set the table.

***Puis** tu peux ranger les fleurs.*
Then you can arrange the flowers.

*C'est une bonne note, **cependant**, ce n'est pas un 20.*
It's a good grade; **however**, it's not a 20. (i.e., the best score possible)

*Elle est végétarienne, **pourtant** elle prendra un peu de poisson de temps en temps.*
She's a vegetarian, **yet** she'll have a little fish once in a while.

*C'est un film qui te plaira. **D'ailleurs** il a reçu un César.*
> You will like the film. **Besides**, it won a César. (French film award)

*Le pauvre bonhomme **n'**a **ni** foyer, **ni** amis.*
> The poor fellow has **neither** home **nor** friends.

Subordinating Conjunctions

It's essential to know which subordinating conjunctions are followed by the indicative and which require the subjunctive. An asterisk signals expressions requiring the subjunctive. Note them with care.

Subordinating conjunctions can be categorized just like the coordinating conjunctions. Temporal conjunctions and conjunctions of sequence include *quand* and *lorsque* (**when**), *dès que* and *aussitôt que* (**as soon as**), *après que* and *avant que** (**before** and **after**), and *tant que*, *tandis que*, and *pendant que* (all variations of **while**).

Conjunctions that convey consequence or cause include *puisque* and *depuis que* (**since**), *parce que* (**because**), and *comme* and *ainsi que* (**as, just as, as well as**). Other conjunctions of consequence are *afin que*,* *de façon que*,* *de manière que*,* *pour que*,* and *de sorte que*,* all of which are variants of **so that** or **in order that**.

The subordinating conjunctions that oppose include *bien que*,* *quoique*,* and *malgré que** (**although, in spite of**).

There are also subordinates that qualify by restricting or limiting. They include: *à moins que** (**unless**), *jusqu'à ce que** (**until**), *pourvu que** (**provided that**), and *de crainte que** and *de peur que** (**for fear that**). Study the following examples carefully:

*Je voudrais être dans sa classe **avant qu'**il **ne** prenne sa retraite.*
> I'd like to be in his class before he retires.

*Je vous ferai signe **dès que** mon vol atterrira.*
> I'll let you know as soon as my flight lands.

*Il viendra **à moins qu'**il ait un match de foot.*
> He'll come unless he has a soccer game.

*Ma sœur est sportive, **tandis que** je suis plutôt sédentaire.*
> My sister is athletic, while (whereas) I'm rather sedentary.

*Ma sœur joue au tennis avec notre frère, **pendant que** je lis.*
> My sister plays tennis with our brother while (during which time) I read.

Drill 33: Coordinating and Subordinating Conjunctions

First select the conjunction needed to convey the English cue. Then provide the required verb form, deciding carefully between the <u>indicative</u> and the <u>subjunctive</u>.

1.   Je vais me mettre au régime _____.
     (until I lose weight)

2.   Papa coupe la viande en petits morceaux _____ le bébé
     (so that)
     _____ les ramasser avec les doigts.
       (can)

3.   Nous irons en France _____ nous _____ le temps et
     l'argent nécessaires.   **(as soon as)**   **(have)**

4.   _____, j'apporte toujours mon vieil appareil
        (When I travel)
     _____ je _____.
       (for fear that)   **(will lose it)**

5.   Ils vont choisir _____ une maison de campagne _____ un
          (either)   **(or)**
     pavillon près de la plage.

6.   Ce complet de l'an dernier ne te va plus, _____ tu as grandi
     d'un mètre!   **(since)**

7.   _____, _____ le donner à ton cadet.
       (Therefore)   **(you can)**

8.   Ils ne nous ont pas invités, _____ cela m'_____ égal.
                                      (yet)   **(is)**

9.   Ils veulent partir de bonne heure demain matin, _____ cela
     me dérange beaucoup.   **(however)**

10. Navré, mais je suis débordé de travail et _____, je ne me
     sens pas très bien.   **(besides)**

Drill 33–Answers and Explanations

1. *jusqu'à ce que je maigrisse* (or *jusqu'à ce que je perde du poids*)
Whichever answer you choose, be sure to note the subjunctive!

2. *afin que / puisse*
Other correct answers include *de façon que*, *de sorte que*, *de manière que*, and *pour que*. All require the subjunctive.

3. *dès que / aurons*
Aussitôt que is also correct. Did you remember to use the future tense here? (See "The Future.")

4. *Quand* (or *Lorsque*) */ de peur que* (or *de crainte que*) */ ne le perde*
Expressions of fear are followed by the subjunctive. Note that both employ the pleonastic *ne*.

5. *soit / soit*
You can also use *ou*, repeated or just once.

6. *depuis que*
You may also use *puisque*.

7. *Donc* (or *Aussi*) */ tu peux* (or *peux-tu*)
Notice the inversion after *aussi*.

8. *pourtant* (or *mais* or *cependant*) *est*
We use the coordinating conjunction *pourtant* to convey **yet**. **But** or **however** work as well.

9. *cependant* (or *toutefois*)
Either coordinator works here. You could also use **but**, *mais*.

10. *d'ailleurs*
You can also use *en plus* here.

NEGATIONS

French negations always have at least two parts, which surround the verb entirely. The first part, *ne*, precedes the verb. The second half of the negation follows the verb directly. Here are the negations that you should know:

ne . . . pas	**not**	*Il ne comprend pas.*
ne . . . guère	**hardly**	*Il ne comprend guère*
ne . . . jamais	**never, not ever**	*Il ne comprend jamais.*
ne . . . point (rarely used today; substitute with *pas du tout*)	**not at all**	*Il ne comprend point.*
ne . . . plus	**no longer, no more**	*Il ne m'aime plus.*
ne . . . rien	**nothing, not anything**	*Il ne comprend rien.*
ne . . . personne	**no one, nobody**	*Il n'aime personne.*
ne . . . , ni . . . ni . . .	**neither, nor**	*Il ne comprend ni toi ni moi.*
ne . . . que	**only**	*Il ne comprend que ça.*
ne . . . nul(le)	**no**	*Il ne comprend nulle question.*
ne . . . nulle part	**nowhere**	*Il ne va nulle part.*
ne . . . aucun(e)	**no, not one, none, not any**	*Il ne comprend aucune question.*

Personne, *rien*, *aucun* + noun, *nul* + noun, and *ni . . . ni* + nouns can also act as subjects. In this case, they are followed directly by *ne*:

Personne ne me comprend.
    Nobody/no one understands me.

Rien ne me plaît.
    Nothing pleases me. (I don't like anything.)

Aucun bulbe n'a fleuri.
    Not one bulb blossomed.

Nul flocon n'est tombé.
    Not one flake fell.

Ni Marc ni Michel ne sont allés.
    Neither Mark nor Michael went.

If a negation appears without a verb, there is no need for *ne*.

Qui est là? Personne.
    Who's there? No one.

Qu'est-ce que tu fais? Rien.
    What are you doing? Nothing.

Je cherche une jupe pas trop courte.
    I'm looking for a not-too-short skirt.

Tu vas venir? Pas moi.
    Are you going to come? Not me.

Il n'aime pas le poisson. Moi non plus.
    He doesn't like fish. Neither do I. (Me neither.)

Positioning Negations

If there is a pronoun in front of the verb, the *ne* will move back to accommodate it so that the negation encircles the pronoun and verb combination.

*Je **ne** me lève **pas**.*
    I'm not getting up.

*Je **ne** la vois **jamais**.*
    I never see her.

In compound tenses the short, self-contained negations wrap around the auxiliary verb. Longer negations, and those that will be combining with nouns, follow the participle. Compare:

*Je **n'ai pas** compris.*
    I didn't understand.

*Il **n'a rien** dit.*
    He said nothing. (He didn't say anything.)

*On **n'est jamais** revenu.*
    We never came back.

*Tu **n'as guère** fini.*
    You've hardly finished.

*Ils **ne** sont **plus** venus.*
    They no longer came. (They didn't come anymore.)

*Vous **n**'avez **guère** fini.*
You've hardly finished.

*Elle **n**'a **vu** personne.*
She didn't see anyone. (She saw no one.)

*Nous **ne** sommes allés **nulle** part.*
We didn't go anywhere. (We went nowhere.)

*Tu **n**'as mangé **ni** tes légumes, **ni** ta viande.*
You ate neither your vegetables nor your meat.

It is possible to combine negative expressions just as we would in English. Place ***plus*** or ***jamais*** first in the series of multiple negations. If they are both in the series, you will hear ***plus jamais*** as well as ***jamais plus***.

*Je **n**'ai **plus rien**.*
I have nothing more.

*Je **ne** vois **plus personne**.*
I don't see anyone anymore.

*Il **ne** comprend **jamais rien**.*
He never understands anything.

*Je **ne** vois **jamais plus personne**.*
I don't ever see anyone anymore.

Drill 34: Negations

Make a sentence with the opposite meaning by using a negation.

1. J'ai un frère.

2. Il fait toujours ses devoirs.

3. Il est jeune et beau.

4. Elle a lu ce roman deux fois. (**Change to say that she read it only once.**)

5. Tout le monde va venir.

6. Il y a encore de la glace au frigo.

7. Nous comprenons complètement.

8. J'ai tout.

9. Elle a beaucoup aimé le film. Nous aussi.

10. Tout lui plaît.

11. Je vois tout le monde tout le temps.

12. Ces jouets se trouvent partout.

13. Elle est déjà prête.

14. Elle partage tout.

15. Tu veux quelque chose.

16. Toutes les filles vont venir. (**Verb must change to singular!**)

17. Tous les garçons sont restés. (**Verb must change to singular!**)

18. Tu as dit quelque chose.

19. Elle a échoué. Moi aussi.

20. J'ai reçu plusieurs invitations.

Drill 34–Answers and Explanations

1.   *Je n'ai **pas** de frère.*
Note the change from *un* to *de*. (The indefinite article is replaced by ***de***
or ***d'*** in a <u>partitive</u> negation.)

2.   *Il **ne** fait **jamais** ses devoirs.*
Jamais is the negative opposite of ***toujours***.

3.   *Il **n'**est **ni** jeune **ni** beau.*
*Ne . . . **ni** . . . **ni** . . .* is needed to negate <u>two</u> adjective traits at the same
time.

4.   *Elle **n'**a lu ce roman **qu'**une fois.*
Notice how ***ne . . . que*** expands to include the verb and its object.

5.   ***Personne** ne va venir.*
Personne provides the negative opposite of ***tout le monde***.

6.   *Il **n'**y a **plus** de glace au frigo.*
Note the loss of the definite article here. **There is no more ice cream**
negates the partitive statement **There is still (some) ice cream**. Therefore
la drops out.

7.   *Nous **ne** comprenons **pas du tout**.*
We create the opposite of **completely** with ***pas du tout*** (**not at all**).

8.   *Je **n'**ai **rien**.*
*Ne . . . **rien*** is the negative opposite of ***tout***.

9.   *Elle **n'**a **point** aimé le film. Nous **non plus**.* (Or *Elle **n'**a **pas** aimé le
film,* or *Elle **n'**a **guère** aimé le film*)
Because there is no exact <u>negative</u> opposite for *beaucoup*, more than one
response is possible. The exact opposite, *peu*, is not a negation.

10.   ***Rien** ne lui plaît.*
Rien is the opposite of ***tout***.

11.   *Je **ne** vois **jamais personne**.*
Personne is the opposite of ***tout le monde***, and ***jamais*** is the opposite of
tout le temps. *Jamais* precedes all other negatives except *plus*.

12.   *Ces jouets **ne** se trouvent **nulle part**.*
Nulle part, **nowhere**, provides the opposite meaning of ***partout***, **everywhere**.

13. *Elle **n'est pas encore** prête.*
    ***Pas encore**, **not yet**, opposes **déjà**, **already**.*

14. *Elle **ne partage rien**.*
    As in question 8, ***rien**, **nothing**, opposes **tout**, **everything**.*

15. *Tu **ne veux rien**.*
    ***Rien** is also the opposite of **quelque chose**, **something**.*

16. ***Aucune** fille **ne va venir**. (or **Nulle** fille **ne va venir**.)*
    Not one girl will come, as opposed to **All the girls will come**, hence the verb change.

17. ***Aucun** garçon **n'est resté**. (or **Nul** garçon **n'est resté**.)*
    The verb must now be singular to match **Not one boy stayed**.

18. *Tu **n'as rien** dit.*
    Observe the placement of this short negation. It wraps around the auxiliary verb.

19. *Elle **n'a pas** échoué. Moi **non plus**.*
    The short negation, ***ne . . . pas***, wraps around the auxiliary. ***Moi non plus***, **Me neither**, provides the opposite of **me too**, ***moi aussi***.

20. *Je **n'ai reçu aucune** invitation.*
    Use a form of ***aucun** or **nul** to negate **plusieurs**.*

THE INFINITIVE

Every possible manifestation of a given verb is represented by the infinitive; hence its name. We differentiate the three basic verb groups by the last two letters of this basic verb form. Thus we speak of *-er* verbs, *-ir* verbs, and *-re* verbs. When you look up the meaning of a verb in the dictionary, its definition will be listed under the infinitive form. English requires two words to make its version of the infinitive. Thus *avoir* means **to have**.

French generally uses the infinitive where English would use a present participle.

> *Je l'ai entendue pleurer.*
>> I heard her crying.

> *Je les ai vus sortir.*
>> I saw them going out.

> *J'adore danser.*
>> I love dancing. (I love to dance.)

> *J'ai envie de dormir.*
>> I feel like sleeping. (I want to sleep.)

In these examples the French infinitive appears after a preposition:

> *Il est parti sans nous dire au revoir.*
>> He left without saying good-bye to us.

> *Lave-toi les mains avant de manger.*
>> Wash your hands before eating.

> *Au lieu d'attendre le lendemain, nous ouvrons nos cadeaux au Réveillon.*
>> Instead of waiting for the next day, we open our gifts on Christmas Eve.

The French infinitive replaces the English present participle used as a noun:

> *Attendre est ennuyant.*
>> Waiting is a bore.

> *Défense de fumer.*
>> No smoking.

> *Mon rêve serait d'aller en France.*
>> Going to France would be my dream.

The immediate future is conveyed whenever an infinitive is preceded by a form of the verb ***aller***:

> *Qu'est-ce que tu vas faire maintenant?*
> What are you going to do now?

Infinitives appear after other verbs in certain set expressions:

> *Je vais chercher une pizza.*
> *aller chercher*: to go get

> *J'ai envoyé chercher une pizza.*
> *envoyer chercher*: to send for

> *J'ai entendu dire qu'elle était revenue.*
> *entendre dire*: to hear that

> *Le bébé a laissé tomber sa tétine.*
> *laisser tomber*: to drop

> *Viens chercher ton argent de poche.*
> *venir chercher*: to come and get

> *Qu'est-ce que cela veut dire?*
> *vouloir dire*: to mean

The infinitive may replace a command form in directions and instructions. This is quite common in recipes:

> *Ajouter le chocolat fondu et bien mélanger.*
> Add the melted chocolate and mix well.

The past infinitive is made with the infinitive of the auxiliary verb (*avoir* or *être*) and the past participle:

> *Après avoir fini mes devoirs, je suis rentré.*
> After finishing my homework, I went home.

> *Il regrettait d'être arrivé en retard.*
> He was sorry for arriving late (for having arrived late).

Drill 35: The Infinitive

Complete the sentence using an infinitive expression:

1. J'ai passé toute la nuit _____.
   (without sleeping)

2. Je voudrais te parler _____.
   (before leaving)

3. _____ deux œufs et _____ les blancs des jaunes.
   (break)   **(separate)**

4. Je t'ai vu _____ le Père Noël !
   (kissing)

5. _____ c'est sa passion.
   (Knitting)

6. Défense d' _____.
   (putting up signs)

7. _____ c'est _____.
   (Seeing)   **(believing)**

8. Qu'est-ce que tu _____ _____ ?
   (mean)

9. Tu _____ _____ _____ tes lunettes.
   (dropped)

10. Je ne me souviens pas d' _____ _____ cela.
    (having written)

Drill 35–Answers and Explanations

1. *sans dormir*
   I spent the whole night without sleeping. Here the English present participle is expressed with an infinitive preceded by a preposition.

2. *avant de partir*
   I'd like to speak to you before leaving. Here is another preposition plus infinitive combination to replace an English present participle.

3. *Casser / séparer*
   Break two eggs and separate the whites from the yolks. The infinitive is commonly used to replace an imperative in instructions.

4. *embrasser*
   I saw you kissing Santa Claus! Note how the English present participle converts to the infinitive here.

5. *Tricoter*
   Knitting is her passion. When a verb is used as a noun, put it in the infinitive form.

6. *afficher*
   Hanging signs is prohibited. Post no bills. Use the infinitive whenever the verb is used as a noun.

7. *Voir / croire*
   Seeing is believing. As in the two preceding problems, these infinitives are used as nouns.

8. *veux dire*
   What do you mean? *Vouloir dire* is one of several fixed expressions constructed with infinitives.

9. *as laissé tomber*
   You dropped your glasses. *Laisser tomber* is a fixed infinitive expression meaning **to drop**.

10. *avoir écrit*
    I don't remember having written that. This is an example of the perfect or past infinitive.

EST-CE À OU DE?

Test questions are sometimes based on which preposition belongs to a given verbal locution. Train yourself to establish the needed preposition (if there is one) whenever you learn a new verb. Here are some common combinations:

*s'abonner **à***	to subscribe to
*abuser **de***	to abuse, overindulge in
*accrocher **à***	to hook or attach to
*s'adosser **à***	to lean on or against
*s'agir **de***	to be about, to be a question of (impersonal)
*aider **à***	to help in, toward
*aimer **à***	to like (with the preposition, only an infinitive can follow; this verb can also be used without the preposition with a person, thing, or infinitive)
*s'amuser **à***	to enjoy, find amusing
*s'amuser **de***	to mock, make fun of
*s'apercevoir **de***	to notice, make fun of
*appartenir **à***	to belong to
*apprendre **à***	to learn, to teach someone
*arriver **à***	to reach, to achieve a result, to find a solution
*arrêter **de***	to stop doing something
*avoir **à***	to have to do
*chercher **à***	to try to
*commander **à** quelqu'un **de** faire quelque chose*	to order someone to do something
*commencer **à***	to begin to
*condamner quelqu'un **à***	to condemn someone to
*consacrer quelque chose **à***	to devote something to
*conseiller **à** quelqu'un **de** faire quelque chose*	to advise someone to do something

continuer à	to continue to
se contenter de	to be content with
craindre de faire quelque chose	to be afraid to do something
croire à (en)	to believe in (Examples: *Il croit à la fin du monde. Il croit en Dieu.*)
dater de	to date from
se débarrasser de	to rid oneself of, to get rid of
décider de	to decide on
se décider à	to make up one's mind to
décourager quelqu'un de faire quelque chose	to discourage someone from doing something
demander à quelqu'un de faire quelque chose	to ask someone to do something
dire à quelqu'un de faire quelque chose	to tell someone to do something
échapper à	to escape, get away from, avoid
s'échapper de	to run away from
écrire quelque chose à quelqu'un	to write something to someone
être à	to belong to
(s')empêcher de	to prevent, to stop
(s')ennuyer de	to be bored with, be annoyed by
enseigner à faire quelque chose	to teach how to do something
enseigner quelque chose à quelqu'un	to teach something to someone
essayer de	to try
se fier à	to trust
s'habituer à	to get used to
hériter de	to inherit something from someone
jouer à	to play a game, play at something
jouer de	to play a musical instrument

(se) méfier de	to be careful, not to trust
(se) moquer de	to make fun of
obéir à	to obey
oublier de faire quelque chose	to forget to do something
parler à	to speak to someone
parler de	to speak about someone or something
proposer à quelqu'un de faire quelque chose	to suggest doing something (to someone)
remercier quelqu'un de (also *pour*) *quelque chose*	to thank someone for something or for doing something
réussir à	to succeed in
songer à	to think of, about
se souvenir de	to remember
supplier quelqu'un de faire quelque chose	to beg someone to do something
tâcher de	to try
téléphoner à	to call someone on the phone
en vouloir à	to bear a grudge against
venir de faire quelque chose	this combination creates the immediate past: to have just

Idioms based on *avoir* also use a preposition:

avoir envie de	to feel like, to want
avoir honte de	to be ashamed of
avoir mal à	to have pain (something hurts)
avoir peur de	to be afraid of

Expressions based on *être* use a preposition as well:

être content de	to be happy with
être fier de	to be proud of
être jaloux de	to be jealous of
être prêt à	to be ready to

Many other prepositions are encountered as integral parts of verbal expressions. Here are just a few examples:

> *Il s'est plongé **dans** l'eau froide.*
> He plunged into the cold water.

> *Est-ce que tu te fâches **contre** moi?*
> Are you angry with me?

> *Elle a fondu **en** larmes.*
> She dissolved into tears.

Drill 36: Using the Correct Preposition after the Verb

Supply the appropriate preposition. Make a contraction with the article if necessary:

1. J'ai essayé _____ échapper _____ chien qui semblait vouloir me mordre.

2. Je devrais écrire _____ mes grands-parents.

3. Ne te fie pas _____ David! C'est un baratineur !

4. J'ai dit _____ Papa _____ nous attendre ici.

5. As-tu remercié ton prof _____ t'avoir aidé ?

6. Elle joue bien _____ piano.

7. Veux-tu jouer_____ cartes avec nous ?

8. Ça m'ennuie _____ l'écouter se plaindre.

9. Mince! Il commence _____ pleuvoir !

10. L'oiseau s'est échappé _____ sa cage.

11. Ne vous moquez pas _____ votre prof !

12. Elle parle _____ sa soeur au téléphone chaque soir.

13. _____ quoi parle-t-il ?

14. L'enfant a supplié son père _____ rester encore quinze minutes à la foire.

15. Débarrasse-toi _____ cette guenille !

16. On n'est pas riche mais cela ne nous empêche pas _____ nous amuser.

17. Il se fâche _____ tout le monde !

18. Elle en veut _____ son frère.

19. J'ai mal _____ pieds !

20. Le bébé cherchait _____ se faire comprendre.

21. Qui t'a enseigné _____ faire du ski comme ça ?

22. Mais dis donc! Je n'ai plus envie _____ bosser !

23. Tâche _____ ne pas déranger Pépé. Il dort.

24. Arrête _____ faire le pitre !

25. Demande _____ enfants _____ rentrer. C'est l'heure du déjeuner.

Drill 36—Answers and Explanations

1. *d' / au*
    I tried to get away from the dog who seemed to want to bite me. *Essayer* uses *de* in front of the infinitive; *échapper* needs *à*.

2. *à*
    I should write to my grandparents. *Écrire* always places *à* in front of its <u>human</u> object.

3. *à*
    Don't trust David. He's a smooth talker! *Se fier* takes *à*.

4. *à / de*
    I told Dad to wait for us here. *Dire* uses *à* for its <u>human</u> object and *de* in front of an infinitive.

5. *de*
    Did you thank your teacher for helping you? *Remercier* uses *de* to thank someone **for doing** something. But in *on remercie le prof **pour** son aide*, **remercier** uses **pour** to thank someone for something (a noun).

6. *du*
    She plays the piano well. *Jouer* always uses *de* with musical instruments.

7. *aux*
    Do you want to play cards with us? *Jouer* uses *à* with sports and games.

8. *de*
    It bores me (It annoys me) to listen to him complain. *S'ennuyer* needs *de* in front of an infinitive.

9. *à*
    Darn! It's starting to rain. *Commencer* uses *à* in front of an infinitive.

10. *de*
    The bird flew away (escaped) from his cage. *S'échapper* requires *de* whereas *échapper* needs *à*. Compare this to question 1.

11. *de*
    Don't make fun of your teacher! *Se moquer* uses *de* in front of its object.

12. *à*
    She speaks to her sister on the phone every night. *Parler* uses *à* to speak **to** a human being.

13. *De*
    What is he talking about? *Parler* uses *de* to speak **of** a person or an object.

14. *de / à*
    The child begged his father to stay another fifteen minutes at the fair. *Supplier* uses *de* in front of an infinitive.

15. *de*
    Get rid of that rag! *Se débarrasser* requires *de* in front of its object.

16. *de*
    We're not rich but that doesn't prevent us from having a good time. *Empêcher* uses *de* before an infinitive.

17. *contre*
    He's mad at (angry with) everyone. *Se fâcher* employs the preposition *contre* before its object.

18. *à*
    She holds a grudge against her brother. *En vouloir* uses *à* in front of its object. If that object is a person, as it is here, that person is an indirect object.

19. *aux*
    My feet hurt! *Avoir mal* uses *à* in front of its object. Contractions are common.

20. *à*
    The baby tried to make himself understood. *Chercher* employs *à* before an infinitive.

21. *à*
    Who taught you to ski like that? *Enseigner* uses *à* in front of an infinitive <u>as well as</u> in front of its human object, making *t'* an <u>indirect</u> object pronoun.

22. *de*
    Hey! I don't feel like cramming anymore! The expression *avoir envie* takes *de* in front of an infinitive or an object. (*J'ai envie d'une glace.*)

23. *de*

Try not to disturb Grampa. He's sleeping. *Tâcher* needs *de* in front of an infinitive.

24. *de*

Stop clowning around! *Arrêter* uses *de* before an infinitive.

25. *aux*

Ask the children to come in. It's time for lunch. *Demander* needs *à* for its <u>human</u> object and *de* in front of an infinitive.

THE PRESENT PARTICIPLE

To make the present participle we go back to the same source that provided the imperfect root: the **nous** form of the present indicative, minus the **-ons**. To this root we add **-ant**, the equivalent of **-ing** in English.

There are only three verbs whose roots are irregular: *avoir* (**ayant**), *être* (**étant**), and *savoir* (**sachant**).

Uses of the Present Participle

1. The present participle is often used as an adjective. It must then, like any other adjective, reflect the gender and number of the noun it modifies:

   un coup écrasant
     a crushing blow

   un professeur exigeant
     a demanding teacher

   une besogne fatiguante
     a tiring task

   des dents éclatantes
     dazzling teeth

2. The French present participle may be used just like its English counterpart; <u>however</u>, its use is much less common in French than it is in English:

   Ne sachant pas la réponse à la dernière question, il a rendu son examen sans y répondre.
     Not knowing the answer to the last question, he turned in his test without answering it.

3. The present participle follows the preposition **en** to tell how <u>another</u> action was completed by the same subject. The two actions, that of the main verb and the participle, are simultaneous:

   Le prof buvaient son café en corrigeant les devoirs.
     The teacher drank his coffee while correcting homework.

   Elle pleurait tout en riant.
     She was crying and laughing at the same time.

Note the word *tout* in front of the participle; this is commonly added to reinforce the simultaneity, especially when the two actions are contradictory, as they are here.

4. ***En* + present participle** can simply express <u>how</u> the main action is achieved. Here the English translation is **by + -ing**:

> *C'est en forgeant qu'on devient forgeron.*
>> By smithing one becomes a blacksmith. (This old proverb is the French version of "practice makes perfect.")

5. ***En* + present participle** is the best construction to translate an English **verb of motion + preposition**, such as **to run up to** or **to skip across**:

> *L'enfant s'est précipité vers son père en courant.*
>> The child ran up to his father.

> *Nous avons traversé le pont en sautillant.*
>> We skipped across the bridge.

6. Use the <u>present participle</u> of ***avoir*** or ***être*** with a <u>past participle</u> to create a compound for an activity that took place before the action of the main verb, like this:

> *Ayant bien travaillé, je me suis endormie satisfaite.*
>> Having worked hard, I fell asleep pleased with myself.

> *Étant déjà tombée une fois, elle descendait l'escalier avec soin.*
>> Having already fallen once, she came down the stairs carefully.

Drill 37: The Present Participle

Supply the correct form of the present participle in the following sentences:

1. C'est une jeune fille _____. (**charming**)

2. Elle tortillait une mèche de cheveux tout en _____ à son petit ami. (**talking**)

3. Je marchais sur la pointe des pieds, _____ que le bébé dormait. (**knowing**)

4. Il nous a salué en _____. (**on his way out**)

5. L'enfant m'a embrassé en _____. (**jumped up to**)

6. _____ à leur examen, les élèves sont partis. (**having passed**)

7. _____ ma clé, je suis revenue la chercher. (**having forgotten**)

8. _____ trop tard, nous sommes rentrés. (**having arrived**)

9. Ils marchaient en _____. (**laughing**)

10. Il est rentré en _____. (**dancing**)

Drill 37–Answers and Explanations

1. *charmante*
She's a charming girl. This is a present participle used as an adjective, therefore it is made feminine to agree with the **girl**.

2. *parlant*
She twirled a lock of hair while talking to her boyfriend. The present participle after *en* conveys that two actions by the same person are taking place simultaneously.

3. *sachant*
I was tip-toeing, knowing that the baby was sleeping. Note the irregular present participle for *savoir*.

4. *sortant*
He waved to us on his way out. *En* + **present participle** is the best way to render an English expression of **motion + preposition**.

5. *sautant*
The child jumped up to kiss me. This problem is similar to the previous one. Use *en* + **present participle** to recreate an English expression of **motion + preposition**.

6. *ayant réussi*
Having passed their exams, the students left. A compound is created with the present participle of the auxiliary verb and the past participle of the main verb.

7. *Ayant oublié*
Having forgotten my key, I came back to get it. This is another example of the past compound.

8. *Étant arrivés*
Having arrived too late, we went home. This past compound uses *être* as an auxiliary verb. Note the anticipatory agreement of the participle *arrivés*.

9. *en riant*
They were walking and laughing (at the same time). There are two simultaneous actions with one subject.

10. *en dansant*
He came home dancing. Here the present participle tells how the main action (**coming home**) was achieved.

THE IMPERATIVE

The command form of a verb is used to tell someone **what to do** or **what not to do**. Therefore we say a command is either <u>affirmative</u> or <u>negative</u>.

A command always involves direct address as you must be speaking to someone to use it. Therefore it exists only in three forms: *tu*, **vous**, and a **nous** form that is used if you want to make a suggestion that includes yourself.

Commands are given in both French and English <u>without</u> a subject pronoun. We use the verb alone, or the verb with an object.

The verb forms used are generally exactly like the *tu*, *nous*, and *vous* forms of the present indicative <u>without</u> the subject pronoun. The only difference takes place in the *tu* form of the *-er* verb. It drops the final letter, *s*, <u>unless in combination</u> with *y* or *en*. The *s* is retained in front of *y* and *en* for ease in pronunciation. There are no other changes in regular commands, just this one. Let's look at some examples of the affirmative command:

Regarde !	**Look!** (note dropped *s*)
Regardez !	**Look!**
Regardons !	**Let's look!**
Ralentis !	**Slow down!**
Ralentissez !	**Slow down!**
Ralentissons !	**Let's slow down!**
Attends !	**Wait!**
Attendez !	**Wait!**
Attendons !	**Let's wait!**

To include an object pronoun in the affirmative command, place it after the verb and attach it to the verb with a hyphen, like this:

Écoute-moi !	*Vas-y !*	*Parle-leur !*
Suivez-moi !	*Lisez-le !*	*Attendez-nous !*
Allons-y !	*Prenons-en !*	*Cherchons-la !*

It is possible to have both a direct and an indirect object pronoun in the same command. In the affirmative command, place the direct object first and attach both objects to the verb and to each other, like this:

Donne-le-moi !	*Rends-la-leur !*	*Achète-les-nous !*
Mettez-les-y !	*Donnez-m'en !*	*Envoyez-les-leur !*
Racontons-la-lui !	*Achetons-leur-en !*	

Note that the order is always direct first, indirect second, then **y**, and then **en**. In the negative command, the verb form is surrounded by a negation:

N'insiste pas !	*Ne pleure plus !*	*Ne maigris plus !*
N'hésitez pas !	*Ne regardez pas !*	*Ne lisez plus !*
Ne fumons point !	*Ne finissons pas !*	*Ne suivons pas !*

We place an object pronoun, or object pronoun pair, in <u>front</u> of the verb in a negative command, much as you would in a regular sentence. See "Object Pronouns" to review the order used here. There are no hyphens in the negative command. Study these examples:

Ne me parle pas !	*Ne me le dis pas !*	*Ne les y pose pas !*
Ne vous en faites pas !	*Ne le leur dites rien !*	*Ne l'y mettez pas !*
Ne l'attendons plus.	*Ne les mangeons pas !*	*Ne la leur envoyons pas !*

The verbs **avoir**, **être**, **savoir**, and **vouloir** have irregular command forms based on the subjunctive:

Aie pitié !	*Sois gentil !*	*Sache la vérité !*
Ayez pitié !	*Soyez gentil(s) !*	*Sachez la vérité !*
Ayons pitié !	*Soyons gentils !*	*Sachons la vérité !*
Veuillez patienter ! (the only form generally used from *vouloir*)		

Drill 38: The Imperative

Change the negative command into an affirmative one. Reposition any pronouns accordingly:

1. N'y va pas !

2. Ne la leur dites pas !

3. N'en prenons pas !

4. Ne nous les envoyez pas !

5. Ne viens pas ici !

Change the affirmative command into a negative one; reposition any pronouns accordingly:

6. Donne-moi ton linge sale.

7. Expliquez-la-nous.

8. Oubliez-le.

9. Allons-y.

10. Mets-toi devant nous.

Drill 38–Answers and Explanations

1. *Vas-y*!
   Go! Compare the two different spellings of *aller* (*va* versus *vas*). In the negative command, the *s* drops from the *tu* form of this *-er* verb, as one would expect. In the affirmative construction, the next word is *y*. The *s* is reattached for smoothness in pronunciation.

2. *Dites-la-leur*!
   Tell it to them! Both pronouns follow the verb in the affirmative command and are attached to the verb and to each other by hyphens. The word order is always <u>direct object</u> before <u>indirect object</u>.

3. *Prenons-en*!
   Let's take some! The pronoun object moves to the rear of the verb and attaches with a hyphen.

4. *Envoyez-les-nous*!
   Send them to us! Pronouns attach to the end of the verb and to each other in the prescribed order of <u>direct</u> before <u>indirect</u> object.

5. *Viens ici*!
   Come here! There are no pronouns to attach. *Ici* is an adverb.

6. *Ne me donne pas ton linge sale*!
   Don't give me your dirty laundry! The disjunctive *-moi* of the affirmative command reverts back to *me* in front of the verb. The **verb + object** unit is wrapped by the negation.

7. *Ne nous l'expliquez pas*!
   Don't explain it to us! Both pronouns precede the verb. Beware, the order is <u>not</u> always direct versus indirect here! Remember the odd little rule. If one pronoun begins with the letter *l*, place it closest to the verb. If both begin with *l*, place them in front of the verb in alphabetical order! *Y* and *en* are always last in the series of pronouns in front of a verb.

8. *Ne l'oubliez pas*!
   Don't forget it! *Le* drops its *e* in front of the verb beginning in a vowel. The negation wraps around the verb and pronoun unit.

9. *N'y allons pas*!
   Let's not go (there)! The pronoun precedes the verb and the negation wraps around them.

10. *Ne te mets pas devant nous!*
    Don't get in front of us! The disjunctive *-toi* reverts back to *te* in the negative command.

REFLEXIVE VERBS

A reflexive verb is one whose subject is also its object, as in the sentence **I cut myself. I** is the subject of **to cut** and **myself** is the object of **to cut**. Most verbs can be both transitive and reflexive. Compare:

<table>
<tr><td>*J'ai lavé le chien.*</td><td>versus</td><td>*Je me suis lavé.*</td></tr>
<tr><td>**I washed the dog.**</td><td></td><td>**I got washed.**</td></tr>
</table>

Here are the reflexive pronouns. Their position relative to the verb is just like any other pronoun object:

<table>
<tr><td>*Je **me** lève.*</td><td>*Je **m'**assieds.*</td></tr>
<tr><td>*Tu **te** lèves.*</td><td>*Tu **t'**assieds.*</td></tr>
<tr><td>*Il **se** lève.*</td><td>*Il **s'**assied.*</td></tr>
<tr><td>*Nous **nous** levons.*</td><td>*Nous **nous** asseyons.*</td></tr>
<tr><td>*Vous **vous** levez.*</td><td>*Vous **vous** asseyez.*</td></tr>
<tr><td>*Ils **se** lèvent.*</td><td>*Ils **s'**asseyent / **s'**assoient*</td></tr>
</table>

Reciprocal Meaning in Plural Forms

The ***nous***, ***vous***, and ***ils*** forms of reflexive verbs often express reciprocity. The plural subjects perform the action and receive the action:

> *Ils s'embrassent.*
>> They kiss each other.
>> They both kiss. (subject)
>> They are both kissed. (object)

Reflexives in the Compound Tenses

Reflexive verbs must be conjugated with ***être*** in the compound tenses. Do not assume, however, that agreement is always made between the past participle and the subject. It is really the function of the reflexive pronoun that determines agreement here. Study these rules carefully:

1. The pronoun most often functions as a direct object. In this case the past participle reflects the gender and number of the pronoun.

    > *Ils **se** sont couchés à minuit.*
    >> They went to bed at midnight.

    > *Je **me** suis assise.*
    >> I sat down. (female)

2. If the reflexive pronoun functions as an indirect object, there is no agreement.

> *Les filles **se** sont parlé.*
> The girls spoke **to** each other.

> *Nous **nous** sommes écrit.*
> We wrote **to** each other.

3. If the reflexive pronoun serves as a possessive marker, it is treated like an indirect object and there is no agreement. Remember how French avoids using possessive adjectives with body parts? This construction allows the body part to be identified as belonging to the subject:

> *Sylvie s'est coupé les cheveux.*
> Sylvie cut **her** hair.

> *Ils **se** sont rasé la barbe.*
> They shaved **their** beards.

> *Nous **nous** sommes lavé les mains.*
> We washed our hands.

Drill 39: Reflexive Verbs

Show agreement if necessary, and leave blank if there is none.

1. Hélène s'est couché_____ tard.

2. Elles se sont haï_____.

3. Ils se sont fait_____ mal.

4. Claudine, tu t'es trompé_____ !

5. Édith s'est limé_____ les ongles.

6. Nous nous sommes, tous les deux, cassé_____ le nez !

7. Il se sont disputé_____.

8. Ils se sont dit_____ au revoir.

9. Régis et Myriam, quand vous êtes-vous marié_____ ?

10. Elle s'est mis_____ à pleurer.

Drill 39–Answers and Explanations

1. **e**
Hélène went to bed late. (Hélène put herself to bed late.) Agreement with pronoun functioning as direct object.

2. **es**
They hated each other. Agreement with pronoun functioning as direct object.

3. **no agreement**
They hurt themselves. (Literally: **They did harm to themselves.**) No agreement with indirect object pronoun.

4. **e**
Claudine, you were mistaken. (Literally: **You fooled yourself.**) Direct object here. Show agreement.

5. **no agreement**
Édith filed her nails. The pronoun simply marks possession here. The direct object is *les ongles*, so the reflexive pronoun is indirect.

6. **no agreement**
Both of us broke our noses! *Le nez* is the direct object, so the reflexive pronoun marks possession.

7. **s**
They argued. This verb is inherently reflexive. That means it is hard to see the direct object nature of the reflexive pronoun, yet there is agreement.

8. **no agreement**
They said goodbye to each other. *Au revoir* is the direct object. The reflexive pronoun is indirect.

9. **s**
Régis and Myriam, when did you get married? Reciprocal verb, when did you marry **each other**? Show agreement.

10. **e**
She began to cry. (Literally: **She put herself to crying**.) Show agreement with the reflexive pronoun, and a direct object here.

MODAL VERBS

The modal verbs are *devoir*, *pouvoir*, *savoir*, *vouloir*, and the impersonal verb *falloir*. They enable, or give modality to, the infinitives that follow them. Mastery of modal verbs will expand and enhance your speaking and writing abilities immeasurably.

The verb *devoir* expresses obligation, probability, or expectation.

> *Je dois chercher les enfants à trois heures.*
> I have to pick up the children at three.

> *Il doit être chez lui.*
> He's probably at home.
> He must be at home.

> *L'avion doit décoller dans un instant.*
> The plane is due to take off in a moment.

When giving advice, use the <u>present conditional</u> of *devoir* to suggest what should or shouldn't be done, and use the <u>past conditional</u> to suggest what should have or should not have been done, like this:

> *Tu devrais te coucher plus tôt.*
> You should get to bed earlier.

> *Vous ne devriez pas être impudents.*
> You shouldn't be insolent.

> *J'aurais dû attendre les soldes.*
> I should have waited for the clearance sales.

> *Nous n'aurions pas dû manger tout cela.*
> We shouldn't have eaten all of that.

The *passé composé* of *devoir* + **infinitive** creates **had to** as well as the supposition **must have**:

> *Mon jean était si abîmé que j'ai dû le jeter.*
> My jeans were so worn out that I had to throw them away.

> *Ils ont dû s'égarer.*
> They must have gotten lost.

The imperfect of *devoir* + **infinitive** expresses what **was supposed** to take place as well as the hypothetical **must have**.

> *Je devais aller à l'école militaire.*
> I was supposed to go to military school.

Elle devait avoir 5 ou 6 ans.
She must have been about 5 or 6.

Pouvoir expresses capability. It is used to seek permission as well:

Elle ne peut pas nager.
She can't swim.

Puis-je m'asseoir ici?
May I sit here?

Il ne pouvait pas nous aider.
He couldn't help us.

J'aurais pu t'aider.
I could have helped you.

The present conditional of **pouvoir** suggests what could be done:

Tu pourrais dire merci.
You could (might) say thank you.

Vouloir relates desire (real or wishful) as well as intention:

Il veut manger avant 7 heures.
He wants to eat before 7:00.

Elle voudrait être célèbre.
She would like to be famous.

Tu as voulu me tromper.
You tried to fool me.

The command form **veuillez** is used to request politely that something be done:

Veuillez raccrocher.
Please hang up.

Savoir + **infinitive** means **to know how**:

Elle sait bien cuisiner.
She really knows how to cook.

Falloir always expresses necessity:

Il faut attendre pour savoir le résultat.
We have to wait to get the results.

Il ne faut pas le déranger.
He must not be disturbed.

The modals may also be used without a following infinitive:

Tu le dois!
    You have to!

Je le sais!
    I know it!

Cela se peut.
    That may (be).

Je ne peux pas!
    I can't!

Il le faut!
    It has to be (done)!

Drill 40: Modal Verbs

Supply the modal verb in the appropriate tense to create the French equivalent of the English cue:

1. _____-tu nous aider plus tard ?
       (Can)

2. Tu _____ en avoir honte !
       (should)

3. Nous _____ finir.
       (must)

4. _____-vous planter les choux ?
   (do you know how)

5. _____ vous asseoir, s'il vous plaît.
   (command—would you please)

6. Nous _____ manger avant de quitter la maison.
       (should have)

7. Tu _____ t'excuser !
       (could)

8. Tu _____ t'excuser !
       (should)

9. Il _____ apprendre à piloter un avion.
       (would like)

10. _____ -je vous aider ?
       (may I)

Drill 40–Answers and Explanations

1. *peux* (or *pourras*, or *pourrais*)
    Can you help us later? (or Will you be able to help us later? or **Would you be able to help us later?)** Any of these tenses could be used, each one with a slightly different meaning.

2. *devrais*
    You should be ashamed! Use the <u>conditional</u> of *devoir* to suggest what **should** be done.

3. *devons*
    We have to (we must) finish. Use the <u>present</u> of *devoir* to tell what **must** be done.

4. *savez*
    Do you know how to plant cabbages? Always use *savoir* + **infinitive** to express **knowing how**.

5. *veuillez*
    Would you please sit down? The *vous* form of the <u>imperative</u> of *vouloir* creates a polite command.

6. *aurions dû*
    We should have eaten before leaving the house. The <u>past conditional</u> of *devoir* is used to express what **should have been** done.

7. *pourrais*
    You could excuse yourself. The <u>conditional</u> of *pouvoir* creates the suggestion of what **could be** done.

8. *devrais*
    You should excuse yourself. Use the <u>conditional</u> of *devoir* to suggest what **should be** done.

9. *voudrait*
    He would like to learn to fly a plane. The <u>conditional</u> of *vouloir* can be used to express a desired goal or intention, what one **would like**.

10. *puis* (or *pourrais*)
    May I help you? (or Could I help you?) Note the special interrogative form of the 1st person (present indicative) of *pouvoir*. Here again, more than one tense could be used, as in question 1.

THE CAUSATIVE CONSTRUCTION

The little formula *faire* + **infinitive** + **person or thing** allows us to express **making** or **having someone do something**, or **having something done**.

If the *faire* + **infinitive** construction has only one object, it will be <u>direct</u>. If *faire* and the infinitive <u>each</u> have an object, the object of *faire* will be <u>indirect</u>. The following examples illustrate both types of constructions. Note in particular that the participle of *faire* remains invariable in the compound past.

Tu fais pleurer ta mère. You make your mother cry.	*Tu **la** fais pleurer.* You make her cry.	*Tu **l'**as fait pleurer.* You made her cry.
Je fais tondre la pelouse aujourd'hui. I'm having the lawn mowed today.	*Je **la** fais tondre aujourd'hui.* I'm having it mowed today.	*Je **l'**ai fait tondre aujourd'hui.* I had it mowed today.
Tu fais faire la robe? Are you having the dress made?	*Tu **la** fais faire?* Are you having it made?	*Tu **l'**as fait faire?* Did you have it made?

These sentences have two objects:

Je fais manger les légumes aux enfants. I make the children eat their vegetables.	*Je **leur** fais manger les legumes.* I make **them** eat their vegetables.	*Je les **leur** fais manger.* I make **them** eat them. (*Les* is the direct object of *manger*.)	*Je les **leur** ai fait manger.* I made **them** eat them.
Je fais couper les cheveux à l'enfant. I have the child's hair cut.	*Je **lui** fais couper les cheveux.* I have **his** hair cut.	*Je les **lui** fait couper.* I have **his** cut. (*Les* is the direct object of *couper*.)	*Je les **lui** ai fait couper.* I had **his** cut.

In a sentence such as *Il fait lire l'histoire à l'étudiant*, confusion is possible. We wonder whether he's having the student read the story, or whether he's having the story read to the student. Because both translations are possible, you can specify that the student is doing the reading by substituting the preposition ***par*** for *à*; thus *Il fait lire l'histoire par l'étudiant* clarifies the student reader.

When making or having a person do something that involves a reflexive verb, we eliminate the reflexive pronoun, like this:

> *Je la fais dépêcher.*
> I make her hurry.

Drill 41: Causative *Faire*

Express these causative sentences in French:

1. He makes his mother worry.

2. I will have the children get up early.

3. I'm having the house repainted.

4. She has the students write.

5. She makes the students speak French.

6. We make him understand.

7. We make him understand French.

8. I have them sing.

9. I have the children drink their milk.

10. I had the boy tell the story.

Drill 41–Answers and Explanations

1. *Il fait inquiéter sa mère.*
    The reflexive pronoun is omitted in the causative construction.

2. *Je ferai lever les enfants de bonne heure.*
    Use the future tense of *faire* and eliminate the reflexive pronoun.

3. *Je fais repeindre la maison.*
    This is the basic causative construction with one object: *faire* + **infinitive** + **person or thing**.

4. *Elle fait écrire les élèves.* (or *les étudiants*)
    This is another basic single object construction.

5. *Elle fait parler français aux élèves.* (or *aux étudiants*)
    Two objects are involved. **French** is the direct object of the verb *parler*, and **the students** becomes the indirect object of *faire*. This construction does give rise to some confusion. Is she making the students speak French or having it spoken to them? You can use *par les élèves* to clarify that the students are speaking.

6. *Nous le faisons comprendre.*
    The single object of *faire comprendre* is the direct object **him**.

7. *Nous lui faisons comprendre le français.*
    With two objects, **French** is the direct object of *comprendre*, and **him** now becomes the indirect object of *faire*.

8. *Je les fais chanter*.
    This is a basic single direct object construction.

9. *Je fais boire leur lait aux enfants.*
    There are two objects: **their milk** is direct and **the children** becomes indirect.

10. *J'ai fait raconter l'histoire par le garçon.*
    This is a past tense construction. We have made clear that the boy told the story by using the preposition *par* instead of *à*.

SAVOIR VERSUS CONNAÎTRE

French has two verbs meaning **to know**. This very same type of differentiation also exists in Spanish, Italian, and Portuguese.

Of the two verbs, *savoir* has the broadest range of use. *Connaître* is restricted to a much narrower application, as we shall see.

The Uses of *Savoir*

1. To express knowing how to do something, always use the verb *savoir* followed by an infinitive.

   > *Elle ne **sait** pas **nager**.*
   > She doesn't know how to swim.

   Note the absence of the adverb *comment* in this construction! It is usually left out with skills. *Comment* is never really necessary, but is occasionally used:

   > *Elle sait le faire.* (or *Elle sait comment le faire.*)
   > She knows how to do it.

2. Use *savoir* when **to know** simply suggests <u>general awareness</u>. This usage includes the following types of usage:

Knowing When	*Je veux **savoir quand** ils viendront.*
	I want to **know when** they're coming.
Knowing Where	*Je ne **sais** pas **où** j'ai laissé mon stylo.*
	I don't **know where** I left my pen.
Knowing Why	***Sais**-tu **pourquoi** elle pleure?*
	Do you **know why** she's crying?
Knowing What	*Il ne **sait** pas **ce qui** se passe.*
	He doesn't know **what's happening**.
	*Je ne **sais** pas **ce que** vous voulez.*
	I don't **know what** you want.
Knowing Which	*Je ne **sais** pas **quel** film choisir.*
	I don't **know which** film to choose.
Knowing Who	***Savez**-vous **qui** a mangé mes beignets?*
	Do you **know who** ate my donuts?
Knowing If	*Nous ne **savons** pas encore **si** nous venons.*
	We don't **know** yet **if** we're coming.
Knowing That	*Tu **sais que** je t'aime.*
	You **know that** I love you.
Knowing How	*Je ne **sais** pas **comment** elle est morte.*
	I don't **know how** she died.

3. We generally use *savoir* for knowing <u>telephone numbers</u> and <u>addresses</u>.

> *Savez-vous mon numéro?*
> Do you know my number?

There is now some overlap with telephone numbers and addresses. Some people do use *connaître* with them.

4. Use *savoir* for knowing something **by heart**, *par cœur*. This usually includes anything that has been memorized or learned by rote, including one's lines for a play, the ABC's, multiplication tables, verb endings, or the capitals of countries.

> *Je dois savoir ce texte pour demain.*
> I have to know these lines by tomorrow.

5. Use *savoir* when the verb **to know** is used alone.

> *Je sais!*
> I know!

> *Je ne sais pas!*
> I don't know!

The Uses of *Connaître*

1. To express **knowing** a person, always use *connaître*. It is the <u>only</u> verb you may use for acquaintance with <u>people</u>.

> *Est-ce que vous connaissez Mme Aubry?*
> Do you know Madame Aubry?

2. To express <u>in-depth knowledge</u>, gained through <u>familiarity</u> due to lengthy association, research, or personal experience, use *connaître*. This usage includes:

Knowing a Place Well	*Je ne **connais** pas très bien **New York**.*
Knowing the Best	*Tu **connais** les **meilleurs** restaurants!*
Knowing the Work of an Artist or Author	*Je **connais** Rimbaud, moi!*
Knowing One's Job	*Après 40 ans, on **connaît** son **métier**!*

Connaître and *Savoir* in the Past Tense

Both verbs take on special meanings in the *passé composé*. *Savoir* takes on the meaning of **finding out**:

> *Je l'ai su par Marie.*
> Marie told me.

> *Nous l'avons su juste hier.*
> We just found out yesterday.

Connaître takes on the meaning of **meeting** for the first time, or **making the acquaintance** of another person:

> *Ils se sont connus à l'université.*
> They met in college.

Drill 42: *Savoir* or *Connaître*?

Complete the sentence with the appropriate form of *savoir* or *connaître*.

1. Il ne _____ pas patiner.

2. Tu _____ où j'habite ?

3. Il veut _____ s'il est censé pleuvoir ce soir.

4. Vous _____ l'œuvre de Berthe Morisot ?

5. Il ne _____ pas mes parents.

6. Je _____ très bien ce quartier.

7. Ils _____ que nous ne pouvons pas venir ce soir.

8. _____-vous quelles chaussures mettre ?

9. Nous _____ qui va gagner.

10. Tu _____, je crois que nous devrions descendre le store.

Drill 42–Answers and Explanations

1. *sait*

    He doesn't know how to skate. Always use *savoir* for knowing **how** to do something.

2. *sais*

    You know where I live? This is a good example of general awareness; knowing **where**. Use *savoir*.

3. *savoir*

    He wants to know whether it's supposed to rain tonight. General awareness; knowing **if**. Use *savoir*.

4. *connaissez*

    Do you know (are you familiar with) the work of Berthe Morisot? **Familiarity** with the work of an artist. Use *connaître*.

5. *connaît*

    He doesn't know my parents. Parents are human beings! Always use *connaître* with people.

6. *connais*

    I know this neighborhood well. Familiarity with a place. Use *connaître*.

7. *savent*

    They know (that) we can't come tonight. General awareness; knowing **that**. Use *savoir*.

8. *Savez*

    Do you know which shoes to wear (to put on)? General awareness; knowing **which**. Use *savoir*.

9. *savons*

    We know who's going to win. General awareness; knowing **who**. Use *savoir*.

10. *sais*

    You know, I think we should pull down the shade. Use *savoir* when the verb is used alone, as it is here.

USING *PLAIRE* AND *MANQUER*

These two verbs present problems for the English speaker because French and English approach what they mean from totally opposite directions.

Let's examine *plaire* first. The actual meaning of *plaire* is **to please**. That is the only thing it means. It does <u>not</u> mean **to like**! When French people use it, it <u>always</u> means **to please**. It is <u>we</u> who say we **like** something. <u>They</u> say it is **pleasing** to them. Sure, what the Frenchman <u>means</u> is that he likes it, but what he <u>says</u> is that it pleases him! If you understand and accept this basic truth, you will save yourself a lot of confusion.

There are some important ramifications to consider. In the English sentence the thing or person being liked is the direct object of the verb. The person who **likes** is the subject of the verb:

> **He** (subject) **likes** (verb) **beer** (direct object).

The French sentence, expressing the same thought, comes out like this:

> *La bière* (subject) *lui* (indirect object) *plaît* (verb).
> Beer is pleasing to him.

The verb *plaire*, which can only mean **to please**, has for its subject the thing that pleases, **beer**. The person who was the subject in the English sentence becomes the indirect object (**to him**) in the French construction. Here's another example:

> **They** (subject) **like** (verb) **girls** (direct object).

The Frenchman thinks and says:

> *Les filles* (subject) *leur* (indirect object) *plaisent* (verb).
> Girls are pleasing to them.

Notice how the verb plaire matches its subject!
Here is one more example:

> **I** (subject) **like** (verb) **you** (direct object).

The same thought, expressed in French:

> *Tu* (subject) *me* (direct object) *plais* (verb).
> You are pleasing to me.

French does have the verb *aimer*, which means **to like** or **to love**. Students tend to stick with it because it's safe and easy. Although the French have both *plaire* and *aimer* at their disposal, more often than not they'll use *plaire*.

When using the verb *manquer* for feeling the absence of someone, we will see a similar pattern unfold. In this usage the verb **manquer** means **to be missing**. Hold that thought! In English **we** miss someone. In French that person **is missing** to us. The same construction that we used with *plaire* now works for *manquer*. Compare:

I miss you.	*Tu me manques.* (subject, indirect object pronoun, verb) **You are missing to me.**
We miss him.	*Il nous manque.* (subject, indirect object pronoun, verb) **He is missing to us.**
I miss them.	*Ils me manquent.* (subject, indirect object pronoun, verb) **They are missing to me.**
Do you miss me?	*Je te manque?* (subject, indirect object pronoun, verb) **Am I missing to you?**
Two chairs are missing.	*Deux chaises manquent.* (subject, verb) or *Il manque deux chaises.* **There are two chairs missing.** (Here **manquer** has the impersonal subject **il**.)

Drill 43: Using *Plaire* and *Manquer*

Match the French sentence with its English translation:

_____	1.	Il lui manque une dent.	A.	**You like him.**
_____	2.	Je leur plais.	B.	**We like you.**
_____	3.	Ils me plaisent.	C.	**We miss you.**
_____	4.	Tu lui manques.	D.	**I like them.**
_____	5.	Il te manque.	E.	**He's missing a tooth.**
_____	6.	Tu lui plais.	F.	**He misses you.**
_____	7.	Il te plaît.	G.	**They like me.**
_____	8.	Nous te plaisons.	H.	**You miss him.**
_____	9.	Vous nous manquez.	I.	**You like us.**
_____	10.	Tu nous plais.	J.	**He likes you.**

Drill 43–Answers

1. **(E)** There is a tooth missing to him. = He's missing a tooth.

2. **(G)** I am pleasing to them. = They like me.

3. **(D)** They are pleasing to me. = I like them.

4. **(F)** You are missing to him. = He misses you.

5. **(H)** He is missing to you. = You miss him.

6. **(J)** You are pleasing to him. = He likes you.

7. **(A)** He is pleasing to you. = You like him.

8. **(I)** We are pleasing to you. = You like us.

9. **(C)** You are missing to us. = We miss you.

10. **(B)** You are pleasing to us. = We like you.

THE PRESENT INDICATIVE

	aimer	*finir*	*vendre*
	to love	**to finish**	**to sell**
je (j')	*aime*	*finis*	*vends*
tu	*aimes*	*finis*	*vends*
il, elle, on	*aime*	*finit*	*vend*
nous	*aimons*	*finissons*	*vendons*
vous	*aimez*	*finissez*	*vendez*
ils, elles	*aiment*	*finissent*	*vendent*

Tips on Pronouncing and Spelling -*er* Verbs

To the ear, there are only <u>three</u> present tense ending sounds for all verbs in the -*er* group. The *je*, *tu*, *il*, <u>and</u> *ils* forms all end in the same sound. It can be [ə] or the final consonant of the stem. The endings of ***nous*** [ɔ̃] and ***vous*** [e] each have their own characteristic sounds. You must remember to pronounce the ***ils*** verb form (*aiment*) <u>exactly like</u> the ***il*** form (*aime*). <u>Never</u> pronounce the -*ent* ending as it sounds in the French word *parent*.

Verbs ending in -*cer*, such as ***agacer***, ***commencer***, and ***placer***, will need a cedilla attached to the *c* whenever it comes in contact with the vowels *a* or *o*. This preserves the soft sound of the *c* in the infinitive, [s]. Examples include the present participle: *en commençant*, as well as conjugated verb forms in various tenses: *nous commençons*.

Verbs ending in -*ger*, such as *manger* and *voyager*, will need the addition of the letter *e* after the *g* when it comes in contact with the same two vowels: *a* and *o*. Again, this preserves the soft sound of the *g* heard in the infinitive, [ʒ]. Examples: *en mangeant*, *nous voyageons*.

-*er* Verbs with Stem Changes

There is only one -*er* verb that is entirely irregular, and that is the verb ***aller*** (**to go**): *vais*, *vas*, *va*, *allons*, *allez*, and ***vont***.

There are four types of spelling changes that occur in regular -*er* verbs. All four changes occur under the <u>same</u> circumstance—before a **silent *e***—and for the <u>same</u> reason—to make a slight change in pronunciation because of that **silent *e***. Where does the **silent *e*** occur? Remember the four forms that share the same ending sound? The *je*, *tu*, *il*, and *ils* forms! Each has a silent *e* appearing <u>after the last consonant of the root</u>. The silent *e* also appears <u>after</u>

the last consonant of the root in the same forms of the present subjunctive, and in every conjugated form of the regular future and conditional tenses.

Here are the four responses to the silent *e*:

1. Verbs that pick up an *accent grave* (*è*). These verbs have unaccented infinitives ending in the vowel *e* + **consonant** + *-er*. Examples include *acheter*, *lever*, *mener*, and *peser*. These verbs all require the *accent grave* in front of the silent *e*.

j'achète	*j'achèterai*	*j'achèterais*
tu lèves	*tu lèveras*	*tu lèverais*

2. Verbs whose accent marks change from (*é*) to (*è*). These infinitives are marked with an acute accent (*é*). Common examples include *espérer*, *préférer*, and *régler*. In conjugation, that accent remains acute when the last consonant of the root is followed by sound, and flips to grave when followed by silent *e*.

j'espère	versus	*nous espérons*
tu préfères	versus	*vous préférez*
ils règlent	versus	*ils ont réglé*

3. Verbs that double their consonants. These verbs have a single consonant in the infinitive, such as *appeler* and *jeter*, and a double consonant in front of silent *e* as follows:

j'appelle	*j'appellerai*	*j'appellerais*
je jette	*je jetterai*	*je jetterais*

   Note that the consonant remains single when followed by a sounded vowel. Compare:

tu appelles	versus	*vous appelez*
il jette	versus	*il a jeté*

4. Verbs whose infinitives end in **vowel** + *-yer*. Examples include *employer*, *essuyer*, *payer*, and *essayer*. The *y* may change to an *i* in front of silent *e*, but it will remain unchanged in front of a sounded vowel. Some writers keep the *y* in both positions. Compare:

tu emploies	versus	*vous employez*
tu employes	and	*vous employez*
elle essuie	versus	*elle essuyerait*
elle essuye	and	*elle essuyerait*

Pronouncing and Conjugating *-ir* Verbs

The *je*, *tu*, and *il* forms all sound alike. The double *ss* of the *ils* form is distinctly pronounced as the <u>final</u> sound of the verb. Once again, it is an error to pronounce the *-ent* that follows the double *ss*.

There is a small subgroup of *-ir* verbs that does not follow the standard conjugation. They are as follows:

dormir (**to sleep**)	*dors, dors, dort, dormons, dormez, dorment*
mentir (**to lie**)	*mens, mens, ment, mentons, mentez, mentent*
partir (**to leave**)	*pars, pars, part, partons, partez, partent*
sortir (**to go out**)	*sors, sors, sort, sortons, sortez, sortent*
(se) sentir (**to feel, smell**)	*sens, sens, sent, sentons, sentez, sentent*
servir (**to serve**)	*sers, sers, sert, servons, servez, servent*

The verbs *offrir* and *souffrir* are conjugated as though they were *-er* verbs as follows:

offrir (**to offer**)	*offre, offres, offre, offrons, offrez, offrent*
souffrir (**to suffer**)	*souffre, souffres, souffre, souffrons, souffrez, souffrent*

The following *-ir* verbs are irregular in the present indicative:

mourir (**to die**)	*meurs, meurs, meurt, mourons, mourez, meurent*
tenir (**to hold**)	*tiens, tiens, tient, tenons, tenez, tiennent*
venir (**to come**)	*viens, viens, vient, venons, venez, viennent*

Pronouncing and Conjugating *-re* Verbs

The *je*, *tu*, and *il* forms all sound alike. In the *ils* form, the consonant that appears in front of the *-ent* ending is distinctly pronounced as the final sound of the verb. Just as it was true of *-er* and *-ir* verbs, it is always wrong to attribute a sound to this *-ent* ending.

There are a number of *-re* verbs that are irregular and should be learned by heart. They are:

battre (**to beat**)	*bats, bats, bat, battons, battez, battent*
boire (**to drink**)	*bois, bois, boit, buvons, buvez, boivent*
conduire (**to drive**)	*conduis, conduis, conduit, conduisons, conduisez, conduisent*
connaître (**to know**)	*connais, connais, connaît, connaissons, connaissez, connaissent*
coudre (**to sew**)	*couds, couds, coud, cousons, cousez, cousent*
craindre (**to fear**)	*crains, crains, craint, craignons, craignez, craignent*
croire (**to believe**)	*crois, crois, croit, croyons, croyez, croient*
dire (**to say, tell**)	*dis, dis, dit, disons, dites, disent*
écrire (**to write**)	*écris, écris, écrit, écrivons, écrivez, écrivent*
être (**to be**)	*suis, es, est, sommes, êtes, sont*
faire (**to do, make**)	*fais, fais, fait, faisons, faites, font*
joindre (**to join**)	*joins, joins, joint, joignons, joignez, joignent*
lire (**to read**)	*lis, lis, lit, lisons, lisez, lisent*
mettre (**to place, put**)	*mets, mets, met, mettons, mettez, mettent*
naître (**to be born**)	*nais, nais, nait, naissons, naissez, naissent*
peindre (**to paint**)	*peins, peins, peint, peignons, peignez, peignent*
plaire (**to please**)	*plais, plais, plaît, plaisons, plaisez, plaisent*
prendre (**to take**)	*prends, prends, prend, prenons, prenez, prennent*
résoudre (**to resolve**)	*résous, résous, résout, résolvons, résolvez, résolvent*
rire (**to laugh**)	*ris, ris, rit, rions, riez, rient*
suffire (**to be enough**)	*suffis, suffis, suffit, suffisons, suffisez, suffisent*

suivre (**to follow**)	*suis, suis, suit, suivons, suivez, suivent*
vaincre (**to conquer**)	*vaincs, vaincs, vainc, vainquons, vainquez, vainquent*
vivre (**to live**)	*vis, vis, vit, vivons, vivez, vivent*

Irregular Verbs Ending in *-oir*

(s')asseoir (**to sit down, to seat**)	*assieds, assieds, assied, asseyons, asseyez, asseyent*
avoir (**to have**)	*ai, as, a, avons, avez, ont*
devoir (**to have to, must**)	*dois, dois, doit, devons, devez, doivent*
falloir (**to be necessary, must**—impersonal)	*faut*
pouvoir (**to be able, can**)	*peux* (*puis-je*), *peux, peut, pouvons, pouvez, peuvent*
pleuvoir (**to rain**—impersonal)	*pleut*
recevoir (**to receive**)	*reçois, reçois, reçoit, recevons, recevez, reçoivent*
savoir (**to know, to know how**)	*sais, sais, sait, savons, savez, savent*
valoir (**to be worth**)	*vaux, vaux, vaut, valons, valez, valent*
voir (**to see**)	*vois, vois, voit, voyons, voyez, voient*
vouloir (**to want**)	*veux, veux, veut, voulons, voulez, veulent*

Drill 44: The Present Indicative

Supply the correct form of the present tense. Make sure your answer agrees with its subject:

1. Quelle boisson _____-tu, limonade ou grenadine ?
   (préférer)

2. Papa _____ tout le monde.
   (connaître)

3. Je _____ en vacances aujourd'hui.
   (partir)

4. À quelle heure _____-ils ?
   (finir)

5. Il _____ profondément.
   (dormir)

6. Mon chaton _____ Minou.
   (s'appeler)

7. Comment _____-vous ?
   (s'appeler)

8. Vous _____ le ballon de travers !
   (jeter)

9. Ils le _____ déjà.
   (savoir)

10. Ne _____-ils pas assister au match ?
    (aller)

11. N'_____-vous pas encore prêts ?
    (être)

12. Qu'est-ce que vous _____ comme dessert ?
    (choisir)

13. _____-tu danser avec moi ?
    (vouloir)

14. Il _____ visite à ses amis.
    (rendre)

15. Nous _____ tôt le soir aux États-Unis.
     (manger)

16. Nous _____ au parc.
     (étudier)

17. Qu'est-ce que tu _____ pour Mémé ?
     (acheter)

18. Qui _____ ces repas ?
     (payer)

19. Tu _____ ton vieux jean ?
     (jeter)

20. Nous _____ notre prof car nous n'écoutons pas toujours.
     (agacer)

21. Où _____-tu comme ça ?
     (aller)

22. Je _____ le même hebdo.
     (recevoir)

23. Quel âge _____-tu ?
     (avoir)

24. Ma chambre _____ sur la cour.
     (donner)

25. Tu _____ en français.
     (répondre)

26. Ce que vous _____ est vrai.
     (dire)

27. Qu'est-ce qu'on _____ ?
     (voir)

28. Que _____-vous ?
     (faire)

29. Elle _____ à ce que ses élèves étudient.
     (veiller)

30. Mes parents _____ les meilleurs restaurants du quartier.
     (connaître)

Drill 44–Answers and Explanations

1. **préfères**

The *accent aigu* of the infinitive becomes an *accent grave* when the *e* that follows the last consonant of its root is not sounded. *Préférer* follows Rule 2 for *-er* verbs with stem changes.

2. **connaît**

Connaître has an irregular conjugation. Only the infinitive and the 3rd person singular get the circumflex accent.

3. **pars**

Partir, dormir, mentir, sentir, and *servir* all follow the same conjugation pattern. They are distant cousins to the standard *-ir* verb family, and follow a distinct, alternative conjugation.

4. **finissent**

Finir is a regular *-ir* verb and follows the standard conjugation. Don't you dare pronounce that *-ent*!

5. **dort**

Dormir follows the alternative *-ir* ends along with *partir, mentir, sentir,* and *servir*.

6. **s'appelle**

Appeler doubles the letter *l* when followed by a silent *e*. This is Rule 3 for *-er* verbs with stem changes.

7. **vous appelez**

Appeler retains a single letter *l* when followed by a sounded *e*.

8. **jetez**

Jeter retains a single *t* when followed by a sounded *e*.

9. **savent**

Savoir has its own irregular conjugation. The only thing regular about this particular verb form is that the *-ent* at the end is silent.

10. **vont**

Aller is the only *-er* verb that is irregular and whose conjugation you must learn by heart. This form brings to mind similar irregulars such as *ont*, *font*, and *sont*.

11. **êtes**

Être is probably one of the first irregular verbs you ever learned. It is essential. Forget taking the AP Exam if you don't know this verb inside and out! It would be easier to nail Jell-O to the ceiling!

12. **choisissez**

Choisir is a regular *-ir* verb and follows the standard conjugation.

13. **Veux**

Vouloir is highly irregular and must be learned by heart.

14. **rend**

Rendre is a regular *-re* verb and follows the standard conjugation.

15. **mangeons**

Like all *-er* verbs whose roots end in *g*, *manger* requires an extra *e* whenever the next letter is *o* or *a*. *Ranger* and *voyager* also work this way.

16. **étudions**

Étudier is a regular *-er* verb and follows the standard conjugation. Remember that when you make the root for an *-er* verb, you only remove the *-er* of the infinitive. Therefore, the root of this verb is *étudi*. It is a common student error to forget that *i*.

17. **achètes**

Acheter picks up a grave accent when a silent *e* follows the last consonant of its root. This is Rule 1 for *-er* verbs with stem changes.

18. **paie** (or **paye**)

The verb *payer* follows Rule 4 for *-er* verbs with stem changes. If the interrogative pronoun *qui* is the subject of the *-er* verb, use the 3rd person singular form of that verb.

19. **jettes**

Jeter doubles its *t* when followed by a silent *e*. This is Rule 3 for *-er* verbs with stem changes.

20. **agaçons**

Like all *-er* verbs whose roots end in *c*, *agacer* requires a cedilla on that *ç* whenever the next letter is *o* or *a*. *Commencer* and *placer* also work this way.

21. **vas**

Part of the irregular conjugation of *aller*, this form is similar to the 2nd person singular conjugation of *avoir*: *as*.

22. **reçois**

Like all verbs ending *-oir*, *recevoir* is irregular.

23. **as**

Like *être*, the verb *avoir* is one of the veritable founding blocks on which French is based. Attempting the AP Exam without knowing every little idiosyncrasy there is to know about this irregular verb would be foolish. Better luck stuffing a garden hose with mashed potatoes!

24. **donne**

Donner is a regular *-er* verb and follows the standard conjugation.

25. **réponds**

Répondre is a regular *-re* verb and follows the standard conjugation.

26. **dites**

Dire is irregular, and the *vous* form is a teacher favorite to catch the unaware!

27. **voit**

Voir is an important irregular conjugation to know by heart.

28. **faites**

Faire is irregular, and the *vous* form, like that of *dire*, often appears on tests to trip up the clueless!

29. **veille**

Veiller is a regular *-er* verb. Use the standard conjugation.

30. **connaissent**

Connaître is irregular. No circumflex is used in this form.

THE FUTURE

The future tense uses one set of universal endings that are applied to all verbs. The regular root is the entire infinitive. What could be easier? Here are samples from each of the three verb groups: Note that the *-re* infinitive drops its final *e* before accepting the endings:

-er: aimer**ai**, aimer**as**, aimer**a**, aimer**ons**, aimer**ez**, aimer**ont**
-ir: finir**ai**, finir**as**, finir**a**, finir**ons**, finir**ez**, finir**ont**
-re: vendr**ai**, vendr**as**, vendr**a**, vendr**ons**, vendr**ez**, vendr**ont**

The following verbs have irregular roots in the future:

aller	*ir-*	*(j'irai)*
avoir	*aur-*	*(j'aurai)*
devenir	*deviendr-*	*(je deviendrai)*
devoir	*devr-*	*(je devrai)*
envoyer	*enverr-*	*(j'enverrai)*
être	*ser-*	*(je serai)*
faire	*fer-*	*(je ferai)*
falloir	*faudr-*	*(il faudra)*
mourir	*mourr-*	*(je mourrai)*
pleuvoir	*pleuvr-*	*(il pleuvra)*
pouvoir	*pourr-*	*(je pourrai)*
savoir	*saur-*	*(je saurai)*
tenir	*tiendr-*	*(je tiendrai)*
venir	*viendr-*	*(je viendrai)*
voir	*verr-*	*(je verrai)*
vouloir	*voudr-*	*(je voudrai)*

You will get to recycle your knowledge of future roots, both regular and irregular, because they are also used in the formation of the conditional.

Use of the Future Tense

This tense is obviously used to express future action, but it is also frequently required in French where English would use the present. This happens when the future is <u>implied</u>. Key words that reliably signal this phenomenon are **quand** and **lorsque**, **when**, and **dès que** and **aussitôt que**, **as soon as**. *Tant que*, **as long as**, may also be followed by the future, if it is implied.

Si can be translated as **if** or **whether**. Again, follow with the future tense only when the future is implied. Study these examples:

> *Où resterez-vous **quand** vous **irez** en France?*
> Where will you stay **when** you go to France?

> *Elle viendra nous voir **lorsqu'**elle **sera** libre.*
> She will come to see us **when** she's free.

> *Je répondrai à votre lettre **dès que** je la **recevrai**.*
> I will answer your letter **as soon as** I receive it.

> *Nous ferons du ski **aussitôt qu'**ils **reviendront**.*
> We'll go skiing **as soon as** they get back.

> *Tu pourras rester **tant que** tu **voudras**.*
> You'll be able to stay **as long as** you want.

> *Je ne sais pas **si** je le **verrai**.*
> I don't know **whether** I'll see him.

Si can also be followed by the present tense when there is no future implication:

> *Je ne sais pas **si** l'auteur **est** toujours vivant.*
> I don't know **if** the author is still alive.

When **whether** and **if** are interchangeable in the English sentence, you must base your tense choice on the presence or absence of a future implication. However, when the word **whether** does not easily replace the word **if** in the English sentence, don't use the future! Here is an example:

> *Tu réussiras ton examen, **si** tu **étudies**.*
> You will ace your exam **if** you study.

The future and the future *antérieur* can also be used for conjecture or supposition, like this:

> *Il y a quelqu'un à la porte, Maman.*
> Mom, there's someone at the door.

> *Ce sera le facteur; j'attends un colis.*
> It's probably the mailman; I'm expecting a package.

> *Tiens, Sandrine aura fait la vaisselle!*
> Oh, Sandrine must have done the dishes!

Drill 45: Present or Future Tense?

Place the indicated verb in the appropriate tense. Look for cues within the sentence to guide your choice.

1. Je vous écrirai dès que je _____.
    (can)

2. Je vous écrirai si je _____.
    (can)

3. Je ne sais pas si elle _____ demain.
    (is coming)

4. Nous irons faire du ski aussitôt qu'il _____.
    (snows)

5. Je resterai fidèle tant qu'il le _____.
    (is)

6. Voulez-vous passer au tabac quand vous _____ en ville?
    (are)

7. J'aurai fini dans un instant si tu _____ m'attendre.
    (want)

8. Téléphone-moi lorsque tu _____.
    (get home)

9. Ils _____ leur maison d'été.
    (will sell)

10. Dites-nous quand vous _____ en France.
    (go)

Drill 45–Answers and Explanations

1. *pourrai*

   I will write to you as soon as I can. Use the future after **as soon as** when the future is implied, which it is here.

2. *peux*

   I will write to you if I can. Use the present tense after *si* (**if**) when it cannot be translated by **whether**.

3. *viendra* (*vient*).

   Je ne sais pas si elle vient demain. Both answers are possible; *si* translates as **if** or **whether**.

4. *neigera*

   We'll go skiing as soon as it snows. Use the future after **as soon as** when the future is implied.

5. *sera*

   I'll remain faithful as long as he is. Use the future after **as long as** when the future is implied.

6. *serez*

   Do you want to stop at the tobacco shop when you're in town? Unlike English, French always uses the future after **when** if the future is implied.

7. *veux*

   I'll be finished in a second if you want to wait for me. Use the present tense here, just as you would in English. *Si* translates only as **if**, and not as **whether**.

8. *rentreras*

   Call me when you get in. French always uses the future after **when** if the future is implied. Compare with question 6.

9. *vendront*

   They will sell their summer house. This is the basic use of the future tense, parallel to English here.

10. *irez*

    Tell us when you go to France. The future is implied; you haven't gone to France yet. In this case use the future after **when**.

THE IMPERFECT

The imperfect uses one set of universal endings for all verbs. The root is made from the *nous* form of the present indicative, <u>minus</u> the *-ons*. There is only one irregular root for the imperfect, and that is *ét-* for the verb *être*. Here are samples of the imperfect construction:

> *-er: aimais, aimais, aimait, aimions, aimiez, aimaient*
> *-ir: finissais, finissais, finissait, finissions, finissiez, finissaient*
> *-re: vendais, vendais, vendait, vendions, vendiez, vendaient*
> *être* (the sole irregular verb in the imperfect): *étais, étais, était, étions, étiez, étaient*

Uses of the Imperfect

1. The imperfect relates <u>continuing</u> action in the past. The action has no discernable beginning or ending within the framework of the sentence. The English translation of the verb invariably uses **was + -ing** or **were + -ing**. The action may be continuing or ongoing in the background while another action takes place.

2. The imperfect is <u>descriptive</u> of a physical or mental state. Actions that take place in the mind, such as **wanting** (*vouloir*), **thinking** (*penser*), **believing** (*croire*), or **fearing** (*craindre*), are generally rendered in the imperfect. Any verb that is <u>weather-related</u> falls into this category. The verb *avoir* in combination with a noun, and the verb *être* plus an adjective or noun are also reliable clues to use the descriptive imperfect.

3. The imperfect relates <u>habitual</u>, <u>customary</u>, or <u>repeated</u> action in the past. The English translation here is **used to** or **would**. There are often clue words in the sentence that suggest repetition, such as *toujours*, *souvent*, or *d'habitude*.

How the *Passé Composé* Is Different

If the past action is <u>completed</u> and clear-cut, having either a distinct beginning or ending within the sentence, we use the *passé composé*. If it is easy to visualize the action being accomplished within the sentence (**he ate the apple**; *il a mangé la pomme*), we render it in the *passé composé*.

In a narrative, it is the *passé composé* that propels the action forward, while the use of the imperfect creates a descriptive pause in the forward progression of the story.

Drill 46: Imperfect or *Passé Composé?*

Supply the most suitable past tense. Study the sentences carefully to determine your choice. Train yourself to pick out hidden clues.

1. Il_____ quand nous _____ ce matin.
   (neiger)   (partir)

2. Elle _____ quand je la (l') _____.
   (pleurer)   (voir)

3. Il _____ la bouteille. Puis, il nous _____ le vin.
   (ouvrir)   (verser)

4. Nous_____ quand le téléphone _____.
   (dormir)   (sonner)

5. Je _____ sortir hier soir mais je (j') _____ épuisé.
   (vouloir)   (être)

6. Ils _____ quand nous _____.
   (s'embrasser)   (entrer)

7. Je _____ quand j'_____ peur.
   (siffler)   (avoir)

8. Nous _____ toujours à l'église le dimanche.
   (aller)

9. _____ le livre que je te (t') _____?
   (lire; tu *form*)   (prêter)

10. J'_____ une 2CV* quand je (j') _____ jeune.
    (avoir)   (être)

   * 2CV: deux-chevaux, *a little car once made by Citroën.*

Drill 46–Answers and Explanations

1.   *neigeait / sommes partis*
   It was snowing when we left this morning. This is a classic combination; the **imperfect** describes the background weather condition, while the *passé composé* conveys the completed action.

2.   *pleurait / ai vue*
   She was crying when I saw her. The **imperfect** is used here to express a continuing or ongoing action, while the *passé composé* plays the only role it can, that of completed action.

3.   *a ouvert / a versé*
   He opened the bottle. Then he poured us the wine. These are two successive completed actions. We can visualize them as they take place. Use the *passé composé* for both. The subject of *verser* is *il*. Don't mistake *nous* for the subject of the verb! It's the indirect object.

4.   *dormions / a sonné*
   We were sleeping when the telephone rang. The **imperfect** expresses the continuing, ongoing background action; the *passé composé* provides the completed action.

5.   *voulais / étais*
   I wanted to go out last night but I was exhausted. Two imperfects. The first one describes an action that takes place in the mind; we don't <u>see</u> it happening. The second one <u>describes a physical state</u>. Remember that *être* + **adjective** and *être* + **noun** are reliable clues for the use of the imperfect.

6.   *s'embrassaient / sommes entrés*
   They were kissing when we came in. The **imperfect** expresses the ongoing background action; the *passé composé* takes care of the completed action.

7.   *sifflais / avais*
   I used to whistle when I was afraid. Two imperfects. The first one is a repetitive or habitual past action; **used to** or **would** convey the English equivalent. The second one describes a mental activity. We don't see it being accomplished. *Avoir* + **noun** is a generally reliable clue for the use of the **imperfect**.

8. *allions*

We would always go to church on Sundays. This activity took place over and over again. It was habitual. *Le dimanche* and *toujours* are neon signs for repeated past action. **Used to** or **would** conveys the English equivalent. Use the **imperfect**.

9. *As-tu lu / ai prêté*

Did you read the book I lent you? These are two completed past actions. Use the *passé composé* for both.

10. *avais / étais*

I had (used to have) a 2CV when I was young. These are two imperfects. The first one describes **what used to be**. The second one describes a <u>physical state</u>. Both *avoir* and *être* are generally put into the **imperfect**.

THE CONDITIONAL

The formation of the present conditional is very simple. Think of it as a charity case; it must borrow both its root formation and its endings from other tenses. From the student's point of view, this provides a welcome breather because there are no new forms to learn or memorize. We simply recombine the <u>future roots</u> with <u>imperfect endings</u> to create the conditional. Here are some examples of regular and irregular formation:

> *-er: aimerais, aimerais, aimerait, aimerions, aimeriez, aimeraient*
> *-ir: finirais, finirais, finirait, finirions, finiriez, finiraient*
> *-re: vendrais, vendrais, vendrait, vendrions, vendriez, vendraient*

Use of irregular future root:

> *aller: irais, irais, irait, irions, iriez, iraient*
> *avoir: aurais, aurais, aurait, aurions, auriez, auraient*
> *être: serais, serais, serait, serions, seriez, seraient*
> *faire: ferais, ferais, ferait, ferions, feriez, feraient*

The Uses of the Conditional

1. When a contrary-to-fact condition is set forth with *si* and the imperfect tense, we follow with the conditional in the result clause, like this:

    > *Si j'avais mes bottes, je les **mettrais** maintenant.*
    > If I had my boots, I'd put them on now.

    > *Si j'étais toi, je n'**attendrais** pas pour commencer.*
    > If I were you, I wouldn't wait to get started.

2. When the introductory clause is in the past tense and we want to express a future event relative to it, we use the conditional, just as we would in English:

    > *Tu as dit que tu m'aiderais.*
    > You said you would help me.

    > *Mémère affirmait toujours qu'elle ne quitterait jamais sa demeure.*
    > Granny always claimed that she would never leave her home.

3. The conditional is used to express something one imagines or dreams of:

> *La voiture dont je rêve serait hors série.*
>   The car of my dreams would be custom built.

4. The conditional tense is used to be polite and to make requests less demanding. This usage parallels English:

> *Je voudrais une omelette aux champignons.*
>   I would like a mushroom omelet.

> *Pourriez-vous m'aider à trouver l'église?*
>   Could you help me find the church?

5. The conditional is used after **au cas où** and **dans le cas où**, both of which translate as **in case**. This is important to know as English follows with the present tense.

> *Voici mon adresse, au cas où tu serais à Paris.*
>   Here's my address in case you are in Paris.

> *Prends ton parapluie dans le cas où il pleuvrait.*
>   Take your umbrella in case it rains.

Drill 47: The Conditional (or the Present)

Place the indicated verb in the appropriate tense. Look for cues with the sentence to guide your choice.

1. Mon homme idéal _____ gentil et tendre.
   (would be)

2. Il disait toujours qu'il _____.
   (would come back)

3. Qu'est-ce que tu _____ à ma place ?
   (would do)

4. Voici un billet de métro au cas où tu en _____ besoin.
   (have)

5. Si j'avais ton âge, j'_____ avec toi.
   (would go)

6. Qui _____ un cornet de glace ?
   (would like)

7. Si on nous avait choisis, nous en _____ contents.
   (would have been)

8. _____-vous m'aider à replier cette carte ?
   (Could you,
   would you be able to)

9. Qui _____ qu'il ait fait cela ?
   (would have believed)

10. Si je ne disais pas la vérité, mes parents le _____.
    (would know)

Drill 47–Answers and Explanations

1. *serait*

   My ideal man would be kind and loving. Here the conditional is used much as it is in English, to express an ideal imagined or dreamed of.

2. *reviendrait*

   He always said he would come back. When the first clause is in the past tense, the conditional will follow to create a future relative to the past action of the first verb. It's easier to see than to explain! This use also parallels English exactly.

3. *ferais*

   What would you do in my place? The conditional is used here just as it would be in English. *À ma place* sets up a contrary-to-fact situation; so the conditional is used for the result.

4. *aurais*

   Here's a subway ticket (just) in case you need it. This use of the conditional after **in case** is particular to French. We would use the present tense in English. *Au cas où* and *dans le cas où* both require the <u>conditional</u>. It is interesting that both English and French imply the future but neither uses it. Beware!

5. *irais*

   If I were your age, I'd go with you. The imperfect in the **if** clause sets up a contrary-to-fact situation; the <u>conditional</u> is used in the subsequent result clause.

6. *aimerait*

   Who would like an ice cream cone? The use of the conditional is literal here. Remember that **who** always uses the 3rd person singular verb form.

7. *aurions été*

   If they had chosen us, we would have been happy about it. The *plus-que-parfait* in the **if** clause sets the stage for the past conditional (*le passé du conditionnel*) in the result clause.

8. *Pourriez*

   Could you (would you) be able to help me fold up this map? This use of the conditional renders the request more polite.

9. *aurait cru*

Who would have believed he'd do that? The conditional is literal here, a verbatim translation of the English. Note the past subjunctive after the interrogative form of *croire* in the past conditional.

10. *sauraient*

If I weren't telling the truth, my parents would know it. A typical construction, the contrary-to-fact **if** clause is in the <u>imperfect</u>, followed by the <u>conditional</u> in the result clause.

COMPOUND TENSES

In the compound tenses, most French verbs use a form of **avoir** as an auxiliary verb along with the past participle of the verb in question. The <u>tense</u> used for the auxiliary varies from one compound past to the next. **Nous avons étudié**, an example from the *passé composé*, is the single equivalent of **we studied**, **we have studied**, and **we did study** in English.

Regular past participles are based on the infinitive root as follows: **aim** + **é** for -er verbs, **fin** + **i** for *-ir* verbs, and **vend** + **u** for *-re* verbs.

There are many irregular past participles in French, just as in English. Like favorite old sneakers that get misshapen from so much use, it is often the most common verbs that fall into this group. Learn these irregular participles by heart. It takes years to learn the irregulars in English. We hear little children say **I buyed**, or **he gived**, and we correct them until they stop.

They are grouped here by similarity:

aperçu	**glimpsed, noticed**	from *apercevoir*
déçu	**disappointed**	from *décevoir*
reçu	**received**	from *recevoir*
assis	**seated**	from *(s')asseoir*
atteint	**achieved, affected**	from *atteindre*
feint	**feigned**	from *feindre*
éteint	**extinguished**	from *éteindre*
peint	**painted**	from *peindre*
eu	**had**	from *avoir*
bu	**drank, drunk**	from *boire*
cru	**believed**	from *croire*
dû	**had to, owed**	from *devoir*
lu	**read**	from *lire*
plu	**pleased**	from *plaire*
plu	**rained**	from *pleuvoir*
pu	**was able**	from *pouvoir*
su	**knew, found out**	from *savoir*
tu	**to have fallen silent**	from *(se) taire*
vu	**saw, seen**	from *voir*
conduit	**drove, driven**	from *conduire*
produit	**produced**	from *produire*

traduit	**translated**	from *traduire*
cousu	**sewed, sewn**	from *coudre*
couru	**ran, run**	from *courir*
craint	**feared**	from *craindre*
plaint	**complained** (also **pitied, felt sorry for**)	from *plaindre*
dit	**said, told**	from *dire*
écrit	**wrote, written**	from *écrire*
décrit	**described**	from *décrire*
été	**was, been**	from *être*

Verbs Conjugated with *Être*

There is a small group of intransitive verbs that use *être* as an auxiliary verb. They are further distinguished from *avoir* verbs in that they must show agreement between the past participle and the subject. That means the gender and number of the subject reflect onto the past participle via additional letters, like this:

> *Marie est tombée.*
>   Marie fell.

> *Nous sommes montés.*
>   We went up.

> *Les filles sont revenues.*
>   The girls came back.

The absence of additional letters means the subject is <u>masculine</u> and <u>singular</u>. This is agreement, too:

> *André est rentré.*
>   Andrew came home.

Here are the seventeen intransitive verbs that require *être* as an auxiliary verb, and which must show agreement between the past participle and the subject. Listing them in this way allows you to see the age-old classroom device: DR + MRS VANDERTRAMPP, a mnemonic to help you recall all seventeen.

Devenir
Rester
+
Monter
Rentrer
Sortir

Venir
Aller
Naître
Descendre
Entrer
Retourner
Tomber
Revenir
Arriver
Mourir
Partir
Passer

Six of these verbs can mutate into transitive verbs by accepting direct objects. Notice their use of *avoir* as auxiliary when used this way:

monter:	*Ils ont monté nos bagages.*
	They brought up our luggage.
descendre:	*J'ai descendu le linge.*
	I brought down the laundry.
passer:	*Il a passé une semaine à Paris.*
	He spent a week in Paris.
sortir:	*Elle a sorti ses devoirs.*
	She took out her homework.
rentrer:	*Tu as rentré tes achats.*
	You brought in your purchases.
retourner:	*Nous avons retourné le matelas.*
	We turned over the mattress.

Observations On Agreement

The following rules of agreement govern <u>all</u> compound tenses:

1. A past participle agrees in gender and number with the <u>subject</u> of all verbs using *être* as auxiliary.

2. A past participle agrees with the <u>preceding direct object</u> of all verbs using *avoir* as auxiliary. The direct object <u>must precede</u> the participle for this to occur:

    > *J'ai mis mes nouvelles chaussures.*
    > I put on my new shoes. (no agreement, doesn't precede)

    > *Je les ai mises.*
    > I put them on.

    > *Quelle robe est-ce que tu as achetée?*
    > Which dress did you buy?

    > *J'adore la robe que tu as achetée.*
    > I love the dress you bought.

3. There is <u>never</u> agreement with an <u>indirect</u> object.

Le Passé Composé

This essential past tense is constructed with the present (indicative) of the auxiliary and a past participle:

> *Nous avons compris la leçon.*
> We understood the lesson.

> *Nous sommes allés au cinema.*
> We went to the movies.

The *passé composé* is the workhorse of the past. It expresses a completed past action in conversation and in informal writing.

Le Plus-Que-Parfait

The past perfect is created with the imperfect of the auxiliary verb and a past participle. It is used for an action that had already taken place previous to another point in the past:

> *J'avais déjà rendu le livre quand tu me l'as demandé.*
> I had already returned the book when you asked me for it.

> *Elle était déjà rentrée quand tu es arrivé.*
> She had already gone home when you arrived.

Le Futur Antérieur

The *futur antérieur* is constructed from the future tense of the auxiliary verb and a past participle. It expresses a future action that will have taken place by some other point in time, as follows:

> *Si nous ne nous dépêchons pas, ils auront fini le repas sans nous.*
> If we don't hurry, they will have finished the meal without us.

> *Si nous ne nous dépêchons pas, ils seront partis sans nous.*
> If we don't hurry, they will have left without us.

Le Conditionnel Passé

The past conditional uses the conditional of the auxiliary verb and a past participle. It expresses what might have taken place, if certain conditions had been met:

> *Si j'avais eu le temps, je l'aurais fait moi-même.*
> If I had had the time, I would have done it myself.

> *Si j'avais eu le temps, je serais allé au concert.*
> If I had had the time, I would have gone to the concert.

Le Passé Du Subjonctif

This compound is made with the present subjunctive of the auxiliary verb and a past participle. It is used in a subordinate clause whose action (1) has taken place prior to that of the main verb or (2) has yet to take place relative to the verb in the main clause:

> *Je doute qu'ils aient trouvé le bon chemin.*
> I doubt they took the right road.

> *Je veux que vous ayez fini tous les exercices avant votre départ.*
> I want you to have finished all of the problems before you leave.

> *J'aurais aimé que vous soyez arrivés plus tôt.*
> I would have preferred that you had arrived earlier.

Le Passé Antérieur

This is a <u>literary</u> tense based on the *passé simple* of the auxiliary verb and a past participle. It has approximately the same meaning as its less formal counterpart, the *plus-que-parfait*. It is restricted to literature or formal writing for an action that **had taken place prior** to the action of the main verb. Expect to see it used along with the *passé simple* like this:

> *Lorsqu'il eut fini son café, il lava sa tasse et la remit sur son crochet.*
> When he had finished his coffee, he washed his cup and put it back on its hook.

Drill 48: Formation of the Compound Tenses: The Auxiliary Verb

Select the correct auxiliary verb. Does the verb require *être* or *avoir*?

1. Elle _____ montée se coucher vers onze heures.
        (est **or** a?)

2. Tu _____ dû finir tes devoirs.
    (serais **or** aurais?)

3. Si je m'_____ dépêché, j'aurais fini avant minuit.
        (étais **or** avais?)

4. Ils _____ morts dans un accident de voiture.
     (sont **or** ont?)

5. Tu t'_____ coupé les ongles.
        (es **or** as?)

6. Vous vous _____ assis.
            (êtes **or** avez?)

7. Elles _____ parties dans une heure.
     (seront **or** auront?)

8. Tes cadeaux m'_____ beaucoup plu.
            (sont **or** ont?)

9. Quelqu'un_____ bu ma bière.
            (sera **or** aura?)

10. Qui _____ pris mes clés?
        (est **or** a?)

Drill 48–Answers and Explanations

1. *est*
    She went up to sleep around eleven. The extra *e* on the end of the participle is a blinking light that signals agreement with subject, the hallmark of verbs conjugated with *être*.

2. *aurais*
    You should have finished your homework. Did you recognize the past participle from the verb *devoir*? *Devoir* is a transitive verb, which means it can accept a direct object. Use *avoir*.

3. *étais*
    If I had hurried, I would have finished before midnight. This is an easy one if you remember that all reflexive verbs use *être* as the auxiliary.

4. *sont*
    They died in a car accident. Agreement with subject is evident in the *s* on the end of the past participle. *Mourir* is an *être* verb.

5. *es*
    You cut your fingernails. This is another reflexive verb. Use *être*!

6. *êtes*
    You sat down. Reflexive again! Choose *être*!

7. *seront*
    They will have left in an hour. The extra *e* + *s* indicate agreement with a feminine plural subject. *Partir* is an *être* verb.

8. *ont*
    I liked your gifts very much. In this sentence *plu* comes from the verb *plaire*, **to please.** It is transitive and must be conjugated with *avoir*.

9. *aura*
    Someone must have drunk my beer. *Boire* requires *avoir* for its auxiliary. Its direct object appears in the sentence (*ma bière*), making *boire* easy to nail as a <u>transitive</u> verb. This is the *futur antérieur* used for conjecture.

10. *a*
    Who took my keys? The keys are the direct object of the verb *prendre*, **to take.** Use *avoir* as auxiliary for this transitive verb.

Drill 49: Formation of the Compound Tenses: The Past Participle

Provide the correct participle. Show agreement where necessary.

1. Elle s'est _____ les cheveux.
      (couper)

2. Elle s'est _____.
      (couper)

3. Si tu avais lu l'histoire, tu aurais _____ la fin.
      (savoir)

4. As-tu vu mes clés? Je les avais _____ sur la table.
      (mettre)

5. Nous leur avons _____ la vérité.
      (dire)

6. L'enfant a _____ les bougies.
      (souffler)

7. J'ai _____ pendant trois heures.
      (dormir)

8. Il n'a pas _____.
      (répondre)

9. As-tu _____ le téléviseur?
      (éteindre)

10. À quelle heure sont-ils _____?
      (partir)

Drill 49–Answers and Explanations

1. *coupé*
   She cut her hair. The past participle of a reflexive verb remains invariable **if** the <u>reflexive pronoun</u> is not the direct object of the verb. Here it serves as a possessive marker for the real direct object, *les cheveux*. See "Reflexive Verbs."

2. *coupée*
   She cut herself. The reflexive pronoun is now the direct object of the verb **to cut**. The participle reflects agreement with it.

3. *su*
   If you had read the story, you would have known the ending. The past participle for *savoir* is irregular. There are many similar two letter participles ending in *u* such as *eu*, *bu*, *dû*, *lu* and *pu*. You will encounter them frequently, so get to know them all.

4. *mises*
   Have you seen my keys? I had left them on the table. *Mettre* uses the irregular participle *mis*. The *e + s* is added to it to reflect the <u>feminine plural direct object</u> that precedes the participle (*les*). This particular agreement is very important because it actually changes the sound of the participle when it is spoken; from [mi] to [miz].

5. *dit*
   We told them the truth. *Dire* uses the irregular participle *dit*. The preceding object in this sentence (*leur*) is <u>indirect</u>. Past participles <u>never</u> agree with <u>indirect</u> objects; this is a hard-and-fast rule worth remembering.

6. *soufflé*
   The child blew out the candles. *Soufflé* is a regular past participle from a typical *-er* verb.

7. *dormi*
   I slept (for) three hours. *Dormi* is a regular past participle from a typical *-ir* verb.

8. *répondu*
   He didn't answer. *Répondu* is a standard past participle from the *-re* verb group.

9. *éteint*

Did you turn off the TV? This is the irregular participle from the verb *éteindre*, **to extinguish, to turn off**. Similar participles include *atteint*, *feint*, and *peint*.

10. *partis*

(At) what time did they leave? A regular *-ir* participle that reflects agreement with its subject, *ils*.

Drill 50: Selection of the Compound Tense

Provide the past compound needed in the sentence.

1. Si elle était venue je l'_____.
    (voir)

2. Nous _____ quand vous reviendrez.
    (partir + déjà)

3. Qu'auriez-vous fait s'il _____?
    (pleuvoir)

4. Je l' _____ vers onze heures.
    (déposer; l' = **her**)

5. Émilie, où étais-tu? Je te (t') _____ partout!
    (chercher)

6. Quand j'_____ le livre, je vous l'enverrai.
    (lire)

7. Ils _____ leur maison d'été l'an dernier.
    (vendre)

8. Il vous _____ ses aventures.
    (raconter)

9. Elle _____ le nez, la pauvre !
    (se casser)

10. Ils _____ hier.
    (se parler)

Drill 50–Answers and Explanations

1. *aurais vue*

If she had come I would have seen her. When the *plus-que-parfait* appears in the **if** clause, as it does here, we must follow with the <u>past conditional</u> in the result clause. Note the agreement between the past participle and its <u>preceding direct object</u>, *l'* = **her.**

2. *serons déjà partis*

We will have already left when you get back. We need the *futur antérieur* here for an action that **will have already taken place before** the second action comes to pass. Because the verb *partir* is intransitive, we conjugate it with *être* as auxiliary and show subject agreement.

3. *avait plu*

What would you have done if it had rained? This sentence contains the same combination of tenses we saw in sentence number 1. The order is reversed, but the formula is the same: the *plus-que-parfait* in the **if** clause and the <u>past conditonal</u> in the result clause. *Plu* is the irregular participle for *pleuvoir*, **to rain.**

4. *ai déposée*

I dropped her off around eleven o'clock. Use the *passé composé* to convey a completed past action with a discernable beginning or ending. The past participle shows agreement with its preceding direct object, *l'* = **her.**

5. *ai cherchée* (or *cherchais*)

I looked for you everywhere! (*passé composé*) **I was looking for you everywhere!** (*imparfait*)You could really use either past tense here, depending on what you want to say.

6. *aurai lu*

When I have read the book, I will send it to you. Use the *futur antérieur* for an action that **needs to take place before** the second action can come to pass. Because the verb is obviously transitive (because of the presence of *le livre*, its direct object), we conjugate with *avoir*.

7. *ont vendu*

They sold their summer house last year. The *passé composé* reports a completed past action here. The verb *vendre* is unmistakably transitive (*maison* = direct object). We use *avoir* as auxiliary.

8. *a raconté*

He told you (all about) his adventures. This is another *passé composé* with another transitive verb. The difficulty here arises in the presence of the indirect object *vous* in front of the verb. Do not mistake it for the subject!

9. *s'est cassé*

She broke her nose, poor thing! This is a completed past action. We use the *passé composé* to report it. *Se casser* is reflexive, so we conjugate with *être* as the auxiliary. Note the lack of agreement! The **nose** is the direct object here, not the reflexive pronoun *se*.

10. *se sont parlé*

They spoke to each other yesterday. This is most likely a completed action. Use *être* as auxiliary with this reciprocal reflexive verb. Note the lack of agreement. The reflexive pronoun *se* is indirect (**to each other**).

THE LITERARY PAST

You must master the *passé simple* to read with understanding. This tense is reserved for written narrative in literature. It is not used in everyday speech, and it is not used in informal writing, such as a letter or an e-mail. The *passé simple* replaces the *passé composé* only in this literary milieu. The meaning of the two tenses is identical. We often see the *passé simple* intertwined with the imperfect in a literary narrative. Translate the *passé simple* just as though it were the *passé composé*.

The formation of the *passé simple* employs three sets of endings. There is one set exclusively for **-er** verbs, one set shared by regular **-ir** and **-re** verbs, and a third set for use with irregular roots, of which there are many. Regular roots are taken from the infinitive, minus the two final letters. Irregular roots, except for **vin-** for *venir* (and its derivatives), end in the vowels **u** or **i**. Here are examples of the three regular formations, followed by the most common irregulars:

> **-er**: *aim**ai**, aim**as**, aim**a**, aim**âmes**, aim**âtes**, aim**èrent***
> **-ir**: *fin**is**, fin**is**, fin**it**, fin**îmes**, fin**îtes**, fin**irent***
> **-re**: *vend**is**, vend**is**, vend**it**, vend**îmes**, vend**îtes**, vend**irent***

Verbs with irregular roots ending in **i**:

acquérir:	*acquis, acquis, acquit, acquîmes, acquîtes, acquirent*
apprendre:	*appris, appris, apprit, apprîmes, apprîtes, apprirent*
comprendre:	*compris, compris, comprit, comprîmes, comprîtes, comprirent*
conduire:	*conduisis, conduisis, conduisit, conduisîmes, conduisîtes, conduisirent*
craindre:	*craignis, craignis, craignit, craignîmes, craignîtes, craignirent*
dire:	*dis, dis, dit, dîmes, dîtes, dirent*
faire:	*fis, fis, fit, fîmes, fîtes, firent*
mettre:	*mis, mis, mit, mîmes, mîtes, mirent*
naître:	*naquis, naquis, naquit, naquîmes, naquîtes, naquirent*
prendre:	*pris, pris, prit, prîmes, prîtes, prirent*
rire:	*ris, ris, rit, rîmes, rîtes, rirent*

Verbs with irregular roots ending in *u*:

apparaître:	*apparus, apparus, apparut, apparûmes, apparûtes, apparurent*
avoir:	*eus, eus, eut, eûmes, eûtes, eurent*
boire:	*bus, bus, but, bûmes, bûtes, burent*
connaître:	*connus, connus, connut, connûmes, connûtes, connurent*
courir:	*courus, courus, courut, courûmes, courûtes, coururent*
croire:	*crus, crus, crut, crûmes, crûtes, crurent*
devoir:	*dus, dus, dut, dûmes, dûtes, durent*
être:	*fus, fus, fut, fûmes, fûtes, furent*
falloir:	*fallut*
lire:	*lus, lus, lut, lûmes, lûtes, lurent*
mourir:	*mourus, mourus, mourut, mourûmes, mourûtes, moururent*
paraître:	*parus, parus, parut, parûmes, parûtes, parurent*
plaire:	*plus, plus, plut, plûmes, plûtes, plurent*
pleuvoir:	*plut*
recevoir:	*reçus, reçus, reçut, reçûmes, reçûtes, reçurent*
savoir:	*sus, sus, sut, sûmes, sûtes, surent*
(se) taire:	*tus, tus, tut, tûmes, tûtes, turent*
vivre:	*vécus, vécus, vécut, vécûmes, vécûtes, vécurent*
vouloir:	*voulus, voulus, voulut, voulûmes, voulûtes, voulurent*

Verbs with irregular roots ending with *n*:

venir:	*vins, vins, vint, vînmes, vîntes, vinrent* (also *convenir, devenir, revenir,* and *tenir*)

Drill 51: *Le Passé Simple*

Change the **boldface** verbs to the *passé simple*, and adjust the pronoun if necessary.

1. Jeanne d'Arc **est née** dans un petit village lorrain.

2. Un jour, elle gardait ses moutons quand elle **a entendu** des voix divines qui lui disaient d'aller sauver la France et de chasser les Anglais hors du pays.

3. Elle **est partie** et **est allée** trouver le dauphin, Charles VII, qu'elle **a réussi** à persuader.

4. Elle **l'a fait** couronner, puis **s'est mise** en tête de son armée.

5. Habillée en homme, elle **a gagné** beaucoup de batailles et **a délivré** la ville assiégée d'Orléans.

6. Elle **a été** trahie, cependant, et les Bourguigons **l'ont capturée** et **l'ont vendue** aux Anglais.

7. Les Anglais **l'ont jugée** et **l'ont condamnée** à mort.

8. Jeanne **est morte** au bûcher.

9. Elle **est devenue** une des plus grandes héroïnes de France.

10. Pendant des années après sa mort, les gens croyaient la revoir. L'église **l'a déclarée** sainte. Peu après le peuple français **l'a choisie** comme sainte patronne.

Drill 51–Answers

1. *naquit*

2. *entendit*

3. *partit / alla / réussit*

4. *le fit / se mit*

5. *gagna / délivra*

6. *fut / la capturèrent / la vendirent*

7. *la jugèrent / la condamnèrent*

8. *mourut*

9. *devint*

10. *la déclara / la choisit*

THE PASSIVE VOICE

The passive voice is generally avoided in French. We will examine various ways to do this. However, it does exist and is made as follows: Conjugate the verb *être* in whatever tense is needed and follow with the past participle of the verb in question. This creates a sentence in which the subject is <u>acted upon</u>. French prefers, whenever possible, an active construction. Here are samples of the passive voice in French:

> *Jean ne pouvait pas faire face à sa mère parce qu'il **a été renvoyé** de l'école.*
> Jean couldn't face his mother because **he was expelled** from school.

> *Vous **serez barrés** à la porte.*
> You **will be denied admittance** at the door.

How To Avoid the Passive Voice

1. If there is no known subject of the action, you can supply an active subject with ***on***:

   > *On m'a chipé mes frites !*
   > My fries have been swiped!

2. You can create an active subject by making the verb reflexive:

   > *Beaucoup de vin se produit en France.*
   > A lot of wine is produced in France.

3. The object of the passive sentence can be made into an active subject:

   > *Sa réception chaleureuse m'a ému.*
   > I was touched by her warm reception.

4. If the subject is a person, you may use the ***se faire*** + **infinitive** construction to keep your sentence in the active voice:

   > *Il s'est fait remplacer par un jeune.*
   > He was replaced by a younger worker.

Drill 52: Avoiding the Passive Voice

Restate the sentence in the active voice:

1. Elle est appelée Aurélie.

2. Ma valise a été ouverte.

3. Il a été renversé par une voiture.

4. Le vin blanc est bu froid.

5. J'ai été surpris de ton cadeau.

6. Nous n'avons pas été invités.

7. Tu avais été oublié.

8. J'ai été refusé.

9. Une nouvelle tour sera construite.

10. Ma nouvelle coiffure n'a pas été remarquée.

Drill 52–Answers and Explanations

1. *Elle s'appelle Aurélie.*
    She is named Aurélie. The reflexive construction works well and is widely used.

2. *On a ouvert ma valise.*
    My suitcase was opened. We supply *On*, an active subject for the unknown individual who opened the suitcase.

3. *Il s'est fait renverser par une voiture.*
    He was hit (run down) by a car. We use *se faire* + **infinitive** to make an active version of **He was run over** (or **hit**) **by a car**.

4. *Le vin blanc se boit froid.*
    White wine is drunk cold. The reflexive works here. You could also supply a subject with *on*.

5. *Ton cadeau m'a surpris.*
    I was surprised by your gift. Turn the **gift** into the subject of the sentence.

6. *On ne nous a pas invités.*
    We weren't invited. Supply an active subject with *On*.

7. *On t'avait oublié.*
    You had been forgotten. Supply an active subject with *On*.

8. *On m'a refusé.*
    I was refused. Supply an active subject with *On*.

9. *On va construire une nouvelle tour* (or *On construira une nouvelle tour*).
    A new tower will be built. Supply an active subject with *On*.

10. *On n'a pas remarqué ma nouvelle coiffure* (or *Personne n'a remarqué ma nouvelle coiffure*).
    My new haircut wasn't noticed by anyone. Supply either active subject.

THE SUBJUNCTIVE

The present subjunctive has one set of universal endings. They are *-e*, *-es*, *-e*, *-ions*, *-iez*, and *-ent*. Its verb forms are generally preceded by the conjunction *que*. In some instances they can also be preceded by *qui*.

Most textbooks give the *ils* form minus the *-ent* as the root. Then the student encounters a myriad of verbs that don't follow the rule. Here I would like to suggest an alternative rule that is more exacting, and to which there are fewer exceptions!

To make the present subjunctive root, look at two different forms of the present indicative: the *ils* form minus the *-ent*, and the *nous* form minus the *-ons*. Compare them. Are they identical? If so, you have a single root for all six forms. If the two roots are different, use the *ils* root for the *je*, *tu*, *il*, and *ils* forms, and the *nous* root for the *nous* and *vous* forms. This rule embraces many verbs that would otherwise be irregular. (There are ten exceptions.) It alerts students to the possibility of more than one root, and it works flawlessly.

Here are examples of the regular formation of the present subjunctive with a single root:

> *-er: aime, aimes, aime, aimions, aimiez, aiment*
> *-ir: finisse, finisses, finisse, finissions, finissiez, finissent*
> *-re: vende, vendes, vende, vendions, vendiez, vendent*

Here are some samples of the regular formation of the present subjunctive with two different roots:

boire:	*boive, boives, boive, buvions, buviez, boivent*
prendre:	*prenne, prennes, prenne, prenions, preniez, prennent*
mourir:	*meure, meures, meure, mourions, mouriez, meurent*
voir:	*voie, voies, voie, voyions, voyiez, voient*
venir:	*vienne, viennes, vienne, venions, veniez, viennent*

Here are the verbs that do not follow the rule, and which you must learn by heart:

avoir (**to have**):	*aie, aies, ait, ayons, ayez, aient*
aller (**to go**):	*aille, ailles, aille, allions, alliez, aillent*
faire (**to do, to make**):	*fasse, fasses, fasse, fassions, fassiez, fassent*
être (**to be**):	*sois, sois, soit, soyons, soyez, soient*
savoir (**to know**):	*sache, saches, sache, sachions, sachiez, sachent*
pouvoir (**to be able**):	*puisse, puisses, puisse, puissions, puissiez, puissent*
valoir (**to be worth**):	*vaille, vailles, vaille, valions, valiez, vaillent*
vouloir (**to want**):	*veuille, veuilles, veuille, voulions, vouliez, veuillent*
falloir (**to be necessary—** impersonal):	*faille*
pleuvoir (**to rain—** impersonal):	*pleuve*

The Subjunctive Mood

The indicative relates actuality or fact. The subjunctive mood allows the speaker to impose his opinion, wish, or emotion onto the verb in the subsequent clause. The construction always uses the conjunction *que* to signal that this is taking place. Remember, however, that *que* figures in lots of expressions that do not require the subjunctive. We will address them as well.

Most of the verbs and expressions with which a speaker can project his fears, doubts, or opinions onto the coming verb can be neatly classified into one of five groups. When deciding whether to use the subjunctive, ask yourself whether the verb or phrase that introduces it fits under one of these broad headings.

Keep in mind that the subjunctive is only needed if the subject of the introductory clause and the subject of the subordinate clause are <u>different</u>. One would <u>never say</u> *je veux que je réussisse*. The subjunctive would be avoided altogether with the much simpler statement *je veux réussir*.

1. *La Volonté*: Will

Is the speaker expressing a want or desire? Is he giving an order or a require-ment, or making a command? Follow with the subjunctive.

> *Je **veux qu'**il **fasse** beau pour le défilé.*
> I **want** the weather to be nice for the parade.

> *Le prof **exige que** nous **parlions** français.*
> The teacher **requires** that we speak French.

> *Papa **insiste pour que** nous **soyons** responsables.*
> Dad **insists** that we be responsible.

2. *Le Doute*: Doubt

Is the speaker expressing doubtfulness? Is he unsure or waivering in cer-tainty? Follow with the subjunctive.

> *Je **doute qu'**ils **puissent** venir.*
> I **doubt** that they can come.

> *Il **se peut qu'**ils **viennent** demain.*
> **Maybe** they'll come tomorrow.

> *Il **est possible qu**'elle ne **veuille** pas venir.*
> It's **possible** that she doesn't want to come.

3. *La Nécessité*: Necessity

Does the speaker think that what is to follow is necessary or required? Use the subjunctive in the subordinate clause.

> *Il **faut que** je **maigrisse**!*
> I **must** lose weight!

> *Il **est nécessaire que** vous **écoutiez** en classe.*
> You **must** listen in class.

4. *L'Émotion*: Emotion

Is the speaker expressing a feeling or emotion, such as fear, happiness or sorrow? Always follow with the subjunctive.

> *Je **regrette qu'**il **pleuve** le jour de leurs noces.*
> I'm **sorry** that it's raining on their wedding day.

> *Je **suis** si **heureux que** tu **sois** là!*
> I'm so **happy** that you're here.

*Nous **sommes tristes que** tu **ailles** à l'hôpital.*
We're **sad** that you're going into the hospital.

*Elle **a peur que** le loup-garou **ne** la **mange**.*
She's **afraid** that the werewolf will eat her. (Notice the **ne**. It is **pleonastic**, which is simply an extra or superfluous word. The pleonastic **ne** heightens the fear in the speaker's tone and is commonly seen when expressing this emotion.)

*Vous **craignez qu'**il n'**échoue**.*
You **fear** that he'll fail. (Again the extra **ne** is added as if to prevent what is feared.)

5. *L'Opinion*: Opinion

Is the speaker giving his opinion regarding what is to follow? Use the subjunctive carefully here as we shall see that some opinions do not require it. Here are the types that do:

*Il **vaut mieux** que*
*Il **est bon** que*
*Il **est juste** que*
*Il **est important** que*
*Il **est étonnant** que*

Verbs and Expressions of Certainty

Think of this as a sixth category: *la certitude*. Verbs and expressions in this group <u>do not</u> use the subjunctive <u>unless</u> they are <u>negated</u> or <u>interrogative</u> (which makes them doubtful).

In a negative question the speaker assumes the listener will agree with his opinion of certainty, and therefore it does not use the subjunctive.

Here are the verbs of certainty. Remember, <u>no subjunctive unless</u> negated or interrogative:

*Je **pense qu'** il neigera.*
I think it will snow.

*Je **ne pense pas qu'** il neige.*
I don't think it will snow. (I don't think it's snowing.)

*Je **crois qu'**il est beau.*
I think he's handsome.

***Croyez-vous qu'**il **soit** beau?*
Do you think he's handsome?

Note: The use of the subjunctive after interrogative *croire* is beginning to slip away. Some speakers now follow with the indicative.

>   *Ne croyez-vous pas qu'il est beau?*
>   Don't you think he's handsome?

>   *J'espère que tu réussiras.*
>   I hope you'll succeed.

>   *Espérez-vous que nous gagnions?*
>   Do you hope we'll win?

Here are some expressions of certainty that work the same way:

il est certain que	**it is certain that**
il est clair que	**it is clear that**
il est évident que	**it is obvious that**
il est probable que	**it is probable that**
il est sûr que	**it is sure that**
il est vrai que	**it is true (***évident***) that**

It should also be noted that *il me semble que* is followed by the indicative, whereas *il semble que* is more doubtful and needs the subjunctive: **it seems to me = *certitude*; but it seems = *doute*.**

Subordinating Conjunctions

There are many conjunctions that must be followed by the subjunctive. Here are some common ones:

afin que	**(so that)**	
à moins que	**(unless)**	uses the pleonastic *ne*
avant que	**(before)**	uses the pleonastic *ne*
bien que	**(although)**	
de crainte que	**(for fear that)**	
de peur que	**(for fear that)**	uses the pleonastic *ne*
de façon que*	**(so that)**	

>   **When *de façon que*, *de manière que*, and *de sorte que* are followed by a result already attained, the indicative is used. When the result is desired but not yet achieved, use the subjunctive.*

de manière que*	**(so that)**
de sorte que*	**(so that)**
en attendant que	**(until)**
jusqu'à ce que	**(until)**

malgré que	(**despite, in spite of**)
pourvu que	(**provided that**)
quel + que + être	(**whatever**)
quelque + adjective or noun + *que*	(**no matter how, no matter what**)

When using *quel + que* (two words), *quel* matches the noun:

> *Quelle que soit sa réponse . . .*
> Whatever his (her) answer . . .

Quelque (one word) is invariable in front of an adjective or adverb, and it agrees in front of a noun:

> *Quelque belle qu'elle soit . . .*
>
> *Quelque difficiles que soient vos circonstances . . . **
>
> *Quelques bijoux qu'elle veuille . . .*

> * Inversion is required when the subject of the verb is not human. Constructions with *quelque . . . que* result in a very formal tone and should be avoided in everyday speech.

quoique	(**although, though**)
sans que	(**without**)

Using the Subjunctive after a Superlative

The subjunctive is used after *seul*, *unique*, *premier*, *dernier*, and **superlative adjectives** if the opinion of the speaker is reflected in the statement. When used to express a fact, they are followed by the indicative:

> *Tu es **le meilleur** ami **qui soit**.*
> You're **the best** friend there is.

> *C'est **la** voiture **la plus rapide** qui a gagné.*
> **The fastest** car won.

> *C'est **le plus joli** quartier que je **connaisse**.*
> It's **the nicest** neighborhood I know.

> *C'est **l'unique** robe qui me **plaise**.*
> It's **the only** dress I like.

> *C'est **la seule** robe bleue que j'ai trouvée.*
> It's **the only** blue dress I found.

The Subjunctive after an Indefinite Antecedent

The subjunctive is used when the desired thing or quality is named but not yet found, like this:

*Nous **cherchons** une maison qui **soit** plus près de l'océan.*
We're looking for a house that is closer to the ocean.

*Connaissez-vous quelqu'un qui **comprenne** le chinois?*
Do you know someone who understands Chinese?

*Y a-t-il un médicament qui **guérisse** cette maladie?*
Is there a drug that cures this disease?

Note that if the desired object has been found, the indicative is used. Compare:

*Elle **cherche** un chapeau qui lui **convienne**.*
She's looking for a suitable hat.

*Elle **a trouvé** un chapeau qui lui convient.*
She found a hat that suits her.

The subjunctive is also required after indefinite expressions:

*Où que tu **ailles**, je te suivrai.*
Wheverever you go, I will follow you.

***Quelque** riche **qu'**il soit, il n'es pas heureux.*
However rich he is, he's not happy.

***Qui que** vous **soyez**, allez-vous en.*
Go away, whoever you are.

***Quoiqu'**il **dise**, nous restons.*
We're staying, no matter what he says.

*Si vite **qu'**il **aille**, il arrive toujours en retard.*
No matter how fast he goes, he always arrives late.

The Subjunctive after a Negative Pronoun

Use the subjunctive after a negative pronoun when expressing an opinion:

*Il n'y a **personne** qui **sache** lui plaire.*
Nobody knows how to please her.

*Il n'y a **rien** qui **vaille**.*
There is nothing worthwhile.

How to Avoid the Subjunctive

The subjunctive is always avoided when both verbs in the sentence have the same subject. This is accomplished by using a simple infinitive or ***de* + infinitive**:

> *Je **regrette de** ne pas pouvoir venir.*
> I'm sorry I can't come.

Most verbs and impersonal expressions can be replaced in a similar manner, even if the subjects of the two verbs are different:

> ***Il vaut mieux** tenir votre enfant par la main.*
> It's better to hold your child's hand.

> ***Il est préférable** d'attendre nos bagages ici.*
> It's better to wait for our bags here.

À + **infinitive** replaces the subjunctive in the superlative construction:

> *Tu es **la seule** personne **à** me comprendre.*
> You are the only person who understands me.

Drill 53: The Subjunctive

Supply the correct form of the subjunctive **or** the indicative, as the case may be. Base your decision on what precedes the *que*.

1.   Je souhaite que vous _____ heureux.
     (être)

2.   Maman veut qu'il nous _____.
     (attendre)

3.   Est-il certain que tu _____ venir?
     (pouvoir)

4.   Il est évident qu'il _____ trop.
     (boire)

5.   Il est clair que vous ne nous _____ pas.
     (écouter)

6.   Il est fâcheux qu'il _____ ce matin.
     (pleuvoir)

7.   Je regrette que nous n'_____ pas de chien.
     (avoir)

8.   Est-il vrai qu'il _____ trop vite?
     (conduire)

9.   Nous cherchons un cadeau qui lui _____ plaisir.
     (faire)

10. Il tient à ce que je lui _____ à haute voix.
     (lire)

11. Je crois que vous _____ étudier davantage.
     (devoir)

12. Il veut rentrer avant que son père ne _____.
     (revenir)

13. Il est urgent que vous _____ ma lettre avant mardi.
     (ouvrir)

14. Il semble qu'elle_____ facilement.
    (rougir)

15. Tu peux prêter ma robe pourvu que tu me la _____.
    (rendre)

16. J'espère que mon cadeau vous _____.
    (plaire)

17. Écrivez de manière que je _____ vous lire.
    (pouvoir)

18. Il faut que tu _____ une matière principale.
    (choisir)

19. Il me semble que vous _____ la vérité.
    (dire)

20. Il se peut que nous _____ le train.
    (prendre)

21. Il n'y a personne qui _____ vous attendre.
    (vouloir)

22. C'est la seule maison que nous _____.
    (posséder)

23. Nous irons où qu'il _____.
    (falloir)

24. C'est dommage qu'il ne _____ pas beau.
    (faire)

25. Connaissez-vous un domestique qui _____ faire la cuisine ?
    (savoir)

Drill 53–Answers and Explanations

1.   *soyez*
     I hope that you will be happy. The speaker projects his wish for happiness onto the subordinate verb. *Souhaiter* is a verb of *volonté* and requires the subjunctive.

2.   *attende*
     Mom wants him to wait for us. *Vouloir*, obviously a verb of *volonté*, requires the subjunctive. Note that *il* is the subject of the verb *attendre*, <u>not</u> *nous*. Remember that a direct object pronoun is placed directly in front of the verb. Students often mistake this object pronoun for a subject. Don't fall into the trap!

3.   *puisses*
     Is it certain that you can come? Here we have an expression of *certitude* in the interrogative, thus it becomes doubtful and requires the subjunctive.

4.   *boit*
     It's obvious that he drinks too much. This is a clear expression of *certitude*. The indicative is required.

5.   *écoutez*
     It's clear that you'e not listening to us. This is another clear-cut expression of *certitude*. Did you recognize the subject of the verb as *vous*? *Nous* is the direct object. The indicative is required.

6.   *pleuve*
     It's unfortunate that it's raining this morning. The speaker's opinion that the rain is unfortunate is reflected in the subjunctive form of *pleuvoir*.

7.   *ayons*
     I'm sorry that we don't have a dog. *Regretter* is a verb of *emotion* requiring the subjunctive.

8.   *conduise*
     Is it true that he drives too fast? An interrogative expression of *certitude* becomes a case for doubt. You must use the subjunctive.

9.   *fasse*
     We're looking for a gift that will please him. The gift being sought has not yet been found, so the existence of this antecedent is then indefinite. Use the subjunctive here.

10. *lise*

He inisists that I read to him aloud. He clearly projects his will (*volonté*) onto the subordinate verb. You must use the subjunctive here.

11. *devez* (or *devriez*)

I think you must or should study more. The verb *croire* is a verb of *certitude*. Use the indicative, either the present or the conditional, here.

12. *revienne*

He wants to be home before his father gets back. *Vouloir* is followed here by the subjunctive of *revenir*.

13. *ouvriez*

It's urgent that you open my letter before Tuesday. This opinion is reflected in the subjunctive that must follow it.

14. *rougisse*

She seems to blush easily. This expression falls under the category of *doute*. Always use the subjunctive after *il semble que*.

15. *rendes*

You can borrow my dress provided that you return it to me. Always use the subjunctive after this subordinating conjunction.

16. *plaît* (or *plaira*)

I hope that my gift pleases or will please you. *Espérer*, like *croire* and *penser*, expresses *certitude*. Use the indicative with these verbs unless they are negated or interrogative. Here either the present or the future is possible.

17. puisse

Write so that I can read (what) you (write). Use the subjunctive after this conjunction because the desired result (**clear handwriting**) has not yet been attained.

18. *choisisses*

You have to choose a major. You must always use the subjunctive after *il faut que* from the category of *nécessité*. This expression is the quintessential example of the subjunctive. Chances are that you will encounter it somewhere on your exam.

19. *dites*

It seems to me that you're telling the truth. The addition of the indirect object pronoun *me* changes an expression of *doute* into an expression of *certitude*. Use the indicative here. Compare this with question 14.

20. *prenions*

Maybe we'll take the train. This is a classic example of *doute*. Use the subjunctive.

21. *veuille*

There's nobody who wants to wait for you. Here we need the subjunctive to follow the negative pronoun *personne*. The person who might wait for you has not been found, and the speaker doesn't think he exists.

22. *possédons*

It's the only house we own. We follow *la seule* with the indicative here because this is a fact, not an opinion.

23. *faille*

We'll go wherever it is necessary. The subjunctive always follows this indefinite, and therefore doubtful, phrase.

24. *fasse*

It's a shame that the weather's not nice. The speaker gives her opinion on the weather. Use the subjunctive.

25. *sache*

Do you know a maid who knows how to cook? This problem is similar to question 9. The existence of the wished-for maid has not yet been confirmed. She is therefore an indefinite antecedent. Use the subjunctive here.

THE IMPERFECT AND PLUPERFECT SUBJUNCTIVE

These tenses are not suitable for everyday speech or informal writing. You are not expected to use them in your written compositions or speech. They are presented here so that you can <u>identify</u> them and <u>understand</u> them when you come upon them in formal texts.

Today, instead of using these two tenses, *l'imparfait du subjonctif*, and the past compound, *le plus-que-parfait du subjonctif*, most French speakers simply substitute with the *passé du subjonctif*, an easy-to-make compound based on the present subjunctive of the auxiliary verb and a past participle.

Modern French has thus streamlined and simplified its use of the subjunctive considerably, relying whenever possible on the present subjunctive or its easy compound, the *passé du subjonctif*. There is also a marked tendency to avoid the subjunctive altogether. Even so, let's take a look at the imperfect subjunctive, just so you will recognize it when you see it.

The Formation of the Imperfect Subjunctive

We will use the same roots we learned for the *passé simple*. The regular roots come from the infinitive, minus the two final letters. All of the irregular roots, except for **vin-** for **venir** (and its derivatives), end in **u** or **i**. You may want to review the list of the irregular roots, which was provided under the heading "The Literary Past."

There are three sets of endings, one exclusively for **-er** verbs, one shared by regular **-ir** and **-re** verbs, and a third set used with all irregular roots.

Here are examples of the three regular conjugations:

> **-er**: *aimasse, aimasses, **aimât**, aimassions, aimassiez, aimassent*
> **-ir**: *finisse, finisses, **finît**, finissions, finissiez, finissent*
> **-re**: *vendisse, vendisses, **vendît**, vendissions, vendissiez, vendissent*

Here are examples of the three types of irregular roots:

avoir	root ends in *i*	*eusse, eusses, **eût**, eussions, eussiez, eussent*
être	root ends in *u*	*fusse, fusses, **fût**, fussions, fussiez, fussent*
venir	root ends in *n*	*vinsse, vinsses, **vînt**, vinssions, vinssiez, vinssent*

Except for the 3rd person singular, none of these forms are used today. Yet if you want to read the great authors of the past, you are bound to encounter them. Here are some simple examples of what to expect:

> *Je regrettais qu'il ne tînt pas sa promesse.*
> I was sorry he didn't keep his promise.

Nous ne savions pas qu'il eût gagné.
We didn't know that he had won.

J'ignorais qu'ils fussent revenus.
I didn't know they had returned.

The similarity between the 3rd person singular of the *passé simple* and the 3rd person singular of the *imparfait du subjonctif* is striking. They are virtually identical except for the circumflex on the latter. Learn those forms well and you will have mastered two important tools for reading.

▼

PRE-EXAM
PRACTICE

From the Editor: This Pre-Exam Practice section contains all the sections found on the AP French Language exam. However, in some sections, more material is provided than is on the actual exam.

AP French
Pre-Exam Practice

ANSWER SHEET

1. Ⓐ Ⓑ Ⓒ Ⓓ
2. Ⓐ Ⓑ Ⓒ Ⓓ
3. Ⓐ Ⓑ Ⓒ Ⓓ
4. Ⓐ Ⓑ Ⓒ Ⓓ
5. Ⓐ Ⓑ Ⓒ Ⓓ
6. Ⓐ Ⓑ Ⓒ Ⓓ
7. Ⓐ Ⓑ Ⓒ Ⓓ
8. Ⓐ Ⓑ Ⓒ Ⓓ
9. Ⓐ Ⓑ Ⓒ Ⓓ
10. Ⓐ Ⓑ Ⓒ Ⓓ
11. Ⓐ Ⓑ Ⓒ Ⓓ
12. Ⓐ Ⓑ Ⓒ Ⓓ
13. Ⓐ Ⓑ Ⓒ Ⓓ
14. Ⓐ Ⓑ Ⓒ Ⓓ
15. Ⓐ Ⓑ Ⓒ Ⓓ
16. Ⓐ Ⓑ Ⓒ Ⓓ
17. Ⓐ Ⓑ Ⓒ Ⓓ
18. Ⓐ Ⓑ Ⓒ Ⓓ
19. Ⓐ Ⓑ Ⓒ Ⓓ
20. Ⓐ Ⓑ Ⓒ Ⓓ
21. Ⓐ Ⓑ Ⓒ Ⓓ

22. Ⓐ Ⓑ Ⓒ Ⓓ
23. Ⓐ Ⓑ Ⓒ Ⓓ
24. Ⓐ Ⓑ Ⓒ Ⓓ
25. Ⓐ Ⓑ Ⓒ Ⓓ
26. Ⓐ Ⓑ Ⓒ Ⓓ
27. Ⓐ Ⓑ Ⓒ Ⓓ
28. Ⓐ Ⓑ Ⓒ Ⓓ
29. Ⓐ Ⓑ Ⓒ Ⓓ
30. Ⓐ Ⓑ Ⓒ Ⓓ
31. Ⓐ Ⓑ Ⓒ Ⓓ
32. Ⓐ Ⓑ Ⓒ Ⓓ
33. Ⓐ Ⓑ Ⓒ Ⓓ
34. Ⓐ Ⓑ Ⓒ Ⓓ
35. Ⓐ Ⓑ Ⓒ Ⓓ
36. Ⓐ Ⓑ Ⓒ Ⓓ
37. Ⓐ Ⓑ Ⓒ Ⓓ
38. Ⓐ Ⓑ Ⓒ Ⓓ
39. Ⓐ Ⓑ Ⓒ Ⓓ
40. Ⓐ Ⓑ Ⓒ Ⓓ
41. Ⓐ Ⓑ Ⓒ Ⓓ
42. Ⓐ Ⓑ Ⓒ Ⓓ

43. Ⓐ Ⓑ Ⓒ Ⓓ
44. Ⓐ Ⓑ Ⓒ Ⓓ
45. Ⓐ Ⓑ Ⓒ Ⓓ
46. Ⓐ Ⓑ Ⓒ Ⓓ
47. Ⓐ Ⓑ Ⓒ Ⓓ
48. Ⓐ Ⓑ Ⓒ Ⓓ
49. Ⓐ Ⓑ Ⓒ Ⓓ
50. Ⓐ Ⓑ Ⓒ Ⓓ
51. Ⓐ Ⓑ Ⓒ Ⓓ
52. Ⓐ Ⓑ Ⓒ Ⓓ
53. Ⓐ Ⓑ Ⓒ Ⓓ
54. Ⓐ Ⓑ Ⓒ Ⓓ
55. Ⓐ Ⓑ Ⓒ Ⓓ
56. Ⓐ Ⓑ Ⓒ Ⓓ
57. Ⓐ Ⓑ Ⓒ Ⓓ
58. Ⓐ Ⓑ Ⓒ Ⓓ
59. Ⓐ Ⓑ Ⓒ Ⓓ
60. Ⓐ Ⓑ Ⓒ Ⓓ
61. Ⓐ Ⓑ Ⓒ Ⓓ
62. Ⓐ Ⓑ Ⓒ Ⓓ

AP French

Pre-Exam Practice

SECTION I: Multiple Choice

Time–1 hour and 25 minutes

Part A: Listening

(Approximate time–25 minutes)

Exchanges

CD 1, Track 1: Exchange Numbers 1–15

1. (A) Non, mais je lui ai parlé pendant 5 minutes.

    (B) Pas que je sache.

    (C) Si, j'ai décroché pendant qu'il parlait et nous avons causé.

    (D) Non, mais il m'a dit qu'il allait téléphoner de nouveau.

2. (A) Ça vaut la peine. Un jour tu regretteras de ne pas l'avoir fait.

    (B) C'est une perte de temps.

    (C) Ça met à la poubelle tous les fichiers importants.

    (D) C'est une distraction, comme un jeu-vidéo.

3. (A) On ne l'a pas décaféiné.

    (B) Ail, champignons, ou fines herbes.

    (C) L'air du Temps ou Je Reviens.

    (D) Framboise, vanille, ou chocolat.

4. (A) J'ai fait de beaux rêves.

    (B) Je n'ai pas fermé l'œil.

    (C) C'était un sommeil profond.

    (D) Je me sens rafraîchi !

5. (A) Bonne idée. L'eau chaude détend les muscles.

    (B) Il vaut mieux se droguer.

    (C) C'est trop coûteux.

    (D) Je descendrai tout de suite au parking.

6. (A) Il y a un chien méchant à côté.

    (B) Il devrait porter une visière.

    (C) Il arrivera plus tôt au fur et à mesure qu'il prend l'habitude.

    (D) C'est la fin du monde !

7. (A) Comme ça je pourrai t'asperger d'eau !

    (B) Tu auras très froid.

    (C) Tu feras le mannequin.

    (D) Le lavage des cheveux est compris.

8. (A) Ça veut dire le petit matin.

    (B) C'est le crépuscule, quand la lumière devient faible et on ne peut pas distinguer de loin entre un chien et un loup.

    (C) C'est midi juste.

    (D) C'est minuit.

9. (A) Tu as raison, nous devrions choisir avec soin un cadeau qui plairait à un officier.

   (B) On fêtera cet honneur aux Invalides parce qu'il a été récemment malade.

   (C) Nous allons tous porter l'uniforme.

   (D) J'espère que la guerre n'aura pas lieu sur place.

10. (A) Mufle ! Ça va ruiner le bois. Enlève-la tout de suite !

    (B) C'est pratique.

    (C) La chaise sera ainsi plus commode.

    (D) Veux-tu la mettre dans ton tiroir, s'il te plaît.

11. (A) Les bonnes choses se font attendre.

    (B) J'ai fait des excuses et il a tout gobé.

    (C) Il l'a pris en disant – Mieux vaut tard que jamais, mais je retire 20 points.

    (D) L'intention vaut le fait.

12. (A) Ça m'est égal si tu veux emprunter un outil, mais 'faut le remettre, c'est ma seule règle !

    (B) J'en achèterai plusieurs la prochaine fois.

    (C) D'accord, j'utiliserai ma clé anglaise.

    (D) Ce n'est pas grave.

13. (A) D'accord, mais tu le dis pour pouvoir dépenser !

    (B) Il est fermé à onze heures du matin.

    (C) D'accord, j'ai besoin d'étudier.

    (D) Nous y pourrons dormir.

14. (A) Elle n'existe pas.

    (B) Je préfère recevoir des lettres en papier.

    (C) J'adore recevoir du courrier électronique.

    (D) Il faudra prendre le temps de la vider si tu veux rester en contact avec tes amis.

15. (A) Achète-moi une nouvelle paire chichiteuse s'il te plaît.

   (B) Je viens de les assouplir, elles me vont si bien !

   (C) Elles sont tout à fait neuves. Je les ai achetées hier.

   (D) C'est la dernière mode pour hommes.

Dialogues

Directions: Listen to the dialogues on your CD. After each one you will hear a series of questions based on what you have just heard. Each question is heard twice. Choose the best answer from the four choices provided and blacken the corresponding letter on your answer sheet. You have only 12 seconds to mark your answer.

CD 1, Track 2: Dialogues

Dialogue Number 1: La Placomusophilie

16. Pourquoi les gens aiment-ils collectionner les plaques de muselet ?

   (A) Elles sont très rares.

   (B) Elles sont innombrables, diverses, décorées de manière intéressante, et ne coûtent rien.

   (C) Elles valent beaucoup d'argent.

   (D) Elles clignotent.

17. Est-ce que ce passe-temps est répandu ?

   (A) Oui, dans le monde entier.

   (B) Pas vraiment, ce sont les Français qui le pratiquent le plus.

   (C) Partout, sauf en France.

   (D) Oui, surtout en Europe.

18. Comment peut-on devenir collectionneur ?

   (A) Il suffit de ne pas jeter la petite capsule quand on ouvre son champagne.

   (B) Il faut s'inscrire à un club.

(C) Il faut s'abonner au périodique.

(D) Il faut acheter sur l'internet.

19. Y a-t-il des sites où l'on peut se renseigner ?

   (A) Oui, mais il y en a très peu.

   (B) Oui, pour enfants.

   (C) Oui, ils sont nombreux, et pour la plupart français.

   (D) Non, ça n'existe pas encore.

Dialogue Number 2: Le Placard

20. Pourquoi le dernier tas ne doit-il pas trop dépasser les autres ?

   (A) Pour qu'il ne se défasse pas.

   (B) Pour être à la même hauteur.

   (C) Parce qu'on veut réduire la quantité de choses retenues.

   (D) Pas de raison spéciale.

21. Est-ce que la femme trouve cette tâche odieuse ?

   (A) Oui c'est pénible.

   (B) Elle déteste nettoyer.

   (C) Oui, c'est une tâche dégoûtante.

   (D) Non, elle aime organiser et y est calée.

22. Que veut dire *trier* ?

   (A) utiliser

   (B) séparer et grouper pour sélectionner

   (C) s'en débarrasser

   (D) entasser

23. Il paraît que le problème n'est pas seulement un manque d'organisation mais aussi que les choses sont . . .

    (A) trop dangereuses.

    (B) trop nombreuses.

    (C) trop vieilles et délabrées.

    (D) puantes.

24. Vont-ils tout ôter au commencement?

    (A) Non, ça va prendre trop de temps.

    (B) Non, ce n'est pas prévu.

    (C) Non, ce n'est pas nécessaire.

    (D) Oui, c'est ce qu'ils vont faire.

Dialogue Number 3: L'Ordinateur

25. Est-ce que cette sorte de perte de document est rare?

    (A) Personne ne le fait.

    (B) Non, cela arrive souvent.

    (C) C'est inouï.

    (D) Oui, c'est rare.

26. La jeune femme a-t-elle sauvegardé son travail?

    (A) Non, elle n'a pas pensé à cela.

    (B) Oui, elle le fait régulièrement.

    (C) Oui, elle a tout copié sur disque.

    (D) Oui, comme d'habitude.

27. Comment pourront-ils revoir le document perdu?

    (A) Ils vont téléphoner à un informaticien.

    (B) C'est impossible parce que les fichiers sont cachés.

    (C) Ils vont ouvrir le fichier provisoire.

    (D) Ils ne savent pas le faire.

28. Comment la jeune femme a-t-elle perdu son document ?

    (A) Elle ne le sait pas.

    (B) Son ordinateur a planté.

    (C) Elle a donné la mauvaise réponse en fermant le fichier.

    (D) Elle a tout effacé.

Dialogue Number 4: Le Violon d'Ingrès

29. Est-ce que la jeune femme est miniaturiste professionnel ?

    (A) Ce n'est que son violon d'Ingrès.

    (B) C'est son métier.

    (C) Elle a sa propre boutique de miniatures.

    (D) Elle y gagne son pain.

30. Quelle sorte de magasin est *Pain d'Épices* ?

    (A) C'est une grande surface.

    (B) C'est une petite boutique de mode.

    (C) C'est un grand magasin comme le Printemps.

    (D) C'est un magasin de jouets.

31. Quel genre de miniatures la jeune femme confectionne-t-elle ?

    (A) Surtout de la nourriture.

    (B) De petits meubles.

    (C) Des habits de poupée.

    (D) Des fleurs et des bouquets miniaturisés.

32. Avoir *les doigts de fée*, est-ce un compliment ?

    (A) Oui. Cela veut dire qu'on est habile avec le travail manuel minutieux.

    (B) Non. On le dit pour se moquer de quelqu'un.

    (C) Non. C'est une exagération.

    (D) Non. Ça montre du dédain.

Part B: Reading

> **Directions:** Read the following passages with care. Each segment is followed by a series of questions or statements to be completed. Choose the best answer, according to what you have read, from the four choices provided. Blacken the corresponding letter on your answer sheet.

La Renault (questions 33–38)

Je la vis se diriger vers moi, tendue, la mâchoire serrée. J'ai su tout de suite que quelque chose n'allait pas. Je posai mon travail et me livrai aux besoins de ma sœur cadette.

Ligne

(5) – Qu'est-ce qu'il y a ? je lui demandai. Tu fais une tête d'enterrement ! – Oh Hélène, je suis vraiment dans le pétrin et je ne sais pas m'en tirer, reprit-elle. Elle lâcha un grand soupir morne avant de continuer. – J'avais des courses à faire ce matin et j'ai pris la Renault de Papa sans la lui demander. Tu sais que j'ai mon permis depuis plus de quatre mois, et que . . . et que . . . . Papa dit lui-même que je suis sage au volant. Rien n'est arrivé . . . sauf

(10) que. . . . Elle hésita comme si elle cherchait le mot juste. Je mis la main sur son épaule pour la rassurer. – Sauf que j'ai oublié de mettre le frein à main quand je l'ai garée. Et alors, tu sais comme notre allée est un peu inclinée . . . il y a une petite bosse, quoi . . . euh, la voiture a dérapé toute seule . . . en arrière, et pendant que j'ouvrais la porte de la maison, elle a percuté la

(15) voiture du voisin qui ralentissait pour se garer. Ce n'est rien de grave, il ne roulait pas très vite . . . mais tu sais . . . Papa . . .

Un ange passa. Nous savions toutes les deux ce qui allait arriver. Notre Papa, comment dirais-je. . . euh, disons que la moutarde lui monte au nez de temps en temps. . . . Je n'osai pas rompre le silence, mais finalement je

(20) fis – Papa ne sera pas fâché que tu aies endommagé la voiture. C'est facile, ça. Tu paieras toutes les réparations et pour la voiture du voisin, Monsieur Blanchard, et pour celle de Papa. – Oui, je sais, fit-elle, tout petit. – Mais il sera furieux que tu l'aies prise sans permission. – Oui, je sais, répéta-t-elle gravement. Je sais exactement ce qu'il dira. Il est question de bonne foi, de

(25) confiance, c'est comme un compte en banque. . . .

Elle m'interrompit. – Combien j'aurai ? demanda-t-elle. – Trois mois minimum, répondis-je. – Première offense, bon record jusqu'à présent, . . . oui, trois mois sans conduire.

33. Qui est la sœur aînée ?

    (A) Hélène

    (B) celle qui a pris la voiture

    (C) on ne le sait pas

    (D) elles ont le même âge

34. Comment leur père recevra-t-il la nouvelle que sa fille ait conduit sa voiture à son insu ?

    (A) Il recevra tranquillement la nouvelle.

    (B) Il se mettra en colère.

    (C) Ça lui sera égal.

    (D) Il lui en fera cadeau.

35. De quoi la sœur est-elle coupable ?

    (A) Elle a totalement gâché la voiture de son père.

    (B) Elle a secoué la confiance que son père avait mise en elle.

    (C) Ce qui est arrivé n'est pas de sa faute, donc elle est innocente.

    (D) Elle a détruit irréparablement le rapport entre son père et elle.

36. Quelle sorte de punition recevra-t-elle, selon sa sœur ?

    (A) Elle ne pourra pas conduire pour trois mois.

    (B) Elle s'excusera auprès de Monsieur Blanchard.

    (C) Elle devra déchirer son permis de quatre mois.

    (D) Elle n'aura jamais plus le droit de toucher à la Renault.

37. Lequel des portraits suivants est celui de leur père ?

    (A) calme, décontracté, indulgent

    (B) farouche

    (C) méfiant

    (D) prévisible, la tête près du bonnet, mais aimable

38. Si l'allée n'était pas inclinée, la voiture aurait-elle dérapé en arrière toute seule ?

   (A) Probablement pas.

   (B) Oui, parce qu'elle a laissé la clé dans l'allumage.

   (C) Elle serait allée en avant.

   (D) Oui, elle aurait sans doute suivi le même chemin.

Les Diamants de la Couronne (questions 39–43)

La notion même des Diamants de la Couronne de France – trésor inviolable et inaliénable, incarnant la puissance et l'éclat de la monarchie – n'apparut que lentement au cours de l'histoire du royaume. Au Moyen Âge, les souverains français, Capétiens directs puis Valois, avaient acquis, conservé ou perdu bien des bijoux et des pierres précieuses. Ainsi s'était constitué, peu à peu, une sorte de trésor appartenant en propre au roi et que rien ne préservait de la dispersion. Il n'en reste aujourd'hui que quelques souvenirs écrits.

[. . .]

C'est une véritable passion que le Roi-Soleil voua aux pierreries. Encouragé par l'exemple de sa mère Anne d'Autriche ainsi que par celui de Mazarin, son parrain, il voyait sans doute dans l'éclat des pierres une manière parfaite de rehausser son lumineux prestige. Son règne marqua l'une des phases les plus brillantes de l'histoire des Diamants de la Couronne, qui bénéficièrent alors d'enrichissements considérables et constituèrent finalement le plus bel ensemble d'Europe. En 1691, la collection ne comportait pas moins de 5.885 diamants, 1.588 pierres de couleur et 488 perles.

[. . .]

Durant la Révolution, le sort s'acharna sur les Diamants de la Couronne. Déposés au Garde-Meuble en 1785 et montrés au public, ils furent volés en septembre 1792 avant d'être retrouvés en grande partie, puis vendus ou mis en gage en 1796. Dès 1800, Bonaparte se soucia de remédier à cette situation. Devenu empereur, il acheta nombre de pierres et fit rédiger l'inventaire du trésor reconstitué.

Les Diamants de la Couronne (Gérard Mabille)
Octavius (Gallimard-Zanardi)

Ligne
(5)
(10)
(15)
(20)

39. Anne d'Autriche était . . .

    (A) une reine capétienne

    (B) la marraine de Mazarin

    (C) la mère de Louis XIV

    (D) la mère de Bonaparte

40. Qui eut l'idée de faire un inventaire des bijoux royaux ?

    (A) Mazarin

    (B) le Roi-Soleil

    (C) le conservateur du Garde-Meuble

    (D) Napoléon

41. Décrivez l'intérêt du Roi-Soleil pour les pierreries.

    (A) Il les adorait et les portait pour mettre en relief son allure person-
         nelle, et l'importance de son statut royal.

    (B) Il visitait de temps en temps leur exposition au Garde-Meuble.

    (C) Il n'avait pas le temps de gérer lui-même la collection de l'État.

    (D) Il voulait vendre sa collection pour augmenter ses rentes.

42. Que sont-elles devenues les premières pierreries moyenâgeuses ?

    (A) On n'a pas de témoignage qu'elles eussent existé.

    (B) Ce trésor a disparu mais nous savons qu'il existait grâce à
         quelques mentions écrites.

    (C) Elles sont en exposition au Louvre.

    (D) Elles ont disparu lors du règne Bourbon.

43. La collection royale de bijoux de 1691 . . .

    (A) était une vaste collection de perles.

    (B) comprenait plus de 5 mille diamants et d'autres pierres précieuses.

    (C) appartenait à la monarchie autrichienne.

    (D) était assez insignifiante.

L'Omelette (questions 44–53)

Réussir une omelette est une des choses les plus faciles qui soient, disent les amateurs . . . et des plus difficiles, vous diront les experts.

Battre vigoureusement les œufs à l'aide d'une fourchette ou d'un fouet en leur ajoutant une cuillerée à soupe d'eau ou de lait pour trois œufs, ainsi qu'une pincée de sel et de poivre. Faire fondre du beurre dans une poêle, verser les œufs battus dedans. Une fois l'omelette cuite, la faire glisser dans un plat en la roulant sur elle-même. Pour qu'elle soit brillante, passer un morceau de beurre à la surface.

De très nombreuses variantes d'omelette existent; en voici quelques-unes:

L'Omelette aux Champignons—Battre les œufs à part. Laver les champignons crus à l'eau vinaigrée et les couper en tranches fines. Les faire rissoler au beurre dans une poêle. Quand ils ont un peu réduit, verser l'omelette dessus.

L'Omelette aux Fines Herbes—Laver, éponger puis hacher finement du persil, du cerfeuil, de la ciboulette et de l'estragon. Les ajouter aux œufs que l'on va battre en omelette.

L'Omelette Espagnole—C'est un plat facile à faire et très agréable l'été. On l'appréciera particulièrement pour un pique-nique, un buffet froid ou un hors-d'œuvre. Battre les œufs dans une terrine. Faire cuire des pommes de terre à l'eau sans les éplucher. Quand elles sont cuites et refroidies, les éplucher et les couper en tranches. Couper en tranche des tomates épépinées et des poivrons. Faire fondre à l'huile mais sans dorer (en mettant un couvercle) des oignons émincés. Verser tous ces ingrédients dans les œufs battus. Ajouter des olives noires, des anchois et des épices. Faire chauffer de l'huile dans une grande poêle (ou un plat allant au four), verser dedans l'omelette et son contenu. Cuire sur feu doux en couvrant ou mieux, si l'omelette est de taille, au four. Quand l'omelette est cuite, la laisser bien refroidir, puis la démouler sur un plat. On la découpe en tranches, comme un gâteau.

Les œufs peints, J. Vinas y Roca (Éditions Fleurus)

Ligne

(5)

(10)

(15)

(20)

(25)

44. Laquelle des omelettes est conseillée comme plat allant au pique-nique ?

    (A) celle aux champignons

    (B) celle aux fines herbes

    (C) l'omelette espagnole

    (D) l'omelette nature

45. Pourquoi l'omelette espagnole serait-elle le meilleur choix à emporter ?

    (A) Elle se mange froide ou tiède et se coupe facilement en tranches.

    (B) Parce que tout le monde aime les anchois.

    (C) Elle se chauffe facilement à la braise.

    (D) On n'a pas besoin de la démouler.

46. Les tomates épépinées doivent être . . .

    (A) hachées dans une terrine.

    (B) émincées finement.

    (C) lavées à l'eau vinaigrée.

    (D) coupées en tranches.

47. Comment sont les oignons que l'on ajoute à l'omelette espagnole ?

    (A) rissolés au beurre

    (B) émincés et fondus à l'huile sans prendre de couleur

    (C) tout crus

    (D) cuits sans couvercle

48. Est-il difficile de réussir une omelette ?

    (A) Oui, ce n'est pas facile.

    (B) Non, c'est très simple.

    (C) Non, surtout pas si vous parlez espagnol.

    (D) Il y a ceux qui disent non et d'autres qui disent le contraire.

49. Faut-il battre les oeufs avec un fouet ?

    (A) Pas forcément, on peut également se servir d'une fourchette.

    (B) Oui, vigoureusement.

    (C) Oui, à part.

    (D) Oui, dans une terrine.

50. Que sont le persil, le cerfeuil, la ciboulette et l'estragon ?

    (A) des verdures

    (B) des herbes

    (C) des épices

    (D) des noms de champignons

51. Combien d'eau devrait-on ajouter à la recette de base ?

    (A) une grande cuillérée

    (B) une petite cuillerée

    (C) il est préférable de mettre du lait

    (D) une pincée

52. L'omelette classique est-elle servie plate ?

    (A) Oui, sur un plat.

    (B) Non, elle est en forme de rouleau.

    (C) Non, elle est démoulée.

    (D) Oui, avec des anchois.

53. Pourquoi passe-t-on un morceau de beurre sur la surface d'une omelette ?

    (A) pour ajouter du goût à la dernière seconde

    (B) pour qu'elle glisse plus facilement

    (C) pour la faire briller

    (D) pour la refroidir un peu

La butte à Petard (questions 54–62)

(1755 – Nouveau-Brunswick) Au cours de sa huitième année de vie dans les bois, Prémélia fête ses vingt ans. Un matin du mois de mai, la jeune femme se hisse sur la grosse branche du hêtre au bord de la forêt.
Le soleil resplendit dans le ciel bleu foncé. La rivière est gonflée par la crue printanière. Le marais est couvert de grandes flaques d'eau, comme des morceaux d'un grand miroir cassé. Prémélia contemple la vallée radieuse, tapissée d'herbes vertes et parsemée de pissenlits. Les bourgeons* sont prêts à éclater tout autour. Quel soulagement après ce dernier hiver, le plus cruel de tous ! La famine et le froid ont failli les tuer. Les vieux en sont encore affaiblis. Le pire, c'est que Rosalie ne mange presque plus. Dernièrement, la vieille femme a beaucoup de peine à endurer les conditions de vie, peu importe les encouragements de Pétard. Le grand-père lui-même perd l'espoir de retourner à la butte. Prémélia ne pense pas qu'ils survivent à un autre hiver.

Quand elle retourne près de la cachette, elle trouve son grand-père assis à sa place favorite, sur un tronc d'arbre mort. Il contemple le sol de son jardin de patates de la petite clairière. Depuis la fois où il avait pu récupérer quelques vieilles patates des vestiges de leur ancienne ferme, il en replante chaque année.

À l'arrivée de Prémélia, Pétard lève la tête, et elle voit qu'il a pleuré. Elle s'agenouille au bord d'une flaque d'eau dans laquelle elle regarde la réflexion de son visage.

– Tu n'as pas besoin de te ruiner les yeux pour voir de quoi tu as l'air. Tu es très belle avec tes habits en cuir, dit Pétard.

Prémélia sourit aux taquineries de son grand-père. – Tu tiens de mon bord de la famille, plaisante-t-il. – Pépère, il fait si beau à la butte; faut que vous veniez à l'arbre.

– Non, j'ai trop mal aux jambes aujourd'hui . . . C'est la 2 811ᵉ journée qu'on passe ici. Maudite guerre ! Ne va-t-elle jamais finir ? Rosalie ne durera plus longtemps. Moi non plus.

– Pépère, ne dites pas ça. Vous ferez votre petit tour au marais en juin pour ramasser de la bonne passe-pierre.** Vous allez goûter les pommes d'août du vieux pommier. Et vous ne pouvez manquer la récolte des meilleures patates au monde !

– Prémélia tu es une jeune femme. Tu survivras.

– Ah, Pépère, vous . . .

– Chut ! Par terre ! chuchote Pétard.

Prémélia se jette à genoux auprès du vieil homme.

– Qu'est-ce qu'il y a ? Des soldats ?

– Regarde, dans les broussailles, là-bas. C'est un homme . . .

Ligne (5) (10) (15) (20) (25) (30) (35) (40)

– Peut-être un colon anglais?

– Non, il est en guenilles. Peut-être un Acadien? Soudain Pétard le reconnaît et crie à tue-tête:

Ligne

– C'est Ti-Pruce! Qu'est-ce que tu fais ici?

(45) Ti-Pruce approche et exclame:

– Si c'est pas le vieux Pétard!

Les deux vieillards s'avancent l'un vers l'autre et s'embrassent.

[. . .]

– Vas-tu nous dire d'où tu sors?

(50) – Je sors des bois, moi aussi, où je me suis caché toutes ces années avec quelques voisins. La semaine dernière, des soldats anglais étaient de passage et ont trouvé notre cachette. Je croyais que nous allions nous faire emprisonner ou tuer, mais ils nous ont dit que nous pouvions sortir des bois, parce que la guerre est finie. L'Angleterre a gagné.

(55) – Elle est finie! Elle est finie, Pépère!

*bourgeons: *buds*
**passe-pierre: *a fleshy, carrot-like root vegetable, often pickled*

La butte à Pétard, Diane Carmel Léger (2004 Bouton d'or Acadie, Canada)

54. Prémélia a vingt ans quand elle va quitter le bois. Quel âge avait-elle quand ils sont entrés en cachette?

(A) C'était une vieille femme.

(B) Elle avait huit ans.

(C) Elle avait douze ans.

(D) Elle y est depuis 1755.

55. Pourquoi la famille s'était-elle réfugiée dans le bois?

(A) Acadiens, ils se cachaient des soldats anglais pendant la guerre.

(B) Parce qu'on a détruit leur ancienne ferme sur la butte.

(C) Ils devaient se cacher des indigènes.

(D) Parce que Ti-Pruce rôdait sur la butte.

56. Pétard craint de ne pas survivre à la guerre. Pourquoi ?

    (A) Parce qu'ils seront tous massacrés.

    (B) Parce qu'il est vieux et vivre dans le bois est très dur, surtout pendant l'hiver.

    (C) Parce que Rosalie mange toutes ses patates.

    (D) Parce qu'ils n'ont que des pissenlits à manger.

57. Ils ont failli périr pendant l'hiver le plus récent à cause de (d') . . .

    (A) un manque de nourriture et le temps gelé.

    (B) un gonflement de la rivière.

    (C) la vallée qui les séparait des autres.

    (D) un colon anglais.

58. Quel est ce *grand miroir cassé* ?

    (A) C'est la vallée tapissée d'herbes vertes.

    (B) C'est le reflet du soleil sur les flaques d'eau du marais.

    (C) Ce sont les bourgeons prêts à éclater.

    (D) C'est la vallée parsemée de pissenlits.

59. Comment Prémélia arrive-t-elle à voir la butte ?

    (A) Elle met ses habits de cuir.

    (B) Elle suit les soldats anglais à leur insu.

    (C) Elle s'agenouille au bord d'une flaque d'eau et regarde le reflet de la butte.

    (D) Elle monte dans un arbre.

60. Où Pétard avait-il planté ses patates ?

    (A) Dans une clairière de la forêt.

    (B) Dans un tronc d'arbre mort.

    (C) Dans un marais.

    (D) Près du vieux pommier.

61. Pourquoi Rosalie et Pétard espèrent-ils retourner à la butte ?

    (A) Pour être plus près du marais.

    (B) C'est là où ils avaient leur ferme.

    (C) Pour ramasser la bonne passe-pierre.

    (D) C'est pour renouveler leur stock de patates.

62. Pourquoi les soldats anglais n'ont-ils pas tué Ti-Pruce et ses voisins quand-ils ont trouvé leur cachette ?

    (A) Parce qu'ils allaient les faire emprisonner.

    (B) Les broussailles étaient trop épaisses pour les voir.

    (C) Ti-Pruce s'est vêtu de guenilles.

    (D) Parce que la guerre était finie.

SECTION II: Free Response
Time–1 hour and 5 minutes

Part A: Writing
Time–20 minutes

Fill In a Word

Directions: In each sentence a single word has been omitted and replaced by a line. Write your answer, **one** single French word, on the line to the right. Make sure the word is correct in form, as well as in meaning and in context. None of your answers will be verbs.

Please note that a response such as *jusqu'à* (or *ce que*) will be considered two words, not one.

Ma ville a déjà fêté **1** 200 ans. **2** rapport **3** d'autres villes américaines, la **4** est vieille. **5** plupart de nos maisons datent du 19ᵉᵐᵉ siècle et ont été construites **6** briques rouges. Nos trottoirs en brique sont difficiles à naviguer à **7** de leur surface inégale. **8** l'hiver ils deviennent glissants mais j'aime leur aspect unique. Il y a de jolis champs tout autour. La campagne est verte et collineuse. **9** automne on peut cueillir des pommes, en été des pêches et des fraises. Il y a un petit centre ville mouvementé, entassé **10** petites boutiques, **11** antiquités, et de bons restaurants. **12** disait Candide, je **13** crois le meilleur des mondes possibles. Ceux **14** habitent ici ont la proximité de New York, Washington et Philadelphie. Il y a des montagnes **15** nord et l'océan **16** l'est.

1. _____
2. _____
3. _____
4. _____
5. _____
6. _____
7. _____
8. _____
9. _____
10. _____
11. _____
12. _____
13. _____
14. _____
15. _____
16. _____

Ma famille habite ici __17__ plus de 40 ans. Trois générations __18__ sont déjà succédées. Mon frère et sa femme Aurélie attendent __19__ premier enfant. Ainsi commencera la __20__ génération.

17. _____

18. _____

19. _____

20. _____

Fill In a Verb

Directions: In each sentence a verb has been omitted and replaced by a line. Supply the missing verb form on the blank to the right. There you will see the infinitive form of the verb you are to use. Read the whole paragraph before choosing your answer. Spelling, agreement, and accent marks must all be accurate for your answer to be correct.

1.

On va déménager la semaine pro-chaine. Notre nouvelle maison ne **1** pas entièrement prête avant la fin du mois, mais il faut quand même qu'on s'en **2** . Il y **3** un petit gîte aux environs de Dijon où nous irons l'attendre. Un entracte paisible entre l'emballage et le déballage! On veut visiter les vignobles tout autour et on **4** commander quelques bonnes bouteilles pour la crémaillère* dont notre bru va nous "surprendre". Évidemment, il faudra que nous **5** pas mal de verres échantillons. Tant mieux!

*crémaillère: *housewarming*

1. _____ (être)
2. _____ (aller)
3. _____ (avoir)
4. _____ (espérer)
5. _____ (goûter)

2.

Je dois donner un petit compte rendu sur *Le Père Goriot*. Je le (l') _6_ et j'ai déjà écrit la plupart de ma présentation. L'inconvénient, c'est que je l'ai déjà rendu à la bibliothèque et je veux vérifier une citation. Qu'est-ce que je vais faire ? C'est simple. Tu _7_ télécharger le livre numérique à l'ordinateur. Comme ça tu _8_ vérifier ta citation sans _9_ ta chambre. Quelle bonne idée ! Merci, tu me (m') _10_ !

6. _____ (lire-déjà)
7. _____ (aller)
8. _____ (pouvoir)
9. _____ (quitter)
10. _____ (sauver)

3.

Claire aime dormir. Elle est très affairée mais elle _11_ le temps de faire un petit dodo chaque après-midi. Elle _12_ 30 minutes après, les cheveux en bataille et une joue rosée, mais rafraîchie après sa petite détente. _13_ la preuve vous-même ! dit-elle toujours. Elle le conseille à tout le monde. _14_-le une fois et vous _15_ combien _16_ mieux.

11. _____ (prendre)
12. _____ (descendre)
13. _____ (faire)
14. _____ (essayer)
15. _____ (voir)
16. _____ (se sentir)

4.

" **17** tous les exercices de la page 50 pour demain. N' **18** pas de remettre la seconde révision de vos thèmes jeudi et **19** que l'interrogation orale **20** lieu mardi prochain. . . . " "Ça me fait râler, franchement le travail qu'elle attend de nous. Le français n'est pas mon unique matière !" "Oui, c'est un boulot énorme mais j'ai parlé à un de ses anciens élèves qui étudie le français à l'université maintenant. Elle se trouve à l'aise dans une classe avancée et avec un prof exigeant. Ne **21** pas. Tu **22** dans un français courant ! Que veux-tu de plus ?"

17. _____ (finir)

18. _____ (oublier)

19. _____ (savoir)

20. _____ (avoir)

21. _____ (pleurnicher)

22. _____ (se plaindre)

5.

Quand j'__23__ petite, j'__24__ des patins à roulettes réglables. On les attachait à l'aide de deux grosses brides en cuir. On y mettait le pied chaussé, on poussait sur les deux extrémités et on vissait à fond avec une clé spéciale. Tous les enfants __25__ leur clé à patins sur une corde autour du cou, tant elle était importante. Si l'enfant __26__ de pointure il __27__ de nouveau ses patins pour accepter son plus grand pied. Les patins étaient lourds et encombrants mais je __28__ là-dedans et je les ai portés pendant des années.

Je n'ai jamais su ce que __29__ mes patins, mais ma mère m'a téléphoné l'autre jour avec une nouvelle surprenante. Lors de la mise d'une moquette toute neuve chez elle, c'est-à-dire dans la maison où je (j')__30__, un des ouvriers __31__ ma vieille clé. En roulant la moquette qu'ils __32__, il la (l')__33__, sur sa corde, exactement comme je la portais autrefois. Je l'__34__ toujours dans ma boîte à bijou. Quelquefois je la glisse autour du cou, je ferme les yeux et je __35__ petite.

23.	_____	(être)
24.	_____	(avoir)
25.	_____	(porter)
26.	_____	(grandir)
27.	_____	(ouvrir)
28.	_____	(voler)
29.	_____	(devenir)
30.	_____	(grandir)
31.	_____	(découvrir)
32.	_____	(reprendre)
33.	_____	(trouver)
34.	_____	(avoir)
35.	_____	(redevenir)

Part B: Essay

Time—40 minutes

Directions: Develop the following topic in French. Prepare a well-conceived, organized, and coherent essay that demonstrates your mastery of verb tenses and illustrates your command of vocabulary. Expect to write at length because short answers do not score well. Be precise and check your work carefully for accents, spelling and agreement.

Essays are evaluated for grammatical accuracy, range and choice of appropriate vocabulary, as well as organization, style, and mastery of syntax.

Tout en admettant qu'une société idéale est irréalisable, décrivez la société dans laquelle vous aimeriez vivre. Quels en seraient, selon vous, les aspects les plus importants ?

Part C: Speaking

Approximate time–15 minutes

Working with a Series of Sketches

Directions: You have one minute and 30 seconds to look at each of the series of pictures below and to answer the questions about them that you will hear on the accompanying audio CD.

CD 1, Track 3: Le Chat

1.   Racontez l'histoire présentée dans ces images. (60 secondes)

2.   Qui a plus peur selon vous ? Le chat ou la fillette ? Pourquoi ? (60 secondes)

3.   La vie des jeunes est pleine de petits périls quotidiens. Même si la crise est banale, elle nous enseigne sur la vie. La fillette, qu'est-ce qu'elle aurait appris ? (60 secondes)

CD 1, Track 4: Samedi Matin

4. Racontez les événements présentés dans ces images. (60 secondes)

5. Comment les taches ménagères sont-elles partagées chez vous ? (60 secondes)

6. D'après vous, les enfants, doivent-ils recevoir de l'argent pour les besognes accomplies ? (60 secondes)

CD 1, Track 5: Le Grand Bal

7. Racontez l'histoire qui se déroule. (60 secondes)

8. Le garçon, est-ce un type nerveux, selon vous? (60 secondes)

9. Donnez votre opinion sur les grands bals lycéens. (60 secondes)

CD 1, Track 6: Le Professeur

10. Racontez l'histoire qui se déroule. (60 secondes)

11. Pourquoi le jeune homme ne s'est-il pas réveillé ? Donnez des raisons vraisemblables. (60 secondes)

12. Commentez la conduite des élèves pendant l'absence de leur professeur. (60 secondes)

CD 1, Track 7: Les Vacances Européennes

13. Décrivez ce qui se déroule dans cette série de dessins. (60 secondes)

14. Avez-vous jamais été en France? Si oui, comment l'avez vous trouvée? Si vous n'avez jamais été en France, que voudriez-vous voir si
vous y alliez? (60 secondes)

15. Vaut-il la peine de faire la queue pour voir quelque chose de vraiment
célèbre? (60 secondes)

CD 1, Track 8: Le Chien Errant

16. Décrivez ce qui se passe dans cette série d'images. (60 secondes)

17. Quelles promesses les enfants auront-ils dû faire à leur mère pour pouvoir garder le chien errant ? (60 secondes)

18. Quel rôle les animaux domestiques peuvent-ils jouer dans la vie familiale ? (60 secondes)

CD 1, Track 9: Les Escargots

19. Décrivez ce qui se passe dans ces scènes. (60 secondes)

20. Avez-vous jamais essayé les escargots ? Si oui, comment les avez-vous trouvés ? Si non, comptez-vous les goûter un jour ? (60 secondes)

21. Devrait-on manger quelque chose que l'on n'aime pas, pour plaire aux autres ? (60 secondes)

CD 1, Track 10: Le Coup de Soleil

22. Dites ce qui se passe dans cette série de dessins. (60 secondes)

23. Comment le garçon aurait-il pu éviter ce coup de soleil? (60 secondes)

24. Expliquez pourquoi ce n'est pas une bonne idée d'aller à la plage tout seul. (60 secondes)

CD 1, Track 11: La Pizza

25. Racontez l'histoire qui se déroule. (60 secondes)

26. Donnez quelques raisons pour lesquelles le troisième garçon ne voudrait pas de saucisse. (60 secondes)

27. Commentez brièvement le vieux dicton *Chacun son goût*. (60 secondes)

Working with One or Two Sketches

> **Directions:** You have one minute and 30 seconds to look at the two pictures below and to answer the questions about them that you will hear on the accompanying audio CD.

CD 1, Track 12: L'Équipe

28. Comparez et contrastez les deux situations. (60 secondes)

29. Comment l'acte de perdre peut nous enseigner? (60 secondes)

30. Pourquoi est-il difficile de perdre en public? (60 secondes)

CD 1, Track 13: Le Dîner

31. Maman doit servir à manger chaque soir. Dégagez les différences évidentes dans la préparation de ces deux repas. (60 secondes)

32. Selon vous est-ce que sa famille sera déçue de ne pas avoir un repas préparé à partir de zéro ? (60 secondes)

33. Croyez-vous que nous, Américains, perdons la tradition du dîner familial ? (60 secondes)

CD 2, Track 1: Les Choristes

34. Dites ce que vous penseriez si vous voyiez le premier dessin sans voir le suivant. (60 secondes)

35. Contrastez l'apparence publique et la réalité. (60 secondes)

36. Est-ce que toutes les vedettes de l'écran et du théâtre sont vraiment aussi parfaites qu'il semble ? Et les mannequins qui apparaissent sur les photos et dans les défilés de mode ? (60 secondes)

CD 2, Track 2: Le Message

37. Comparez et contrastez les deux scènes. (60 secondes)

38. Discutez les progrès qui permettent l'échange immédiat des messages aujourd'hui. (60 secondes)

39. Imaginez les progrès futurs en ce qui concerne la communication. (60 secondes)

CD 2, Track 3: Le Mangeoir

40. Comparez et contrastez les deux scènes. (60 secondes)

41. D'après vous, a-t-on pendu ce mangeoir pour attirer les écureuils? (60 secondes)

42. Les choses finissent souvent à servir de manière non voulue dans la vie. Quelquefois c'est gênant mais cela peut aussi mener au bon. En pouvez-vous signaler un exemple de la vie actuelle? (60 secondes)

CD 2, Track 4: La Bagarre

43. Comparez et contrastez les deux scènes. (60 secondes)

44. Comment est-il possible de faire la paix après une dispute ? (60 secondes)

45. Est-ce que les garçons se disputeront de nouveau ? (60 secondes)

CD 2, Track 5: Le Téléphone

46. Décrivez ce qui arrive. (60 secondes)

47. Quand on est impatient chaque seconde semble durer une éternité. Commentez cet aspect de la vie. (60 secondes)

48. Avez-vous jamais renoncé à une idée longtemps contemplée, pour la trouver tout d'un coup possible? (60 secondes)

CD 2, Track 6: Le Loisir

49. Comparez et contrasez les deux scènes. (60 secondes)

50. Tout le monde apprécie et recherche un moment pour se détendre. Le loisir joue-t-il un rôle important dans votre vie? (60 secondes)

51. Comment aimez-vous passer votre temps libre? (60 secondes)

AP French
Pre-Exam Practice

ANSWER KEY

Section I: Multiple Choice
Part A: Listening

Exchanges

1.	(B)	5.	(A)	9.	(A)	13.	(A)
2.	(A)	6.	(C)	10.	(A)	14.	(D)
3.	(D)	7.	(A)	11.	(C)	15.	(B)
4.	(B)	8.	(B)	12.	(A)		

Dialogues

16.	(B)	21.	(D)	26.	(A)	31.	(A)
17.	(B)	22.	(B)	27.	(C)	32.	(A)
18.	(A)	23.	(B)	28.	(C)		
19.	(C)	24.	(D)	29.	(A)		
20.	(C)	25.	(B)	30.	(D)		

Part B: Reading

33.	(A)	41.	(A)	49.	(A)	57.	(A)
34.	(B)	42.	(B)	50.	(B)	58.	(B)
35.	(B)	43.	(B)	51.	(A)	59.	(D)
36.	(A)	44.	(C)	52.	(B)	60.	(A)
37.	(D)	45.	(A)	53.	(C)	61.	(B)
38.	(A)	46.	(D)	54.	(C)	62.	(D)
39.	(C)	47.	(B)	55.	(A)		
40.	(D)	48.	(D)	56.	(B)		

Section II: Free Response
Part A: Writing

Fill In a Word

1. ses
2. Par
3. à
4. mienne
5. La
6. de (*or* en)
7. cause
8. Pendant
9. En (*or* L')
10. de
11. d'
12. Comme
13. le (*or* la)
14. qui
15. au
16. à
17. depuis
18. se
19. leur
20. quatrième (*or* prochaine)

Fill In a Verb

1. sera
2. aille
3. a
4. espère
5. goûtions
6. ai déjà lu
7. vas
8. pourras (*or* peux)
9. quitter
10. as sauvé(e)
11. prend
12. descend
13. Faites
14. Essayez
15. verrez
16. sentirez
17. Finissez
18. oubliez
19. sachez
20. aura
21. pleurniche
22. te plains
23. étais
24. avais
25. portaient
26. grandissait
27. ouvrait
28. volais
29. sont devenus
30. ai grandi
31. a découvert
32. reprenaient
33. a (*or* avait) trouvée
34. ai
35. redeviens

Note: Please see "Detailed Explanations of Answers" for examples of response to Section II, Part B (Essay) and Part C (Speaking).

Detailed Explanations of Answers

Pre-Exam Practice
Section I
Part A: Listening

1. **(B)**   The first speaker states that whoever was on the phone hung up before he could answer it. The second speaker asks if a message was left on the answering machine. Answers (A) **I spoke to him for 5 minutes**; (C) **I picked up while he was recording and we chatted**; and (D) **He said he would call back**, could not have taken place. Only (B) **Not that I know of**, makes sense.

2. **(A)**   He says he'll back up his files this morning. Better safe than sorry, she answers; I should do it too but never take the time. His rejoinder would most likely be (A) **It's worth the trouble and someday you'll be sorry that you didn't do it.** He wouldn't say that **it's a waste of time** (B). It doesn't **send important files to the trash can** (C), and it's nothing **like a video game** (D).

3. **(D)**   He asks if she'd like to taste an Esquimau (brand) popsicle. She asks what the flavors are. The best answer is (D) **Raspberry, vanilla, or chocolate.** Less likely would be (A) **They don't have decaf**, or (B) **Garlic, mushroom, or herb.** Answer (C) gives the names of two famous French perfumes.

4. **(B)**   He couldn't sleep at all last night. She says that must be why you look exhausted. The next comment will be (B) **I didn't sleep a wink.** He didn't **have sweet dreams** (A), it wasn't **a deep sleep** (C), and he doesn't **feel refreshed** (D).

5. **(A)**   His back hurts; he did too much today. She recommends a long, hot shower. The best answer is (A) **Good idea, hot water relaxes the muscles.** Eliminate (B) **it's better to take drugs**, (C) **it's too expensive**, and (D) **I'll go right down to the parking lot.**

6. **(C)** She asks if the mail has arrived yet. No, there's a new mailman and he's slow. (C) is the best answer, **He'll get here earlier as he gets used to his route.** The other choices were (A) **There's a nasty dog next door**, (B) **He should wear a visor**, and (D) **It's the end of the world!**

7. **(A)** He asks if she would like to help him wash the car this morning. She says yes, and she'll put on her bathing suit first because it's sunny. His most likely comeback is (A) **Then I'll be able to squirt you!** The other choices were (B) **You'll be cold**, (C) **You'll be like a model**, and (D) **Hair wash is included.**

8. **(B)** He says they got home this evening between **dog** and **wolf**. She says she doesn't understand what that means. He explains that (B) **It's twilight, when it would be hard to tell the difference between a dog and a wolf in the fading light.** The other choices were (A) **In the early hours**, (C) **Exactly noon**, and (D) **Midnight.**

9. **(A)** Didier is to be promoted to major in April. His mother is so proud of him and has invited them to the ceremony at Les Invalides. Besides being a famous tourist site that houses the tomb of Napoleon, Les Invalides also serves as the French army's national headquarters, much like our Pentagon. His mother has every reason to be proud because his rise through the ranks has been swift. He is very young to become a major. The best answer is (A) **You're right, we should take special care in choosing a gift that would please an officer.**

10. **(A)** She asks where he left his wet beach towel. On the wooden chair in the kitchen, he answers. The best answer is (A): she calls him a **boor** or **yokel**, the idea being that he should know better, and she explains that **the wet towel will ruin the wood, so he should remove it immediately.** She will not respond that **it's handy** or **convenient** (B), even though he must have thought it was. She will not say that **the chair will be more comfortable that way** (C). She will not ask him to **please put the wet towel in his drawer** (D).

11. **(C)** He turned in his paper late. She knows his teacher is pretty tough. She asks what he said, and whether he accepted it. The most likely answer is (C), **He accepted it, saying better late than never, but took off twenty points.** A tough teacher would not have said that **good things are worth waiting for** (A). Nor would he have said (D) **meaning to is as good as doing.** Answer (B) is the least likely. Although the student may have made up excuses, a sharp teacher would not have fallen for them.

12. **(A)**   He wants to know who borrowed his hammer and didn't put it back. She used it but doesn't remember where she left it. The best answer is (A) **I don't mind if you want to borrow a tool, but ya' gotta put it back! That's all I ask! (It's my only rule.)** He will not answer (B) **I'll buy several of them**, (C) **Okay, I'll use my monkey wrench**, or (D) **No big deal.**

13. **(A)**   The air-conditioner is on the fritz, and he's suffocating from the heat. She suggests they go to the mall where they'll be cool and comfortable. Answer (A) is the most likely rejoinder on his part: **Okay, but you're just saying that so you can shop (spend)!** The mall would not be **closed at 11 AM** (B). He wouldn't answer that **he needs to study** (C). They certainly can't **plan on sleeping there** (D).

14. **(D)**   He sent her an e-mail but got it right back as undeliverable. She thinks her mailbox is probably full. Answer (D) is his most likely response: **You'll have to take the time to empty it if you want to stay in touch with your friends.**

15. **(B)**   He's begging her not to throw out his slippers. She says they're awful and stinky. His response will be (B) **I just got them broken in; they're just right.** He will not ask her **to buy him a really frilly new pair** (A). He cannot claim **they're brand-new and that he just bought them** (C). They are certainly **not the latest fashion for men** (D).

16. **(B)**   People collect the little champagne caps because **there are so many different kinds. The varied designs are interesting and they don't cost a thing.** (B) is the correct answer. They are not **rare** (A). They're not **worth a lot of money** (C), and they don't **twinkle** (D).

17. **(B)**   This hobby is little known outside of France. Answer (B) is the best choice: **Most collectors are French.** It is not **worldwide** (A). (C) means **everywhere <u>but</u> France.** (D) means **especially in Europe.**

18. **(A)**   You can become a collector **simply by not discarding the little cap when you open up the champagne.** (A) is the correct answer. You don't have **to join a club** (B), **subscribe to a newsletter** (C), or **buy on the Internet** (D).

19. **(C)**   **There are lots of Internet sites, and most of them are French.** (C) is the best answer.

20. **(C)**   The pile of things he's going to keep shouldn't be too much bigger than the piles of things to throw away, to sell, or to give away. They want **to reduce the number of things he keeps in the closet.** The best answer is (C).

21. **(D)**   She doesn't mind doing the job at all. It is not **tiresome** (A). She doesn't **hate to clean** (B). She doesn't think **it's a disgusting chore** (C). (D) is the best answer: **She likes to organize and she's very good at it.**

22. **(B)**   The verb *trier* means **to go through** or **sort through.** The best answer is (B), **to group or separate in order to choose or classify.** It does not mean **to use** (A), **to get rid of** (C), or **to pile** (D).

23. **(B)**   He has too much stuff! The best answer is (B). There are just **too many** things in the closet. They may be **dangerous** (A), **old and dilapidated** (C), or even **smell bad** (D), but none of those conditions creates an avalanche every time the door is opened.

24. **(D)**   They are going to remove everything from the closet. She will vacuum it, wipe down the shelves, and throw away all of the bent hangers while he sorts through his belongings. (D) is the correct answer.

25. **(B)**   It is not **rare** (D) or **unheard of** (C) to lose a document. **No one does** (A) is certainly not the correct answer. The best choice is (B) **it happens often.**

26. **(A)**   She doesn't **back up routinely** (B). She didn't **copy to disk** (C). It's not **usual for her** (C). The best answer is (A) **She didn't think of it.**

27. **(C)**   They're going **to open the temporary file.** (C) is the correct answer. They're not going **to call a tech** (A). (B) is also incorrect. The files are hidden but it's **not impossible to get to them.** (D) is incorrect because he knows what to do and shares this information with her.

28. **(C)**   She lost her document by answering **yes** when she should have answered **no.** (C) is correct, **She gave the wrong answer when closing the file.** She knows what she did, so (A) is wrong. Her computer didn't **freeze**, (B). She didn't **erase everything** (D).

29. **(A)** She is not a professional miniaturist. It's not **her job** or **profession** (B). She doesn't **have her own shop** (C). She doesn't **earn her living** making minis (D). (A) is the best answer: **It's just her hobby.**

30. **(D)** *Pain d'Épices* (gingerbread) is a **toy store.** (D) is the correct answer. It's not a **big store** like Wal-Mart (A). It's not a **big department store** (C). It's not a **little dress shop** (B).

31. **(A)** She makes mostly tiny little **foods** out of clay, which she then bakes. The correct answer is (A). She doesn't make **furniture** (B), **doll clothes** (C), or **flowers** (D).

32. **(A)** Yes, it would be a compliment. It means that one is very good at making things that require a lot of fine detail and manual dexterity, such as crafts, knitting, or crochet. The correct answer is (A). It is not **mocking** (B) or **disdainful** (D). It is not an **exaggeration** (C).

Part B: Reading

33. **(A)** She speaks of tending to the needs of her *cadette*, her **little sister.** The correct answer is (A), **Hélène** is older.

34. **(B)** Hélène uses the idiom that **mustard rises up to his nose** to describe their father. He's a bit of a hothead. The correct answer is (B) **He will be angry.**

35. **(B)** **She's shaken the trust that her father had placed in her.** The correct answer is (B). She did not **totally ruin her father's car** (A). What happened really was **her fault,** so (C) is incorrect. She hasn't **irreparably destroyed her entire relationship with her father** (D).

36. **(A)** **She'll lose her driving privileges for three months.** The correct answer is (A). She may **have to apologize to Monsieur Blanchard,** but that will not be the extent of her punishment. (B) is not correct. Eliminate (C); she won't be **made to tear up her four-month-old driver's license.** Eliminate (D); Hélène doesn't predict that **she'll never be allowed to touch the Renault again.**

37. **(D)** He's predictable, hotheaded, but loveable. The correct answer is (D). Eliminate (B); he is neither **timid** nor **wild.** Eliminate (C); he is not **suspicious.**

38. **(A)** If the driveway had been flat rather than on an incline, the car would **probably not** have rolled backward (into the street) all by itself. The correct answer is (A). She did not **leave the key in the ignition** (B). It wouldn't **have gone forward** (C), or **taken the same path** (D).

39. **(C)** She was the **mother of the Sun King.** The correct answer is (C).

40. **(D)** It was **Napoleon Bonaparte**'s idea to make an inventory of the royal jewels. The correct answer is (D).

41. **(A)** **He loved gems and wore them to accentuate his personal style and the importance of his royal status.** The correct answer is (A).

42. **(B)** **The treasure has disappeared, but we know of its existence thanks to a few written references to it.** The correct answer is (B).

43. **(B)** The royal collection **included more than five thousand diamonds and other precious gems.** The correct answer is (B).

44. **(C)** The **Spanish omelet** is the one recommended for a picnic. The correct answer is (C).

45. **(A)** It would be the best choice because **it can be eaten cold and is easily cut into slices.** The correct answer is (A).

46. **(D)** The seeded tomatoes must be **cut into slices.** The correct answer is (D). They are not supposed to be **chopped** (A), **finely minced** (B), or **washed in vinegar water** (C).

47. **(B)** They're to be **minced and softened in oil without browning.** The correct answer is (B).

48. **(D)** **There are those who say it's not hard and others who say the the opposite.** The correct answer is (D).

49. **(A)** **Not necessarily; you can also use a fork.** The correct answer is (A).

50. **(B)**   Parsely, chervil, chives, and tarragon are **herbs.** The correct answer is (B). They are not **vegetables** (A), **spices** (C), or the **names of mushrooms** (D).

51. **(A)**   The recipe calls for a **tablespoon.** The correct answer is (A).

52. **(B)**   No, it's **rolled** or **in the form of a roll.** The correct answer is (B). Eliminate (A) **Yes, on a plate,** (C) **It is unmolded,** and (D) **Yes, with anchovies.**

53. **(C)**   Run a piece of butter over the surface of the hot omelet **to make it shine.** (C) is the correct answer.

54. **(C)**   She's now twenty and has been in the woods with her family for eight years. That means she was **twelve** when they went into hiding. (C) is the correct answer.

55. **(A)**   **They're Acadian and were hiding from the English soldiers during the war.** The best answer is (A).

56. **(B)**   **He's old and living in the woods is very hard, especially during the winter.** The correct answer is (B).

57. **(A)**   They almost perished last winter due to **a lack of food and the freezing weather.** (A) is the correct answer.

58. **(B)**   **It's the reflection of the sun on the puddles in the marsh.** (B) is the correct answer.

59. **(C)**   She hoists herself up onto a big branch on the beech tree at the edge of the forest. (C) is the correct answer: **She climbs a tree.**

60. **(A)**   He's planted his sweet potatoes **in a clearing in the forest.** The correct answer is (A).

61. **(B)**   **That is where they had their farm.** (B) is the right answer.

62. **(D)**   They didn't kill Ti-Pruce and his neighbors **because the war had ended.** The correct answer is (D).

Section II
Part A: Writing

Fill In a Word

1. *ses*
    Ma ville uses the 3rd-person possessor. It is plural to match *200 ans.* Thus, **my town has already celebrated its two hundredth anniversary.**

2. *Par*
    Supply the preposition *par* to complete the French expression meaning **compared with.**

3. *à*
    Complete the expression meaning **compared with** using the preposition *à.*

4. *mienne*
    La mienne is a possessive pronoun referring to the unnamed feminine singular town. It translates as **mine.**

5. *La*
    The word *plupart* requires the feminine article.

6. *de* (or *en*)
    The majority of the nineteenth-century houses were built **of** red brick. This meaning is conveyed by the prepositions *de* or *en.*

7. *cause*
    The brick sidewalks are hard to walk on **because of** or **due to** their uneven surface.

8. *Pendant*
    They become slippery **during** the winter. We might have said *en hiver,* but the presence of the article *l'* in front of *hiver* prevents its use here.

9. *En* (or *L'*)
    Use *en* in front of all seasons except *printemps*. We say *en été, en automne,* and *en hiver,* but *au printemps.* If you supply the definite article, (*L'*) you create the idea of repetition, **every fall.**

10. *de*
    Here *de* is used to mean jammed **with** little shops.

11. *d'*
    Use *d'* to continue the list of what the town center is jammed **with.**

12. *Comme*

Just as (or **Like**) **Candide used to say** requires *comme.*

13. *le* (or *la*)

Complete Candide's saying with an object pronoun. The pronoun object may refer to *le monde,* which is masculine, or to *la ville,* which is feminine.

14. *qui*

The demonstrative pronoun *ceux* signals that a relative pronoun will follow. It refers to the subject of the verb *habiter*, so we choose *qui.*

15. *au*

Use the preposition *à* to make the directional term **to the north.** It contracts with *le* to produce *au.*

16. *à*

Use the preposition *à* to make the directional term **to the east.**

17. *depuis*

This action began in the past and continues to the present day. My family **has been living** here for more than 40 years. The present tense of the verb *habiter* is a tip-off that *depuis* is part of this construction.

18. *se*

The verb *succéder* is made reflexive to suggest that the successive generations have followed **each other.** Supply the reflexive pronoun here.

19. *leur*

Use the possessor *leur* for the child they will have together. **My brother and his wife are expecting their first child.**

20. *quatrième* (or *prochaine*)

The generation to come will be the **fourth** one, or simply the **next** one.

Fill In a Verb

1. *sera*

The future is literal here; the house **will not be** ready.

2. *aille*

A subjunctive is needed after *il faut que. Aller* is one of the ten irregulars that must be learned by heart.

3.   ***a***

Use the present indicative of *avoir* to complete the idiom for **there is,** *il y a.*

4.   ***espère***

This present indicative form of *espérer* takes the *accent grave* when a silent *e* follows the last consonant of the root.

5.   ***goûtions***

Use the subjunctive after the subordinating conjunction *il faut que.* Here it appears in the future tense: faudra.

6.   ***ai déjà lu***

Use the *passé composé* here for this clearly completed action. **I've already read it and I've already written most of my presentation.**

7.   ***vas***

Use the present tense of *aller* here to create the immediate future. **You're going to download the digital book on the computer.**

8.   ***pourras*** (or ***peux***)

You could answer with either the future or the present of *pouvoir* here.

9.   ***quitter***

Always use the infinitive form of the verb after *sans.* **That way you'll be able to (you can) check your quote without leaving your room.**

10.   ***as sauvé(e)***

Use the *passé composé* to create the meaning **Thanks, you've saved me.**

11.   ***prend***

This is the present tense of the regular verb *prendre.* **She takes the time to have a little nap each afternoon.**

12.   ***descend***

Stay with the present tense here. **She comes down 30 minutes later, her hair disheveled, one pink cheek, but refreshed after her little rest.**

13.   ***Faites***

This is a command form. It is Claire telling others, **Try it out yourself!** *Une preuve* is a piece of evidence or proof. The expression *faire la preuve* is frequently heard in TV commercials and always appears in advertising and on product packaging. It means **test it and prove it to yourself.**

14. ***Essayez***
Another command form, **Try it once . . .**

15. *verrez*
Follow the command with the future tense for *voir*.

16. *sentirez*
Complete the command with the future tense for *sentir*.

17. ***Finissez***
This is a command form. The teacher is giving instructions. You may have hesitated about which form of the command to choose because the teacher could be speaking to an individual rather than to a group. Reading a little further, we come upon the words *vos thèmes*. She is clearly addressing the whole class.

18. *oubliez*
Use the command form for *oublier* here.

19. *sachez*
One more command form, for *savoir*.

20. *aura*
Use the future tense of *avoir* because the oral exam **will take place next Tuesday.**

21. *pleurniche*
The student has just complained to a classmate about the workload this teacher piles on her pupils. The latter is now speaking back to him, so use the familiar form of the command. Don't forget to drop the *s* of this regular *-er* verb. *Pleurnicher* means **to snivel** or **whine.**

22. *te plains*
This is the present tense of a reflexive verb, so you need to include the reflexive pronoun *te*. **You're complaining in fluent French! What more do you want!**

23. *étais*
Use the imperfect here: **When I was little . . .**

24. *avais*
Continue using the imperfect: **I used to have adjustable roller-skates.**

25. *portaient*
The wearing of the skate key around the neck took place many times. Use the <u>imperfect</u> for an activity that was repeated in the past.

26. *Grandissait*

Use the imperfect here: **If the child grew a foot size . . .**

27. *ouvrait*

Continue the sentence with the imperfect: **he would open up his skates again . . .**

28. *volais*

The imperfect is used here to mean **I used to fly in them.**

29. *sont devenus*

Use the *passé composé* here. **I never knew what happened to my skates.**

30. *ai grandi*

Use the *passé composé* for **the house where I grew up.** That action has been completed. The narrator is an adult.

31. *a découvert*

This is another completed action. **One of the workers discovered my old key.**

32. *reprenaient*

Use the <u>imperfect</u> for a continuing past action within the framework of the sentence: **While rolling the carpet they were taking up . . .**

33. *a* (or *avait*) *trouvée*

Use the *passé composé* to mean **he found it on its cord, just as I used to wear it.** Or use the *plus-que-parfait* to mean **he had found it.**

34. *ai*

Use the present tense here: **I still have it in my jewelry box.**

35. *redeviens*

Use the present tense here because it has already been established in the sentence with *glisse* and *ferme*. **Sometimes I slip it around my neck, close my eyes, and become little again.**

Part B

Two Sample Essay Answers

Read the following essays to see how a student might have answered this question. You will note different ability levels in the two responses. Try to critique the essays yourself and then read the evaluations that follow to see how they might be graded.

Sample Essay 1

Depuis toujours, l'homme se bat pour trouver la société idéale. Personne ne partagera jamais le même avis à propos de la meilleure forme de gouvernement. Les guerres, les différences d'opinion lors des votes, les attentats, etc en sont la preuve. Mais il semble cependant qu'il y ait plusieurs aspects sur lesquels la majorité est d'accord. Même si l'on a des débats sur comment les atteindre, les buts envisagés semblent être similaires.

Je pense par exemple, que nul homme ne peut honnêtement dire qu'il est contre l'égalité de tous. Je crois que chacun devrait avoir les mêmes droits, la même chance de réussir. Il faut que personne ne se sente rejeté, ou ne ressente de l'injustice envers lui. Dans ma société idéale, personne n'aurait de problème d'argent, tout le monde aurait un emploi qui lui plait et auquel il est doué et tout le monde recevrait une éducation complète.

Je crois la première raison pour laquelle une société parfaite est impossible, ce n'est pas la forme de gouvernement comme le pensent beaucoup. Je crois que c'est plutôt le fait que toute société est composée d'individus uniques et qui ont chacun des besoins différents. Le principe d'une société idéale, c'est de répondre aux besoins de chacun.

Sample Essay 2

Dans la société où je veux vivre, il n'y a pas de pauvres et il n'y a pas de crime. Tout le monde peut faire ce qu'il veut et personne n'est mécontent. En fait, il n'y a même pas d'argent et tout est gratuit. Tout le monde dépend de l'aide des autres. Il n'y a pas besoin de gouvernement parce qu'il n'y a pas de crime. Tout le monde est pareil. Il n'y a pas de gens qui ont plus de pouvoir que les autres. Aussi, il n'y a pas besoin de loi. Il n'y a pas de prison. Tout le monde fait le bien, donc il n'y a pas besoin de punition.

Aussi, tout le monde connaît tout le monde, et ils sont tous amis. Alors, il n'y a pas de gens qui se sentent rejetés. Tout le monde est heureux parce qu'ils ont beaucoup d'amis et tout le monde les aide quand ils ont des problèmes. Les vieux et les jeunes ont les mêmes droits et sont tous contents.

Jamais c'est possible d'avoir une société comme ça. C'est impossible, mais c'est la société que je veux parce qu'elle est parfaite.

Evaluation of Sample Essay 1

This is a nicely written essay, but there are errors. A missing accent on *plaît* is not as troublesome as *Je crois la première raison*. The relative pronoun is missing; this is commonly acceptable in English, but not in French. *Je crois que la première raison* would have been better.

The student states his ideas clearly and well. Verb tenses are masterfully employed. This essay would receive high marks.

Evaluation of Sample Essay 2

This essay is disappointing. Only the present tense is used, when the subject of the essay clearly invites the use of the conditional. The essay is poorly organized and fails to impress. It would not earn more than a low-average score.

Part C: Sample Answers to Speaking Questions

Le Chat

Here is how a student might have answered the questions that accompany the sketches:

(1) On voit un chat dans un arbre. Il garde son équilibre sur une haute branche, étant monté à la poursuite d'un oiseau.

Son propriétaire, une petite fille, saisit son dilemme avant qu'il ne s'en aperçoive lui-même.

L'oiseau s'envole et maintenant le chat ne sait pas descendre.

Un pompier, que la fille aura appelé, monte son échelle pour sauver le chat.

Le pompier s'en va, on voit s'éloigner son grand camion. Le chat est sauvé et la petite fille en est contente.

(2) Je crois que c'est la fille qui a plus peur, parce que c'est elle qui se rend compte du péril. Elle comprend que son chat ne pourra pas descendre tout seul. C'est pour ça qu'elle a averti un adulte. Aussi est-elle responsable de son chat.

(3) Elle aurait découvert qu'elle était capable de faire face au danger. Elle a montré du sang froid et a pu résoudre son problème. Ce sont des leçons utiles, advienne que pourra. Espérons aussi qu'elle apprendra à mieux surveiller son chat.

Samedi Matin

Here is how a student might have answered the questions that accompany the sketches:

(4) C'est un samedi matin au mois de juin. On voit un garçon sur le point de quitter la maison. Il a son ballon de foot sous le bras. Sa mère est devant l'évier.

Il paraît que sa chambre est en désordre. Sa mère exige qu'il la range avant de pouvoir sortir.

Il monte l'escalier à contrecœur. Il faut qu'il fasse ce que sa mère lui dit.

On voit le fatras de sa chambre. Le lit n'est pas fait et ses affaires traînent partout. Même le cadre est de travers.

Sa chambre est en ordre. Sa mère en devra être contente. Le garçon est libre maintenant. Il a fini sa besogne. Il joue au foot, souriant.

(5) Chez nous chacun a quelques tâches à la semaine parce que Maman est prise hors de la maison. Elle est infirmière et travaille à plein temps. Je tonds la pelouse quand il fait beau. Je descends la poubelle et je m'occupe du chien. Papa prépare le dîner et mes sœurs font la vaisselle.

(6) Selon moi, les enfants doivent accomplir de petites tâches ménagères sans être payés. S'ils reçoivent un peu d'argent de poche chaque semaine, tant mieux; c'est l'idée de payer qui me déplaît. Je préfère qu'ils fassent leurs besognes comme membres de l'équipe, la famille.

Le Grand Bal

Here is how a student might have answered the questions that accompany the sketches:

(7) Il est évident que le garçon aime la fille sans qu'elle le sache. Il ne lui parle pas.

L'année scolaire tire à sa fin. Le grand bal aura lieu le 10 mai. Chaque garçon voulant y aller devra avoir le courage de demander à une fille de l'accompagner. Celle-là cherchera une robe de soirée inoubliable et passera des heures avec ses copines à discuter coiffure et parure.

Les deux filles parlent du grand événement. Celle de gauche a déjà sélectionné sa robe; elle sait avec qui elle sortira. On reconnaît la fille à droite, celle pour qui le jeune homme a le béguin. Elle aussi a trouvé une robe mais on ne l'a pas encore invitée.

Voilà le jeune homme de nouveau. Cette fois elle a tourné la tête vers lui. Elle le voit. Il semble maladroit auprès d'elle mais il faudra qu'il ouvre la bouche.

Il fait appel à tout son courage et lui pose la question. Elle accepte son invitation. C'était beaucoup plus facile qu'il ne le croyait. Ils iront au bal ensemble.

(8) Pas forcément. Je crois que c'est une question de trac parce qu'il aime beaucoup la fille et n'est pas expérimenté dans les affaires du cœur. Il hésite parce qu'il n'a aucune idée comment s'y prendre. Il a sans doute le cœur qui bat dans les oreilles et les paumes humides.

(9) Les frais sont trop élevés pour les jeunes. Payer les billets, louer un smoking, acheter des fleurs pour la fille, obtenir un moyen de transport luxueux comme une limousine; tout cela est trop coûteux. D'autre part c'est une occasion qui ne vient qu'une fois dans la vie. C'est un haut point de la jeunesse.

Le Professeur

Here is how a student might have answered the questions that accompany the sketches:

(10) Un jeune homme se réveille à huit heures. Il a l'air surpris et inquiet. Il sera en retard pour son boulot.

Il s'habille hâtivement. Pas question de se doucher ou de se raser ce matin. Il est déjà huit heures cinq.

Il se précipite vers la porte en jetant un coup d'œil vers sa montre. Il a une serviette et il porte une cravate. Il se dépêche pour aller travailler quelque part.

C'est une salle de classe. Les enfants font à leur gré parce qu'il n'y a pas de surveillant adulte. Le professeur n'est pas encore là. On jette des avions en papier, on dessine au tableau noir, on fait le poirier.

Le professeur entre dans la salle de classe. Les élèves sont assis comme si de rien n'était. Les quelques moments de liberté sont terminés. On reprendra la leçon comme normal.

(11) Se sera-t-il réveillé et puis rendormi? Il vit seul. Une mère, une femme ou un camarade de chambre l'aurait réveillé de nouveau. Il se peut qu'il se soit couché trop tard la veille et qu'il n'ait pas assez dormi. Peut-être qu'il s'est trompé de jour, méprenant un jour ouvrable pour un samedi ou dimanche.

(12) Même les meilleurs étudiants sont capables de faire des bêtises quand le prof n'est pas là. Je trouve leur conduite tout à fait normale. Au moins, personne ne s'est pas fait mal et ils n'ont pas endommagé leur salle de classe. S'il y avait eu un accident sérieux, leur jeune professeur en aurait été responsable.

Les Vacances Européennes

Here is how a student might have answered the questions that accompany the sketches:

(13) On voit une jeune famille à bord d'un avion en route pour l'Europe. Ils songent à tous les endroits célèbres qu'ils verront; la tour de Pise, la tour Eiffel, la corrida.

Une fois arrivés en Espagne, ils assistent à la corrida renommée. Le jeune fils en est comblé, c'était toujours son rêve.

En Italie ils voient de tout près la célèbre tour de Pise. La mère en est fort contente. La petite se demande quand elle verra sa tour Eiffel.

La famille arrive sur le sol français! La petite fille verra bientôt la tour de 1889!

La tour Eiffel est resplendissante! Elle ne déçoit jamais les touristes. Dommage que la fillette qui en avait tant rêvé se soit assoupie dans les bras de sa maman.

(14) Je n'ai pas encore visité la France. J'ai été une fois au Canada avec mes parents et j'ai pu me faire comprendre dans les restaurants, ce dont mes parents étaient très fiers. Si j'allais en France je crois que j'aimerais visiter Lascaux pour voir les dessins préhistoriques sur les murs des cavernes. Je n'aime pas tellement les grandes villes et les visites aux musées ne me disent pas grand'chose non plus.

(15) Je n'aime pas attendre, moi, et je déteste faire la queue. J'ai des amis qui attendent des heures pour avoir un billet de concert, pas moi. Si j'étais au Louvre et il fallait faire la queue pour voir la Joconde, par exemple, j'irais regarder un autre chef-d'œuvre moins connu mais plus accessible. Ce n'est pas le seul trésor du Louvre !

Le Chien Errant

Here is how a student might have answered the questions that accompany the sketches:

(16) Deux enfants rentrent de l'école à pied. Ils portent tous les deux un sac à dos plein de livres. Un peu plus loin on voit un chien qui semble les suivre.

Les enfants se sont arrêtés. On voit le chien de plus près. Il n'a pas de collier mais semble gentil et en bonne santé.

C'est le coup de foudre. Le garçon se laisse lécher par son nouvel ami.

Les enfants veulent adopter le chien comme le leur. Ils veulent le garder mais doivent convaincre leur mère. Elle considère. Les enfants la supplient et le chien attend poliment.

Il semble qu'elle ait dit oui. Ses enfants l'embrassent. Elle sourit. Il y a un nouveau membre de la famille.

(17) Ils auront promis de partager toute responsabilité de leur nouveau compagnon. Ce sont eux qui devront le nourrir et le sortir. Ce sont eux qui garderont propre sa niche.

(18) Les animaux domestiques enseignent la patience et la tolérance. Ils renforcent les liens familiaux. Ils nous aiment tels quels. On apprécie leurs excentricités, on soulage leur craintes. On les aime; on les

voit vieillir et on les perd. Toutes les leçons importantes de la vie peuvent s'apprendre auprès d'eux.

Les Escargots

Here is how a student might have answered the questions that accompany the sketches:

(19) Un jeune couple dîne dans un restaurant de luxe. La jeune femme aime les escargots et suggère que son compagnon les commande aussi. Il a l'air douteux.

Le plat est servi, les escargots en coquille. Le jeune homme ne sait pas les aborder.

La jeune femme montre comment ça se fait avec les pinces pour tenir la coquille et la petite fourchette pour en sortir l'escargot. Il l'observe.

Il essaie de faire comme elle mais une coquille s'envole de l'assiette. Il est gêné.

Elle sourit parce que c'est marrant. Il trouve ça moins drôle qu'elle.

(20) Je n'ai jamais essayé les escargots. Cependant j'en ai souvent entendu parler. Je ne sais pas si je les aimerai mais je crois que je suis assez curieux/curieuse pour vouloir les essayer au moins une fois.

(21) Il y a ceux qui disent toujours ce qu'ils n'aiment pas, ou bien ce à quoi ils ne toucheront pas. Ils s'attendent à ce que leur hôte satisfasse leurs besoins particuliers. Moi, je suis plutôt de ces gens qui mangeraient quoique ce soit, même si je ne l'aimais pas, si mon hôte me l'offrait. C'est la moindre des choses pour montrer que je suis content/contente d'être leur invité(e).

Le Coup de Soleil

Here is how a student might have answered the questions that accompany the sketches:

(22) Un jeune homme va passer l'après-midi à la plage. Il porte une chaise pliante et un livre. Il fait beau. Je crois qu'il cherche un endroit pour s'installer.

Il s'installe en plein soleil. Il commence à lire. Dans l'arrière-plan deux enfants commencent la construction d'un château de sable.

Il s'endort. Son livre abandonné reste ouvert sur sa poitrine.

Le temps passe. Les enfants ont fait beaucoup de progrès sur leur château. À son insu il commence à prendre couleur.

Les enfants s'en sont allés, laissant leur grand château de sable terminé. Le garçon s'est réveillé. Il est debout; l'air surpris et confus. Il a un drôle de coup de soleil avec l'impression du livre ouvert sur la poitrine.

(23) Il s'est installé directement sous le soleil. Il aurait dû penser à porter une ombrelle. Il n'a pas mis de crème protectrice. Il s'est endormi et ne faisait pas attention aux rayons nocifs du soleil.

(24) Le jeune homme des dessins n'avait pas de boisson froide non plus. Il est très facile de vite se déshydrater à la plage si on ne boit pas. On peut s'endormir ou même pire perdre conscience sur la plage. C'est une meilleure idée d'aller au bord de la mer avec un compagnon. Un ami l'aurait peut-être réveillé avant qu'il n'ait reçu ce coup de soleil. Il ne faut jamais se baigner seul.

La Pizza

Here is how a student might have answered the questions that accompany the sketches:

(25) Trois garçons ont l'idée de commander une grande pizza à partager entre eux.

Le premier envisage une pizza aux champignons. Ses copains n'aiment pas du tout cette idée.

Le second propose une pizza à la saucisse. Les deux autres ne semblent pas d'accord.

Le troisième dit que le broccoli lui plairait. Ça va pour le garçon qui avait suggéré les champignons mais Monsieur Saucisse en a l'air horrifié. Ils ne peuvent pas se mettre d'accord.

La solution est simple. Au lieu de commander une grande pizza, ils peuvent en commander trois petites. Comme ça ils auront chacun leur choix.

(26) Il se peut tout simplement qu'il n'aime pas le goût. Peut-être est-il allergique à un des ingrédients. Il est aussi possible qu'il soit végétarien.

(27) On ne peut jamais se mettre d'accord en ce qui concerne la question du goût. Le goût varie selon l'individu. Justement, le proverbe existe parce que ce phénomène est universel et fait partie de la condition humaine.

L'Équipe

Here is how a student might have answered the questions that accompany the sketches:

(28) Les membres de l'équipe sont exubérants ! Ils viennent de gagner un championnat. Pour eux c'est un rêve atteint ! Ils sont fiers, orgueilleux, contents. Ils ont probablement passé des heures d'entraînement ensemble. C'est un moment à savourer. C'est la victoire !

Maintenant ils sont très déçus. Ils ont sûrement perdu un match important. Perdre n'est jamais facile. Eux aussi ils s'étaient entraînés, et avaient rêvé. Ils essaient d'analyser ce qui vient d'arriver. Ils se demandent pourquoi ils n'ont pas gagné. C'est une grande déception. Ils secouent la tête, ils essaient de se conforter l'un l'autre.

(29) On ne peut pas s'attendre à gagner tout le temps. Quoique l'on fasse de son mieux, on va perdre de temps en temps. C'est la vie. Il est bon d'accepter cet aspect de la réalité et d'essayer d'examiner objectivement comment atteindre un meilleur résultat la prochaine fois. Une réussite est toujours plus douce chez ceux qui ont déjà goûté la défaite.

(30) C'est très dur de perdre devant son entraîneur, ses amis et ses parents. Si on échoue à un examen écrit en classe on a, au moins, le luxe d'apprendre la mauvaise nouvelle en privé. On a le temps de s'habituer à l'idée, de se rendre compte des erreurs commises, et de mettre sa figure publique. Quand on apprend en même temps que les

spectateurs qu'on n'a pas réussi, c'est bien plus embarrassant. C'est un coup cruel et dur à supporter.

Le Dîner

Here is how a student might have answered the questions that accompany the sketches:

(31) La mère a préparé un repas à partir de zéro. Elle a consulté ses livres de recettes, elle a utlilsé des cuillères et un tas de bols. Elle a dû trouver tous les ingrédients, il a fallu les mésurer et les combiner. Ça lui a coûté beaucoup de temps et d'effort.

La prochaine fois on la voit au volant. Elle passe vite chez MacDo et achète un dîner tout fait. Elle ne sera pas obligée de passer des heures à laver la vaisselle et à nettoyer la cuisine.

(32) Toute famille aime un bon repas préparé par Maman, mais dans le va-et-vient de tous les jours on peut se contenter de manger vite de temps en temps. Les jeunes ont souvent des obligations telles que les leçons de danse ou de musique, les matchs de foot, les répétitions de choeur. On n'a pas toujours le temps de savourer longuement son repas. Sa famille mangera volontier ce repas vitesse.

(33) Il devient de plus en plus difficile de pouvoir s'asseoir tous ensemble pour le dîner traditionnel. Tout le monde travaille, semble-t-il, la mère, le père, et souvent les enfants adolescents aussi. Tout le monde a un horaire différent. Je crois que cela sape la tradition du dîner en famille. En France l'heure du dîner a lieu plus tard qu'ici et chacun peut faire ce qu'il a à faire avant de se réunir le soir.

Les Choristes

Here is how a student might have answered the questions that accompany the sketches:

(34) Les membres d'une troupe chorale chantent. Je ne vois rien de remarquable. Ils portent tous la même robe de chœur. Ils sont en rangée. Je dirais qu'ils ont tous à peu près la même taille.

Maintenant je vois que la dernière de droite est beaucoup plus petite que les autres chanteurs. Elle se tient debout, élévée à la hauteur des autres à l'aide d'une caisse ou d'une boîte solide. Cette divergence de taille se cacherait facilement pendant le programme parce que la prochaine rangée de chanteurs dissimulerait les pieds de ceux qui sont derrière.

(35) Je crois que des trucs pareils sont très répandus pour améliorer l'apparence publique. Je sais aussi que les speakerines qui semblent si parfaites à la télé portent souvent des tennis ou sont même pieds-nus pendant l'émission. Elles peuvent s'accorder un peu de confort parce que personne ne verra leurs pieds. Méfiez-vous de l'apparence publique, elle est souvent truquée.

(Although *truc* is a common <u>slang</u> word for a thing whose name we can't recall at the moment—a **thingy** or a **whatsit**—here it is used to mean a trick of the trade.)

(36) Carrément pas ! Nous savons tous que les éditeurs peuvent effacer et retoucher toutes les prises. Ils corrigent les dents ternies, les cheveux trop clairsemés. Ils éffacent les boutons, les cicatrices, les tatouages. Les mannequins sont couverts de maquillage trompeur. Aujourd'hui c'est un véritable art de cacher au public tous les petits défauts des vedettes.

Le Message

Here is how a student might have answered the questions that accompany the sketches:

(37) Une jeune femme écrit une lettre à la plume d'oie. On voit sur son bureau un pot d'encre et des lettres scéllées à la cire. Comme éclairage elle n'a qu'une bougie et la lumière naturelle près de la fenêtre. Dehors, on entrevoit une calèche qui souligne que ce n'est pas le temps moderne.

Une jeune fille moderne s'assied devant la même fenêtre. Il y a une voiture garée dehors. Elle est en train d'envoyer ou de recevoir un message électronique. Son ordinateur domine le bureau. On voit aussi le clavier et la souris. Il y a une lampe électrique à côté. Il y a une affiche au mur. C'est une scène de nos jours.

(38) Je sais combien de temps il faut compter pour écrire une lettre à la main, et pour trouver et écrire l'adresse. Il faut la timbrer et la mettre

à la poste aussi. Je le sais parce que mes parents m'obligent de re-mercier ainsi si, par exemple, je reçois un cadeau important de mes grands-parents. Ça prend du temps et ce n'est pas avec une plume d'oie, c'est avec un stylo moderne. Et puis il y a le délai entre la remise à la poste et la réception à la destination voulue. Je n'y pense pas souvent mais les progrès sont vraiment ahurissants.

(39) On parle déjà des ordinateurs qui seront de plus en plus miniaturi-sés. Un jour on les portera au poignet, comme la montre. On pourra envoyer des voix et des photos instantanément aussi. Ça commence déjà. On dit qu'ils pourront également traquer les mouvements des personnes et que nos parents sauront toujours où on est.

Le Mangeoir

Here is how a student might have answered the questions that accompany the sketch:

(40) Quelqu'un a pendu un mangeoir à oiseaux. Les voilà profitant d'un goûter impromptu. Il y a des graines et de petites noix dans une sorte de tuyau percé de petits trous. Il y a des perches pour se balancer. Nous avons un mangeoir un peu pareil chez nous. Maman aime re-garder les oiseaux quand elle fait la vaisselle devant la fenêtre.

(41) Ensuite on voit un écureuil, la tête en bas, accroché au mangeoir. Il y cramponne de toutes ses forces grâces à ses pattes menues. Il a les joues presque bourrées.

C'est un visiteur que l'on n'a pas invité. C'est un rongeur goulu qui mangera tout si on ne le chasse pas. Il est très tenace et renvoit toujours les oiseaux, c'est-à-dire les hôtes espérés. S'il arrive deux écureuils, il se disputeront au lieu de partager. Ils adorent les grains de tournesol.

(42) Le propriétaire du mangeoir sera vêxé quand il apprendra que c'est un gros écureuil qu'il nourrit. Quelquefois, les choses destinées à un but finissent à en servir un autre. Tout le monde a vu la vieille baignoire plantée de fleurs dans un jardin. Idem les vieilles bottes de soldat. De plus en plus, on découvre qu'un médicament prescrit pour une seule maladie est aussi efficace pour d'autres conditions.

La Bagarre

Here is how a student might have answered the questions that accompany the sketch:

(43) C'est une bagarre entre deux garçons qui luttent furieusement. On ne voit pas très bien ce qui se passe parce que les coups s'enchaînent très rapidement. Il est difficile de prédire qui gagnera et qui perdera.

Ensuite on voit que tous les deux se sont fait assez mal. Toujours impossible de dire qui aura gagné. Il me semble qu'il n'y a vraiment pas de vainqueur et que les deux garçons se sont battus jusqu'à ce qu'ils en étaient trop épuisés pour continuer. Ils ne sont plus vexés. Ils sourient et s'en vont amis.

(44) Je crois qu'il est toujours possible de faire la paix *si l'on veut. Vouloir,* c'est l'essentiel. Il faut admettre son propre rôle dans le malentendu. Il faut pardonner à l'autre. Il faut reléguer la dispute au passé. On doit vouloir recommencer, faire table rase et continuer ensemble, respectueux l'un de l'autre et peut-être un peu plus sages.

(45) S'ils continuent leur amitié ils vont sans doute se disputer de nouveau. C'est tout à fait normal. Cependant, au fur et à mesure qu'ils se connaissent, il deviendra de plus en plus facile de résoudre leurs conflits sans se battre. Ils se connaîtront mieux. Ils apprendront à respecter leurs différences et à tolérer le point de vue de l'autre. Ils sauront éviter les disputes sans se déchirer. Il est question de maturité qui vient avec l'expérience.

Le Téléphone

Here is how a student might have answered the questions that accompany the sketch:

(46) Il y a une jeune fille assise dans un fauteuil à côté du téléphone. Elle attend un appel.

Le temps passe mais le téléphone ne sonne pas. Elle reste là, elle regarde fixement et le téléphone et l'horloge.

Elle abandonne finalement son poste de spectatrice. Le téléphone sonne.

(47) Cela est vrai quand je m'ennuie en classe. Si le professeur n'est pas intéressant, les aiguilles de l'horloge ne semblent même pas bouger. Plus il est barbant, plus le temps ralentit. En revanche, si je m'amuse beaucoup à faire quelque chose, je ne fais pas attention au passage du temps et j'ai l'impression que ça passe très vite.

(48) Oui, cela m'arrive tout le temps. Je cherche longtemps tel foulard mais je ne le trouve nulle part. Dès que j'en mets un autre que j'aime moins, je trouve celui que je voulais d'abord, mais je n'ai plus le temps de changer de foulard et je sors avec mon second choix autour du cou.

Le Loisir

Here is how a student might have answered the questions that accompany the sketch:

(49) La jeune fille se perd dans un livre. Elle lit assise, clouée sans bouger. Elle porte des lunettes qui donnent l'impression de lectrice vouée. Si elle est comme moi, elle est capable de commencer et de finir une histoire dans une longue mais seule séance.

Le jeune homme est monté sur son vélo. Il porte le casque aérodynamique des fana de bicyclette. Il prend plaisir à aller aussi vite que possible.

(50) Je travaille dur, ça fait partie de mon caractère. Mon frère et ma sœur ont ce même acharnement face au travail. Nous le tenons de notre père, celui qui travaille le plus passionnément de tous. J'oublie souvent de laisser aller et quand je travaille sans cesse il m'arrive quelquefois des maux de tête et des insomnies. Alors là, je me rends compte que je devrais ralentir un peu. Le loisir ne m'a jamais été naturel. Il faut que je l'ajoute à mon horaire consciemment.

(51) J'adore lire. J'aime voyager et j'aime recevoir aussi souvent que possible. Je suis extrêmement paresseuse quand il s'agit de bouger. Je resterais toujours assise ou allongée si je n'avais pas peur de de devenir une souche. Je fais un peu de jogging mais c'est tout à fait forcé. Je le fais parce que je crois devoir le faire. Ce n'est pas pour le plaisir. C'est une obligation que je m'impose.

▼
PRACTICE TEST 1

AP French

Practice Test 1

ANSWER SHEET

1. Ⓐ Ⓑ Ⓒ Ⓓ	26. Ⓐ Ⓑ Ⓒ Ⓓ	51. Ⓐ Ⓑ Ⓒ Ⓓ
2. Ⓐ Ⓑ Ⓒ Ⓓ	27. Ⓐ Ⓑ Ⓒ Ⓓ	52. Ⓐ Ⓑ Ⓒ Ⓓ
3. Ⓐ Ⓑ Ⓒ Ⓓ	28. Ⓐ Ⓑ Ⓒ Ⓓ	53. Ⓐ Ⓑ Ⓒ Ⓓ
4. Ⓐ Ⓑ Ⓒ Ⓓ	29. Ⓐ Ⓑ Ⓒ Ⓓ	54. Ⓐ Ⓑ Ⓒ Ⓓ
5. Ⓐ Ⓑ Ⓒ Ⓓ	30. Ⓐ Ⓑ Ⓒ Ⓓ	55. Ⓐ Ⓑ Ⓒ Ⓓ
6. Ⓐ Ⓑ Ⓒ Ⓓ	31. Ⓐ Ⓑ Ⓒ Ⓓ	56. Ⓐ Ⓑ Ⓒ Ⓓ
7. Ⓐ Ⓑ Ⓒ Ⓓ	32. Ⓐ Ⓑ Ⓒ Ⓓ	57. Ⓐ Ⓑ Ⓒ Ⓓ
8. Ⓐ Ⓑ Ⓒ Ⓓ	33. Ⓐ Ⓑ Ⓒ Ⓓ	58. Ⓐ Ⓑ Ⓒ Ⓓ
9. Ⓐ Ⓑ Ⓒ Ⓓ	34. Ⓐ Ⓑ Ⓒ Ⓓ	59. Ⓐ Ⓑ Ⓒ Ⓓ
10. Ⓐ Ⓑ Ⓒ Ⓓ	35. Ⓐ Ⓑ Ⓒ Ⓓ	60. Ⓐ Ⓑ Ⓒ Ⓓ
11. Ⓐ Ⓑ Ⓒ Ⓓ	36. Ⓐ Ⓑ Ⓒ Ⓓ	61. Ⓐ Ⓑ Ⓒ Ⓓ
12. Ⓐ Ⓑ Ⓒ Ⓓ	37. Ⓐ Ⓑ Ⓒ Ⓓ	62. Ⓐ Ⓑ Ⓒ Ⓓ
13. Ⓐ Ⓑ Ⓒ Ⓓ	38. Ⓐ Ⓑ Ⓒ Ⓓ	63. Ⓐ Ⓑ Ⓒ Ⓓ
14. Ⓐ Ⓑ Ⓒ Ⓓ	39. Ⓐ Ⓑ Ⓒ Ⓓ	64. Ⓐ Ⓑ Ⓒ Ⓓ
15. Ⓐ Ⓑ Ⓒ Ⓓ	40. Ⓐ Ⓑ Ⓒ Ⓓ	65. Ⓐ Ⓑ Ⓒ Ⓓ
16. Ⓐ Ⓑ Ⓒ Ⓓ	41. Ⓐ Ⓑ Ⓒ Ⓓ	66. Ⓐ Ⓑ Ⓒ Ⓓ
17. Ⓐ Ⓑ Ⓒ Ⓓ	42. Ⓐ Ⓑ Ⓒ Ⓓ	67. Ⓐ Ⓑ Ⓒ Ⓓ
18. Ⓐ Ⓑ Ⓒ Ⓓ	43. Ⓐ Ⓑ Ⓒ Ⓓ	68. Ⓐ Ⓑ Ⓒ Ⓓ
19. Ⓐ Ⓑ Ⓒ Ⓓ	44. Ⓐ Ⓑ Ⓒ Ⓓ	69. Ⓐ Ⓑ Ⓒ Ⓓ
20. Ⓐ Ⓑ Ⓒ Ⓓ	45. Ⓐ Ⓑ Ⓒ Ⓓ	70. Ⓐ Ⓑ Ⓒ Ⓓ
21. Ⓐ Ⓑ Ⓒ Ⓓ	46. Ⓐ Ⓑ Ⓒ Ⓓ	71. Ⓐ Ⓑ Ⓒ Ⓓ
22. Ⓐ Ⓑ Ⓒ Ⓓ	47. Ⓐ Ⓑ Ⓒ Ⓓ	72. Ⓐ Ⓑ Ⓒ Ⓓ
23. Ⓐ Ⓑ Ⓒ Ⓓ	48. Ⓐ Ⓑ Ⓒ Ⓓ	73. Ⓐ Ⓑ Ⓒ Ⓓ
24. Ⓐ Ⓑ Ⓒ Ⓓ	49. Ⓐ Ⓑ Ⓒ Ⓓ	74. Ⓐ Ⓑ Ⓒ Ⓓ
25. Ⓐ Ⓑ Ⓒ Ⓓ	50. Ⓐ Ⓑ Ⓒ Ⓓ	75. Ⓐ Ⓑ Ⓒ Ⓓ

AP French
Practice Test 1

Total Test Time—2 hours and 30 minutes

SECTION I: Multiple Choice

Time–1 hour and 25 minutes

Part A: Listening

(Approximate time–25 minutes)

Exchanges

> **Directions:** Listen to the following series of brief exchanges between two speakers. You will hear each exchange twice. Then, based on what you have just heard, choose the most likely rejoinder from the four choices you are given below. Blacken the corresponding letter on your answer sheet.

CD 2, Track 7: Exchange Numbers 1–15

1.   (A) Le mal de mer n'est pas un problème.

     (B) Les paquebots sont de plus en plus luxueux aujourd'hui.

     (C) J'ai peur de m'ennuyer s'il n'y a pas de jeunes gens.

     (D) Tu crois, des vacances en pleine mer !

2.   (A) Elle peut tailler mon crayon aussi.

     (B) La fourmi n'est pas prêteuse.

     (C) On a le même teint rose.

     (D) Tu as raison, et elle le fera nettoyer avant.

3. (A) Est-ce qu'on a la clime ?

    (B) Je mettrai une chemise aux manches courtes.

    (C) J'aime bien ta salade maraîchère aux œufs durs.

    (D) Ton cassoulet est appétissant.

4. (A) D'accord, ça te tente de faire du camping dans un bois frais et ombragé ?

    (B) D'accord, veux-tu faire du bateau à voile ?

    (C) On pourrait faire du ski nautique.

    (D) Tu mettras ton imper.

5. (A) Emmène-moi chez le médecin tout de suite.

    (B) Cherche mon écharpe s'il te plaît.

    (C) Parfait ! On mangera et tu pourras conduire après.

    (D) Je respire à peine !

6. (A) Je les verserai dans mon compte bancaire.

    (B) Le distributeur est en panne.

    (C) S'il te plaît ! Ce n'est qu'un prêt, Papa !

    (D) Mais j'ai des dettes de jeu, Papa !

7. (A) La grande roue me donne le vertige !

    (B) La barbe à papa est trop sucrée.

    (C) Les montagnes russes !

    (D) Il fallait faire la queue pendant une demi-heure.

8. (A) C'est mon nouvel appareil numérique qui permet de tout faire à l'ordinateur !

    (B) Je suis photographe expérimenté.

    (C) Il y a une puce spéciale.

    (D) Il faut compter environ trois heures.

9.   (A) On doit le remuer au moins trois fois pendant la cuisson.

     (B) Je le saupoudrai quand même d'un peu de cannelle.

     (C) Un parfum appétissant se répand dans la cuisine.

     (D) Il y a des ciseaux spéciaux pour couper la vigne ligneuse de la grappe.

10. (A) Quel dommage! Au moins, elle a ce magnifique anneau comme souvenir de leur vie ensemble.

     (B) Et pourtant je n'ai pas vu de bague de fiançailles.

     (C) Quelle sorte de lune de miel ont-ils faite?

     (D) Invitons-la à nos noces.

11. (A) Je peux le ramasser en rentrant.

     (B) Courage! Je t'emmènerai au centre commercial pour te remonter un peu le moral.

     (C) Moi aussi, j'ai subi une déprime profonde.

     (D) Il fait trop chaud pour mettre ton pull.

12. (A) Il plane comme un aigle.

     (B) Il paraît que la cabine est un peu serrée.

     (C) Il est capable de voler plus vite que le son.

     (D) Quelle déception! Je ne le savais pas.

13. (A) Tu aimes cette coiffure?

     (B) Carrément pas! Il fait trop froid pour sortir tête mouillée.

     (C) Je les ferai couper en frange.

     (D) Mais oui, ils sont naturels! Je suis blonde depuis la petite enfance.

14. (A) Même les oiseaux ne la supportent pas!

     (B) On va suffoquer tous les deux!

     (C) Ce citron pressé est rafraîchissant et je me sens mieux à l'ombre, merci!

     (D) C'est un cas d'urgence, je m'étouffe!

15. (A) Je n'ai aucune idée !

    (B) Ne vous en faites pas, les voilà, près de la photocopieuse.

    (C) Je devais les faire doubler à la quincaillerie.

    (D) On n'a pas de domestique, c'est ma femme qui fait le ménage.

Dialogues

> **Directions:** Listen to the dialogues on your CD. After each one you will hear a series of questions based on what you have just heard. Each question is heard twice. Choose the best answer from the four choices provided and blacken the corresponding letter on your answer sheet. You have only 12 seconds to mark your answer.

CD 2, Track 8: Dialogues

Dialogue Number 1: Le Départ

16. Finissez cette phrase: "Il est evident que . . ."

    (A) que ce couple ne s'entend pas très bien.

    (B) que Monsieur s'inquiète plus que Madame.

    (C) que ce couple a souvent voyagé ensemble.

    (D) qu'ils vont à Orly et pas à Charles de Gaulle.

17. N'auront-ils pas faim s'ils partent si tôt ?

    (A) Après avoir tout réglé, ils peuvent prendre le petit déjeuner près de leur porte de départ.

    (B) Ils vont faire leur repas avant de partir.

    (C) Madame préparera des sandwichs rapides.

    (D) On leur a conseillé de ne pas manger avant le vol.

18. Comment savons-nous que leur départ sera tranquille et pas pressé ?

    (A) Monsieur s'occupera de réserver un taxi le soir précédent.

    (B) Ils n'auront pas besoin de se hâter parce qu'ils n'ont pas de valises.

    (C) Il n'y aura pas d'inconvénient s'ils arrivent en retard.

    (D) Ils ont bien planifié jusqu'au dernier détail.

19. Partagent-ils la responsabilité également ?

   (A) En effet c'est Madame qui fait tout. Monsieur n'y songe même pas.

   (B) Oui, ils ont chacun quelques devoirs particuliers.

   (C) Madame ne doit pas se soucier, Monsieur n'oublie jamais rien.

   (D) C'est leur agent de voyage qui en est responsable.

Dialogue Number 2: La Poupée

20. Dans quel rayon se trouve ce couple ?

   (A) Ils sont parmi les jouets.

   (B) Ils cherchent des produits solaires.

   (C) C'est probablement le rayon bricolage.

   (D) C'est le rayon des appareils ménagers.

21. Combien de petites filles ont-ils selon vous ?

   (A) Ils ont une fille de 23 ans.

   (B) Leur seule fille a déjà grandi.

   (C) Ils n'ont qu'une petite fille à l'âge des poupées.

   (D) Ils en ont deux.

22. Est-ce qu'ils sont d'accord sur cet achat ?

   (A) Le mari est moins enthousiaste que la femme.

   (B) Ils en sont tous les deux émerveillés.

   (C) Ils hésitent à cause du prix.

   (D) Non, le mari croit que sa femme est trop dépensière.

23. Quelles sortes de vacances vont-il faire ?

   (A) Ils visiteront tous les châteaux de la Loire pour éveiller des fantaisies de princesse.

   (B) Ils resteront en ville pour assister au Guignol et pour monter au manège féerique.

   (C) La famille ira, sans doute, au bord de la mer.

   (D) Ce sont les musées qu'ils vont faire ensemble.

24. C'est une nouveauté, cette poupée ?

(A) C'est vieux comme le monde !

(B) Oui, tout à fait !

(C) Non, toutes les fillettes en ont déjà. C'est vieux jeu.

(D) Oui, ils ont vu la poupée à la télé, et sont venus expressément pour la chercher.

Dialogue Number 3: Les Voisins

25. Croyez-vous que ces gens aient aimé être parents ?

(A) Ils en avaient ras le bol.

(B) Ça leur était pénible.

(C) Ils chérissent les souvenirs de cette époque de leur vie.

(D) Ils se souviennent à peine d'être parents.

26. Qu'est-ce qu'ils ressentent à part la bonne volonté ?

(A) la nostalgie

(B) la curiosité

(C) l'envie

(D) l'inquiétude

27. Comment le jeune couple va-t-il recevoir l'amitié de leurs voisins ?

(A) Ils en seront reconnaissants mais choisiront eux-mêmes le nom de leur enfant.

(B) Ils n'auront besoin de personne.

(C) Ils s'en mettront à leurs propres parents.

(D) Ils refuseront leur aide.

28. Les jeunes parents, comment savent-ils élever un enfant ?

(A) Ils ne se trompent jamais.

(B) Ils demandent aux voisins ce qu'ils devront faire.

(C) Les enfants évoluent à leur gré.

(D) Ils se laissent guider par l'instinct et l'exemple des proches.

Dialogue Number 4: Au Revoir au Franc

29. Presque tout le monde a gardé quelques francs. Pourquoi?

    (A) Pour les dépenser au cas où le franc reviendrait.

    (B) Parce que perdre son argent national, c'est un peu comme perdre un vieil ami et on voulait en avoir un souvenir.

    (C) Pour en faire des boutons.

    (D) Pour devenir eux aussi numismates.

30. En fin de compte l'euro réjouit le cœur du numismate. Comment?

    (A) Il s'ennuyait du franc.

    (B) Il n'avait jamais aimé le bonnet phrygien.

    (C) Il s'intéresse plus aux billets.

    (D) Il y aura beaucoup de nouvelles pièces à acquérir.

31. Le changement monétaire était le plus dur pour qui?

    (A) Pour les jeunes parce qu'ils n'avaient pas l'expérience.

    (B) Pour les immigrés.

    (C) Pour ceux qui utilisaient le franc depuis le plus longtemps.

    (D) Chez les collectionneurs.

32. Où peut-on commander une collection belle épreuve, selon vous?

    (A) à la Monnaie.

    (B) à la caisse.

    (C) à la banque.

    (D) à la Bourse.

Part B: Reading

Directions: Read the following passages with care. Each segment is followed by a series of questions or statements to be completed. Choose the best answer, according to what you have read, from the four choices provided. Blacken the corresponding letter on your answer sheet.

Questions 33–38

Il y avait à Montmartre, au troisième étage du 75 *bis* de la rue d'Orchampt, un excellent homme nommé Dutilleul qui possédait le don singulier de passer à travers les murs sans en être incommodé. Il portait un binocle, une petite barbiche noire, et il était employé de troisième classe au ministère de l'Enregistrement. En hiver, il se rendait à son bureau par l'autobus, et, à la belle saison, il faisait le trajet à pied, sous son chapeau melon.

Dutilleul venait d'entrer dans sa quarante-troisième année lorsqu'il eut la révélation de son pouvoir. Un soir, une courte panne d'électricité l'ayant surpris dans le vestibule de son petit appartement de célibataire, il tâtonna un moment dans les ténèbres et, le courant revenu, se trouva sur le palier du troisième étage. Comme sa porte d'entrée était fermée à clé de l'intérieur, l'incident lui donna à réfléchir et, malgré les remontrances de sa raison, il se décida à rentrer chez lui comme il en était sorti, en passant à travers la muraille. Cette étrange faculté, qui semblait ne répondre à aucune de ses aspirations, ne laissa pas de le contrarier un peu et, le lendemain samedi, profitant de la semaine anglaise, il alla trouver un médecin du quartier pour lui exposer son cas. Le médecin put se convaincre qu'il disait vrai, et, après examen, découvrit la cause du mal dans un durcissement hélicoïdal de la paroi strangulaire du corps thyroïde. Il prescrivit le surmenage intensif et, à raison de deux cachets par an, l'absorption de poudre de pirette tétravalente, mélange de farine de riz et d'hormone de centaure.

Le Passe-Muraille, Marcel Aymé

33. Dutilleul, est-il marié ?

(A) Oui, depuis sa quarante-troisième année.

(B) Oui, sa femme travaille au ministère de l'Enregistrement.

(C) Non, il n'a pas de femme.

(D) Oui, se marier représentait un surmenage intensif, prescrit par son médecin.

34. Quel est le ton de l'auteur envers le médecin?

    (A) légèrement moqueur

    (B) respectueux

    (C) admirateur

    (D) tout à fait mécontent

35. Comment décririez-vous la vie de Dutilleul jusqu'à ce moment?

    (A) une vie déréglée, sans la moindre routine

    (B) une vie louche et pas respectable

    (C) une vie plutôt banale et monotone

    (D) une vie vagabonde et bohémienne

36. De quel genre de littérature s'agit-il?

    (A) C'est une biographie.

    (B) C'est une fantaisie.

    (C) C'est un roman à clé.

    (D) C'est une critique.

37. Comment Dutilleul pénètre-t-il le mur?

    (A) Il tâtonne plusieurs fois le mur dans l'obscurité.

    (B) Il s'installe dans le vestibule.

    (C) Il monte au troisième étage.

    (D) Ni lui ni le lecteur ne le sait exactement.

38. D'habitude, portait-il un chapeau en allant au bureau?

    (A) Oui, un canotier.

    (B) Oui, une sorte de béret.

    (C) Oui, un chapeau à l'anglaise.

    (D) Non, point de chapeau.

Questions 39–46

Il existe depuis plus de 200 cent ans un rapport entre mon pays natal et mon pays élu, tour à tour susceptible et tendu, mais au fond fraternel. Depuis le 11 septembre, 2001, et dans le sillon pénible qui le suivit, je le ressens
plus solidement que jamais. Je crois que dans les moments les plus difficiles,
(5) on entrevoit mieux ce que c'est qu'un véritable ami. Ce jour-là, quand on nous a arraché le cœur, qui est venu nous tendre la main et nous soutenir dans notre douleur ?

Anéantie par la peur blanche et l'angoisse d'une mère dont le seul enfant venait de s'installer à Manhattan dans le quartier même du WTC, je vis
(10) pénétrer ma panique par les larges épaules de Jacques Chirac, venu à l'aide de son ami Rudi Giuliani. Soulagement maternel, comme deux pierres auxquelles je pouvais m'accrocher pendant que les murs s'effondraient. Tous les deux nous ont fortifiés sous le bras élevé de "la Liberté éclairant le monde", celle-ci cadeau inoubliable du peuple français au mien.

(15) Le juillet suivant j'étais ravie de pouvoir visiter le musée Bartholdi à Colmar, non seulement pour le voir et l'apprécier, mais aussi pour chuchoter tout bas un merci sincère.

Plusieurs preuves de ce lien fraternel m'attendaient tout au long de ma visite estivale. En regardant le défilé du 14 juillet en direct de Paris, je fus
(20) émerveillée de voir invités non seulement les pompiers newyorkais mais aussi presque 200 cadets de West Point qui allaient également fêter avec leurs homologues français, les 200 ans de Saint-Cyr. Il faut admettre que je pleure devant tous les défilés où qu'ils soient, même s'il s'agit de petits bonhommes tenus par la main de maman, mais cette fois-ci j'ai laissé couler
(25) des larmes et fières et reconnaissantes.

Quelques jours plus tard, je me trouvais à Annecy où le Maire-adjoint savoyard nous a accueillis à bras ouverts. Cette femme a présidé la cérémonie du renouvellement des vœux de mariage de mes amis, la main sur le cœur, sans lire les paroles qu'elle prononçait.

(30) Elle nous a parlé de cette même parenté incontestable entre la France et son cadet fougueux, mon pays. Ses paroles éloquentes précisaient simplement ce lien familial même avec ses piques lancées, ses chamailleries et bagarres, ses moues innombrables et ses mésententes banales. Qui pourrait s'en douter ? La France et les États-Unis, deux branches qui jaillissent du même tronc,
(35) sont férocement liés et dévoués, tous les deux, à la Liberté.

Après la cérémonie émouvante, déroulée comme un conte de fée, il m'a fallu du temps pour remettre le pied sur terre, et pour ralentir le moulin à larmes qui allait vider à fond mes canaux lacrymaux surmenés.

Je venais de me remettre quand j'ai appris que la ville d'Annecy avait
(40) offert une de ses célèbres cloches en fonte de bronze à la capitale de chaque

état américain. Qui aurait jamais imaginé une telle largesse ? Rien que pour partager avec nous ce que les Anneciens estimaient leur meilleure chose, leur cloche, la même qu'entendaient leurs aïeux, et qu'entendraient leurs petits-fils. Ils ont donné ce dont ils étaient le plus fiers, et qui, avec sa voix métallique, répéterait leur aveu d'amitié.

Cette nouvelle a failli déclencher chez moi une troisième ondée lacrymose mais j'ai réussi à supprimer cet essor plutôt bovin de mon caractère en ruminant discrètement le beau geste que je venais de découvrir.

La France, si petite en superficie, par rapport à mon pays, évoque en moi une mère fine et menue, dont l'énorme fils la dépasse en taille mais qui porte partout sur son jeune être à la fois costaud et maladroit les traces de sa mère et de son amour. Cet amour se traduit non seulement par les grands gestes mais aussi dans le petit va-et-vient de tous les jours. Je l'ai constaté cent fois, face à face au Français. Qu'il soit alsacien, auvergnat, breton, normand, périgordin, ou savoyard, je l'aime bien, . . . mon semblable, mon frère.

Ligne (45)

(50)

(55)

39. La narratrice de ce passage est . . .

    (A) née franco-américaine.

    (B) mère.

    (C) new-yorkaise.

    (D) Maire-adjoint d'Annecy.

40. Elle raconte ses expériences lors d'un voyage . . .

    (A) en Alsace et en Savoie.

    (B) à Paris le 14 juillet.

    (C) en Normandie.

    (D) à Manhattan.

41. Saint-Cyr est une école . . .

    (A) polytechnique.

    (B) internationale.

    (C) de droit.

    (D) militaire.

42. Quel est le lien entre *la Liberté éclairant le monde* et les cloches anneciennes ?

    (A) Ce sont des cadeaux du peuple français aux Américains.

    (B) La narratrice les a vues pendant ses vacances.

    (C) Elles remontent à deux cents ans.

    (D) Elles ont été construites de métaux similaires.

43. Quelles circonstances provoquaient les larmes de la narratrice ?

    (A) la visite au Musée Bartholdi

    (B) un quelconque défilé, et la cérémonie à Annecy

    (C) le don des cloches

    (D) la petite superficie de la France

44. Est-ce que le Président de la République est venu aux États-Unis après le 11 septembre ?

    (A) Oui, il a fait le tour de toutes les capitales.

    (B) Oui, il est venu à New York.

    (C) Non, mais il a invité les pompiers à venir à Paris.

    (D) Non, mais il a invité 200 cadets de West Point.

45. Qui est *l'énorme fils costaud et maladroit* ?

    (A) C'est Bartholdi, le sculpteur.

    (B) C'est le fils unique de la narratrice.

    (C) C'est la personnification des États-Unis.

    (D) C'est le symbole du pompier courageux de New York.

46. Il est clair que cette narratrice est . . .

    (A) historienne.

    (B) chauvine.

    (C) trop larmoyante pour se faire comprendre.

    (D) francophile.

Questions 47–54

Au bout de trois heures de route, Loiseau ramassa ses cartes: "il fait faim", dit-il. Alors sa femme atteignit un paquet ficelé d'où elle fit sortir un morceau de veau froid. Elle le découpa proprement par tranches minces et
Ligne fermes, et tous deux se mirent à manger. "Si nous en faisions autant" dit la
(5) comtesse. On y consentit et elle déballa les provisions préparées pour les deux ménages. C'était, dans un de ces vases allongés dont le couvercle porte un lièvre en faïence, pour montrer qu'un lièvre en pâté gît au-dessous, une charcuterie succulente, où de blanches rivières de lard traversaient la chair brune du gibier, mêlée à d'autres viandes hachées fin. Un beau carré de
(10) gruyère, apporté dans un journal, gardait imprimé: "fait divers" sur sa pâte onctueuse.

Les deux bonnes sœurs développèrent un rond de saucisson qui sentait l'ail; et Cornudet, plongeant les deux mains en même temps dans les vastes poches de son paletot sac, tira de l'une quatre œufs durs et de l'autre le
(15) croûton d'un pain. Il détacha la coque, la jetta sous ses pieds dans la paille et se mit à mordre à même les œufs, faisant tomber sur sa vaste barbe des parcelles de jaune clair qui semblaient, là-dedans, des étoiles.

Boule de Suif, dans la hâte et l'effarement de son lever, n'avait pu songer à rien; et elle regardait, exaspérée, suffoquant de rage, tous ces gens qui
(20) mangeaient placidement. Une colère tumultueuse la crispa d'abord, et elle ouvrit la bouche pour leur crier leur fait avec un flot d'injures qui lui montait aux lèvres; mais elle ne pouvait pas parler tant l'exaspération l'étranglait.

Personne ne la regardait, ne songeait à elle. Elle se sentait noyée dans le mépris de ces gredins honnêtes qui l'avaient sacrifiée d'abord, rejetée ensuite,
(25) comme une chose malpropre et inutile. Alors elle songea à son grand panier tout plein de bonnes choses qu'ils avaient goulûment dévorées, à ses deux poulets luisants de gelée, à ses pâtés, à ses poires, à ses quatre bouteilles de Bordeaux; et sa fureur tombant soudain comme une corde trop tendue qui casse, elle se sentit prête à pleurer. Elle fit des efforts terribles, se raidit,
(30) avala ses sanglots comme les enfants, mais les pleurs montaient, luisaient aux bords de ses paupières, et bientôt deux grosses larmes se détachant des yeux se roulèrent lentement sur ses joues.

Boule de Suif, Guy de Maupassant

47. Est-que tous les voyageurs dans la diligence déjeunent ?
    (diligence = *stagecoach*)

    (A) Oui, tous mangent placidement.

    (B) Non, les bonnes sœurs s'abstiennent.

    (C) Non, la comtesse ne touche à rien.

    (D) Tout le monde mange sauf Boule de Suif.

48. Pourquoi cette dernière est-elle à jeun ?

    (A) Elle n'aime pas son sobriquet et veut maigrir.

    (B) Elle n'a vraiment pas faim.

    (C) Elle n'a rien apporté et personne ne partage avec elle.

    (D) Elle n'aime pas manger en route.

49. Qu'est-ce qui est arrivé le jour où elle avait son panier et les autres n'avaient rien à manger ?

    (A) Elle n'avait que quelques miettes, pas assez pour partager.

    (B) Elle a partagé avec eux tout ce qu'elle avait là-dedans.

    (C) Elle a offert à manger mais ils ont tous refusé poliment.

    (D) Personne ne voulait manger ce jour-là.

50. Quelle est l'attitude de Boule de Suif envers ses compagnons ?

    (A) Elle n'ose pas leur parler à cause de sa grande timidité.

    (B) Elle les observe d'un air curieux mais indifférent.

    (C) Outragée, elle brûle d'une colère silencieuse mais aiguë.

    (D) Détachée, elle ne s'intéresse guère à leur repas.

51. Qu'est-ce qu'elle laisse entendre quand Boule de Suif les appelle "gredins honnêtes" ?

    (A) son mépris et leur hypocrisie

    (B) leur niveau social supérieur au sien

    (C) que le voyage donne faim

    (D) qu'elle les estime

52. Pourquoi Boule de Suif pleure-t-elle?

    (A) parce qu'elle a honte

    (B) parce qu'elle a faim

    (C) parce qu'elle se sent blessée par leur dédain

    (D) parce qu'elle se sent dépaysée

53. L'auteur décrit longuement toute la nourriture qu'ils vont consommer. À quoi servent ces détails?

    (A) Ça montre sa maîtrise évocatrice.

    (B) Ça sert à éveiller l'appétit du lecteur.

    (C) Ça hausse l'effet du repas abondant sur le passager qui n'y participe pas et sur le lecteur qui la plaint.

    (D) Cela indique que l'écrivain est lui-même gourmand.

54. Le comportement des passagers montre . . .

    (A) que Boule de Suif n'aurait pas dû oublier son panier.

    (B) qu'ils sont répréhensibles et manquent d'humanité.

    (C) qu'ils sont honnêtes et bien élevés.

    (D) que Boule de Suif ne mérite pas leur attention.

Questions 55–60

Le soleil semble me suivre, une brise rafraîchissante me salue. Midi juste. Église de la Madeleine, une prière brève mais fervente, un cierge allumé, un remerciement sincère. Je traverse le marché aux fleurs, et traîne un peu devant la vitrine magnifique de Hédiard. Puis je me lance vers la boutique de Maille pour remplir de moutarde fraîche mon pot en grès. La jeune vendeuse me gronde poliment parce que je n'ai plus mon bouchon. Un euro de plus sur le prix de ma moutarde piquante. Juste assez de temps pour sélectionner quelques cadeaux de dernière minute. Je rentre demain matin, hélas. Que dites-vous? Si mes amis n'aiment pas la moutarde? Ma parole! Un ami anti-moutardiste? Rassurez-vous, je n'en ai point. Une fois dehors, je louche au soleil éclatant. Quand je rouvre les yeux, je me trouve installée face à une petite table couverte de lin blanc, de porcelaine fine. Ah, qu'est-ce qu'on est bien chez Fauchon! Assiette d'agrumes, saupoudrée de gros sucre, café crème, petit pichet d'eau froide. Comme celle qui fréquente ce salon de

Ligne

(5)

(10)

(15) thé somptueux tous les jours, je contemple ma chance entre les bouchées citronnées et délicieuses que je m'offre. Le bon Dieu ne me chasse pas; je lambine. Je lui dis d'une toute petite voix frêle que je ne veux pas tellement rentrer.

    Le lendemain matin, à l'aéroport Charles de Gaulle on annule mon vol.
(20) On s'excuse en me donnant un bon gratuit pour quatre repas et une jolie chambre d'hôtel. La plupart des passagers s'agacent. Moi, je commence à rigoler. On se la coule douce ! Après tout ce n'est pas la mer à boire. Je mettrai les moutardes au frais.

55. Quel temps fait-il pendant ce récit ?

    (A) Il fait beau et frais.

    (B) Le ciel est couvert.

    (C) C'est l'hiver.

    (D) C'est une journée grisâtre.

56. D'après vous, cette femme avait-elle été chez Maille avant ?

    (A) Oui, elle a même rapporté son pot vide.

    (B) Non, elle préfère les moutardes de Hédiard.

    (C) Non, elle va toujours chez Fauchon pour la moutarde.

    (D) Oui, mais c'est la première fois qu'elle fait un achat.

57. Comment réagit-elle quand son vol est annulé ?

    (A) Elle s'agace parce que c'est inopportun.

    (B) Elle s'inquiète parce que sa famille sera incommodée.

    (C) Elle se demande comment elle pourra payer son logement ce soir-là.

    (D) Elle est surprise mais sereine, voire contente.

58. Quelle sorte de déjeuner s'offre-t-elle son dernier jour à Paris ?

    (A) un déjeuner coûteux avec plusieurs plats élégants

    (B) un tout petit déjeuner léger mais exquis

    (C) une assiette froide aux crevettes

    (D) le plat du jour comprenant boisson et dessert.

59. Où se trouvent les boutiques de Fauchon, Maille et Hédiard?

(A) près de l'église de la Madeleine

(B) dans un quartier industriel

(C) près de l'aéroport Charles de Gaulle

(D) dans des champs de moutarde

60. Pourquoi la femme rigole-t-elle en apprenant que son vol est annulé?

(A) Elle se moque de ceux qui s'en agacent.

(B) Parce qu'elle ne veut pas encore quitter Paris et c'est comme si Dieu intervenait.

(C) Parce qu'elle ira au bord de la mer.

(D) Elle trouve l'aéroport amusant.

Questions 61–69

Chaque jour, pour se construire, se dépenser et se renouveler, notre corps a besoins de nutriments. Les nutriments sont des molécules utilisées par les cellules de l'organisme; c'est lors de la digestion des aliments consommés que les nutriments sont obtenus et rendus utilisables.

Les Produits Laitiers—Cette famille regroupe les laits, les yaourts, les spécialités laitières, les fromages blancs, les desserts lactés, les petits-suisses,* les crèmes desserts et, bien sûr tous les fromages. Leurs caractéristiques nutritionnelles: protéines d'origine animale; graisses d'origine animale; calcium, phosphore, vitamines du groupe B, surtout B_2 et B_{12}.

Les Viandes-Poissons-Œufs—Cette famille, appelée *les VPO*, regroupe l'ensemble des viandes (bœuf, veau, agneau, mouton, porc, volailles, abats, gibier . . .) l'ensemble des produits marins (poissons, crustacés, mollusques, coquillages . . .), certaines charcuteries et les œufs. Leurs protéines et graisses sont d'origine animale. Aussi acides gras essentiels (pour les poissons); fer (surtout pour la viande rouge); phosphore; zinc; vitamines du groupe B; vitamine D (pour les poissons gras); vitamine A (pour les abats).

Les Fruits et Légumes—Cette famille regroupe les légumes frais, les fruits frais et secs, les fruits oléagineux frais et secs (avocats, noix, noisettes, amandes . . .) et les aliments dérivés: jus de légumes, soupes, jus de fruits, compotes. . . . Leurs caractéristiques nutritionnelles: eau; glucides simples; graisse d'origine végétale (uniquement pour les fruits oléagineux); fibres alimentaires; vitamine C; bêta-carotène (provitamine A) vitamine B_9; (les fruits et légumes sont la deuxième source alimentaire de calcium après les

Ligne

(5)

(10)

(15)

(20)

Ligne produits laitiers); magnésium (surtout pour les fruits oléagineux secs); fer
(25) (ce fer d'origine végétale est moins bien absorbé que celui qui est présent
dans les aliments d'origine animale).

*petits-suisses: small individual portions of fresh cheese with the consis-
tency of yogurt, featured at breakfast or eaten as a snack*

Calories, Stéphane Dupré: Dormonval, CH Lucerne S.A.E.P.

61. Lequel serait un fruit oléagineux ?

   (A) le fruit de mer

   (B) le veau

   (C) la noisette

   (D) le jaune d'œuf

62. Le yaourt appartient à quel groupe alimentaire ?

   (A) les VPO

   (B) c'est un produit laitier

   (C) c'est un légume sec

   (D) c'est un produit marin

63. Que mangeriez-vous comme source de fibre alimentaire ?

   (A) un fromage

   (B) de la volaille

   (C) un fruit ou un légume

   (D) un œuf

64. Lequel n'est pas un produit de mer ?

   (A) les mollusques

   (B) les avocats

   (C) les crustacés

   (D) les coquillages

65. Qu'est-ce qui rend les nutriments utilisables ?

    (A) les fibres

    (B) les graisses

    (C) le phosphore

    (D) le processus de la digestion

66. Quelle serait une bonne source de la vitamine D, selon cet article ?

    (A) tous les poissons

    (B) quelques poissons

    (C) les œufs

    (D) les glucides simples

67. La viande rouge est une bonne source de (d') . . .

    (A) fer.

    (B) calcium.

    (C) fibre alimentaire.

    (D) acides gras essentiels.

68. Pourquoi le fer d'origine végétale est-il moins bon que le fer d'origine animale ?

    (A) La quantité est négligeable.

    (B) Il diminue notre calcium.

    (C) Son absorption est moins efficace.

    (D) C'est trop oléagineux.

69. Comment peut-on être sûrs d'obtenir les acides gras essentiels ?

    (A) en prenant assez de glucides simples

    (B) en mangeant les fruits et les légumes

    (C) en mangeant surtout les graisses

    (D) en mangeant souvent du poisson

Questions 70–75

Un homme épouvantable entre et se regarde dans la glace.

– Pourquoi vous regardez-vous au miroir, puisque vous ne pouvez vous y voir qu'avec déplaisir? L'homme épouvantable me répond:

Ligne

(5)

– Monsieur, d'après les immortels principes de 89, tous les hommes sont égaux en droits; donc je possède le droit de me mirer; avec plaisir ou déplaisir, cela ne regarde que ma conscience.

Au nom du bon sens, j'avais sans doute raison; mais, au point de vue de la loi, il n'avait pas tort.

Le Miroir, Charles Baudelaire (Petits Poèmes en Prose)

70. À quels immortels principes l'homme épouvantable fait-il allusion?

(A) à la Déclaration des Droits de l'Homme de 1789

(B) à l'Exposition Universelle de 1889

(C) à l'avènement d'Henri IV en 1589

(D) à l'an 89 avant Jésus Christ

71. À quelle conclusion sur la loi le narrateur semble-t-il nous mener?

(A) que la loi favorise les beaux

(B) que la loi protège les laids

(C) que la loi n'est pas bonne

(D) que la loi ne peut pas nous protéger de nous-mêmes

72. Quel est le ton de l'auteur?

(A) Le ton est ironique et spirituel.

(B) Le ton est grave.

(C) C'est choquant.

(D) Le ton est sérieux.

73. Selon le raisonnement du narrateur l'homme ne devrait pas se regarder parce que (qu') . . .

    (A) il n'a pas de principes.

    (B) son reflet ne va pas lui plaire.

    (C) c'est contre la loi.

    (D) la glace est épouvantable.

74. Selon l'homme épouvantable se regarder dans la glace . . .

    (A) est son droit, garanti par la loi.

    (B) lui semble une bonne idée.

    (C) plait à sa conscience.

    (D) appelle au bon sens.

75. L'auteur pose une question à l'homme épouvantable et une question voilée au lecteur. Que serait cette dernière ?

    (A) Reconnaissez-vous une dualité dans la condition humaine ?

    (B) Qui a raison ?

    (C) Les laids ont-ils les mêmes droits que les autres ?

    (D) Doit-on avoir des miroirs dans des endroits publics ?

SECTION II: Free Response
Time–1 hour and 25 minutes

Part A: Writing
(Approximate Time–20 minutes)

Fill In a Word

> **Directions:** In each sentence a single word has been omitted and replaced by a line. Write your answer, **one** single French word, on the line to the right. Make sure the word is correct in form, as well as in meaning and in context. None of your answers will be verbs.
>
> Please note that a response such as *jusqu'à* (or *ce que*) will be considered two words, not one.

1.

Depuis __1__ Michel a fêté ses seize ans, il ne pense qu'__2__ obtenir son permis de conduire. Chaque dimanche il conduit avec son père et essaie __3__ garer la voiture plusieurs fois. Son père est patient et Michel fait __4__ progrès. Il croit pouvoir passer son permis __5__ un mois. S'il réussit du premier coup, il __6__ sera très content. Ce serait __7__ ailleurs un accomplissement __8__ il pourrait être fier. S'il ne réussit pas d'emblée, il continuera à s'entraîner avec son père jusqu'à __9__ qu'il atteigne son but. Pour l'instant, il étudie son manuel et songe __10__ sa réussite.

1. _____
2. _____
3. _____
4. _____
5. _____
6. _____
7. _____
8. _____
9. _____
10. _____

2.

Maman vient __11__ exiger __12__ je range ma chambre. Je dois nettoyer toutes les surfaces couvertes __13__ poussière, __14__ qui ne sera pas facile à cause de tous les bibelots que je devrai enlever d'abord. __15__ tâche pénible !

11. _____

12. _____

13. _____

14. _____

15. _____

Fill In a Verb

Directions: In each sentence a verb has been omitted and replaced by a line. Supply the missing verb form on the blank to the right. There you will see the infinitive form of the verb you are to use. Read the whole paragraph before choosing your answer. Spelling, agreement, and accent marks must all be accurate for your answer to be correct.

À l'âge de cinq ans, petite Caroline **1** princesse magique. La métamorphose intérieure **2** lieu subitement, du jour au lendemain. Néanmoins, il **3** plusieurs trajets à Monoprix pour réussir sa parure complète. Jour après jour, elle **4** toujours en tenue de princesse magique. Elle **5** sa robe à paillettes avec sa pèlerine assortie, sa couronne en papier d'aluminium et sa baguette en plastique rose.

Les marchandes lui **6** souvent la révérence, souriant. M. duCreuil, le boulanger, la **7** avec panache et un petit pain sucré. Le confisier, M. LaFitte, lui **8** un bonbon quotidien, qu'il **9** sur un petit plat en argent massif étincelant.

Quelquefois, en rentrant du marché, la petite souveraine devait **10** sa baguette entre les dents, pour pouvoir **11** tendrement de ses doigts potelés, une marguerite offerte par Mme Crespin (la fleuriste), tout en tenant de l'autre menotte la main maternelle.

1. _____ (devenir)
2. _____ (avoir)
3. _____ (falloir)
4. _____ (sortir)
5. _____ (exiger)
6. _____ (faire)
7. _____ (saluer)
8. _____ (réserver)
9. _____ (offrir)
10. _____ (mettre)
11. _____ (empoigner)

Un beau jour le règne de Caroline __12__ de manière ignominieuse. Quand sa mère __13__ ses atouts habituels de princesse, Caroline lui __14__, "Maman, je ne peux plus mettre ces loques ni-aises où que j'__15__ ! Je préfère mettre ma salopette".

12. _____ (se terminer)

13. _____ (étaler)

14. _____ (prononcer)

15. _____ (aller)

Part B: Essay
Time—40 minutes

Directions: Develop the following topic in French. Prepare a well-conceived, organized, and coherent essay that demonstrates your mastery of verb tenses and illustrates your command of vocabulary. Expect to write at length because short answers do not score well. Be precise and check your work carefully for accents, spelling, and agreement.

Essays are evaluated for grammatical accuracy, range, and choice of appropriate vocabulary, as well as organization, style, and mastery of syntax.

(A similar question appeared on an actual past exam.)

Le rôle essentiel des jeunes, c'est de remettre toujours en question l'autorité. Discutez cette opinion.

Part C: Speaking

Approximate time—15 minutes

Working with a Series of Sketches: Perdre du poids

Directions: You have one minute and 30 seconds to look at the series of five pictures below and to answer the questions about them that you will hear on CD 2, Track 9.

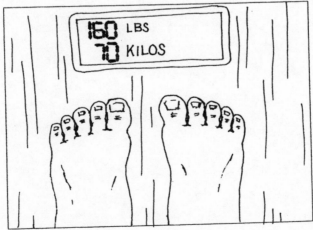

1. Racontez l'histoire présentée dans cette série d'images. (60 secondes)

2. Expliquez pourquoi beaucoup de gens ont de la difficulté à suivre un régime. (60 secondes)

3. Selon vous, quels sont les attributs nécessaires pour réussir à son but, quel qu'il soit? (60 secondes)

Working with One or Two Sketches: Au Volant

Directions: You have one minute and 30 seconds to look at the two pictures below and to answer the questions that you will hear about them on CD 2, Track 10.

1. Contrastez comment ces deux personnes se comportent au volant. (60 secondes)

2. Qui est le meilleur conducteur selon vous ? (60 secondes)

3. Est-il possible de bien faire attention à la route en tenant un portable ou une boisson à la main ? (60 secondes)

AP French
Practice Test 1

ANSWER KEY

Section I: Multiple Choice
Part A: Listening

Exchanges

1.	(C)	5.	(C)	9.	(B)	13.	(B)
2.	(D)	6.	(C)	10.	(A)	14.	(C)
3.	(C)	7.	(C)	11.	(B)	15.	(B)
4.	(A)	8.	(A)	12.	(D)		

Dialogues

16.	(C)	21.	(C)	26.	(A)	31.	(C)
17.	(A)	22.	(B)	27.	(A)	32.	(A)
18.	(D)	23.	(C)	28.	(D)		
19.	(B)	24.	(B)	29.	(B)		
20.	(A)	25.	(C)	30.	(D)		

Part B: Reading

33.	(C)	44.	(B)	55.	(A)	66.	(B)
34.	(A)	45.	(C)	56.	(A)	67.	(A)
35.	(C)	46.	(D)	57.	(D)	68.	(C)
36.	(B)	47.	(D)	58.	(B)	69.	(D)
37.	(D)	48.	(C)	59.	(A)	70.	(A)
38.	(C)	49.	(B)	60.	(B)	71.	(D)
39.	(B)	50.	(C)	61.	(C)	72.	(A)
40.	(A)	51.	(A)	62.	(B)	73.	(B)
41.	(D)	52.	(C)	63.	(C)	74.	(A)
42.	(A)	53.	(C)	64.	(B)	75.	(A) or (B)
43.	(B)	54.	(B)	65.	(D)		

Section II: Free Response
Part A: Writing

Fill In a Word

1.	que	9.	ce
2.	à	10.	à
3.	de	11.	d'
4.	du	12.	que
5.	dans (*or* en)	13.	de
6.	en	14.	ce
7.	d'	15.	Quelle
8.	dont		

Fill In a Verb

1.	est devenue	9.	offrait
2.	a eu	10.	mettre
3.	a fallu	11.	empoigner
4.	sortait	12.	s'est terminé
5.	exigeait	13.	a étalé
6.	faisaient	14.	a prononcé
7.	saluait	15.	aille
8.	réservait		

Note: Please see "Detailed Explanations of Answers" for examples of response to Section II, Part B (Essay) and Part C (Speaking)

Detailed Explanations of Answers

Practice Test 1

Section I

Part A: Listening

1. **(C)** The speaker has stated that she's going on a cruise with her parents but that she's a little worried. As we consider the answer choices we should be looking for a statement that explains **why** she's worried. She says that **seasickness** is **not** a problem so we eliminate answer (A). A comment about the **luxury of modern cruise liners** (B) doesn't help either. Answer (D) is an exclamation about a vacation at sea. Only answer (C) sheds light on what is bothering her: **She's afraid she'll be bored if there aren't any other young people.**

2. **(D)** The speaker tells her husband that Sophie wants to borrow her pink suit, the one he likes best. He says that as long as she returns it, he sees no problem. Answers (A) **She can sharpen my pencil, too,** (B) **The ant is not a borrower,** and (C) **We have the same pink complexion,** should all be eliminated because none is germane to the conversation. She agrees with her husband in answer (D): **You're right, and she will have it cleaned before returning it.**

3. **(C)** The woman will prepare something light for dinner because it's so hot. The man reminds her that he likes **her garden salad with hard-boiled eggs** in answer (C). The tasty *cassoulet* is a heavy meat and beans stew served hot. Eliminate answer (D). (A) and (B), comments about **air-conditioning** and **short-sleeved shirts,** don't really have anything to do with their topic, which is what they are going to eat.

4. **(A)** When he suggests they go to the beach for the weekend, she asks if they couldn't plan something else. She's already had a bad sunburn this summer and she's worried about her skin. Answer (A) is a suggestion **to go camping in cool, shaded woods,** the perfect solution. **Water-skiing** and

sailing would still expose her to full sun. **Putting on a raincoat** is obviously not the solution, either.

5.   **(C)**   The driver complains that he's hungry and that his neck hurts. He suggests they look for a rest stop. She agrees. Answer (C) **Perfect! We'll eat and you can drive afterwards,** makes more sense than (A) **Take me to the doctor,** (B) **Get me my scarf,** or (D) **I can hardly breathe.**

6.   **(C)**   The daughter tells her father she needs thirty euros and points out that he has his credit card. He tells her that the ATM is not a magic wishing well. Answer (C), **Please, it's just a loan, Dad!** is her best chance to get the money. Certainly better than telling him **she will deposit it in her account** (A), that **the ATM is out of service** (B), or that **she has gambling debts.**

7.   **(C)**   **The roller coaster!** (C) is the best answer to the question asked: What was your favorite ride (at the Parc Astérix)? The **Ferris wheel makes him dizzy,** (A) so that's not it. **Cotton candy is too sugary** (B) and standing in line for half an hour (D) do not answer the question either.

8.   **(A)**   **It's my new digital camera that lets me do everything on the computer** (A) is the best answer to the question asked: How were you able to develop them so quickly? The other choices are somewhat plausible but much less likely: (B) **I'm an experienced photographer,** (C) **There's a special chip,** and (D) **It takes about three hours.**

9.   **(B)**   She feels like making rice pudding. He asks her not to put raisins in it because he likes it plain. Answer (B) is the best response, **She'll just sprinkle a little cinnamon on top.** Answer (A) gives recipe instructions, (B) mentions the **delicious aroma,** and (C) describes **grape scissors.**

10.   **(A)**   She thinks Madame Saulnier's wedding ring is the most beautiful she's ever seen. She would like to congratulate her husband on his choice of ring but learns that the woman is a widow. Answer (A) is the best response, **What a shame! At least she has this magnificent ring as a memento of their life together.** Comments about an **engagement ring** (B), the **honeymoon** (C), and a suggestion to **invite her to their own wedding** (D) are less to the point.

11.   **(B)**   She has the blues and the dry cleaner has lost her favorite sweater. Answer (B) is the best response: **Come on, I'll take you to the mall to cheer you up.** The other choices were an offer to **pick up the sweater on**

the way home (A), that he, too, **suffered a major depression** (C), and **it's too hot to wear your sweater** (D).

12. **(D)** He always wanted to fly aboard the Concorde. She tells him that he's missed his chance. The Concorde has been retired. (C) **What a disappointment, I didn't know** is the best answer. The other comments, **She soars like an eagle** (A), **The cabin is a little tight** (B), and **It can fly faster than the speed of sound** (C), all miss the point that the mighty Concorde is no more.

13. **(B)** She has just washed her hair and her hairdryer is on the fritz. He suggests she let it dry naturally. (B) is the best response, **Absolutely not, it's too cold to go out with a wet head.** The other rejoinders, **Do you like this hairdo?** (A), **I'll cut bangs** (C), and **I'm a natural blonde since childhood** (D), don't follow logically.

14. **(C)** He complains that it's so hot he can't breathe. She says come sit under the awning and I'll bring you a cold drink. Answer (C) is the best rejoinder, **This lemonade is refreshing and I feel better in the shade, thanks!** The other choices, **Even the birds can't stand it!** (A), **We're both going to suffocate!** (B), and **It's an emergency, I'm suffocating!** (D), are further exaggerations about the heat.

15. **(B)** He asks his secretary if she's seen his keys. She asks which ones, his office keys or his house keys? The best rejoinder is (B) **Never mind, there they are, near the photocopier.** The other choices were (A) **I have no idea,** (C) **I was supposed to make duplicates at the hardware store,** and (D) **We don't have a maid, my wife does the housekeeping.**

16. **(C)** It's obvious that this couple **has traveled together often.** (C) is the correct answer. They get along fine, which eliminates answer (A). Monsieur is **not worried more than Madame** (B), and there is no mention of the airport they're headed for (D).

17. **(A)** (A) is the best answer: **After settling everything, they can have breakfast near their departure gate.** They are not planning **to eat before they leave** (B). There is no mention of **making sandwiches** (C), and no one has **advised them not to eat before flying** (D).

18. **(D)** We know they will have a smooth, unhurried departure because **they have planned so well.** (D) is the best answer. There is no need for a

taxi, so eliminate (A). Rule out (B) because they will have put their **luggage** in the car by morning. (C) is not correct either because they must not **be late.**

19. **(B)** They do share responsibility equally. **Each has his own duties.** (B) is the best answer. (A) suggests that **Madame does everything,** which is not the case. (C) suggests that it is he who takes care of everything. (D) states that their **travel agent takes responsibility for all the details.**

20. **(A)** They're in the toy aisle. (A) is the correct answer. They are not **looking for sun creams** (B). They're not in the **do-it-yourself aisle** (C). They are certainly not in **appliances** (D).

21. **(C)** They mention having **only one little girl who is at the age for dolls.** (C) is the correct answer. She is **not yet grown up,** so disregard answers (A) and (B). They do not have **two** little girls (D). Christiane is their daughter's playmate.

22. **(B)** They agree on the purchase because both think it's **marvelous.** (B) is the correct answer. The husband is just as crazy about the doll as his wife, so (A) is not a good choice. Eliminate (C) and (D) because they are not concerned about **price** or how much is being spent.

23. **(C)** **The family will undoubtedly be going to the shore.** (C) is the correct answer. Their excitement about bringing along a doll that can tan certainly suggests this. There is no mention of **fairy princess castles** (A), nor of **Punch and Judy** or **merry-go-rounds** (B). They are not planning on **museum** outings (D).

24. **(B)** **Absolutely!** (B) is the best answer. The doll is entirely new to them, a novelty. It is not **as old as the hills** (A), nor is it **passé** (C). They did not know about the doll before they spotted it in the store. (D), which says they saw it advertised **on TV,** is therefore not correct.

25. **(C)** **They cherish their memories of that time in their life.** (C) is the best answer. They speak fondly of being parents. They were not **fed up with** parenthood (A). Nor was it **bothersome** (B). (D), which says **they can hardly remember being parents,** should also be disregarded because their recall is quite vivid.

26. **(A)** Besides genuine goodwill toward their new neighbors, the couple is definitely feeling **nostalgic** about their early years as parents. (A) is the best answer. The other choices were **curiosity** (B), **envy** (C), and **worry** (D).

27. **(A) They will be grateful but will choose their child's name on their own.** (A) is the best answer. All we know about the young couple is that she is pregnant, they have no relatives to help them, and that they are both extremely nice. We can assume that they will be pleased with their neighbors' kindnesses, and gracious enough to listen to their well-meaning suggestions about names. Eliminate (B), which says **they won't need anyone,** and (C), because they have no **parents to turn to.** They will certainly not **refuse the help** of their good-hearted neighbors, (D).

28. **(D)** How do young parents know how to raise their children? **They follow their instincts and the example of loved ones.** (D) is the best choice. Eliminate (A), which says **they never make mistakes,** and (B), because it's not just a matter of **asking the neighbors what to do.** (C), **Letting the kids figure it out for themselves,** is usually a recipe for disaster.

29. **(B) Because losing one's national currency is a little like losing an old friend. They wanted to keep a remembrance or souvenir of the franc.** (B) is the best choice. (A) suggests they were **kept to spend in case the franc should come back into circulation.** (C) **to make buttons** out of them and (D) **to become coin collectors themselves** are not discussed.

30. **(D) There will be lots of new coins to collect.** (D) is the best answer. The gentlemen is happy about the new euro after all because he is, at heart, a collector. He doesn't say that **he was bored with the franc** (A). He doesn't say that **he had never liked Marianne's floppy cap** (B), and he wasn't **more interested in bills** than coins (C).

31. **(C)** Learning a new currency was hardest on **those who had used the franc for the longest time.** (C) is the best answer. The other choices were (A) **young people** and (B) **immigrants,** neither of whom would have had much experience with, or allegiance to, the franc. (D) **Coin collectors** would have had no more difficulty than any other group, and as we saw in the previous question, might have welcomed the change more than most.

32. **(A)** The best place to try to order a proof set of coins is **at the mint**. (A) is the best answer. Other choices were (B) **at the cash register,** (C) **at the bank,** and (D) **at the stock exchange.**

33. **(C)** **Dutilleul is not married.** (C) is the correct answer. We know that he lives alone in *un petit appartement de célibataire*, **a little bachelor apartment.** We rule out answer (A), that he has been married **since the age of 43,** and (B), that **his wife works in the Bureau of Records.** We must also eliminate answer (D) because he did not marry in order to put himself **under great stress, as prescribed by his physician.**

34. **(A)** The author clearly **pokes fun** at doctors. (A) is the correct answer. The tone is tongue-in-cheek and gently mocking. The doctor's diagnosis is a lengthy, impossible-to-decipher mishmash of medical terms, meant to impress and confuse his poor patient. His prescription for intense overwork along with pills containing rice flour and centaur hormones rounds out the portrait of a charlatan.

35. **(C)** **A rather unremarkable and monotonous life** (C) is the correct answer. Dutilleul's life is one of rigid routine. He is very neat, proper, and dependable; a quiet little nothing of a man. There is nothing **wild** (A), **seedy** (B), or **bohemian** (D) about his existence.

36. **(B)** With Dutilleul walking through walls and swallowing pills made from centaur hormones, this is clearly a **fantasy.** (B) is the correct answer. Rule out (A) **biography,** (C) **novel with real people thinly disguised,** and (D) **criticism.**

37. **(D)** Dutilleul **isn't really sure** how he goes through the wall. Because he doesn't know how it happens, neither does the reader. (D) is the best choice. (A) is a close runner-up because **he was feeling around in the dark** when it first happened, but we don't know if he actually touched the wall, or if he did, how many times.

38. **(C)** Yes, he always wore a little *chapeau melon,* or **bowler,** the classic English businessman's hat. (C) is the best answer. The other choices were (A) **a straw hat,** (B) **a type of beret,** and (D) **no hat at all.**

39. **(B)** The only thing the narrateur reveals about herself in this passage is that she has one child. She is a **mother.** (B) is the best answer. She is not **half French** (A), **from New York** (C), or **Assistant Mayor of Annecy** (D).

40. **(A)** She's telling about a trip she took to Colmar and Annecy. (A) is the correct answer. She mentions watching the Bastille Day parade **live** from Paris, but doesn't say she went there. There is nothing to suggest she went to Normandy or Manhattan.

41. **(D)** St-Cyr is a **military school.** (D) is the correct answer. We realize this when we read that 200 West Point cadets had come to Paris to celebrate St-Cyr's 200th anniversary with their *homologues français,* **their French counterparts.**

42. **(A)** The Statue of Liberty and the bells from Annecy are **both gifts from the people of France to the Americans.**

43. **(B)** **Any parade** will make her cry, she says, and the **wedding ceremony** of her friends in Annecy. The correct answer is (B). She is moved by her **visit to the Bartholdi museum** (A), and by **the gift of the bells** (C), but neither brings her to tears. The **surface area of France,** although small compared to that of the United States (D), is nothing to cry about either.

44. **(B)** Jacques Chirac **came to New York** shortly after 9/11. The correct answer is (B). The narrator reports seeing him with Rudy Giuliani. He did not **tour all of the capitals,** so rule out answer (A). Both (C) and (D) say that he did not come but invited American **firefighters** and **cadets** to Paris.

45. **(C)** The author speaks of France as a slight mother whose robust but awkward young son is larger than she. He bears an unmistakable resemblance to her, and to their common ancestor, liberty. The image **personifies the United States.** The correct answer is (C).

46. **(D)** The author is very fond of France and all things French. The correct answer is (D) **francophone.** The other choices were (A) **historian,** (B) **chauvinist,** and (C) **too tearful to make herself understood.**

47. **(D)** **They all eat except Boule de Suif.** The answer is (D). (A) is wrong, because one person is not eating. (B) is wrong because **the good sisters** are working on their garlic sausage. (C) is wrong because **the countess** is lunching on *pâté* of hare, and a big square of Swiss cheese.

48. **(C)** In her haste **she hasn't brought anything to eat and no one offers to share with her.** (C) is the correct answer. She is not **trying to lose**

weight (A). She is **very hungry,** so (A) is wrong. She didn't mind **eating while riding** the day she did have her provisions with her so (D) is wrong.

49. **(B)** **She shared everything that she had in her basket with them.** (B) is the correct answer. She shared an enormous feast that included, among other things, two whole chickens and four bottles of Bordeaux. Therefore (A) is wrong. (C) and (D) are both wrong because no one refused and all of them partook.

50. **(C)** She is **livid, burning with a silent but piercing anger.** The answer is (C). It is not **timidity** that keeps her quiet (A). She is not **indifferent** (B) or **detached** (D). She is furious and deeply offended.

51. **(A)** She calls them **upstanding wretches.** Their behaviour is *gredin,* **mean** and **underhanded.** She uses *honnêtes,* **decent** and **honorable,** ironically. They are hypocrites and she despises them. The correct answer is (A).

52. **(C)** They eat in front of her as though she weren't even present. They do not acknowledge her previous generosity. They deny her **humanity.** She cries **because she is so hurt by their callous disdain.** The correct answer is (C).

53. **(C)** The author's detailed description of the food and its aroma heightens the anguish of the simple, good-hearted little woman who is watching them eat while she is hungry and has nothing. The reader cannot help but take her side. The correct answer is (C).

54. **(B)** Their behavior **is reprehensible and shows their utter lack of humanity.** The correct answer is (B).

55. **(A)** **The weather is beautiful and cool.** There's a refreshing breeze. The correct answer is (A). The sky is not **cloudy** (B). It is not **winter** (C). It's sunny, not **gray** (D).

56. **(A)** Yes, she is a return customer. She has even brought her empty stoneware crock to be refilled. The correct answer is (A).

57. **(D)** She is **surprised** that her flight has been cancelled **but she's not upset at all.** She's actually happy about it because she doesn't really want to leave Paris yet. The correct answer is (D).

58. **(B)**   She's ordered a salad of citrus fruits and a coffee with cream. There's not much to it but it's delicious. The correct answer is (B). She did not order **an expensive lunch with many elegant courses** (A). She is not having **shrimp** (C). She did not order **the special of the day with drink and dessert included** (D).

59. **(A)**   All three shops are **near the Madeleine,** where she lit a candle and said a prayer. The correct answer is (A).

60. **(B)**   We know that **she doesn't really want to leave Paris** (*hélas*), and that she prayed briefly at the Madeleine. She laughs because **it's as if God had answered her prayer.** The correct response is (B).

61. **(C)**   The correct answer is (C). The **hazelnut,** along with the other nuts and the avocado, is considered a fatty, or oil-bearing, "fruit." The other choices, (A) **seafood,** (B) **veal,** and (D) **egg yolk,** are not.

62. **(B)**   Yogurt is a **dairy product.** The correct answer is (B).

63. **(C)**   The best source of dietary fiber would be answer (C), **a fruit or a vegetable.** Not **cheese** (A), **poultry** (B), or **egg** (D).

64. **(B)**   **Mollusks** (A), **crustaceans** (C), and **shellfish** (D) are all seafood. **Avocados** are not. The correct answer answer is (B).

65. **(D)**   Nutrients are released during **the digestion process** of food that has been consumed. The correct answer is (D).

66. **(B)**   Only fatty fish are cited as providing vitamin D; therefore the correct answer is (B) **some fish,** not (A) **all fish,** (C) **eggs,** or (D) **simple sugars.**

67. **(A)**   The article cites red meat as being a good source of **iron.** The correct answer is (A). Red meat is not acknowledged as being a good source of **calcium** (B), **dietary fiber** (C), or **essential fatty acids** (D).

68. **(C)**   It is **not as readily absorbed** as iron from an animal source. The best answer is (C).

69. **(D)**   The best way to ensure that one gets enough of the essential fatty acids is to **eat fish often.** The correct answer is (D).

70. **(A)** He refers to the **Declaration of the Rights of Man and Citizen,** which states that all citizens are equal in the eyes of the law. The correct answer is (A).

71. **(D)** The man with the horrible appearance insists on his right to look at himself in the mirror, thus exposing himself to the painful knowledge that he is hideous. (D) is the correct answer. **The law cannot protect us from ourselves.**

72. **(A)** The author presents his conundrum with wit. It is **clever** and **ironic.** He knows neither side of the argument can be denied. The correct answer is (A). He also seems to enjoy the dilemma.

73. **(B)** The narrator tells the hideous man that he shouldn't look at himself because **he won't like his reflection.** The correct answer is (B).

74. **(A)** The man with the dreadful appearance feels that it's his right to look at himself, a right guaranteed by the law, and so he will look at himself no matter how displeasing it may be. The correct answer is (A).

75. **(B)** or **(A)** On the surface, the question the author deftly poses to the reader is (B) **Who is right,** the narrator or the hideous man? On another level, he seems to ask **whether we recognize an essential duality in the nature of things** (A). Either answer is acceptable. His use of the mirror is an excellent ploy to convey these divergent realities.

Section II
Part A: Writing

Fill In a Word

1.   *que*
    Que completes this conjunction, meaning **ever since**.

2.   *à*
    The verb *penser* requires the preposition *à* when it means, **to think of** or **about**, if an opinion is not going to follow. If that were the case, *penser* would require *de*.

3.   *de*
    Essayer requires the preposition *de* in front of an infinitive.

4.   *du*
    The partitive is needed here. Michel makes **some** progress.

5.   *dans* (or *en*)
    Dans is the preposition of choice when **in** refers to a period of time that has not yet taken place. *En* is also possible.

6.   *en*
    The pronoun *en* stands for an inanimate object of the preposition *de* (*être content de*).

7.   *d'*
    Here the *d'* added to *ailleurs* changes its meaning from **elsewhere** to **besides**.

8.   *dont*
    Dont is the only relative pronoun possible here, that is, for an object introduced by *de* (*être fier de*).

9.   *ce*
    Ce is needed here to complete the subordinating conjunction **until:** *jusqu'à ce que*.

10. *à*
    Songer requires *à* before an infinitive.

11. *d'*
    The immediate past is created by inserting *de* between *venir* and an infinitive: **Mom has just . . .**

12. *que*

The verb *exiger* (**to demand, to require**) is always followed by the subordinating conjunction *que* + <u>subjunctive</u> if the coming verb is conjugated and not in the infinitive. Were an infinitive to follow, *exiger* would take *de*.

13. *de*

The preposition *de* is frequently used after a past participle acting as an adjective. Here it means **covered with dust**.

14. *ce*

Ce completes the relative pronoun *ce qui*, or **which**.

15. *Quelle*

The interrogative adjective serves here to make an exclamation in French. Note the lack of article in the construction: **What a tiresome, boring task!** Like all adjectives, *quelle* reflects the gender and number of the noun it modifies.

Fill In a Verb

1. *est devenue*

Use the *passé composé* for an action whose beginning takes place within the sentence. If the passage were part of a more formal literary text, the *passé simple* would be used instead.

2. *a eu*

Use the *passé composé* for an action whose ending takes place within the sentence.

3. *a fallu*

Although the trips to Monoprix were repeated (*plusieurs* trajets = **numerous trips**), the goal of putting together her outfit has been accomplished.

4. *sortait*

Jour après jour and *toujours* make clear that this action was repeated many times. Use the <u>imperfect</u>.

5. *exigeait*

This sentence further clarifies her repeated behavior. In English the verb is translated as **she would demand.** Use the <u>imperfect</u>.

6. *faisaient*

The female merchants **used to** or **would** curtsy. Use the <u>imperfect</u>.

7. *saluait*

The baker **would** greet her with flair. Use the <u>imperfect</u>.

8. *réservait*

Use the <u>imperfect</u> because M. LaFitte did these actions **daily.** *Quotidien* is a clue!

9. *offrait*

Again, use the <u>imperfect</u> for a habitual action.

10. *mettre*

Use the <u>infinitive</u> form to follow a modal verb.

11. *empoigner*

This also follows a modal verb, so the <u>infinitive</u> form is needed.

12. *s'est terminé*

Use the *passé composé* for an action that ends within the sentence.

13. *a étalé*

Use the *passé composé* to express what her mother **did.** Don't be misled by *habituels,* which refers to her **usual** attire.

14. *a prononcé*

Use the *passé composé* to express what Caroline **said.**

15. *aille*

Use the <u>subjunctive</u> after the subordinating conjunction *où que*.

Part B

Two Sample Essay Answers

Read the following essays to see how a student might have answered this question. You will note different ability levels in the two responses. Try to critique the essays yourself and then read the evaluations that follow to get a feel for how they would be graded.

Sample Essay 1

Il n'y a pas de doute que les jeunes évoluent beaucoup. On entend souvent l'expression "Ah! Les jeunes d'aujourd'hui!" Ils paraissent plus rebelles qu'ils ne l'étaient avant et selon certains, moins bien élevés. Je crois que cela est du à la croissante importance de la presse dans notre société. En effet, les jeunes sont plus au courant qu'ils ne l'étaient avant des évènements qui ont lieu dans le monde. Alors, ils se rendent compte de ce qu'ils vont hériter.

Je crois qu'en effet, ils sentent le besoin de s'assurer de l'efficacité du système, car ce sont eux qui seront les victimes des erreurs d'aujourd'hui. C'est leur devoir de se tenir informés du fonctionnement du monde puisqu'ils devront un jour être en charge eux-mêmes sans l'aide de leurs parents.

Cependant, ils semblent parfois ignorer que le monde ne leur appartient pas encore. Ils ne se rendent pas toujours compte de l'importance de "l'expérience" qu'ont ceux qui ont vécu plus longtemps et ont parfois du mal à simplement faire confiance aux gens plus âgés quand cela est nécessaire.

Sample Essay 2

Je suis d'accord avec cette opinion. Je crois que les jeunes doivent remettre toujours en question l'autorité. Ils ne sont pas l'autorité, mais ils vont l'être. Je crois qu'ils doivent préparer le monde qui est à eux. Je crois que les jeunes sont le futur et qu'ils sont responsables du monde.

Je crois que ce que font les gens aujourd'hui est important pour ce que le monde va être plus tard. Ils doivent faire attention qu'ils sont contents. S'ils ne sont pas contents aujourd'hui, il va être trop tard pour changer plus tard, et alors ils ne seront pas contents plus tard.

Je crois que même si les vieux sont responsables aujourd'hui, les jeunes sont les vrais responsables parce que le monde va être à eux plus tard. Les vieux doivent savoir que les jeunes ont le droit de décider des choses parce que le monde va être à eux. Quand les vieux ne sont plus là, il faut que les jeunes soient biens tout seuls. Alors il faut que les jeunes remettent en question l'autorité pour être surs que l'autorité sera bien quand ils seront vieux et qu'ils auront le monde.

Evaluation of Sample Essay 1

This student has written a coherent essay in which he attempts to answer the question in a nice, direct, matter-of-fact style. The student deftly and correctly employs the phrase *qu'ils ne l'étaient avant*. This demonstrates very good mastery of many elements. However, the identical phrase is then repeated, and that is a detractor. A different turn of phrase would have been a better choice.

There is an accent mark missing on the past participle of *devoir*, *Je crois que cela est dû*, but it is a small error. The student earns high marks for supporting his opinions nicely. The student is a skilled speller and is remarkably adept at showing agreement. Although it is not a perfect essay, it is quite well written and would probably earn a satisfactory score.

Evaluation of Sample Essay 2

The second essay is mediocre. The student fills up space by restating portions of the question. The essay is disorganized and very repetitive. The sentence *il va être trop tard pour changer plus tard, et alors ils ne seront pas contents plus tard* is a clunker! Although it doesn't contain any technical errors, one wonders whether the student bothered to reread it to see how it sounds. There are a few bright spots, but the overall impression is that the student used a lot of words to say very little. It would not receive more than a middling score.

Part C: Sample Answers to Speaking Questions

Perdre du Poids

Here is how a student might have answered the questions that accompany the sketches:

(1) Une jeune femme hésite devant le pèse-personne. Elle s'est enveloppée d'une serviette en éponge et on voit son embonpoint. Elle est dodue. C'est le 2 janvier. Elle aura résolu de perdre du poids.

On voit qu'elle pèse soixante-dix kilos.

Elle résout de ne plus manger de choses calorifiques. Elle semble dire au revoir à la pizza. Il n'y aura plus de bonbons, plus de glaces, plus de desserts sucrés.

Le temps passe. C'est le 2 février. Elle mange des carottes, elle boit de l'eau. Elle s'entraîne. On la voit courir dans la rue.

Deux mois se sont écoulés. Elle se pèse de nouveau. Elle est visiblement plus mince. Elle sourit parce qu'elle est contente de son effort et de son résultat. Elle pourra même mettre son maillot de bain assez révélateur.

(2) Ce n'est pas facile parce que c'est long. On ne voit pas l'effet du jour au lendemain. Il faut se priver pendant longtemps. Si on relâche son effort une fois, il est difficile de reprendre la volonté de continuer. Les gens nous invitent. Les fêtes se succèdent. Il est extrêmement dur de rester fidèle à son régime.

(3) Je crois que le mot clé c'est la persévérance; qu'il s'agisse d'un régime ou d'un autre but personnel. La patience y est pour beaucoup aussi. Atteindre un but, faire un changement permanent dans sa vie, c'est long. On y arrive péniblement, pas à pas. Il ne faut pas se décourager. On doit être jusqu'au-boutiste, fidèle à son idée même quand ce n'est plus facile.

Au Volant

Here is how a student might have answered the questions that accompany the sketches:

(1) Le jeune homme au volant ne porte pas de ceinture de sécurité; son passager non plus. C'est la chose la plus frappante selon moi, puisque je mets automatiquement ma ceinture chaque fois. Il tient son portable à la main gauche. Il ne regarde même pas la route devant lui; il parle à la jeune fille à côté. Il est évident qu'ils sont en train de manger, de parler, et d'écouter de la musique. Je vois deux pailles dans la boisson, ce qui indique qu'il doit tourner la tête vers la droite pour boire. La fille ne fait pas attention à la route non plus. Personne ne regarde la route ! Le rétroviseur est de travers, et ainsi inutile.

Le second conducteur a attaché sa ceinture de sécurité. La jeune fille qui l'accompagne a bouclé la sienne également. Il tient très fermement le volant des deux mains. Lui et son passager regardent droit devant eux. Ils font attention à la route, à la circulation, à leur chemin. Il n'y a pas de distractions dangereuses à l'intérieur de la voiture. On ne mange pas. S'il y a de la musique, elle n'est pas trop forte. Si quelqu'un klaxonne, ou s'il y a une sirène, il l'entendra. Le rétroviseur est positionné de façon à être utile. On ne voit pas de portable.

(2) Le passager peut aider le conducteur avec les directions ou bien si on cherche une adresse. Il ne faut pas qu'il détourne l'attention de la route. Son comportement peut nuire s'il bouge beaucoup, s'il crie ou rigole trop fort. S'il tire l'attention du conducteur sur lui-même, ça peut mener à un accident.

(3) Le jeune homme qui ne fait pas attention à la route est celui qui risque de percuter sa voiture. Au volant on conduit, rien d'autre !

PRACTICE TEST 2

AP French
Practice Test 2

ANSWER SHEET

1. (A) (B) (C) (D)	26. (A) (B) (C) (D)	51. (A) (B) (C) (D)
2. (A) (B) (C) (D)	27. (A) (B) (C) (D)	52. (A) (B) (C) (D)
3. (A) (B) (C) (D)	28. (A) (B) (C) (D)	53. (A) (B) (C) (D)
4. (A) (B) (C) (D)	29. (A) (B) (C) (D)	54. (A) (B) (C) (D)
5. (A) (B) (C) (D)	30. (A) (B) (C) (D)	55. (A) (B) (C) (D)
6. (A) (B) (C) (D)	31. (A) (B) (C) (D)	56. (A) (B) (C) (D)
7. (A) (B) (C) (D)	32. (A) (B) (C) (D)	57. (A) (B) (C) (D)
8. (A) (B) (C) (D)	33. (A) (B) (C) (D)	58. (A) (B) (C) (D)
9. (A) (B) (C) (D)	34. (A) (B) (C) (D)	59. (A) (B) (C) (D)
10. (A) (B) (C) (D)	35. (A) (B) (C) (D)	60. (A) (B) (C) (D)
11. (A) (B) (C) (D)	36. (A) (B) (C) (D)	61. (A) (B) (C) (D)
12. (A) (B) (C) (D)	37. (A) (B) (C) (D)	62. (A) (B) (C) (D)
13. (A) (B) (C) (D)	38. (A) (B) (C) (D)	63. (A) (B) (C) (D)
14. (A) (B) (C) (D)	39. (A) (B) (C) (D)	64. (A) (B) (C) (D)
15. (A) (B) (C) (D)	40. (A) (B) (C) (D)	65. (A) (B) (C) (D)
16. (A) (B) (C) (D)	41. (A) (B) (C) (D)	66. (A) (B) (C) (D)
17. (A) (B) (C) (D)	42. (A) (B) (C) (D)	67. (A) (B) (C) (D)
18. (A) (B) (C) (D)	43. (A) (B) (C) (D)	68. (A) (B) (C) (D)
19. (A) (B) (C) (D)	44. (A) (B) (C) (D)	69. (A) (B) (C) (D)
20. (A) (B) (C) (D)	45. (A) (B) (C) (D)	70. (A) (B) (C) (D)
21. (A) (B) (C) (D)	46. (A) (B) (C) (D)	71. (A) (B) (C) (D)
22. (A) (B) (C) (D)	47. (A) (B) (C) (D)	72. (A) (B) (C) (D)
23. (A) (B) (C) (D)	48. (A) (B) (C) (D)	73. (A) (B) (C) (D)
24. (A) (B) (C) (D)	49. (A) (B) (C) (D)	74. (A) (B) (C) (D)
25. (A) (B) (C) (D)	50. (A) (B) (C) (D)	75. (A) (B) (C) (D)
		76. (A) (B) (C) (D)

AP French
Practice Test 2

Total Test Time—2 hours and 30 minutes

SECTION I: Multiple Choice

Time–1 hour and 25 minutes

Part A: Listening

(Approximate time–25 minutes)

Exchanges

Directions: Listen to the following series of brief exchanges between two speakers. You will hear each exchange twice. Then, based on what you have just heard, choose the most likely rejoinder from the four choices you are given below. Blacken the corresponding letter on your answer sheet.

CD 3, Track 1: Exchange Numbers 1–15

1. (A) C'est le gagnant du tour qui porte le maillot jaune.

   (B) Super ! Nous aurons le temps de voir les deux émissions avant de dîner.

   (C) On a déjà trop de feuilles.

   (D) Tu crois que ça suffit ?

2. (A) Je ne sais pas très bien la manœuvrer.

   (B) Elle accueille aisément quatre personnes.

   (C) N'est-ce pas ?! Voici la clé. Allez, viens, tu peux faire l'essai de route !

   (D) Les sièges sont larges et l'intérieur est spacieux.

3. (A) Il va mieux mais les deux yeux sont très pochés.

   (B) Il sera à l'hôpital pour des mois.

   (C) En fait, il respire mieux maintenant.

   (D) Il est beau à en mourir.

4. (A) D'accord, mais c'est plus intéressant à quatre. Je bats.

   (B) D'accord, voici l'échiquier et les pièces.

   (C) Mais non, il manque le fou noir !

   (D) Mais non, on n'a pas assez de temps !

5. (A) Elle est sûrement morte.

   (B) Quelle bonne astuce ! Elle roule !

   (C) Je crois que c'est irréparable.

   (D) Je vais la jeter dans la poubelle !

6. (A) Nous aurions pu être riches !

   (B) La moisson se fait tard cette année.

   (C) Pourquoi les as-tu endommagés ?

   (D) Je ne sais plus les titres.

7. (A) . . . gêné !

   (B) . . . confus !

   (C) . . . âgé !

   (D) . . . orgueilleux !

8. A) Je refuse leur invitation.

   (B) Comment ? Il ne fait jamais chaud en Provence.

   (C) Ne t'inquiète pas. Il fait frais le soir et en plus ils ont la clime.

   (D) Tu prendras une pilule.

9. (A) Hâtons-nous de finir et j'inviterai tout le monde pour la fête des rois.

    (B) D'accord, c'est donc certain pour le Nouvel An.

    (C) Ça va alors pour les étrennes.

    (D) Meilleurs vœux de la saison.

10. (A) C'est vrai, mon petit réveil, mais fais un effort.

    (B) Le train est parti à l'heure.

    (C) C'est parce que je somnolais sur le quai.

    (D) Notre lit est défoncé.

11. (A) Des poissons rouges ?

    (B) Des tricycles alors ? Je leur apprendrai comment les entretenir, et tu n'auras pas à nettoyer un clapier.

    (C) Hmm, un chiot alors ?

    (D) Ben, une chèvre ?

12. (A) C'est facile. Je le ferai moi-même demain matin.

    (B) Il faudra remplacer d'abord le pare-brise.

    (C) C'est facile si tu ouvres le capot.

    (D) Il faudra attacher les ceintures.

13. (A) Tu as peut-être raison . . . et la tenue blanche coûte beaucoup moins cher qu'un cuivre ou un violon.

    (B) Allons en Corée !

    (C) Ils donneront tous les trois des récitals musicaux.

    (D) On aura notre propre trio !

14. (A) Oh Papa, tu es si ringard !

    (B) Merci Papa, tu l'aimeras !

    (C) Toutes mes copines seront jalouses de moi !

    (D) J'ai déjà choisi une boucle diamantée !

15. (A) Oh, pardon, je me suis trompée.

    (B) Si ! Tu ronfles et tu m'empêches de dormir. Veux-tu te coucher sur le canapé, je t'en prie !

    (C) Tu es somnambule !

    (D) Fais de beaux rêves, chéri !

Dialogues

> **Directions:** Listen to the dialogues on your CD. After each one you will hear a series of questions based on what you have just heard. Each question is heard twice. Choose the best answer from the four choices provided and blacken the corresponding letter on your answer sheet. You have only 12 seconds to mark your answer.

CD 3, Track 2: Dialogues

Dialogue Number 1: Le Portefeuille

16. Où la dame avait-elle laissé son portefeuille ?

    (A) . . . sur le tableau de bord.

    (B) . . . au fond de son sac.

    (C) . . . au magasin de tout à l'heure.

    (D) . . . à la station-service.

17. Qu'est-ce qu'elle venait de faire ?

    (A) . . . des courses dans un hypermarché.

    (B) . . . l'inspection annuelle de la voiture.

    (C) . . . une conversation au portable.

    (D) . . . le revêtement des sièges.

18. Son mari, va-t-il récupérer le portefeuille à sa place ?

    (A) Oui, tout de suite.

    (B) Non, il n'en a pas envie.

    (C) Pas possible. Il faut qu'elle y aille elle-même.

    (D) Non, il va déballer les achats.

19. Pourquoi son mari cherche-t-il dans la voiture?

    (A) Au début il semble plausible d'y trouver le portefeuille.

    (B) Pour vérifier qu'elle n'ait pas endommagé les sièges.

    (C) Pour chercher le reste des paquets.

    (D) Pour vider le portefeuille de son contenu.

Dialogue Number 2: Le Bleu

20. Selon vous, est-ce que cette fille taquine souvent?

    (A) Non, elle est assez réservée.

    (B) Non, jamais.

    (C) Sans le vouloir, peut-être.

    (D) Oui, constamment.

21. Où était ce bleu?

    (A) au front, entre les yeux

    (B) sur la tempe

    (C) sur le nez

    (D) au-dessus de l'œil gauche

22. Pourquoi ne pouvait-il pas voir le râteau?

    (A) Parce qu'il ne fait jamais attention.

    (B) Parce que la terre était couverte de feuilles.

    (C) Parce que c'était un vieux râteau.

    (D) Parce qu'il avait besoin que quelqu'un l'aide.

23. Où travaillait-il?

    (A) sur une pelouse plantée d'arbres

    (B) dans sa niche de bricoleur

    (C) au sous-sol

    (D) devant la cheminée extérieure

24. Est-il sérieux en demandant si le bleu fait ressortir la couleur de ses yeux ?

    (A) Il cherche un compliment.

    (B) C'est de la vanité masculine.

    (C) Il dit ça pour blaguer.

    (D) Il a les yeux marron.

Dialogue Number 3: Le Prêt

25. Quel est le ton de la femme ?

    (A) moqueur

    (B) encourageant

    (C) dédaigneux

    (D) distrait

26. Que veut dire *PDG* ?

    (A) Prince de Galles

    (B) pattes de grand-père

    (C) président-directeur général

    (D) procureur de guimauve

27. Qu'est-ce qu'il devra faire, ce Monsieur, après l'ouverture de son studio ?

    (A) gagner assez d'argent pour rembourser son emprunt

    (B) ouvrir d'autres succursales

    (C) acheter un cadeau pour sa femme

    (D) changer de cravate

28. Est-ce que sa femme partage ses idées pour l'avenir ?

    (A) Elle ne se mêle pas aux affaires.

    (B) Elle le soutient sincèrement.

    (C) Elle préfère chercher le tire-bouchon.

    (D) Elle ouvrira son propre commerce.

Dialogue Number 4: Au Restaurant

29. La femme se laisse-t-elle convaincre par les propos de son mari ?

    (A) Pas du tout.

    (B) Elle goûtera seulement une bouchée de viande.

    (C) Il réussit à la persuader.

    (D) Elle commence à croire comme lui.

30. Pourquoi ne doit-elle pas prendre de viande ?

    (A) Elle craint la vache folle.

    (B) Elle n'aime pas le gras.

    (C) Elle veut maigrir.

    (D) Elle doit baisser le niveau de ses lipides.

31. Qu'est-ce que c'est que le Charolais ?

    (A) du bœuf renommé pour sa chair tendre

    (B) un vin rouge allant aux entrecôtes

    (C) une cuisson à point

    (D) un plat régional

32. Qu'est-ce qu'elle commande ?

    (A) de la charcuterie

    (B) des pâtes

    (C) des légumes variés

    (D) des fruits de mer

Part B: Reading

> **Directions:** Read the following passages with care. Each segment is followed by a series of questions or statements to be completed. Choose the best answer, according to what you have read, from the four choices provided. Blacken the corresponding letter on your answer sheet.

Questions 33–39

Le Mi-Rhin (blotti entre le Bas-Rhin et le Haut-Rhin) est très peu connu, parce que, si l'on bat la paupière en le passant, on ne le verra guère, tant il est petit. Les citoyens, poupées, marionnettes et quelques pantins montagnards
Ligne sont bien contents et fiers de leur petit royaume riquiquais. Protégé par
(5) des montagnes tout autour, leur lac étincelant bifurqué, Deux Gouttes, se pelotonne entre les collines vosgiennes. Les indigènes y jouissent des quatre saisons, de leurs plats régionaux, et de leurs traditions anciennes.

La patronne bénévole de ce 101ième département de France, c'est la Comtesse Marie-Honnête, seule héritière d'une vaste fortune d'une très ancienne
(10) famille de marionnettes à gaine. Justement, faute de pieds, les générations les unes après les autres, ont-elles pu économiser au point de vue chaussures, puisqu'il n'était pas question de chausser une famille sans-pieds. Aucune dépense chez le cordonnier, ni pour chaussettes, bottes ou sandales portées par un enfant ayant deux pieds, depuis la petite enfance jusqu'à la majorité:
(15) songez-y cher lecteur, et vous saurez comment une famille zérojambiste peut accumuler autant de biens, voire un trésor inestimable, en moins de 700 ans. Issue de cette souche aisée mais sans titre, notre Marie-Honnête n'avait que 18 ans quand elle s'est liée avec Timothée, Comte de Tantpys. Mariée quelques années plus tard, Marie ne savait pas grand'chose du monde, et
(20) même moins au sujet des hommes. Pleine de confiance, souriante, un peu écervelée, elle ne comprenait pas les silences de son mari taciturne, mais croyait y voir un homme sérieux. Elle s'est consacrée à l'enseignement des jeunes de leur pays, à gérer leur petit royaume et aux tâches ménagères qui semblaient remplir sa petite vie. Après une trentaine d'années dans la salle
(25) de classe, elle s'est mise à rêver un peu, à voyager, à écrire et à se lier amitié un peu partout dans le monde entier.

Après la disparition du Comte, on l'appelait tout simplement "la bonne veuve", ce qui lui convenait. Le peuple ne savait pas, cependant, que son mari n'était pas mort, mais tout simplement parti avec quelques midinettes
(30) pour un rendez-vous avec le démon de midi. Après quatre ans de conduite peu seyante, il a fondé un comté de l'autre côté de la montagne, avec une marionnette à fil qui ressemblait si fortement à Marie-Honnête que l'on aurait dit son sosie. On dit que le royaume de l'au-delà est pareil au premier

Ligne   jusqu'au dernier détail, sauf pour l'absence du partenaire original.

(35)   Marie-Honnête, douce de nature et sans rancœur, et qui avait su depuis longtemps faire tourner son petit monde toute seule, se contente de sa petite vie actuelle, de ce côté de la montagne, et profite de son indépendance pour s'épanouir et découvrir des choses dont elle n'aurait jamais rêvées auparavant.

(40)   Récemment elle a eu l'occasion et la chance de voyager avec un groupe de professeurs humains à travers la France. Comme le nain du jardin du père d'Amélie Poulain, elle a eu des aventures. N'ayant ni organes ni estomac, notre héroïne pouvait se régaler de la merveilleuse cuisine française à son gré, sans faire trop attention aux calories. Malheureusement, sa compagne

(45)   humaine en est sortie un peu plus arrondie qu'elle ne l'aimerait. Ne la plaignez-vous pas ? Elle se mettra au régime tandis que la Comtesse garde si aisément sa minceur de jeunesse.

33. Marie-Honnête est d'origine . . .

   (A)   normande.

   (B)   parisienne.

   (C)   alsacienne.

   (D)   basque.

34. Les ancêtres de Marie-Honnête étaient . . .

   (A)   pantins.

   (B)   poupées.

   (C)   nains.

   (D)   riches.

35. Où le mari de la *bonne veuve* est-il enterré ?

   (A)   de l'autre côté de la montagne

   (B)   près de Deux Gouttes

   (C)   il vit toujours

   (D)   dans les Vosges

36. Quels sont les avantages d'être marionnette à gaine?

    (A) On n'a pas besoin de se chausser et on peut manger quoi que ce soit.

    (B) On peut vivre 700 ans.

    (C) On connaîtra personnellement le démon de midi.

    (D) On aura toujours un sosie.

37. Quel métier Marie-Honnête exerçait-elle?

    (A) Elle était tout simplement midinette.

    (B) Elle était professeur.

    (C) Elle était marionnette à fil.

    (D) Elle faisait uniquement du travail bénévole.

38. Comment est-elle devenue Comtesse?

    (A) Elle a épousé un comte.

    (B) C'est un titre honoraire.

    (C) Son royaume est un comté.

    (D) C'était son droit héréditaire.

39. Le Mi-Rhin est il grand en superficie?

    (A) Le Mi-Rhin est plus grand que le Haut-Rhin mais moins grand que le Bas-Rhin.

    (B) Le Mi-Rhin est un département de taille moyenne.

    (C) Le Mi-Rhin est minuscule.

    (D) Le Mi-Rhin est le troisième département en superficie.

Questions 40–46

Cyril se releva d'un bond, honteux, bien entendu. Je me relevai à mon tour, plus lentement en regardant Anne. Elle se tourna vers Cyril et lui parla doucement comme si elle ne le voyait pas: "Je compte ne plus vous revoir", dit-elle. Il ne répondit pas, se pencha sur moi et me baisa l'épaule, avant de s'éloigner. Ce geste m'étonna, m'émut comme un engagement. Anne me fixait, avec ce même air grave et détaché comme si elle pensait à autre chose. Cela m'agaça: si elle pensait à autre chose, elle avait tort de tant parler. Je

Ligne

(5)

me dirigea vers elle en affectant un air gêné, par pure politesse. Elle enleva
machinalement une aiguille de pin de mon cou et sembla me voir vraiment.
Je la vis prendre son beau masque de mépris, ce visage de lassitude et de
désapprobation qui la rendait remarquablement belle et me faisait un peu
peur: "Vous devriez savoir que ce genre de distractions finit généralement
en clinique", dit-elle.

Elle me parlait debout en me fixant et j'étais horriblement ennuyée. Elle
était de ces femmes qui peuvent parler, droites, sans bouger; moi, il me
fallait un fauteuil, le secours d'un objet à saisir, d'une cigarette, de ma jambe
à balancer, à regarder balancer. . . .

    – Il ne faut pas exagérer, dis-je en souriant. J'ai juste embrassé Cyril, cela
    ne me traînera pas en clinique . . .

    – Je vous prie de ne pas le revoir, dit-elle comme si elle croyait à un mensonge.
    Ne protestez pas: Vous avez dix-huit ans, je suis un peu responsable de
    vous à présent et je ne vous laisserai pas gâcher votre vie. D'ailleurs, vous
    avez du travail à faire, cela occupera vos après-midi.

Elle me tourna le dos et repartit vers la maison de son pas nonchalant. La
consternation me clouait au sol. Elle pensait ce qu'elle disait: mes arguments,
mes dénégations, elle les accueillerait avec cette forme d'indifférence pire
que le mépris, comme si je n'existais pas, comme si j'étais quelque chose
à réduire et non pas moi, Cécile, qu'elle connaissait depuis toujours, moi,
enfin, qu'elle aurait pu souffrir de punir ainsi. Mon seul espoir était mon
père. Il réagirait comme d'habitude: "Quel est ce garçon, mon chat? Est-il
beau au moins et sain? Méfie-toi des salopards, ma petite fille". Il fallait
qu'il réagît en ce sens, ou mes vacances étaient finies.

Le dîner passa comme un cauchemar.

    [. . .]

"J'aimerais que vous donniez quelques conseils avisés à votre fille,
Raymond. Je l'ai trouvée dans le bois de pins avec Cyril, ce soir, et ils
semblaient du dernier bien".

Mon père essaya de prendre cela à la plaisanterie, le pauvre. "Que me
dites-vous là? Que faisaient-ils?"

    – Je l'embrassais, criais-je avec ardeur. Anne a cru . . . Je n'ai rien cru du
    tout, coupa-t-elle. Mais je crois qu'il serait bon qu'elle cesse de le voir
    quelque temps et qu'elle travaille un peu sa philosophie.

    – La pauvre petite, dit mon père . . . ce Cyril est gentil garçon, après tout?

    – Cécile est aussi une gentille petite fille, dit Anne. C'est pourquoi je serais
    navrée qu'il lui arrive un accident. Et étant donné la liberté complète
    qu'elle a ici, la compagnie constante de ce garçon et leur désœuvrement,
    cela me paraît inévitable. Pas vous?"

Bonjour tristesse, Françoise Sagan

Ligne
(10)
(15)
(20)
(25)
(30)
(35)
(40)
(45)

40. Quelle sorte d'*accident* Anne craint-elle ?

    (A) un accident de voiture

    (B) une grossesse inattendue ou un mariage prématuré

    (C) un incendie dans le bois des pins

    (D) une noyade

41. Comment décririez-vous l'attitude d'Anne pendant qu'elle affronte Cécile ?

    (A) détachée mais persévérante

    (B) stridente et frénétique

    (C) exagérée et sans fondement

    (D) frivole

42. Pourquoi Cécile se sent-elle *horriblement ennuyée* pendant qu'Anne lui parle dans le bois ?

    (A) Elle n'a pas de fauteuil.

    (B) Elle se trouve face à face avec Anne pendant que celle-ci parle de sa conduite avec Cyril. Personne ne lui avait parlé comme ça avant.

    (C) Elle voulait fumer une cigarette.

    (D) Elle a très peur d'Anne.

43. Comment Anne s'exprime-t-elle ?

    (A) Elle fait allusion à ce qu'elle veut sans le dire.

    (B) Elle est calme, confiante, directe et tenace.

    (C) Elle ménace et crie fort.

    (D) Elle hésite et bégaye.

44. Le bois des pins se trouve près de la maison où Cécile, son père et Anne se sont installés pour . . .

    (A) suivre un stage.

    (B) la nuit.

    (C) vivre.

    (D) passer leurs vacances.

45. D'après Cécile, comment se déroule le dîner ce soir-là ?

    (A) gaiement, avec des plaisanteries

    (B) lentement

    (C) de manière insupportable

    (D) vite

46. Que diriez-vous sur le rapport entre Cécile et son père ?

    (A) Son père est très stricte en ce qui concerne sa fille.

    (B) Son père l'aime bien mais ne sait vraiment pas ce qui se passe entre Cécil et Cyril.

    (C) Son père surveille chaque mouvement qu'elle fait.

    (D) Cécile et son père ne s'entendent pas très bien.

Questions 47–54

Pendant des siècles, les Basques étaient un peuple de pasteurs qui ne s'intéressaient pas vraiment à la mer. Vers la fin du Moyen Âge, les pasteurs ont découvert la mer et ont commencé à quitter leurs côtes. La légende veut *Ligne* que ce soit les Normands qui aient appris aux Basques à construire des (5) bateaux. Cela est possible, car les Normands, descendants des Vikings, et grands marins depuis toujours, descendaient régulièrement jusqu'à la côte basque.

Quoiqu'il en soit, un beau jour, certains bergers se sont transformés en pêcheurs timides. Ils chassaient les baleines dans le Golfe de Biscaye.

(10) Graduellement, les baleines se sont éloignées des côtes et il fallait les poursuivre plus loin. Les marins basques, sans instruments de navigation, allaient de plus en plus loin. Tellement loin qu'ils traversaient l'océan jusqu'à des terres inconnues. Leur seul but: la pêche. Ils n'avaient, semble-t-il, aucun souci d'explorer et encore moins d'annexer de nouveaux mondes.

Ligne

(15)   Un jour, le Génois Christophe Colomb, écoutant le récit d'un marin basque, eut l'idée d'une nouvelle route des Indes. Quelques années plus tard, mais cent ans après les marins Basques, il découvrit l'Amérique. Son pilote était un Basque qui s'appelait Lacotza.

[. . .]

(20)   L'origine de la langue des Basques, euskara, est un mystère que personne n'a encore pu éclaircir. C'est une langue qui ne ressemble à rien de connu. Elle ne ressemble surtout pas au français ni à l'espagnol. Tour à tour les spécialistes ont essayé de l'apparenter à l'hébreu, au japonais, à l'arabe et même à des langues africaines. Toujours sans succès. Mais, ce que les

(25) experts ont découvert, c'est que le basque est probablement la langue la plus ancienne qui se parle dans le monde aujourd'hui.

    Des études faites à l'aide d'ordinateurs ont révélé que le basque se parle par un très petit groupe depuis peut-être 20 000 à 25 000 ans. (Le français n'a pas mille ans.) C'est une langue qui a résisté à la latinisation, la francisation

(30) et à l'hispanisation qui a eu lieu tout autour des Basques.

En Mouvement, Marie Galanti (D.C. Heath and Company)

47. Les Normands sont supposés issus des ancêtres . . .

    (A) basques.

    (B) nordiques.

    (C) génois.

    (D) pasteurs.

48. Que cherchaient les marins basques ?

    (A) les plus grandes créatures marines

    (B) de petits poissons allant à la poêle

    (C) une nouvelle route aux Indes

    (D) de nouvelles terres

49. Les parleurs basques, sont-ils nombreux ?

    (A) La langue vient de disparaître.

    (B) Il y a autant de parleurs basques que de japonais.

    (C) Il y en a très peu, seulement la petite population basque.

    (D) Personne ne le parle. C'est une langue écrite.

50. La langue basque est . . .

    (A) une langue sémitique.

    (B) une langue indo-européenne.

    (C) une langue dont les origines nous restent inconnues.

    (D) une langue moyenâgeuse.

51. Que faisaient-ils, les Basques, avant de découvrir la mer ?

    (A) la pasteurisation

    (B) ils menaient une vie agricole

    (C) ils étaient chasseurs

    (D) ils tenaient des troupeaux de moutons

52. Si un peuple s'hispanise, les gens . . .

    (A) subissent l'influence de la langue espagnole.

    (B) commencent à parler français.

    (C) retiennent leur langue natale.

    (D) oublient leur propre langue.

53. Les marins basques, ont-ils, selon cet auteur, atteint le nouveau monde ?

    (A) Non, ce sont les Vikings qui y sont allés.

    (B) Oui, récemment.

    (C) Oui, 100 ans avant Christophe Colomb.

    (D) Non, ils sont restés surtout dans le Golfe de Biscaye.

54. Est-ce que l'euskara remonte aux langues africaines ?

    (A) Oui, surtout aux langues arabes.

    (B) À vrai dire, on ne le sait pas.

    (C) Non, c'est une langue romane.

    (D) Les origines sont plutôt germaniques.

Questions 55–60

Genévrier *Juniperus communis*—Petit pin pouvant atteindre 6 m de hauteur. Le feuillage vert épineux des arbres femelles est parsemé de petites baies, d'abord vertes, puis bleu-noir à maturation, plus ternes les années suivantes. Les baies contiennent un antiseptique et une huile puissante diurétique utilisée pour soigner la cystite, et, en aromathérapie, pour éliminer les toxines. L'huile diluée peut être frottée sur les tempes pour diminuer les douleurs rhumatismales ou névralgiques mais son utilisation interne doit être effectuée avec grande prudence et jamais pendant une grossesse. Les baies parfument le gin et les sauces. Protégé dans le Nord-Pas-de-Calais.

Saule blanc *Salix alba*—Arbre gris argenté aux branches ascendantes pouvant atteindre 25 m de hauteur. Feuilles étroites, velues et argentées devenant progressivement d'un vert terne à partir du sommet. Les chatons apparaissent avec les feuilles, mâles et femelles sont sur des arbres différents. Pousse au bord des rivières et des cours d'eau. Fraîches ou séchées, l'écorce a été longtemps utilisée pour soigner les rhumes, les douleurs, et aussi comme calmant. À l'origine on a expliqué son efficacité par son aptitude à pousser sans aucun problème dans des endroits humides. Bien connu aujourd'hui comme possédant les composants de base de l'aspirine, laquelle est désormais produite de façon synthétique.

Houblon *Humulus lupulus*—grimpant vivace, souvent cultivé, aux tiges volubiles* pouvant atteindre 6 m de hauteur. Les feuilles opposées sont larges, pourvues de 3 à 5 lobes et couvertes de poils raides. Plantes unisexes, mâles avec des grappes de fleurs rameuses et femelles avec des cônes à l'aspect de papier. Les cônes sont utilisés pour soigner les maladies du foie et du système digestif. Un oreiller rempli de cônes de houblon, est, paraît-il, un remède contre l'insomnie. Le houblon est néanmoins surtout connu pour son utilisation d'agent de goût dans la bière et est cultivé à grande échelle commerciale pour les brasseries. Seules les têtes pourvues de fruits sont utilisées.

Orme *Ulmus rubra* – Arbre à feuilles caduques pouvant atteindre 30 mettre de hauteur. Feuilles profondément incisées et doublement dentées, dont la surface est d'aspect rêche,** la forme ovale avec une base dissymétrique. Les fruits vert-jaune ont l'aspect du papier. Originaire des sous-bois humides de l'Amérique du Nord orientale. L'intérieur de l'écorce est blanc et gluant. Réduite en poudre, elle sert à préparer une tisane épaisse et mucilagineuse pour les maux de gorge, la toux et les ulcères. Également appliquée sur les blessures et les brûlures. Ôter l'écorce interne abîme et peut même tuer l'arbre. L'accroissement des besoins en écorce a provoqué l'utilisation, beaucoup moins efficace, de l'écorce externe.

*volubile = twining
**rêche = rough

Plantes Aromatiques et Médicinales, Poches Nature, B. Press (Les Éditions du Carrousel)

55. Laquelle de ces plantes est une vigne tenace ?

   (A) le genévrier

   (B) le saule

   (C) le houblon

   (D) l'orme

56. Le saule a-t-il des baies ?

   (A) Oui, bleu foncé.

   (B) Non, des chatons.

   (C) Non, des cônes.

   (D) Non, des fruits vert-jaune.

57. Quelle plante prête son goût à une boisson célèbre ?

   (A) le houblon

   (B) le saule

   (C) le genévrier

   (D) l'orme

58. Laquelle de ces plantes serait membre de la famille des pins ?

   (A) le genévrier

   (B) le saule

   (C) le houblon

   (D) l'orme

59. Quel arbre pousse de préférence au bord d'un ruisseau ou d'un fleuve ?

    (A) le genévrier

    (B) le saule

    (C) le houblon

    (D) l'orme

60. Comment sont les feuilles du saule ?

    (A) larges et dentées

    (B) étroites

    (C) dissymétriques

    (D) lisses

Questions 61–71

    – Mesdemoiselles, annonce la mauvaise rousse, sortez vos livres et vos cahiers, nous allons être forcées de nous réfugier à l'école maternelle, provisoirement.

Ligne
(5)   Aussitôt toutes les gamines s'agitent comme si le feu était à leur bas; on se pousse, on se pince, on remue les bancs, les livres tombent, nous les empilons dans nos grands tabliers. La grande Anaïs me regarde prendre ma charge, portant elle-même son bagage dans ses bras, puis elle tire lestement le coin de mon tablier et tout croule.

(10)   Elle conserve son air absent et considère attentivement trois maçons qui se lancent des tuiles dans la cour. On me gronde pour ma maladresse, et deux minutes après, cette peste d'Anaïs recommence la même expérience sur Marie Belhomme qui, elle, s'exclame si bruyamment qu'elle reçoit quelques pages d'histoire ancienne à copier. Enfin notre meute bavarde et piétinante traverse la cour et entre à l'école maternelle. Je fronce le nez:
(15) c'est sale, nettoyé à la hâte pour nous, ça sent encore l'enfant mal tenu. Pourvu que ce *provisoire* ne dure pas longtemps !

    [. . .]

    Nous retournons à l'ancienne classe avec le bruit d'un troupeau de bœufs échappés, et nous transportons les tables, si vieilles, si lourdes, que nous
(20) heurtons et accrochons un peu partout, dans l'espoir qu'une d'elles au moins se disloquera complètement et tombera en morceaux vermoulus. Vain espoir ! Elles arrivent entières; ce n'est pas notre faute.

Claudine à l'école, Willy et Colette

61. Pourquoi, selon vous, les filles doivent-elles changer de salle de classe ?

    (A) L'école maternelle vient d'être rénovée.

    (B) Vus les maçons dans la cour, il s'agit des travaux.

    (C) Leur salle de classe est trop bruyante.

    (D) Leurs tables sont vermoulues.

62. Décrivez ce déménagement.

    (A) C'est ordonné et calme.

    (B) Les jeunes filles sont silencieuses et graves.

    (C) On dirait un ballet gracieux de jeunes filles éphémères.

    (D) C'est un sauve-qui-peut bovin.

63. Décrivez le comportement de la grande Anaïs.

    (A) C'est une gamine méchante.

    (B) Elle est gentille.

    (C) Elle est maladroite à cause de sa taille.

    (D) Elle est distraite.

64. Qui serait la mauvaise rousse ?

    (A) Claudine, la narratrice

    (B) la grande Anaïs

    (C) le professeur

    (D) Marie Belhomme

65. Qui est responsable de transporter les meubles d'une salle de classe à l'autre ?

    (A) les ouvriers de la cour

    (B) les enfants de la maternelle

    (C) les professeurs

    (D) les filles elles-mêmes

66. Est-ce que le professeur surveille de près ce qui se passe entre ses élèves ?

   (A) Elle doit plutôt surveiller les tuiles dans la cour.

   (B) Pas assez bien. Elle gronde un enfant innocent et punit un autre en laissant aller le coupable.

   (C) Aussi bien que possible, étant vu le tumulte.

   (D) Elle est allée préparer l'autre salle.

67. À part les modernités qui nous sont disponibles aujourd'hui, est-ce que ce qui se passe dans une salle de classe a beaucoup changé ?

   (A) Oui. Il n'y a plus de farceurs parmi les élèves.

   (B) Oui. Les élèves sont moins bruyants aujourd'hui.

   (C) Non. De petites scènes entre élèves s'échappent à nos profs aussi et n'importe quelle distraction serait accueillie avec autant d'enthousiasme par nos élèves actuels.

   (D) Non, mais les frasques espiègles n'arrivent plus.

68. Les filles ont-elles réussi à casser une des vieilles tables ?

   (A) Oui, en la heurtant un peu partout.

   (B) Oui, en la piétinant.

   (C) Non, elles sont toutes restées entières.

   (D) Oui, en morceaux vermoulus.

69. Qu'est-ce que c'est que *la meute bavarde et piétinante, le troupeau de bœufs échappés* ?

   (A) Ce sont les élèves.

   (B) Ce sont des animaux tenus à côté de l'école.

   (C) Ce sont les quelques garçons de la classe.

   (D) C'est le son des tuiles qui tombent par terre.

70. Pourquoi Claudine (la narratrice) ne veut-elle pas rester trop longtemps à l'école maternelle ?

   (A) Elle n'aime pas son professeur.

   (B) Elle veut regarder travailler les maçons dans la cour.

   (C) C'est sale et en plus ça sent mauvais.

   (D) Elle ne veut pas qu'on la croie plus jeune qu'elle ne l'est.

71. Cette histoire se déroule en 1899. Que portaient les écolières à l'époque ?

   (A) des sacs à dos

   (B) des uniformes

   (C) de grands tabliers

   (D) des robes courtes

Questions 72–76

Passé Simple—Ce fut midi. Les voyageurs montèrent dans l'autobus. On fut serré. Un jeune monsieur porta sur sa tête un chapeau entouré d'une tresse, non d'un ruban. Il eut un long cou. Il se plaignit auprès de son voisin
Ligne   des heurts que celui-ci lui infligea. Dès qu'il aperçut une place libre, il se
(5)   précipita vers elle et s'y assit.

Je l'aperçus plus tard devant la gare Saint-Lazare. Il se vêtit d'un pardessus et un camarade qui se trouva là lui fit cette remarque: il fallut mettre un bouton supplémentaire.

Télégraphique—BUS BONDÉ STOP JNHOMME LONG COU
(10)   CHAPEAU CERCLE TRESSÉ APOSTROPHE VOYAGEUR INCONNU SANS PRÉTEXTE VALABLE STOP QUESTION DOIGTS PIEDS FROISSÉS CONTACT TALON PRÉTENDU VOLONTAIRE STOP JNHOMME ABANDONNE DISCUSSION POUR PLACE LIBRE STOP QUATORZE HEURES PLACE ROME JNHOMME ECOUTE CONSEILS
(15)   VESTIMENTAIRES CAMARADE STOP DÉPLACER BOUTON STOP SIGNÉ ARCTURUS.

   Tanka—L'autobus arrive
   Un zazou à chapeau monte
   Un heurt il y a
(20)   Plus tard devant Saint-Lazare
   Il est question d'un bouton

Exercices de style, Raymond Queneau

72. Dans son livre, Queneau raconte la même brève histoire 99 fois et de 99 manières différentes. Ces trois extraits témoignent que le lecteur trouvera . . .

   (A) de l'humour dans les permutations du récit.

   (B) plusieurs descriptions de l'état d'âme du jeune homme.

   (C) l'importance de la mise en place d'un bouton.

   (D) que tous les moyens de transports sont serrés à Paris.

73. Plus elle est racontée plus elle devient drôle parce que le lecteur . . .

   (A) commence à aimer les individus mentionnés.

   (B) veut connaître tous les placements possibles d'un bouton.

   (C) anticipe les changements comme s'il s'agissait d'un jeu.

   (D) croit que les évènements vont changer.

74. À part les changements de style, l'histoire est tout à fait . . .

   (A) comique.

   (B) banale.

   (C) tragique.

   (D) littéraire.

75. Que peut-on trouver à la Place Rome ?

   (A) la gare Saint-Lazare

   (B) un magasin de chapeaux à tresses

   (C) des italiens aux longs cous

   (D) des boutons de pardessus

76. Chaque récit finit par la mention . . .

   (A) du bouton de son pardessus.

   (B) de son chapeau.

   (C) de la place libre.

   (D) de son cou.

SECTION II: Free Response
Time–1 hour and 5 minutes

Part A: Writing
Time–20 minutes

Fill In a Word

Directions: In each sentence a single word has been omitted and replaced by a line. Write your answer, **one** single French word, on the line to the right. Make sure the word is correct in form, as well as in meaning and in context. None of your answers will be verbs.

Please note that a response such as *jusqu'à* (or *ce que*) will be considered two words, not one.

1.

L'été dernier je suis allée à Paris pour améliorer mon français. **1** mon départ j'ai ramassé mes dictionnaires et tous les livres **2** je croyais avoir besoin. Dans ma hâte je n'ai pas pu trouver mon Grevisse, le livre de grammaire **3** je me fiais le plus. Heureusement j'ai pu **4** acheter un nouveau dès mon arrivée. Je suis allée directement à la FNAC pour remplacer mon fidèle Grevisse. Je l'ai trouvé **5** les références.

Contente de mon achat, je suis montée au rayon papeterie pour chercher **6** cahiers quadrillés. J'**7** ai choisi quelques-uns **8** couvertures vives. J'aime noter les mots **9** j'apprends dans ces petits calepins. Une fois rentrée dans ma chambre d'hôtel, je me suis amusée à remplir plusieurs pages **10** que je regardais la télé.

1. _____
2. _____
3. _____
4. _____
5. _____
6. _____
7. _____
8. _____
9. _____
10. _____

2.

De __11__ les ponts __12__ traversent la Seine, __13__ que j'aime le plus, c'est le pont Alexandre III. J'adore ses magnifiques réverbères branchés. Ils font penser __14__ une allée d'arbres __15__ fonte.

11. _____

12. _____

13. _____

14. _____

15. _____

Fill In a Verb

Directions: In each sentence a verb has been omitted and replaced by a line. Supply the missing verb form on the blank to the right. There you will see the infinitive form of the verb you are to use. Read the whole paragraph before choosing your answer. Spelling, agreement, and accent marks must all be accurate for your answer to be correct.

Après __1__ sa tarte aux myrtilles de son moule, Maman l'__2__ près de la fenêtre ouverte pour qu'elle __3__ un peu. Les baies __4__ au soleil et un parfum délicat __5__ au nez. Une belle réussite, elle __6__ se l'avouer. Satisfaite de son effort, elle __7__ faire quelques petites courses. __8__ moins d'une heure plus tard, elle __9__ un clin d'œil vers son œuvre culinaire. Il ne __10__ qu'une croûte creuse! L'auteur de ce crime n'__11__ aucune trace bleue, rien que le pâté en croûte dénudé.

Qui __12__ résister à sa célèbre croûte légère et moelleuse? Tout d'un coup elle __13__ à rire. Elle __14__ vers le jardin, munie d'un pichet d'eau fraîche, sa boîte à recettes et un crayon.

Câline __15__ sous l'ombre du grand chêne. L'énorme caniche blanche __16__ l'air rassasié; son museau bleuâtre __17__ rire. Maman __18__ l'eau fraîche dans son bol en __19__ "Comment aurais-je pu __20__ ma pâte?"

1. _____ (retirer)
2. _____ (poser)
3. _____ (refroidir)
4. _____ (chatoyer)
5. _____ (monter)
6. _____ (devoir)
7. _____ (sortir)
8. _____ (revenir)
9. _____ (jeter)
10. _____ (rester)
11. _____ (laisser)
12. _____ (pouvoir)
13. _____ (se mettre)
14. _____ (se diriger)
15. _____ (ronfler)
16. _____ (avoir)
17. _____ (faire)
18. _____ (verser)
19. _____ (murmurer)
20. _____ (améliorer)

Part B: Essay

Time–40 minutes

> **Directions:** Develop the following topic in French. Prepare a well-conceived, organized, and coherent essay that demonstrates your mastery of verb tenses and illustrates your command of vocabulary. Expect to write at length because short answers do not score well. Be precise and check your work carefully for accents, spelling, and agreement.
>
> Essays are evaluated for grammatical accuracy, range, and choice of appropriate vocabulary, as well as organization, style, and mastery of syntax.

Certains affirment que, dans le monde moderne, il est impossible d'être toujours honnête. Partagez-vous cette opinion? Justifiez votre point de vue.

Part C: Speaking

Approximate time–15 minutes

Working with a Series of Sketches: La Glace

Directions: You have one minute and 30 seconds to look at the series of five pictures below and to answer the questions about them that you will hear on CD 3, Track 3.

1. Racontez ce qui arrive dans cette série de dessins. (60 secondes)

2. Bien que les rapports entre frères et sœurs ne soient pas toujours
    harmonieux d'un jour à l'autre, comment la sœur aînée réagit-elle ?
    (60 secondes)

3. D'après vous, quelles sont les responsabilités des aînés envers leurs
    cadets ? (60 secondes)

Working with One or Two Sketches: Les Oignons

> **Directions:** You have one minute and 30 seconds to look at the two pictures below and to answer the questions that you will hear about them on CD 3, Track 4.

1.   Comparez et contrastez ce que vous penseriez si vous voyiez le premier dessin sans voir le suivant. (60 secondes)

2.   Les apparences sont souvent trompeuses. Commentez l'idée de ne pas trop vite tirer une conclusion. (60 secondes)

3.   Avez-vous jamais pleuré de joie ? Pourquoi pleure-t-on si on est heureux ? (60 secondes)

AP French
Practice Test 2

ANSWER KEY

Section I: Multiple Choice
Part A: Listening

Exchanges

1.	(B)	5.	(B)	9.	(A)	13.	(A)
2.	(C)	6.	(A)	10.	(A)	14.	(A)
3.	(A)	7.	(C)	11.	(B)	15.	(B)
4.	(A)	8.	(C)	12.	(A)		

Dialogues

16.	(C)	21.	(A)	26.	(C)	31.	(A)
17.	(A)	22.	(B)	27.	(A)	32.	(C)
18.	(C)	23.	(A)	28.	(B)		
19.	(A)	24.	(C)	29.	(A)		
20.	(D)	25.	(B)	30.	(D)		

Part B: Reading

33.	(C)	44.	(D)	55.	(C)	66.	(B)
34.	(D)	45.	(C)	56.	(B)	67.	(C)
35.	(C)	46.	(B)	57.	(A) or (C)	68.	(C)
36.	(A)	47.	(B)	58.	(A)	69.	(A)
37.	(B)	48.	(A)	59.	(B)	70.	(C)
38.	(A)	49.	(C)	60.	(B)	71.	(C)
39.	(C)	50.	(C)	61.	(B)	72.	(A)
40.	(B)	51.	(D)	62.	(D)	73.	(C)
41.	(A)	52.	(A)	63.	(A)	74.	(B)
42.	(B)	53.	(C)	64.	(C)	75.	(A)
43.	(B)	54.	(B)	65.	(D)	76.	(A)

Section II: Free Response
Part A: Writing

Fill In a Word

1. Avant
2. dont
3. auquel
4. en
5. parmi (*or* dans)
6. des
7. en
8. aux
9. que
10. pendant (*or* alors)
11. tous
12. qui
13. celui
14. à
15. en

Fill In a Verb

1. avoir retiré
2. a posée
3. refroidisse
4. chatoyaient
5. montait
6. a dû (*or* devait)
7. est sortie
8. Revenue
9. a jeté
10. restait
11. avait laissé
12. aurait pu
13. s'est mise
14. s'est dirigée
15. ronflait
16. avait
17. faisait
18. a versé
19. murmurant
20. améliorer

Note: Please see "Detailed Explanations of Answers" for examples of responses to Section II, Part B (Essay) and Part C (Speaking).

Detailed Explanations
of Answers

Practice Test 2
Section I
Part A: Listening

1.   **(B)**   She asks what's on TV. He says Channel 2 has her soap opera at 5 pm, followed by the game show "The Weakest Link." (B) is the most likely response. **Great! We'll have time to see both programs before dinner.**

2.   **(C)**   She's delighted with her new car. He recognizes it as one he's read about and which got excellent reviews. When he sees that she bought a convertible, he's very impressed. She says it's small and very easy to park. That eliminates the idea that she's having trouble **handling it** (A), that **it can easily accommodate four people** (B), and that the **interior is spacious** with **wide seats** (D). **Come on, you can take a test drive** (C) is the best response.

3.   **(A)**   His brother broke his nose yesterday. She says **the poor thing!** and asks how he's doing. The best response is (A) **he's better but he's got two black eyes.** One is not hospitalized **for months** with a broken nose (B). He is not in fact **breathing better** than he did before (C). His looks are not **to die for** at the moment (D).

4.   **(A)**   He asks if she wants to play checkers or chess. She feels he always wins at both games. She suggests Belote, a card game. (A) is the most likely rejoinder: **All right, but it's more fun with four people. I'll shuffle.** This makes more sense than (B) **Here's the chess board and the pieces,** or (C) that **the black bishop is missing.** If they have enough time to play chess, they certainly have **enough time** to play a hand of cards. That eliminates answer (D).

5.   **(B)**   Something's wrong with the mouse; the cursor doesn't respond. He wonders how he will he be able to get online to read his e-mail. She says

it's just dust inside the mouse and tells him how to open and clean it. The most likely answer is (B) **What a good tip; it's moving now!** The mouse is not **dead** (A), nor is it **unfixable** (C). It doesn't need to be **thrown out** (D).

6. **(A)**   The girl tells her father that she saw a Fantomas book just like her grandfather's on the Internet. It was worth 200 euros. No kidding, says her father. Too bad it's the only one I have left. I had to throw the rest of them away due to mildew. (A) **We could have been rich!** is the best answer.

7. **(C)**   The daughter shows her father a funny-looking doll that her grandmother gave her. She's never seen one like it. Her father can't believe she's never heard of Bécassine. This really makes him feel **old!** A child who's never heard of Bécassine in France would be like one who's never heard of Raggedy Ann in the United States. The correct answer is (C).

8. **(C)**   They've been invited to spend time at the home of friends in Provence. The husband doesn't tolerate the heat in the south of France very well. (C) is the wife's most likely rejoinder: **Don't worry, it's cool in the evening, and besides, they have air-conditioning.**

9. **(A)**   Aunt Mireille wants to know whether they can host the family for the traditional Christmas Eve dinner this year. They're doing renovations to their home and the wife wonders whether the work will be finished by then. He says maybe by New Year's Eve. (A) is the best response: **Let's hurry up and finish and I'll invite everyone for King's Day** (Epiphany, January 6th). If the construction won't be finished until New Year's Eve, they most likely won't be ready to entertain the very next day, so answers (B) and (C) are not feasible. Answer (D) **Season's Greetings,** is not a plausible choice either.

10. **(A)**   He's hurrying her as she gets ready to go out. She reminds him that he overslept this morning; if it hadn't been for her he would have missed his train. (A) is the most likely retort: **That's true, my little alarm clock, but make an effort.** He doesn't want to be late tonight.

11. **(B)**   He wants to buy a rabbit for their children to let them have an enjoyable pet and to teach them to be responsible. She thinks it's a bad idea. After the novelty wears off, she'll be the one taking care of it. She asks him to think of another gift. (B) is probably the only suggestion he makes that she'll agree to: **What about tricycles? I'll teach them how to maintain them, and you won't have to clean a rabbit hutch.** The other suggestions,

goldfish (A), a **puppy** (C), and a **goat** (D), are likely to need as much care as a rabbit.

12. **(A)** The driver's side windshield wiper is making an annoying screech. She asks whether it can be fixed. The correct answer is (A) **It's easy, I'll do it myself tomorrow morning.** It's not necessary to replace the whole **windshield** (B). You don't need to **open the hood** to work on a wiper (C). **Seat belts** are not required to change a wiper blade (D).

13. **(A)** Sylvie wants karate lessons. Her mother had hoped she'd learn a musical instrument, like her two brothers. The father says let her do what she wants to do. They have enough musicians. Answer (A) is the most plausible rejoinder: **Maybe you're right . . . and the white outfit will cost a lot less than a horn or a violin.**

14. **(A)** The daughter wants permission to get her navel pierced. Her father says not while he still walks the earth. Her most likely response is (A) **Oh, Dad, you're so old-fashioned!**

15. **(B)** She says he snores. He says she's exaggerating; he just breathes deeply. The best rejoinder is (B): **You do too snore and it's keeping me awake. Would you please sleep on the couch!**

16. **(C)** At first she can't remember where she left her wallet. Eventually she realizes that she must have left it **in the store she's just come from.** (C) is the correct answer.

17. **(A)** She's just done some shopping in a **big-box store** like Wal-Mart. (A) is the correct answer. She didn't **have the car inspected** (B). She wasn't **talking on her cell phone** (C). She didn't **have the seats reupholstered** (D).

18. **(C)** Her husband offers to pick up the found wallet for her, but store policy says she must appear in person to get it back. (C) is the correct answer. **She must go there herself.**

19. **(A)** Her husband goes to look in the car because **it seems a likely place to find the wallet at first.** (A) is the correct answer. It's not **to see whether she's damaged the seats** (B). It's not **to get the rest of the packages** (C). It's not **to empty the wallet of its contents** (D).

20. **(D)**   Yes, she teases him **all the time.** (D) is the correct answer. She is not **reserved** (A). (B) says she **never** teases. (C) says **maybe she does it unknowingly.** While her zingers are not mean-spirited, she does deliver them knowingly and gleefully.

21. **(A)**   The correct answer is (A) **in the middle of the forehead, between the eyes.**

22. **(B)**   He couldn't see the rake **because the ground was covered with leaves** up to his calves. (B) is the best answer.

23. **(A)**   He wasn't working in his **little handyman area** (B). He wasn't **in the basement** (C). There is no mention of a **chimney** (D). He must have been working **on an outdoor surface planted with trees,** such as a lawn. (A) is the correct answer.

24. **(C)**   He is joking when he asks whether she thinks the black-and-blue mark brings out the blue of his eyes. (C) is the correct answer. **He says it to joke around.**

25. **(B)**   The wife is very supportive of her husband on this important day. Her tone is **encouraging**. (B) is the correct answer.

26. **(C)**   **PDG** is the approximate equivalent of **CEO** in English. It stands for general director or president of a company. (C) is the correct answer. The other choices were (A) **Prince of Wales,** (B) **sideburns,** and (D) **procurer of marshmallow!**

27. **(A)**   Once his studio has opened, he'll have **to earn enough money to pay back the loan.** (A) is the best answer. **Opening other branches** (B) might come afterward. Answer (C) is **to buy a gift for his wife,** and (D) is **to change his tie.**

28. **(B)**   Yes, **her support is sincere.** (B) is the best answer. She does share his dream.

29. **(A)**   She is **not convinced at all.** The correct answer is (A). She doesn't think he should order the beef, and she will not eat it herself.

30. **(D)**   Her cholesterol is too high. (D) is the correct answer. **She must lower the level of fats in her blood.**

31. **(A)** Her husband says there is nothing better in the whole world than Charolais beef. Charolais are never herded. They are allowed to graze naturally, in small groups. Their **tender flesh** is the pride of the French beef industry. The correct answer is (A).

32. **(C)** She orders artichokes, grated carrots, and celeriac. (C) is the correct answer: **various vegetables.**

33. **(C)** Marie supposedly comes from the Mi-Rhin. This tiny department would be located between the two real Rhine departments that make up **Alsace.** The correct answer is (C).

34. **(D)** Over the centuries her family was able to amass a great fortune. As finger puppets they never had to buy footwear. The correct answer is (D). They were **rich.**

35. **(C)** Even though the people call her the good widow, **her husband is still alive.** Remarried, he lives on the other side of the Vosges mountains. The correct answer is (C).

36. **(A)** The best answer is (A): **You don't have to wear shoes, and you can eat whatever you want without fear of gaining weight.** The other choices were **You can live 700 years** (B), **You'll get to meet the midlife crisis demon personally** (C), and **You'll always have a double** (D).

37. **(B)** She dedicated herself to the education of children. **She was a teacher.** (B) is the best answer. She was not a *midinette,* a **feather-brained young girl** or **bimbo** (A). She was not a **string puppet**, like her former husband's second wife (B). (D) says **she only did volunteer work,** but we know she spent 30 years in the classroom.

38. **(A)** Her husband was titled. **She married a count.** (A) is the best answer. It was not **an honorary title** (B), and she did not **inherit** the title. Eliminate answers (C) and (D). Her family was wealthy but not noble.

39. **(C)** The Mi-Rhin is so **tiny** that you will miss it if you blink your eyes when you pass by. (C) is the best answer.

40. **(B)** Anne is not worried about a **car accident** (A), **a fire in the pine forest** (C), or **a drowning** (D). She thinks Cécile and Cyril spend entirely

too much time together unsupervised. She fears **an unplanned pregnancy or teenage marriage.** The correct answer is (B).

41. **(A)**   She does not scream; she is not **agitated** (B). She did discover the young couple alone together in the pine forest. *Ils semblaient du dernier bien* suggests they were in an intimate embrace. Eliminate answers (C) and (D) because her worries are not **unfounded** or **frivolous.** When she confronts Cécile she is very controlled. Her manner is very cool and detached, but she is relentless. The best answer is (A) **detached but tenacious.**

42. **(B)**   When Cécile says she hopes for her father's **usual** reaction to her behavior with this young man, we sense that he has been quite permissive up to this point. He has never set limits and never asked many questions about what she's been up to. She is quite unused to parental control, and she finds it very unsettling. The best answer is (B): **She is face to face with Anne, who confronts her about her conduct with Cyril. No one had ever spoken to her like that before.**

43. **(B)**   She is **direct, calm,** and **unrelenting.** The correct answer is (B).

44. **(D)**   Anne speaks of the complete freedom Cécile has **here.** This suggests they are not currently at their permanent residence. *Le désœuvrement,* **the idleness** of the two teenagers suggests an unstructured day. They are not in school. (D) is the best answer. They have come to this house **on vacation.**

45. **(C)**   The dinner feels like **a nightmare,** *un cauchemar,* to Cécile. The best answer is (C). It is **unbearable.**

46. **(B)**   Cécile's father is not **strict,** (A). He does not **keep watch over every move she makes** (C). She and her father get along fine, so (D) can't be right. The best answer is (B): **Her father loves her but doesn't really know what's going on between Cécile and Cyril.**

47. **(B)**   The text tell us that the Normans, descendants of the Vikings, taught the Basques how to build boats. The correct answer is (B) **Nordic.**

48. **(A)**   The early Basque fishermen were looking for whales in the Bay of Biscay. The correct answer is (A) **the largest sea creatures.**

49. **(C)** Euskara has not **just disappeared** (A). There are not **as many speakers of this language as there are speakers of Japanese** (B). It is a spoken language, not just **written.** Eliminate answer (D). The best answer is (C). **There are very few speakers of Euskara, only the small Basque population.**

50. **(C)** Euskara has stumped the experts for centuries. Because it does not fit into **any** known family of languages, **its origins remain unknown** to us. The best answer is (C).

51. **(D)** They did not **sterilize milk** (A). They did not **farm** (B). They were not **hunters** (C). **They kept flocks of sheep.** The correct answer is (D).

52. **(A)** The correct answer is (A). They **undergo the influence of the Spanish language and culture.**

53. **(C)** She reports that they reached the New World **100 years before Christopher Columbus.** The correct answer is (C).

54. **(B)** No one has been able to prove that Euskara dates back to Africa. There is no evidence to suggest that its origin is **Arabic** (A). It is not a **Romance language** (C). It is not **Germanic** (D). The correct answer is (B) **To tell the truth, we don't know.**

55. **(C)** Only one plant is described as a clinging vine. The correct answer is (C) **hops.**

56. **(B)** The willow does not have berries. It has downy, hanging flowers called **catkins.** The correct answer is (B).

57. **(A) or (C)** **Juniper** berries are used to flavor gin (A). **Hops** is an ingredient in beer (C). Both answers are correct.

58. **(A)** Only the **juniper** is an evergreen or conifer. The correct answer is (A).

59. **(B)** The **willow** likes to grow beside rivers and streams. The correct answer is (B).

60. **(B)**   The leaves are (B) **narrow.** They are not **broad and toothed** (A). They are not **asymmetric** (C). They are **fuzzy**, *velues,* not **smooth** (D).

61. **(B)**   **What with builders** throwing tiles in the courtyard below, the students are probably **vacating** their classroom for some kind of construction project. The correct answer is (B). We know **the kindergarten is not freshly renovated** (A). The girls **cause the noise** in their classroom, so (C) is not the answer. (D) is also wrong because they take **their worm-eaten tables** with them.

62. **(D)**   It's like a stampede of **cattle** when the girls exit their classroom. They're loud, they push and trample, and they bump into things, pinch each other, and drop their books as they go. (D) is the correct answer. It is not **orderly** (A). They are not **quiet and serious** (B). Their movement in no way resembles a **graceful ballet** (C).

63. **(A)**   Anaïs is a **nasty** troublemaker with a knack for getting away with her pranks. (A) is the correct answer.

64. **(C)**   Claudine refers to her **teacher** as **the bad redhead.** The correct answer is (C).

65. **(D)**   The correct answer is (D). **The girls** move the tables into the kindergarten room.

66. **(B)**   The teacher is **not watching closely enough** to see that Anaïs caused both Claudine and Marie Belhomme to drop their books. They had piled them into their big aprons in order to carry them. Anaïs pulled on each apron to make all of books give way. The teacher scolded Claudine for her clumsiness and assigned extra work to Marie, who had let out a yell when Anaïs tugged on her apron. The correct answer is (B).

67. **(C)**   (A) is not correct because there are still **practical jokers** today. Students are just **as noisy today** as they were when Claudine was in school, so (B) is not correct. **Mischievous pranks** still take place, so (D) is wrong. The correct answer is (C). **Teachers still sometimes miss what's going on, and kids still welcome with enthusiasm any kind of distraction.**

68. **(C)**   The correct answer is (C). **All of the tables remained intact,** in spite of their poor, worm-eaten condition and the rough handling of the girls who banged them into everything as they moved them.

69. **(A)** The author describes the girls as a loud and trampling pack of hounds. She also refers to them as herd of escaped oxen. (A) is the correct answer; she's referring to **the students.** There are no real **animals nearby** (B). There aren't any **boys in the class** (C). She's not referring **to the sounds made by tiles dropping** (D).

70. **(C)** She doesn't want to stay because **it's so dirty and it smells bad.** (C) is the correct answer.

71. **(C)** The correct answer is (C): the girls wore **big pinafores** to school. These were large aprons that covered the bodice as well as the skirt and were worn over one's regular dress. They didn't wear **backpacks** (A), **uniforms** (B), or **short dresses** (D).

72. **(A)** Queneau retells the same story in a variety of literary styles. The reader is entertained as the same tale reappears, each time in new garb. The **variations** are often **funny.** (A) is the correct answer.

73. **(C)** The reader knows that none of **the events in the story will change,** so (D) is not the correct answer. We never learn much at all **about the characters,** so (A) is not correct. No one is really that interested in **button placement** (B). The correct answer is (C) **The reader begins to anticipate the changes the author will make as though it were a game.**

74. **(B)** The actual story, which is told over and over again, is not in itself **funny** (A). It is not **tragic** (C) or **literary** (D). It is utterly **ordinary** and **mundane.** The correct answer is (B).

75. **(A)** We know that the story is the same, no matter how it is told. If *Saint-Lazare* is mentioned as the location in two excerpts and *Place Rome* in the other one, they must be the very same location. (A) is the correct answer.

76. **(A)** All 99 variations end with the young man's friend suggesting that he move **the button on his overcoat,** this being said in front of the *gare Saint-Lazare*, *Place Rome*. The correct answer is (A).

Section II
Part A: Writing

Fill In a Word

1. *Avant*

   The context of the sentence suggests the need for the preposition *avant* to specify that these activities took place **before** departure.

2. *dont*

   We use the relative pronoun *dont* to link **the books** to the verbal expression *avoir besoin de* (**to need**). This is the case because **the books** are the object of the preposition *de*.

3. *auquel*

   A relative pronoun is needed to connect **the grammar book** to the clause **I trusted the most.** Because this verb, *se fier,* requires *à* before an infinitive, we contract *à* + *lequel* to create *auquel,* literally **to which.**

4. *en*

   Happily I was able to buy another one **of them.**

5. *parmi* (or *dans*)

   The preposition *parmi* expresses **among.** *Dans* means **in.**

6. *des*

   Use the partitive article to express **some graph paper notebooks.**

7. *en*

   The pronoun *en* stands for the object of the preposition *de* in a number expression. **I chose a few of them.**

8. *aux*

   The preposition *à* contracts with *les* in this common construction to mean **with bright covers.**

9. *que*

   The two clauses connect smoothly with a relative pronoun. Although both *qui* and *que* can be translated as **which,** we must choose *que* to reflect that **the words** *(les mots)* are the object of the verb **to learn** *(apprendre).*

10. *pendant* (or *alors*)

    The preposition *pendant,* when used with *que,* creates the conjunction **while,** or **at the same time.** *Alors que* also works.

11. ***tous***

We know from the context of the sentence that the adjective **all** is needed. *Tous* agrees with the masculine plural *ponts.*

12. ***qui***

A relative pronoun is needed to connect **the bridges** to the clause that follows. This time we need *qui* to convey that **the bridges** is the <u>subject</u> of the verb *traverser.*

13. ***celui***

The masculine singular demonstrative pronoun *celui* is used to mean **the one.** It is followed by the relative pronoun *que* (**which**) as the <u>object</u> of the verb *aimer.*

14. ***à***

The verb *penser,* when not used to give an opinion, requires the preposition *à* before its object.

15. ***en***

The **branched streetlamps** on the bridge make the narrator think of a path lined with **trees cast in metal.** Complete the phrase with the preposition *en.*

Fill In a Verb

1. ***avoir retiré***

The preposition *après* + <u>infinitive</u> + <u>past participle</u> creates the French equivalent of **after having done something,** here **after removing.**

2. ***a posée***

The *passé composé* conveys a simple, completed past action: **she placed it near the open window.** The extra *e* on the end of the participle reflects that the preceding direct object is feminine and singular (*l'* = **it,** *sa tarte*).

3. ***refroidisse***

The subjunctive is required after the conjunction *pour que.*

4. ***chatoyaient***

The imperfect is used to **describe** what **was going on. The berries shimmered in the sunlight while a delicate aroma rose up.**

5. ***montait***

Continue the description with another imperfect tense: **while a delicate aroma rose up.** Notice how the narrative stops in order to **describe.** We are not moving forward in the story. We pause to look at the scene.

6. *a dû* (or *devait*)

Either tense works here. The *passé composé* emphasizes that she **had** to admit it, whereas the <u>imperfect</u> complements a verb that takes place in the mind.

7. *est sortie*

Use the *passé composé* to pick up the narrative again. It is easy to visualize this completed action taking place.

8. *Revenue*

A <u>past participle</u> functioning as an adjective, *revenue* is feminine and singular.

9. *a jeté*

She glanced is a simple, completed action that propels the narrative forward. Use the *passé composé*.

10. *restait*

The imperfect is used to describe **what was left of** the pie. This is not an <u>action</u> that can be visualized as in the case of the *passé composé*. This is a description of the state of the pie! It stops the forward momentum of the narrative.

11. *avait laissé*

Use the *plus-que-parfait* to state what **had taken place** prior to finding the hollowed-out crust.

12. *aurait pu*

Use the *passé du conditionnel*: **Who would have been able to resist her tender, flaky crust?**

13. *s'est mise*

Tout d'un coup (**all of sudden**) sets the stage for an action to **begin.** Use the *passé composé*.

14. *s'est dirigée*

An action whose beginning can be visualized, this verb is <u>reflexive</u> and therefore conjugated with *être* in the *passé composé*. **She headed toward the garden.**

15. *ronflait*

The imperfect paints the scene. We stop to see what was going on. These are continuing actions or states of being. **Câline was snoring.**

16. *avait*

The scene description continues: **The enormous white poodle looked stuffed** (she appeared to have eaten her fill).

17. *faisait*

Another imperfect verb: **her blue snout made one laugh** (looked silly).

18. *a versé*

Maman poured fresh water into her bowl (completed action, *passé composé*).

19. *murmurant*

While Maman was pouring, she was **murmuring** (*en* + present participle).

20. *améliorer*

Maman wonders how she **could have improved her pastry** (infinitive after the modal verb *pouvoir*).

Part B

Two Sample Essay Answers

Read the following essays to see how a student might have answered this question. You will note different ability levels in the two responses. Try to critique the essays yourself and then read the evaluations that follow to get a feel for how they would be graded.

Sample Essay 1

On nous a toujours dit que l'honnêteté était une qualité. Il semble cependant que les gens honnêtes sont de plus en plus rares. On remarque en effet par exemple, que tous les politiciens sont malhonnêtes d'une façon ou d'une autre. On s'attend à ce qu'ils mentent et on sait qu'une fois élus, ils n'accompliront pas tout ce qu'ils ont promis. Les mensonges paraissent de moins en moins mal vus.

Mais cela ne concerne pas seulement les politiciens. Tous les jours, chacun est témoin ou même coupable d'un mensonge. La plupart des gens exagèrent leur CV, certains se voient obligés de tricher pour réussir aux examens, d'autres inventent des qualités pour vendre un produit, etc. . . .

La malhonnêteté a des formes de plus en plus variées. On peut même aller jusqu'à parler par exemple, du maquillage. Celui-ci n'est-il pas une forme de déguisement? Pourtant, pour un entretien, pour beaucoup de métiers, pour passer à la télé, etc., le maquillage est obligatoire.

La malhonnêteté a tout simplement pris une place plus importante dans notre société, et est aujourd'hui parfois considérée plutôt un talent qu'un défaut.

Sample Essay 2

Les gens aujourd'hui sont malhonnêtes. Il n'y a personne qui ne ment jamais. Chaque jour, tout le monde ment et tout le monde entend un mensonge. Les gens mentent à propos de tout. Les gens mentent pour des choses importantes et pour des choses pas importantes. C'est une habitude.

Il y a des gens qui mentent plus que d'autres. Il y a aussi beaucoup de criminels. Les criminels sont des gens pas honnêtes. Dans le monde moderne, je crois qu'il y a plus de criminels qu'avant. Il y a des façons d'être malhonnête pire que d'autres. Parfois on ment pour quelque chose qui n'est pas important et parfois être malhonnête peut être voler. Il y a des gens qui ne sont pas punis même s'ils sont malhonnêtes parce que personne ne s'en rend pas compte.

Il faut faire attention parce que les gens sont souvent malhonnêtes. Il faut faire attention à qui on fait confiance. A chaque fois qu'on fait quelque chose, il faut vérifier qu'on n'est pas malhonnête. Il faut faire plus attention qu'avant, parce que c'est plus facile d'être malhonnête aujourd'hui qu'avant.

Evaluation of Sample Essay 1

This student has written a good essay. There are some flaws. In the sentence beginning with ***On remarque en effet par exemple***; either *en effet* or *par exemple* would suffice. The student effectively uses the term ***CV*** for **curriculum vitae**. The essay is organized and the student supports his opinion with examples from real life. The writing shows good verb mastery and evidences a varied vocabulary. This essay would surely receive a satisfactory score.

Evaluation of Sample Essay 2

The second essay is not badly written but is less sucessful than the first one. The student states that he thinks there are more criminals today than previously; yet a supportive statement does not follow. ***Les criminels sont des gens pas honnêtes*** is childish, and hardly needs to be stated. The phrase ***parce que personne ne s'en rend pas compte*** should not include the word ***pas***. *Personne* + *ne* complete the negation. The range of vocabulary is not impressive. This is a very average essay and would not score as well as the first one.

Part C: Sample Answers to Speaking Questions

La Glace

Here is how a student might have answered the questions that accompany the sketches:

(1) Un monsieur achète deux cornets de glace à deux boules. Ses filles attendent patiemment leur petit plaisir. Les deux sœurs n'ont pas la même taille. La grande est probablement l'aînée; la petite, la cadette.

Dans ce dessin les deux fillettes raffolent de leurs glaces. Elles ont l'air bien content.

On voit trébucher la cadette en traversant la rue. Les boules de glace se dégagent du cornet et tombent par terre.

La voilà agenouillée, toute en pleurs, à côté de son trésor gâché. Elle était si contente tout à l'heure.

Sa sœur lui offre son cornet. Le père semble content de ce geste généreux. Il met la main sur le dos de sa fille aînée comme s'il voulait montrer son approbation silencieuse. La petite s'arrête de pleurer. Elle aura une glace, grâce à sa sœur.

(2) Elle réagit de manière spontanée. Elle voit sa sœur en détresse et elle veut la soulager. Elle ne réfléchit pas. C'est un acte altruiste.

(3) Je crois que l'aîné doit servir de modèle pour ses cadets. Ceux-ci suivront son exemple, ou bon ou mauvais. Puisqu'il exerce une si grande influence sur eux, même sans le vouloir, il faut qu'il montre le bon chemin.

Les Oignons

Here is how a student might have answered the questions that accompany the sketches:

(1) On voit une jeune femme toute en pleurs. Il semble qu'elle pleure toutes les larmes de son corps, tant elles sont abondantes. On se demande ce qui ne va pas. Est-il question de mauvaises nouvelles ou d'une grande déception? On ne saurait deviner la cause de sa détresse, mais on s'inquiète et on la plaint.

Maintenant on voit qu'elle est tout simplement en train de couper un tas d'oignons pour en faire une soupe. Je connais la recette parce que nous l'avons préparée dans ma classe de français il y a deux ans. Il faut trancher finement et cela provoque une grande irritation aux yeux. Les larmes commencent donc à couler.

(2) Si on ne savait pas qu'elle coupait les oignons, on croirait qu'elle était en détresse. Aussitôt vu le second dessin, on comprend que ce n'est rien de grave. C'est très banal; elle coupe des oignons. Il vaut mieux savoir tous les faits et tous les détails avant de tirer une conclusion.

(3) J'ai remarqué que presque toutes les filles qui gagnent une couronne de beauté pleurent. Les athlètes victorieux font souvent la même chose. Les parents et les grands-parents, eux aussi, pleurent à la naissance d'un enfant, et aux noces familiales. Je ne sais pas, à vrai dire, pourquoi cela arrive, mais c'est ainsi; je l'ai souvent constaté et cela m'arrive de temps en temps. Je devine que c'est une forte émotion d'être comblé de joie, et que la force du sentiment y est aussi pour quelque chose.

PRACTICE TEST 3

AP French
Practice Test 3

ANSWER SHEET

1. Ⓐ Ⓑ Ⓒ Ⓓ
2. Ⓐ Ⓑ Ⓒ Ⓓ
3. Ⓐ Ⓑ Ⓒ Ⓓ
4. Ⓐ Ⓑ Ⓒ Ⓓ
5. Ⓐ Ⓑ Ⓒ Ⓓ
6. Ⓐ Ⓑ Ⓒ Ⓓ
7. Ⓐ Ⓑ Ⓒ Ⓓ
8. Ⓐ Ⓑ Ⓒ Ⓓ
9. Ⓐ Ⓑ Ⓒ Ⓓ
10. Ⓐ Ⓑ Ⓒ Ⓓ
11. Ⓐ Ⓑ Ⓒ Ⓓ
12. Ⓐ Ⓑ Ⓒ Ⓓ
13. Ⓐ Ⓑ Ⓒ Ⓓ
14. Ⓐ Ⓑ Ⓒ Ⓓ
15. Ⓐ Ⓑ Ⓒ Ⓓ
16. Ⓐ Ⓑ Ⓒ Ⓓ
17. Ⓐ Ⓑ Ⓒ Ⓓ
18. Ⓐ Ⓑ Ⓒ Ⓓ
19. Ⓐ Ⓑ Ⓒ Ⓓ
20. Ⓐ Ⓑ Ⓒ Ⓓ
21. Ⓐ Ⓑ Ⓒ Ⓓ
22. Ⓐ Ⓑ Ⓒ Ⓓ
23. Ⓐ Ⓑ Ⓒ Ⓓ
24. Ⓐ Ⓑ Ⓒ Ⓓ
25. Ⓐ Ⓑ Ⓒ Ⓓ

26. Ⓐ Ⓑ Ⓒ Ⓓ
27. Ⓐ Ⓑ Ⓒ Ⓓ
28. Ⓐ Ⓑ Ⓒ Ⓓ
29. Ⓐ Ⓑ Ⓒ Ⓓ
30. Ⓐ Ⓑ Ⓒ Ⓓ
31. Ⓐ Ⓑ Ⓒ Ⓓ
32. Ⓐ Ⓑ Ⓒ Ⓓ
33. Ⓐ Ⓑ Ⓒ Ⓓ
34. Ⓐ Ⓑ Ⓒ Ⓓ
35. Ⓐ Ⓑ Ⓒ Ⓓ
36. Ⓐ Ⓑ Ⓒ Ⓓ
37. Ⓐ Ⓑ Ⓒ Ⓓ
38. Ⓐ Ⓑ Ⓒ Ⓓ
39. Ⓐ Ⓑ Ⓒ Ⓓ
40. Ⓐ Ⓑ Ⓒ Ⓓ
41. Ⓐ Ⓑ Ⓒ Ⓓ
42. Ⓐ Ⓑ Ⓒ Ⓓ
43. Ⓐ Ⓑ Ⓒ Ⓓ
44. Ⓐ Ⓑ Ⓒ Ⓓ
45. Ⓐ Ⓑ Ⓒ Ⓓ
46. Ⓐ Ⓑ Ⓒ Ⓓ
47. Ⓐ Ⓑ Ⓒ Ⓓ
48. Ⓐ Ⓑ Ⓒ Ⓓ
49. Ⓐ Ⓑ Ⓒ Ⓓ
50. Ⓐ Ⓑ Ⓒ Ⓓ

51. Ⓐ Ⓑ Ⓒ Ⓓ
52. Ⓐ Ⓑ Ⓒ Ⓓ
53. Ⓐ Ⓑ Ⓒ Ⓓ
54. Ⓐ Ⓑ Ⓒ Ⓓ
55. Ⓐ Ⓑ Ⓒ Ⓓ
56. Ⓐ Ⓑ Ⓒ Ⓓ
57. Ⓐ Ⓑ Ⓒ Ⓓ
58. Ⓐ Ⓑ Ⓒ Ⓓ
59. Ⓐ Ⓑ Ⓒ Ⓓ
60. Ⓐ Ⓑ Ⓒ Ⓓ
61. Ⓐ Ⓑ Ⓒ Ⓓ
62. Ⓐ Ⓑ Ⓒ Ⓓ
63. Ⓐ Ⓑ Ⓒ Ⓓ
64. Ⓐ Ⓑ Ⓒ Ⓓ
65. Ⓐ Ⓑ Ⓒ Ⓓ
66. Ⓐ Ⓑ Ⓒ Ⓓ
67. Ⓐ Ⓑ Ⓒ Ⓓ
68. Ⓐ Ⓑ Ⓒ Ⓓ
69. Ⓐ Ⓑ Ⓒ Ⓓ
70. Ⓐ Ⓑ Ⓒ Ⓓ
71. Ⓐ Ⓑ Ⓒ Ⓓ
72. Ⓐ Ⓑ Ⓒ Ⓓ
73. Ⓐ Ⓑ Ⓒ Ⓓ
74. Ⓐ Ⓑ Ⓒ Ⓓ
75. Ⓐ Ⓑ Ⓒ Ⓓ

AP French

Practice Test 3

Total Test Time—2 hours and 30 minutes

SECTION I: Multiple Choice

Time–1 hour and 25 minutes

Part A: Listening

Approximate time–25 minutes

Exchanges

> **Directions:** Listen to the following series of brief exchanges between two speakers. You will hear each exchange twice. Then, based on what you have just heard, choose the most likely rejoinder from the four choices you are given below. Blacken the corresponding letter on your answer sheet.

CD 3, Track 5: Exchange Numbers 1–15

1. (A) Ce que tu dis est vrai.

    (B) Il n'est pas question de te rembourser.

    (C) C'est mon saint patron.

    (D) Je te jure, tu auras ton argent dans une quinzaine.

2. (A) Oui, figure-toi, troisième fois.

    (B) Ce sont les premières noces.

    (C) Ils vont simplement vivre à deux cette fois.

    (D) Ils n'auront pas d'invités.

3. (A) Tu es gentil, mais je n'ose pas mettre ce short.

   (B) Je suis forte parce que je fais des haltères.

   (C) Mes cuisses sont minces.

   (D) Les cuisses me font mal.

4. (A) On a droit au tarif réduit.

   (B) J'ai déjà réservé nos billets.

   (C) C'est pour ça, j'adore la publicité préliminaire.

   (D) Il n'y a plus de strapontins.

5. (A) J'ai eu une augmentation.

   (B) J'en avais marre !

   (C) C'était un poste intéressant.

   (D) J'étais bien vu par mes supérieurs.

6. (A) J'ai déjà bien considéré.

   (B) Je ne vois pas les reflets.

   (C) Je vois double.

   (D) Je l'ai fait faire.

7. (A) Tu exagères, mais j'aimerais bien le connaître.

   (B) Il fait trop froid pour nager !

   (C) Je reste maître de la décision, moi.

   (D) Est-il aussi maître d'hôtel ?

8. (A) Elle collectionne beaucoup.

   (B) Elle a le cœur sentimental, comme toutes les mères.

   (C) Évidemment, elle organise les affaires.

   (D) Elle se croît conservatrice.

9. (A) Tout est soldé en ce moment; on fera une affaire.

   (B) Je mettrai tous les achats sur compte.

   (C) On ne vit qu'une fois.

   (D) On a l'intention de faire des extravagances inouïes.

10. (A) La fête de la Sainte Valentin est sympa !

   (B) En dépit de ton sarcasme, c'est un mois insupportable.

   (C) Tu as ton anniversaire le 28.

   (D) Le mois de février suit le mois de janvier.

11. (A) La poste est fermée à cause des travaux.

   (B) On mettra toutes les photos dans un album.

   (C) D'accord, je descendrai leurs albums philatélistes.

   (D) Ils gagneront ainsi leur badge numismate.

12. (A) Si, je deviens chauve comme un caillou.

   (B) D'accord, je resterai glabre.

   (C) Je me raserai deux fois par jour.

   (D) Même sans cheveux ?

13. (A) D'accord, je leur en parlerai demain.

   (B) Tu m'aiderais à bosser comme ça ? C'est super !

   (C) Ils n'en seront pas contents.

   (D) C'est surtout Papa qui en sera déçu.

14. (A) N'importe quel soulier !

   (B) Moi aussi, je voudrais changer de chaussures.

   (C) Ne pourrais-tu pas mettre tes tennis ? Il fait si beau ce soir.

   (D) Mets tes bottes !

15. (A) Pas vraiment, j'ai l'habitude.

   (B) Je suis à bout.

   (C) J'ai eu un siège en bout de rangée.

   (D) J'ai soufflé les bougies tout à l'heure.

Dialogues

> **Directions:** Listen to the dialogues on your CD. After each one you will hear a series of questions based on what you have just heard. Each question is heard twice. Choose the best answer from the four choices provided and blacken the corresponding letter on your answer sheet. You have only 12 seconds to mark your answer.

CD 3, Track 6: Dialogues

Dialogue Number 1: Les Étoiles

16. Si les étoiles sont éblouissantes, comment sont-elles ?

   (A) argentées, métalliques

   (B) à peine visibles

   (C) éclatantes, brillantes

   (D) clignotantes

17. Que fera le couple après avoir prononcé *santé* ?

   (A) . . . ils trinqueront leurs verres

   (B) . . . ils rempliront leurs verres

   (C) . . . ils poseront leurs verres

   (D) . . . ils videront leurs verres

18. Quand son époux lui manque, que fait la femme ?

   (A) Elle regarde les étoiles et songe à son mari.

   (B) Elle se verse un vin frais.

   (C) Elle balaie la terrasse.

   (D) Elle regarde surtout Rigel.

19. Décrivez le ciel cette nuit-là.

    (A) Le ciel est couvert.

    (B) L'obscurité est cloutée de diamants scintillants.

    (C) Il y a de l'orage dans l'air.

    (D) L'horizon n'est pas distinct.

Dialogue Number 2: L'Au Pair

20. Est-ce que ce couple va rentrer en Angleterre ?

    (A) Non, ils feront des vacances méditerranéennes.

    (B) Oui, avec leurs deux enfants.

    (C) Non, ils feront les pays scandinaves.

    (D) Non, ils feront une traversée atlantique.

21. Pourquoi la jeune fille veut-elle devenir au pair ?

    (A) Elle ne veut pas commettre d'impair.

    (B) Pour quitter ses parents.

    (C) Pour devenir anglaise.

    (D) Pour pouvoir voyager, apprendre et gagner de l'argent.

22. Comment sont les enfants de ce couple ?

    (A) Ils sont jumeaux.

    (B) Ce sont de petits morveux.

    (C) Ils sont mignons et très bien élevés.

    (D) Ce sont des enfants terribles.

23. Est-ce que la fille finit par convaincre son père ?

    (A) Il promet de considérer sa demande.

    (B) Non, elle va trop lui manquer.

    (C) En fin de compte, oui.

    (D) Oui, mais sa mère est contre l'idée.

24. Quels progrès personnels la fille envisage-t-elle ?

   (A) Elle croit pouvoir apprendre la cuisine italienne.

   (B) Elle se voit plus forte dans les langues étrangères.

   (C) Elle aura le temps de bachoter.

   (D) Elle se voit plus mondaine.

Dialogue Number 3: Le Manuel de Latin

25. Comment expliqueriez-vous le geste d'Aubain ?

   (A) C'était un geste considéré.

   (B) C'était une envie adolescente de se défouler.

   (C) C'était probablement un acte anarchiste.

   (D) C'était pour impressionner sa cadette.

26. Pourquoi ne peut-il pas récupérer son manuel ?

   (A) Parce que le manuel a atterri sur une surface inaccessible.

   (B) Parce qu'il l'avait déchiré avant de le jeter.

   (C) Parce qu'il ne sait pas où il est.

   (D) Parce que le manuel est tombé dans les buissons.

27. Aurait-il jeté son manuel de manière préconçue ?

   (A) C'était un acte prémédité et délibéré.

   (B) C'était plutôt une envie subite.

   (C) Oui, c'était pour montrer à ses parents qu'il ne voulait plus étudier.

   (D) C'était pour montrer qu'il aurait mieux aimé le français.

28. Que dira le père à son fils à propos de cet acte, selon vous.

   (A) Il soulignera l'importance du latin dans la vie actuelle.

   (B) Il expliquera la fabrication des manuels.

   (C) Il montrera à son fils comment monter l'échelle.

   (D) Il parlera du besoin de réfléchir avant d'agir.

Dialogue Number 4: La Caravane

29. Quel est l'essentiel, selon la femme ?

    (A) De monter et descendre la tente sans difficulté.

    (B) De choisir elle-même leur itinéraire.

    (C) De pouvoir continuer à faire du camping même quand ils en seront moins capables.

    (D) De pouvoir dormir sous les étoiles.

30. Qu'est qu'elle entend, en disant *pile* ?

    (A) Elle veut dire *exactement* !

    (B) Elle veut dire qu'ils sont encore jeunes.

    (C) Elle veut dire qu'il faut arrêter la voiture.

    (D) Elle veut dire *trop tard* !

31. D'après vous, vont-ils éventuellement s'acheter une caravane ?

    (A) Non, le mari est carrément contre l'idée.

    (B) Oui, probablement.

    (C) Oui, s'il pleut.

    (D) Non, ce n'est pas du camping.

32. Pourquoi devraient-ils considérer l'achat d'une caravane selon le raisonnement féminin ?

    (A) Parce qu'elle va bouder s'il n'y consent pas.

    (B) Parce que son mari aime conduire.

    (C) Parce qu'ils n'ont plus l'âge de tout faire.

    (D) Parce qu'elle n'aime pas cuisiner lors de leurs trajets.

Part B: Reading

Directions: Read the following passages with care. Each segment is followed by a series of questions or statements to be completed. Choose the best answer, according to what you have read, from the four choices provided. Blacken the corresponding letter on your answer sheet.

Questions 33–38

Périgueux est la capitale de la Dordogne. J'y ai fait ma première visite lors d'une réunion de profs de langue il y a à peu près cinq ans. N'ayant jamais entendu parler de cette ville avant, je n'avais aucune idée de ce qui m'attendait. Alors elle m'a séduite d'emblée. Ébahie par ses ruelles médiévales et ses vieux bâtiments blottis les uns contre les autres, je me laissais traînasser sur son sol gallo-romain.

Saint-Front, sa cathédrale imposante, s'étale comme un énorme berger hâlé surveillant son troupeau de vieilles maisons dociles. Le calme est palpable et la paix semble pénétrer jusqu'aux os. On essayait d'imaginer vivre dans un tel lieu féerique, presque irréel, et dont la beauté sereine est difficile à mettre au jour, mais lisible aux yeux de mes compagnons. Inutiles, tous nos efforts d'avaler Périgueux d'un seul coup. Il vaudrait mieux grignoter ici et là, se demandant tout au long de ce festin pour l'âme si l'on vit ou si l'on rêve.

Après s'être baladées à travers ses rues festonnées de fleurs, quelques-unes de me nouvelles compagnes et moi, nous nous sommes métamorphosées en bande bruyante de jeunes filles aux rires bébêtes. C'était dans cet état altéré que nous avons dîné ensemble dans un petit restaurant qui allait devenir notre auberge préférée: Au Bon Bien. Oubliant notre anglais, nos vies banales, nos ankyloses et notre âge, nous sommes devenues de vraies convives animées. Il y a un vieux dicton français: "À table on ne vieillit pas". Ce soir-là j'ai constaté qu'à table on peut également rajeunir.

Ligne (5), (10), (15), (20)

33. Les *maisons* sont *dociles* comme des . . .

 (A) moutons.

 (B) jeunes filles rieuses.

 (C) profs de langue.

 (D) sirènes périgordiens.

34. Contrastez Périgueux et Paris:

    (A) Périgueux est plus animé et vif.

    (B) Périgueux est plus tranquille.

    (C) Périgueux est beaucoup plus moderne.

    (D) Les gratte-ciel de Périgueux s'étalent plus haut.

35. Comment décririez-vous l'ambiance de Périgueux et son effet sur l'auteur?

    (A) cacophonique et déconcertante

    (B) sombre et déprimante

    (C) paisible et tranquillisante

    (D) audacieuse et stimulante

36. A-t-il fallu beaucoup de temps pour que l'auteur apprécie cette ville?

    (A) Oui, mais peu à peu elle commençait à l'aimer.

    (B) Oui, il a fallu du temps parce que c'était sa première visite et elle ne savait pas ce à quoi s'attendre.

    (C) Non, elle l'a aimée dès la première vue.

    (D) Il paraît qu'elle ne s'y est jamais habituée.

37. Comment l'auteur et ses compagnes se sentent-elles changées sous l'effet magique de cette ville?

    (A) Elles se sentent plus religieuses à cause de Saint-Front.

    (B) Elles ne sont pas conscientes d'un changement.

    (C) Elles se sentent plus jeunes et insouciantes.

    (D) Elles éprouvent un sentiment ankylosant.

38. Combien de fois ces femmes ont-elle mangé Au Bon Bien pendant leur séjour ?

    (A) une fois, cette magique soirée-là décrite par l'auteur

    (B) plusieurs fois

    (C) une seule fois, étant renvoyées à cause du bruit qu'elles faisaient lors de leur premier repas

    (D) deux fois seulement, la nourriture était moins bonne la seconde fois

Questions 39–45

Le moteur, à chaque plongée, vibrait si fort que toute la masse de l'avion était prise d'un tremblement comme de colère. Fabien usa ses forces à dominer l'avion, la tête enfoncée dans la carlingue,* face à l'horizon gyroscopique car, au-dehors, il ne distinguait plus la masse du ciel de celle de la terre, perdu dans une ombre où tout se mêlait, une ombre d'origine des mondes. Mais les aiguilles des indicateurs de position oscillaient de plus en plus vite, devenaient difficiles à suivre. Déjà le pilote, qu'elles trompaient, se débattait mal, perdait son altitude, s'enlisait peu à peu dans cette ombre. Il lut sa hauteur, "cinq cents mètres". C'était le niveau des collines. Ils les sentit rouler vers lui leurs vagues vertigineuses. Il comprenait aussi que toutes les masses du sol, dont la moindre l'eût écrasé, étaient comme arrachées de leur support, déboulonnées, et commençaient à tourner, ivres, autour de lui. Et commençaient, autour de lui, une sorte de danse profonde et qui le serrait de plus en plus.

Il en prit son parti. Au risque d'emboutir, il atterrirait n'importe où. Et, pour éviter au moins les collines, il lâcha son unique fusée éclairante. La fusée s'enflamma, tournoya, illumina une plaine et s'y éteignit: c'était la mer.

La femme de Fabien téléphona.

    – Fabien a-t-il atterri ?

Le secrétaire qui l'écoutait se troubla un peu:

    – Qui parle ?

    – Simone Fabien.

    – Ah, une minute . . .

Le secrétaire, n'osant rien dire, passa l'écouteur au chef de bureau.

    – Qui est là ?

    – Simone Fabien.

    – Ah, que désirez-vous Madame ?

    – Mon mari, a-t-il atterri ?

Ligne
(5)
(10)
(15)
(20)
(25)

Ligne

(30) Il y eût un silence qui dût paraître inexplicable, puis on répondit simplement:

    – Non.

    – Il a du retard?

    – Oui . . .

(35) Il y eut un nouveau silence.

    – Oui . . . du retard.

    – Ah! . . .

C'était un "Ah" de chair blessée. Un retard, ce n'est rien . . . ce n'est rien . . . mais quand il se prolonge . . .

(40)   – Ah! . . . Et à quelle heure sera-t-il ici?

    – À quelle heure sera-t-il ici? Nous . . . nous ne savons pas.

*carlingue: *cabin*

Vol de Nuit, Antoine de Saint-Exupéry

39. Combien de fusées éclairantes reste-t-il?

    (A) Il y en a un nombre vertigineux.

    (B) Il n'y en a plus.

    (C) Il y en a quelques-unes que Fabien devra arracher avec soin de sorte qu'elles ne se déclenchent pas trop tôt dans la carlingue.

    (D) Il en a mais elles sont toutes éteintes.

40. Les aiguilles de position sont-elles déboulonnées?

    (A) Non, mais elles oscillaient si vite que Fabien ne pouvait les lire qu'à peine.

    (B) Oui, elles se sont détachées complètement de leur cadran.

    (C) Il y a quelque chose qui bloque leur mouvement.

    (D) Elles sont cassées et ne bougent plus.

41. Le pilote savait-il qu'il volait au-dessus de la mer avant de déclencher sa fusée?

    (A) Justement, il la cherchait.

    (B) Il le savait grâce à l'horizon gyroscopique.

    (C) Oui, il sentait venir vers lui les ondes et les vagues.

    (D) Il se croyait au-dessus d'un terrain collineux.

42. Fabien pourra-t-il atterrir?

   (A) Sans doute.

   (B) Il faudra d'abord continuer sa descente.

   (C) À moins d'un miracle, ce sera probablement impossible.

   (D) Il pourra atterrir sur le ventre.

43. Qu'est-ce qu'on entend chez Mme Fabien par son *"Ah" de chair blessée?*

   (A) En dépit de son espoir, elle comprend que son mari est en péril.

   (B) Elle est surprise que son mari soit en retard.

   (C) Fabien s'est fait mal.

   (D) Elle devra attendre jusqu'au lendemain pour le revoir.

44. Le chef du bureau, sait-il pourquoi Mme Fabien a téléphoné?

   (A) Non, c'est pourquoi il demande *"Que désirez-vous?"*

   (B) Oui, il sait exactement pourquoi elle a téléphoné mais il se sent mal à l'aise et maladroit.

   (C) Il croit qu'elle veut savoir les conditions atmosphériques.

   (D) Il pense qu'elle veut vérifier l'heure de son atterrissage.

45. Pourquoi l'hésitation de la part du secrétaire d'abord, et puis du chef, en parlant à Madame Fabien?

   (A) Ils sont tous les deux très affairés et préoccupés.

   (B) Il y avait beaucoup d'appels ce soir-là.

   (C) Mme Fabien téléphone souvent et ça les embête.

   (D) Ni l'un ni l'autre ne veut transmettre de mauvaises nouvelles.

Questions 46–53

   Le faisan est un grand oiseau à longue queue. Le mâle adulte est facilement reconnaissable: corps bronze irisé bien marqué, queue fauve avec barre brun foncé, très longue. Tête vert bouteille brillant avec plaque faciale écarlate.

Ligne
(5)
Femelle gris-fauve avec stries plus sombres, queue plus courte. Habite les champs cultivés, bruyères, buissons et bois ouverts. Répandu.

   Le tridactyle* est une mouette de taille moyenne à ailes minces. Adulte, principalement blanc. Ailes gris pâle. Pointe des rémiges noire sans

tache blanche. Bec jaune citron. Petit. Pattes nettement noires. Immature:
semblable mais avec un collier noirâtre. Marque noire *M* sur les ailes et
queue peu échancrée à pointe noire visible en vol. Grégaire. Vol léger. Ailes
longues et minces. Très bruyant en colonie, cri caractéristique "*kitti-oueik*"
qui lui vaut son nom anglais, Kittiwake. Niche en colonie sur les falaises
maritimes, parfois les bâtiments. En hiver, généralement au large. Quelques
spécimens dans les eaux côtières. Répandu.

Le colombin* est un pigeon familier de taille moyenne. Adulte et immature,
dessus et dessous gris sourd uniforme. Adulte, reflets métalliques verts sur
la nuque et roses sur la potrine. Bec sombre et court. Pattes rougeâtres.
Grégaire. Roucoulement bruyant "*cou-ouh*", surtout au printemps. Niche
dans des trous d'arbres, dans les bois et les champs cultivés, parfois sur les
côtes. Répandu.

Le rossignol phylomème* est un chanteur incomparable. Adulte, dessus
brun olive à queue marquante, longue, rousse, arrondie. Dessous fauve pâle
presque blanc sur le ventre, sans marques. Pattes relativement longues et
fortes correspondant aux habitudes terrestres. Cri doux "*hui-iit*". Chant
fort, long, mélodieux, liquide, très varié avec quelques imitations d'autres
oiseaux, souvent émis nuit et jour. Habite les bois à buissons denses et
fourrés marécageux. Répandu.

*tridactyle, colombin, phylomène: *species*

Oiseaux Poches Nature, J. Flegg (Les Éditions du Carrousel)

46. Les oiseaux décrits dans le passage précédent sont . . .

    (A) des espèces menacées.

    (B) très rares.

    (C) assez communs.

    (D) étrangers.

47. Quel oiseau compteriez-vous voir au bord de la mer?

    (A) le faisan

    (B) la mouette

    (C) le rossignol

    (D) le pigeon

48. Lequel des oiseaux roucoule ?

    (A) le faisan

    (B) la mouette

    (C) le rossignol

    (D) le pigeon

49. Le Kittiwake est . . .

    (A) un faisan anglais.

    (B) une mouette.

    (C) un rossignol.

    (D) un colombe.

50. Quel oiseau a la plus belle voix ?

    (A) le faisan

    (B) la mouette

    (C) le rossignol

    (D) le pigeon

51. De quelle couleur est la plaque faciale du faisan ?

    (A) rouge vif

    (B) vert bouteille

    (C) jaune citron

    (D) gris pâle

52. Est-ce que les pattes des oiseaux varient ?

    (A) Seulement de couleur.

    (B) Elles sont toutes noires.

    (C) Oui, et les becs aussi.

    (D) Les pattes ne se distinguent pas les unes des autres.

53. Quel oiseau copie la chanson des autres de temps en temps ?

   (A) le faisan

   (B) la mouette

   (C) le rossignol

   (D) le pigeon

Questions 54–60

Un beau jour, dans notre île, les mots se sont révoltés. C'était il y a bien longtemps, au début du siècle. Je venais de naître. Un matin, les mots ont refusé de continuer leur vie d'esclaves. Un matin, ils n'ont pu accepter d'être
Ligne convoqués, à n'importe quelle heure, sans le moindre respect et puis rejetés
(5) dans le silence. Un matin, ils n'ont plus supporté la bouche des humains. J'en suis sûr, vous n'avez jamais pensé au martyre des mots. Où mijotent les mots avant d'être prononcés ? Réfléchissez une seconde. Dans la bouche. Au milieu des caries et des vieux restes de veau coincé entre les dents: empuantis par la mauvaise haleine ambiante, écorchés par des langues pâteuses, noyés dans
(10) la salive acide. Vous accepteriez, vous, de vivre dans une bouche? Alors, un matin les mots se sont enfuis. Ils ont cherché un abri, un pays où vivre entre eux, loin des bouches détestées. Ils sont arrivés ici, une ancienne ville minière, abandonnée depuis qu'on n'y trouvait plus d'or. Ils s'y sont installés. Voilà, vous savez tout. Je vais vous laisser jusqu'à ce soir, j'ai ma chanson à finir.
(15) Vous pouvez les regarder tant que vous voudrez, les mots ne vous feront pas de mal. Mais ne vous avisez pas d'entrer chez eux. Ils savent se défendre. Ils peuvent piquer pire que des guêpes et mordre mieux que des serpents.

   [. . .]

Alors il faut que je vous dise: quand ils sont libres d'occuper leur temps
(20) comme ils le veulent, au lieu de nous servir, les mots mènent une vie joyeuse. Ils passent leurs journées à se déguiser, à se maquiller et à se marier.

Du haut de ma colline, je n'ai d'abord rien compris. Les mots étaient si nombreux. Je ne voyais qu'un grand désordre. J'étais perdue dans cette foule. J'ai mis du temps, je n'ai appris que peu à peu à reconnaître les principales
(25) tribus qui composent le peuple des mots. Car les mots s'organisent en tribus, comme les humains. Et chaque tribu a son métier.

Le premier métier, c'est de désigner les choses. Vous avez déjà visité un jardin botanique ? Devant toutes les plantes rares, on a piqué un petit carton, une étiquette. Tel est le premier métier des mots: poser sur toutes les choses
(30) du monde une étiquette, pour s'y reconnaître. C'est le métier le plus difficile. Il y a tant de choses et des choses compliquées et des choses qui changent sans arrêt! Et pourtant, pour chacune il faut trouver une étiquette. Les mots

chargés de ce métier terrible s'appellent les *noms*. La tribu des noms est la tribu principale, la plus nombreuse.

La grammaire est une chanson douce, Erik Orsenna

54. Les mots croient que l'intérieur de la bouche humaine est . . .

(A) un peu serré mais commode.

(B) un abri tiède et rassurant.

(C) une prison dégoûtante.

(D) un endroit agréable.

55. Pourquoi les mots ont-ils révolté ?

(A) Ils en avaient marre de leur servitude.

(B) Ils sont juste partis aux îles en vacances.

(C) Pour organiser un attentat contre l'humain.

(D) Parce qu'ils sont nés loquaces.

56. Pourquoi leur ville adoptée avait-elle été abandonnée ?

(A) Elle est devenue trop délabrée pour y vivre.

(B) Elle était trop près de la mer et a été inondée.

(C) Son trésor s'est épuisé.

(D) Ses habitants sont tous morts de la peste au début du siècle.

57. Les articles, les adjectifs, et les adverbes, que seront-ils d'après vous ?

(A) des esclaves

(B) comme les noms, d'autres tribus de mots

(C) des ouvriers mineurs

(D) des naufragés

58. Quel est le métier des noms ?

(A) de ramasser les étiquettes du jardin botanique

(B) de convoquer les autres tribus

(C) de signaler chaque chose du monde d'une manière unique et distincte.

(D) de grouper les choses

59. Pourquoi les noms sont-ils si nombreux ?

(A) Parce qu'ils sont membres de la tribu principale.

(B) Parce que ce sont des guerriers féroces qui ont vaincu les petites tribus.

(C) Parce qu'ils sont venus les premiers.

(D) Parce qu'il y a tant de choses sur la terre qui doivent être nommées.

60. Les mots sont-ils capables de faire mal ?

(A) Non, ils sont inoffensifs.

(B) Non, ils ne sont bons à rien.

(C) Oui, ils peuvent piquer et mordre.

(D) Oui on peut s'étouffer en parlant.

Questions 61–70

Ils allèrent dans une forêt fort épaisse, où à dix pas de distance on ne se voyait pas l'un l'autre. Le Bûcheron se mit à couper du bois et ses enfants à ramasser les broutilles pour faire des fagots. Le père et la mère, les voyant occupés à
Ligne travailler, s'éloignèrent d'eux insensiblement, et puis s'enfuirent tout à coup
(5) par un petit sentier détourné. Lorsque ces enfants se virent seuls, ils se mirent à crier et à pleurer de toute leur force. Le Petit Poucet les laissait crier, sachant bien par où il reviendrait à la maison; car en marchant, il avait laissé tomber le long du chemin les petits cailloux blancs qu'il avait dans ses poches. Il leur dit donc, ne craignez point mes frères; mon Père et ma Mère nous ont laissés ici,
(10) mais je vous ramènerai bien au logis, suivez-moi seulement, ils le suivirent, et il les mena jusqu'à leur maison par le chemin qu'ils étaient venus dans la forêt. Ils n'osèrent d'abord entrer, mais ils se mirent tous contre la porte pour écouter ce que disaient leur Père et leur Mère.

Ligne
(15) Dans le moment que le Bûcheron et la Bûcheronne arrivèrent chez eux, le Seigneur du Village leur envoya dix écus qu'il leur devait il y avait longtemps, et dont ils n'espéraient plus rien. Cela leur redonna la vie, car les pauvres gens mouraient de faim. Le Bûcheron envoya sur l'heure sa femme à la Boucherie. Comme il y avait longtemps qu'elle n'avait mangé, elle acheta trois fois plus de viande qu'il n'en fallait pour le souper de deux personnes.
(20) Lorsqu'ils furent rassasiés, la Bûcheronne dit:

– Hélas! Où sont maintenant nos pauvres enfants? Ils feraient bonne chère de ce qui nous reste là. Mais aussi, Guillaume, c'est toi qui les as voulu perdre; j'avais bien dit que nous nous en repentirions. Que font-ils maintenant dans cette Forêt? Hélas! mon Dieu, les Loups les ont peut-être
(25) mangés! Tu es bien inhumain d'avoir perdu ainsi tes enfants.

Le Petit Poucet, Charles Perrault

61. Quel était le métier de Guillaume, le père de la famille?

(A) Il servait au Seigneur du Village.

(B) Il était boucher.

(C) Il coupait le bois.

(D) Il forgeait les écus.

62. Pourquoi les parents ont-ils laissé leurs enfants dans la forêt?

(A) Ils étaient si pauvres qu'ils ne pouvaient plus les nourrir.

(B) Les enfants étaient tous des voyous insupportables.

(C) Ils ne l'ont pas fait exprès.

(D) Ils avaient l'intention de les reprendre plus tard.

63. Comment Petit Poucet a-t-il pu ramener ses frères?

(A) Il connaissait très bien la forêt.

(B) Il a allumé une torche.

(C) Il avait jeté de petits cailloux reconnaissables le long du sentier.

(D) Caché, il avait suivi ses parents et savait quel chemin prendre.

64. Quel évènement change le sort de la famille pauvre ?

    (A) Le couple reçoit le paiement d'une dette oubliée.

    (B) Les enfants trouvent un trésor caché dans la forêt.

    (C) Le Seigneur du Village leur lègue son château.

    (D) Le Roi les appelle à sa cour.

65. Que font-ils de cette aubaine ?

    (A) Ils rétablissent la maison.

    (B) Ils la cachent derrière la maison.

    (C) Ils deviennent philanthropes.

    (D) Ils achètent à manger.

66. Que dit la Bûcheronne à son mari ?

    (A) que ses enfants lui manquent et qu'elle regrette de les avoir abandonnés

    (B) qu'ils devraient avoir d'autres enfants

    (C) que la maison leur sera trop grande sans les enfants

    (D) qu'elle n'a plus d'appétit

67. Qui avait pris la décision de perdre les enfants dans la forêt ?

    (A) les deux parents

    (B) le père

    (C) la mère

    (D) les enfants eux-mêmes ont voulu s'échapper

68. La mère regrette-elle la décision ?

    (A) Oui, beaucoup, elle craint que les loups ne les mangent.

    (B) Pas encore.

    (C) Non, elle est contente de s'en être débarrassé.

    (D) Oui, un tout petit peu.

69. Est-ce que les parents reprendront leurs enfants en découvrant qu'ils sont tous là, près de la porte ?

(A) Oui, mais à contre cœur.

(B) Oui, à bras ouverts, et la mère leur donnera à manger.

(C) Non, ils sont bannis à tout jamais.

(D) Non, les enfants devront demeurer ailleurs.

70. Perrault est célèbre dans le monde entier pour sa collection de contes. Tout le monde connaît l'histoire du Petit Chaperon rouge, de Cendrillon, et de la Belle au bois dormant. De quel genre littéraire s'agit-il ?

(A) C'est de la poésie.

(B) Ce sont des contes de fée.

(C) Ce sont des pièces théâtrales.

(D) C'est un journal intime.

Questions 71–75

Monsieur Rodin

Comme je n'ai rien à faire je vous écris encore. Vous ne pouvez pas vous figurer comme il fait bon à l'Iselette. J'ai mangé aujourd'hui dans la salle du milieu (qui sert de serre) où l'on voit le jardin des deux côtés. Mme Courcelles m'a proposé (sans que j'en ai parlé le moins du monde) que si cela vous était agréable vous pourriez y manger de temps et même toujours (je crois qu'elle en a une fameuse envie) et c'est si joli là !

Je me suis promené dans le parc, tout est tondu, foin, blé, avoine, on peut faire le tour partout, c'est charmant. Si vous êtes gentil, à tenir votre promesse, nous connaîtrons le paradis. Vous aurez la chambre que vous voulez pour travailler. [. . .] La vieille m'a dit que je pouvais prendre des bains dans la rivière, où sa fille et la bonne en prennent, sans aucun danger. Avec votre permission j'en ferai autant car c'est un grand plaisir et cela m'évitera d'aller aux bains chauds à Azay. Que vous seriez gentil de m'acheter un petit costume de bain bleu foncé avec des galons blancs, en deux morceaux blouse et pantalon (taille moyenne), au Louvre ou au Bon Marché (en serge) ou à Tours ! [. . .]

Je vous embrasse. Camille

Lettre écrite à Auguste Rodin *par* Camille Claudel

71. La salle à manger dont elle parle, a-t-elle des fenêtres ?

    (A) Oui, mais les volets sont fermés.

    (B) Les murs sont en verre puisque c'est une serre.

    (C) Non, il n'y a pas de trouée.

    (D) Oui, elle a des fenêtres mais il n'y a rien de joli à regarder.

72. Camille veut que Rodin . . .

    (A) vienne passer du temps à Iselette.

    (B) aille à Tours.

    (C) se baigne à Azay.

    (D) reste à Paris.

73. Quelle faveur demande-t-elle au maître ?

    (A) de lui trouver un maillot de bain

    (B) de sculpter Mme Courcelles et sa fille

    (C) de venir enseigner

    (D) de tondre le foin

74. Serait-elle satisfaite d'un costume quelconque ?

    (A) Oui, puisque c'est lui qui va le sélectionner.

    (B) Non, il faut qu'il soit en serge bleu foncé aux galons blancs.

    (C) Oui, du moment qu'il soit utilisable.

    (D) Non, parce qu'elle a l'intention de le mettre aux bains chauds d'Azay.

75. Que semble-t-elle faire à Iselette ?

    (A) Elle s'ennuie beaucoup et n'aime pas le lieu.

    (B) Elle se détend et prend plaisir dans son oisiveté.

    (C) Elle travaille furieusement.

    (D) Elle écrit ses mémoires.

SECTION II: Free Response
Time–1 hour and 5 minutes

Part A: Writing
Time–20 minutes

Fill In a Word

Directions: In each sentence a single word has been omitted and replaced by a line. Write your answer, **one** single French word, on the line to the right. Make sure the word is correct in form, as well as in meaning and in context. None of your answers will be verbs.

Please note that a response such as *jusqu'à* (or *ce que*) will be considered two words, not one.

Mireille fait **1** boum pour **2** 14 juillet et elle nous invite **3** . **4** s'amusera **5** elle et **6** on ira voir les feux d'artifice ensemble. Chacun doit apporter **7** chose **8** manger. Son frère **9** je t'ai déjà parlé, viendra aussi. Il fait son service militaire **10** il a un congé de trois jours. **11** avoir assisté **12** spectacle, tout **13** monde reviendra chez nous pour trinquer une **14** fois avant **15** se quitter.

1. _____
2. _____
3. _____
4. _____
5. _____
6. _____
7. _____
8. _____
9. _____
10. _____
11. _____
12. _____
13. _____
14. _____
15. _____

Fill In a Verb

Directions: In each sentence a verb has been omitted and replaced by a line. Supply the missing verb form on the blank to the right. There you will see the infinitive form of the verb you are to use. Read the whole paragraph before choosing your answer. Spelling, agreement, and accent marks must all be accurate for your answer to be correct.

1.

Gisèle **1** la porte pour voir si son journal quotidien **2**. Elle **3** le lire chaque matin en **4** son café. Pas encore là! Déçue, elle **5** la porte et **6** dans un fauteuil près de la fenêtre, les pieds élevés, à **7** sa tradition matinale.

2.

En **8** chez elle, Marie-Noël **9** le message suivant sur son répondeur: "Salut Ma-No, c'est moi, Didier. **10**, si tu **11** libre demain soir, je voudrais venir te **12** vers 18 heures. On donne le nouveau film de Jean-Pierre Jeunet au Pathé et je **13** que ça te plairait. **14**-moi dès que tu **15**".

1. _____ (ouvrir)
2. _____ (arriver)
3. _____ (aimer)
4. _____ (boire)
5. _____ (fermer)
6. _____ (s'asseoir)
7. _____ (guetter)
8. _____ (rentrer)
9. _____ (trouver)
10. _____ (écouter)
11. _____ (être)
12. _____ (ramasser)
13. _____ (croire)
14. _____ (rappeler)
15. _____ (pouvoir)

3.

"Dédé, __16__ un ange et __17__ chercher mon sac. Tu le __18__ pendu sur le crochet derrière la porte. Merci, mon trésor. __19__ , voici une pièce de deux euros pour ta tirelire". "Tu es gentille Maman, mais je ne __20__ pas accepter ta pièce. Tu es ma mère, je t'aime, et il faut qu'un fils __21__ sans intérêt, tu sais". "Qu'est-ce que j' __22__ ? Est-ce que je rêve? Tu es bien mon fils André, le même qui __23__ de l'argent à tout bout de champs ?" "C'est pour les scouts, Maman. J' __24__ de gagner mon badge bénévole. Il faut que je __25__ à autrui pendant 24 heures".

16. _____ (être)

17. _____ (aller)

18. _____ (trouver)

19. _____ (tenir)

20. _____ (pouvoir)

21. _____ (agir)

22. _____ (entendre)

23. _____ (réclamer)

24. _____ (essayer)

25 . _____ (penser)

Part B: Essay

Time–40 minutes

> <u>Directions:</u> Develop the following topic in French. Prepare a well-conceived, organized, and coherent essay that demonstrates your mastery of verb tenses and illustrates your command of vocabulary. Expect to write at length because short answers do not score well. Be precise and check your work carefully for accents, spelling, and agreement.
>
> Essays are evaluated for grammatical accuracy, range, and choice of appropriate vocabulary, as well as organization, style, and mastery of syntax.

Dans une société qui devient de plus en plus technologique, quel est l'importance des arts (cinéma, danse, littérature, musique, sculpture, peinture, etc.) dans votre vie ?

Part C: Speaking

Approximate time–15 minutes

Working with a Series of Sketches: Les Bonbons

> **Directions:** You have one minute and 30 seconds to look at the series of five pictures below and to answer the questions about them that you will hear on CD 3, Track 7.

1. Racontez ce qui se déroule dans ces images. (60 secondes)

2. Croyez-vous que ces bonbons soient à la fillette ? Si non, à qui ? (60 secondes)

3. La fillette devrait-elle être punie parce qu'elle a chipé des bonbons qui ne lui appartenaient ? (60 secondes)

Working with One or Two Sketches: La Croissance

Directions: You have one minute and 30 seconds to look at the two pictures below and to answer the questions that you will hear about them on CD 3, Track 8.

1. Comparez et contrastez les deux dessins. (60 secondes)

2. Discutez les rôles changeants de mère et de fils avec le passage du temps. (60 secondes)

3. Dévéloppez un lien entre le jeune arbre et le jeune homme, tous les deux nourris par la même *mère*. (60 secondes)

AP French
Practice Test 3

ANSWER KEY

Section I: Multiple Choice
Part A: Listening

Exchanges

1.	(D)	5.	(B)	9.	(A)	13.	(B)
2.	(A)	6.	(A)	10.	(C)	14.	(C)
3.	(A)	7.	(A)	11.	(C)	15.	(A)
4.	(C)	8.	(B)	12.	(D)		

Dialogues

16.	(C)	21.	(D)	26.	(A)	31.	(B)
17.	(A)	22.	(C)	27.	(B)	32.	(C)
18.	(A)	23.	(C)	28.	(D)		
19.	(B)	24.	(B)	29.	(C)		
20.	(A)	25.	(B)	30.	(A)		

Part B: Reading

33.	(A)	44.	(B)	55.	(A)	66.	(A)
34.	(B)	45.	(D)	56.	(C)	67.	(B)
35.	(C)	46.	(C)	57.	(B)	68.	(A)
36.	(C)	47.	(B)	58.	(C)	69.	(B)
37.	(C)	48.	(D)	59.	(D)	70.	(B)
38.	(B)	49.	(B)	60.	(C)	71.	(B)
39.	(A)	50.	(C)	61.	(C)	72.	(A)
40.	(A)	51.	(A)	62.	(A)	73.	(A)
41.	(A)	52.	(C)	63.	(C)	74.	(B)
42.	(C)	53.	(C)	64.	(A)	75.	(B)
43.	(A)	54.	(C)	65.	(D)		

Section II: Free Response
Part A: Writing

Fill In a Word

1. une
2. le
3. tous
4. On
5. chez
6. puis (*or* alors)
7. quelque
8. à
9. dont
10. mais
11. Après
12. au
13. le
14. autre (*or* dernière)
15. de

Fill In a Verb

1. a ouvert
2. était arrivé
3. aimait
4. buvant
5. a fermé
6. s'est assise
7. guetter
8. rentrant
9. a trouvé
10. Écoute
11. es
12. ramasser
13. crois (*or* croyais)
14. Rappelle
15. pourras
16. sois
17. va
18. trouveras
19. Tiens
20. peux (*or* pourrai *or* pourrais)
21. agisse
22. j'entends
23. réclame
24. essaie (*or* essaye)
25. pense

Note: Please see "Detailed Explanations of Answers" for examples of responses to Section II, Part B (Essay) and Part C (Speaking).

Detailed Explanations
of Answers

Practice Test 3
Section I
Part A: Listening

1. **(D)** She asks for a loan of 50 *balles*. (The word *balles* was slang for the former French currency denomination, the *franc*. It was used the way we would say 10 bucks instead of 10 dollars. Today it means euros.) He refuses her. She won't pay him back until *Saint Glinglin*. The French sometimes refer to the feast day of a saint for a calendar date. (St Sylvestre to mean "New Year's Eve" is a good example). There is no Saint Glinglin. People say this when they mean **never.** It's the equivalent of **when hell freezes over,** or **in a month of Sundays.** What will she say next? The best choice is (D), **I swear you'll have your money back in two weeks.**

2. **(A)** Her sister is getting married again. Saying that every woman should have **a middle husband** suggests that this is a third marriage rather than a second one. The correct answer for the next comment she will make is (A), **Imagine, third time.**

3. **(A)** She thinks her thighs are too heavy. Her husband says he doesn't like those skinny models and that she's beautiful, a real woman. The most likely response from her is **You're sweet (kind) but I don't dare put on these shorts.** (A) is a better answer than (B), **I'm strong because I lift weights,** (C) **My thighs are thin,** or (D) **My thighs hurt me.**

4. **(C)** Everyone is waiting for them at the movie theatre. He suggests they hurry. No need to rush, she says, they'll save us seats and there's a series of advertisements and commercials before the feature film. The choices are (A) **We get a reduced price,** (B) **I've already reserved our tickets,** (C) **That's why we should hurry, I love the opening commercials,** and (D) **There aren't any more flip-down seats on the end of the aisles.** Answer (C) makes the best sequitur.

5.   **(B)**   Getting a raise (A), having an interesting job (C), and being well thought-of by one's superiors (D) are not reasons for quitting. The best rejoinder is (B), **I couldn't stand it anymore.**

6.   **(A)**   She's thinking about having laser surgery to correct her vision. She's worthless without glasses and doesn't want to wear them anymore. The operation can't be reversed. He warns her to think it over carefully before having it done. Her next response is most likely (A), **I've already thought it over carefully.**

7.   **(A)**   She thinks the lifeguard is cute. He says she thinks **all** lifeguards are cute. **It's too cold to swim** (B) is not what she would say next. (C), **I'm in charge of the decision,** doesn't follow either. Nor does the question, (D) **Is he also a maître d'?** (A) is the best answer: **You exaggerate, but I'd still like to meet him.**

8.   **(B)**   She says, here are my baby booties. Mom had them in a box, wrapped in tissue paper. I think that's so touching. That's nothing, he says. She has our baby teeth in an envelope. (B) is the next logical comment: **She's sentimental, like all mothers.** The other choices are (A), **She has a lot of collections,** (C) **She's organizing things,** and (D) **She thinks she's a museum curator.**

9.   **(A)**   She's going to the mall with Mado and they'll grab a bite there. She asks her husband to feed the kids and the dog. He says no problem but not to spend too much. The best rejoinder is (A), **Everything's on sale now and we'll get a good bargain.** The other answers are certainly not what her husband wants to hear: **I'll charge everything we buy** (B), **You only live once** (C), and **We intend to make wildly extravagant purchases** (D).

10.   **(C)**   She complains about a dark and dreary day. February seems endless to her. He quips, Gee! and I thought it was the shortest month! Her comeback will not be **Valentine's Day is nice** (A), **Your birthday is the 28th** (B), or **February is the month after January** (D). Her retort is most likely to be (C), **In spite of your sarcasm, February is an unbearable month.**

11.   **(C)**   He's going to help the boys with their coin collections after school this afternoon. They will organize everything. She says, Great idea! She'll clear off the dining room table so they can work there. The next comment will be (C), **I'll bring down their coin albums.** This makes more sense than

(A) **The post office is closed for renovations**, (B) **We'll put all the photos in the albums,** or (D) **They'll earn their Stamp badge (for Scouts) this way.**

12. **(D)** He thinks he's beginning to lose his hair and asks if she doesn't think his hairline is receding. She says it's not that noticeable and that he can always grow a beard. Then she says she'll always love him, no matter how he looks. The most likely remark to follow is the question **Even without hair?** Answer (D) makes more sense than (A) **Yes, I'm bald as an egg** (in French, one is bald as a pebble), (B) **Okay, I'll remain clean-shaven,** or (C) **I'll shave twice a day.**

13. **(B)** She's flunked her chemistry test and is worried about telling their parents. She says her life is over. He got an A on his test and offers to help her study every night for two weeks, the amount of time they have before the next test. He says she'll pass it next time around, no need to worry their parents. The next most likely comment is (B), **You would help me to study like that? That's great!**

14. **(C)** She suggests they take a walk and get some air. He was just about to put on his slippers. What will she say next? The most likely remark is (C), **Couldn't you put on your sneakers? It's such a beautiful evening.** The other answers do not make suitable sequiturs. **It doesn't matter what shoe** (A), **I'd like to change shoes, too** (B), and (D), **Put on your boots.**

15. **(A)** She's just walked 3 kilometers and feels great. He asks if she isn't out of breath. (A) is the best rejoinder: **Not really, I'm used to it.**

16. **(C)** *Éblouissant* means dazzling. It does not mean **silvery** or **metallic** (A). It does not mean **barely visible** (B). It does not mean **blinking** (D). The correct answer is (C) **dazzling, brilliant.**

17. **(A)** After toasting **they will clink their glasses together.** The correct answer is (A).

18. **(A)** When she misses her husband **she looks at the stars,** which she knows he can see too, no matter how far away, and **she thinks of him.**

19. **(B)** The night sky is clear and dark. It's not **cloudy** (A). There is no **storm brewing** (C). Since the horizon is not described, (D) is not cor-

rect. (B) is the best answer, **The darkness is studded with sparkling diamonds.**

20. **(A)** They are not going home to England **with their two children** (B). They are not planning to visit **Scandinavian countries,** either (C). They are not planning **a trans-Atlantic crossing** (D). They will be spending time in Italy and Greece. The best answer is (A), **They'll have a Mediterranean vacation.**

21. **(D)** The best answer is (D), **She wants to be able to travel, learn, and earn money.** The other choices are less logical. **She doesn't want to make a blunder** (A), **She wants to leave her parents** (B), and **to become an English citizen** (C).

22. **(C)** The children are not **twins** (A). They are not **snotty-nosed** (B), or **badly behaved** (D). The correct answer is (C). **They're cute and well-mannered.**

23. **(C)** **When all is said and done, yes.** The best answer is (C), as he does eventually agree. He has already considered her request, so we eliminate (A). He will miss her but has been persuaded by her promise to stay in touch daily, so eliminate (B). Her mother is not against the idea, so eliminate (D).

24. **(B)** She may **learn to cook Italian style** (A), but that is not a goal she speaks of. She won't be taking a course, so she doesn't need to worry about **having the time to cram** (C). The experience probably will **make her more worldly** (D), but she doesn't realize it at this point. When trying to persuade her father to give his permission, she points out that she will be able to improve her English and learn Italian. (B) is the best answer, **She imagines she will get better at foreign languages.**

25. **(B)** It was most likely **not well thought-out** (A). It wasn't the **act of an anarchist** (C). He probably wasn't just trying to impress his little sister (D). (B) is the most likely answer, **It was an adolescent urge to let off steam.**

26. **(A)** He did <u>not</u> **tear up the book before he threw it** (B). He <u>does</u> know where it landed, so (C) is not correct. The Latin textbook did not **fall into the bushes** (D). He couldn't get it because it landed on the roof. The correct answer is (A).

27. **(B)** It was not **premeditated** (A). It was not just **to show his parents that he didn't want to study anymore** (C). It wasn't **to show that he would have preferred French** (D). The correct answer is (B), **It was just a sudden urge.**

28. **(D)** The most likely answer is (D), His father will probably talk about **the need to think before doing something like that**.

29. **(C)** The correct answer is (C). What matters to her most is **being able to continue their camping trips even when they are older and less physically capable** of doing all the chores that tent-camping involves.

30. **(A)** Pile means **exactly** in French. It's like saying **Bingo!** when someone is right on target in English. The correct answer is (A).

31. **(B)** The husband admits that his back hurt him last year and he remembers getting soaked one night when it rained hard. He has agreed to look at trailers with his wife. She really wants one. This couple will probably eventually choose a trailer. The best answer is (B), **Yes, probably.**

32. **(C)** There's nothing to suggest **she will pout if he doesn't agree** (A). We don't know whether **her husband likes to drive** or not, so (B) is not the correct answer. She doesn't seem to mind cooking on their outings; in fact she's enthusiastic about the real kitchen a trailer would have. The answer is not (D). The best answer is (C). According to her, they are getting too old to set up and take down the tent at each stop. She'd also like a real bed and a reliable shelter from bad weather.

33. **(A)** If the cathedral rises up over the houses like a huge weather-beaten shepherd, the houses would then be like a flock of **sheep.** The best answer is (A).

34. **(B)** The author is struck by the serenity of Périgueux. It is quieter and **calmer** than Paris. The best answer is (B).

35. **(C)** She describes a feeling of palpable calm as well as a peacefulness that penetrates one's very core. The correct answer is (C).

36. **(C)** She liked Périgueux *d'emblée*. The correct answer is (C), **She liked it as soon as she saw it.** She didn't need **to warm up to it little by**

little (A). It didn't **take a while** (B). To say that **she never got used to it** (D) is certainly not the case.

37. **(C)**   They laugh loudly and giggle like a bunch of schoolgirls. The correct answer is (C), **They feel younger and more carefree.**

38. **(B)**   **It was to become their favorite restaurant** suggests that they would eat there again and again. The correct answer is (B), **many times. They were not thrown out for making too much noise the first time they ate there** (C). Because she says it became their favorite haunt, we may assume the food was consistently good. Eliminate (D) as a suitable answer. Answer (A) says they ate there just once.

39. **(A)**   He uses **his only flare,** *son unique fusée.* There are **none left.** He only had one to begin with. (A) is the correct answer.

40. **(A)**   The hands of the altimeter did not come loose but **they were fluctuating so fast he could hardly read them.** The correct answer is (A).

41. **(A)**   The pilot could no longer distinguish the sky from the earth. He thought that dizzying hills were rolling toward him. He did not realize that he was flying over water until he lit the flare. The correct answer is (A), **He thought he was flying over hilly terrain.**

42. **(C)**   Both Fabien and the reader realize that he will not be able to land safely. The correct answer is (C), **Failing a miracle, it will probably be impossible.**

43. **(A)**   She utters this tiny little syllable, which rises up from her as though torn from wounded flesh. **She understands that her husband is in great danger.** The correct answer is (A).

44. **(B)**   Of course he knows why she called; Fabien's plane is lost; he should have landed by now. He uses the trite formula **What can I do for you?** (A) as though there were nothing wrong. He knows she's not calling **to check on atmospheric conditions** (C). He knows it's not **to confirm his arrival time** (D). The correct answer is (B), **He knows exactly why she called but feels very ill at ease and awkward speaking to her.**

45. **(D)**   They hem and haw but not because they are **very busy and preoccupied** (A). It is not because **there were a lot of calls that evening** (B).

It is not because **Mme Fabien annoys them with frequent calls** (C). The correct answer is (D), **Neither one of them wants to be the bearer of the sad news** that Fabien's plane has gone down.

46. **(C)**   The pheasant, the sea gull, the nightingale, and the pigeon are all **quite common.** The correct answer is (C). None of them is **endangered** (A), **rare** (B), or **foreign** (D).

47. **(B)**   Even if you didn't already know that **the gull** is a seaside bird, the text tell us it likes to roost on *falaises maritimes,* **seaside cliffs.** The correct answer is (B).

48. **(D)**   The pigeon makes a cooing sound. The French verb, *roucouler,* is one of the most perfect examples of onomatopoeia that exist. When pronounced correctly, it sounds exactly like a pigeon's coo. The correct answer is (D), **the pigeon.**

49. **(B)**   This is a gull whose English name is based on the sound of its call. The correct answer is (B), **a gull.**

50. **(C)**   The nightingale is described in the article as being an incomparable singer. Its beautiful song is unmatched. The correct answer is (C).

51. **(A)**   The pheasant has a distinctive scarlet facial patch. The correct answer is (A), **bright red.**

52. **(C)**   (A) is incorrect because the feet vary in size as well as color. (B) is also wrong because they are not all black. (C) is the best answer, **Yes, they vary, and so do the beaks.** (D) is wrong because it suggests all bird feet are the same.

53. **(C)**   The nightingale apparently enjoys singing so much that it occasionally includes the songs of other birds in its repertory. The correct answer is (C), **the nightingale.**

54. **(C)**   The human mouth is described as a very vile, bad-smelling place. It is not **a little crowded but comfortable** (A). It is not **a warm and reassuring shelter** (B). It is not **an agreeable place** (D). The correct answer is (C), **a disgusting prison.**

55. **(A)** The words got tired of having to be constantly at the beck and call of ungrateful humans who used them and never even began to appreciate them. They rose up like freed slaves in revolt. They couldn't stand their constrained and indentured status, their **slavery.** The correct answer is (A).

56. **(C)** Their adopted town was once a gold-mining center, abandoned when all of the gold had been mined. The correct answer is (C), **Its treasure had been exhausted.** It hadn't become just **too dilapidated to live there** (A). It hadn't been flooded out because **it was too close to the sea** (B). Its inhabitants did not **all die of the plague at the beginning of the century** (D).

57. **(B)** The correct answer is (B), **Like the nouns, they are other tribes of escaped words.**

58. **(C)** The job of nouns has always been **to name all of the things in the world in a distinctly unique way.** The correct answer is (C). Their traditional job was not **to collect the nametags from botanical gardens** (A). It was not **to convene the other tribes** (B). It was not **to group things** (D).

59. **(D)** Their tribe is the biggest and most powerful **because there are so many things on earth that must be named.** (D) is the correct answer. It is not **because their tribe is the principal one,** even though it is (A). Their warriors did not **vanquish smaller tribes** (B). It is not **because they arrived on the island first** (C).

60. **(C)** The best answer is (C), **They can sting and bite.** They are not **innocuous** (A) or **good for nothing** (B). One doesn't usually **choke on words** (D).

61. **(C)** The correct answer is (C), **He was a woodcutter.** He did not **work for the *Seigneur*** (A), he was not **a butcher** (B), and he didn't **make coins** (D).

62. **(A)** The correct answer is (A), **They were so poor they could no longer feed them.** The children weren't **hoodlums** (B). The parents deliberately left them behind, so (C), which says they didn't do it on purpose, is incorrect. Eliminate (D) because they did not **intend to pick them up later on.**

63. **(C)**   He didn't know the forest that well (A). He didn't have a torch to light (B). He didn't hide to watch which path his parents took (D). The correct answer is (C), **He threw little pebbles which he would be able to recognize again all along the path** they took into the forest.

64. **(A)**   As soon as the couple got back to their house, they received 10 coins, in payment for a debt which they had long ago stopped hoping to be paid for. (A) is the correct answer.

65. **(D)**   **They buy food** with their windfall. The correct answer is (D). They don't **refurbish the house** (A), or **hide it behind the house** (B). They don't use it **to help others** (C).

66. **(A)**   The wife clearly misses her children and says she's sorry they abandoned them. She's also worried about what will become of them in the forest. The correct answer is (A).

67. **(B)**   It was the father who decided to leave the children in the forest, not **the mother** (C). The corrrect answer is (B). It wasn't a joint decision (A), and the children didn't **want to run away** (D).

68. **(A)**   **The mother very much regrets leaving the children and fears they will be eaten by wolves.** The correct answer is (A).

69. **(B)**   The correct answer is (B), **They will take the children back with open arms and the mother will feed them** as soon as they come in.

70. **(B)**   The correct answer is (B). Little Red Riding Hood, Cinderella, and Sleeping Beauty are all fairy tales.

71. **(B)**   **The walls of the dining room are made of glass because it is a greenhouse.** The correct answer is (B).

72. **(A)**   She wants him **to come spend time with her at Islette.** She tells him how beautiful it is, how welcome he would be, and that he can have any room he'd like. The correct answer is (A).

73. **(A)**   She wants him **to buy her a bathing suit** so she can go bathing in the river like Mme Courcelle's daughter and maid do. The correct answer is (A).

74. **(B)** She tells him exactly what the bathing suit must be like. **It must be dark blue serge with white braid trim. Two pieces, size medium.** She doesn't want him to pick one out for her (A); she wants him to find her the one she has described. The correct answer is (B). Answer (C), just something she can use, is not correct because she has specified exactly what she wants. She is not planning to wear the bathing suit to the hot baths at Azay because she doesn't like to go there at all (D).

75. **(B)** **She's relaxing and enjoying her free time** (idleness). The correct answer is (B), She takes walks in the park, enjoys meals in the beautiful greenhouse dining room, writes letters, and will go bathing as soon as she gets a swim suit.

Section II
Part A: Writing

Fill In a Word

1. *une*
 Boum is feminine when it means **party** and masculine when it means **bang.** Use the **indefinite** article to say that **Mireille is having a party.**

2. *le*
 Calendar dates are always masculine. Use the definite article for **the 14th of July.**

3. *tous*
 What would fit into this slot? An adverb would work, but none seems to fit the context we have. The adjective **all** fits the context, so we supply it in the masculine plural form to match *nous.*

4. *On*
 This verb form needs a third person subject, so we supply the general *on.*

5. *chez*
 The preposition *chez* fits in front of the disjunctive pronoun *elle* to make **at her place.**

6. *puis* (or *alors*)
 An adverb of time is needed here. Both *puis* and *alors* (meaning **then**) will work. You could also use *ensuite or après.*

7. *quelque*
 Supply the indefinite pronoun *quelque* to begin this common expression.

8. *à*
 Complete the common expression **something to eat** with the preposition *à.*

9. *dont*
 Here *dont* means **about whom.** It connects a direct object, *frère,* to the verb that governs it, *parler.* It is used instead of *que* because **to speak of** (or **about**) involves the preposition *de,* even though it isn't visible.

10. *mais*

A coordinating conjunction is needed to link these two clauses. **But** fits the context nicely.

11. *Après*

The combination of **infinitive + past participle** requires the preposition *après* to make the equivalent of the English gerund **after attending.**

12. *au*

The verb *assister* requires the preposition *à* before its object. Here it contracts with *le* to produce *au.*

13. *le*

Tout le monde is an idiom for **everyone.**

14. *autre* (or *dernière*)

Use one of these adjectives to suggest **another** or **a last** time.

15. *de*

Avant uses *de* in front of an infinitive.

Fill In a Verb

1. *a ouvert*

Gisèle opened the door. The *passé composé* expresses an action whose completion is easy to visualize within the confines of the sentence.

2. *était arrivé*

Use the *plus-que-parfait* (**had arrived**) for an action that was to have taken place prior to the opening of the door.

3. *aimait*

Chaque matin is a clue to use the imperfect for this habitual action.

4. *buvant*

Place a present participle after *en* to create a simultaneous activity, **while drinking her coffee.**

5. *a fermé*

Fermer is conjugated with *avoir* because it is transitive, that is, capable of accepting a direct object, **the door.**

6. *s'est assise*

S'asseoir, a reflexive verb, is conjugated with *être.*

7. **guetter**

The preposition *à* (from *s'asseoir à*) signals that an infinitive is to follow.

8. **rentrant**

The preposition *en* calls for the present participle. This makes the equivalent of the English gerund **on coming home.**

9. **a trouvé**

Use the *passé composé* for the simple completed action **she found.**

10. **Ecoute**

With no subject pronoun in sight, a command form is clearly needed. Use the familiar form because *tu* appears in the next part of the sentence. Remember to drop the *s* in this *-er* command.

11. **es**

Use the present tense here, just as you would in English. **If you are free tomorrow night.**

12. **ramasser**

Always use an infinitive form after a modal verb such as *vouloir*: **I would like to come pick you up around 6 o'clock.**

13. **crois** (or **croyais**)

Use the <u>present</u> to say **I think / I believe you would like it.** The <u>imperfect</u> conveys **I thought you would like it.** Either tense is plausible here.

14. **Rappelle**

This is another *-er* command form with a dropped *s* in the *tu* form: **Call me back as soon as you can.**

15. **pourras**

Use the future after *dès que* here.

16. **sois**

An affirmative command is needed here. Note that the *être* command form is irregular and must be learned by heart.

17. **va**

Another affirmative command is needed here. The fact that there are no subject pronouns for these verbs is a tip-off.

18. **trouveras**

A literal need for the future; **You will find it.**

19. **Tiens**

Use the *tu* form of the command here because the woman is speaking to her son.

20. **peux** (or **pourrai** or **pourrais**)

The present tense of *pouvoir* gives the literal translation for **I can't.** It would also be possible to use the future tense, **I won't be able.** The conditional would work too, **I couldn't.**

21. **agisse**

Always use the subjunctive after *il faut que*.

22. **j'entends**

Use the present tense here, **What's this I hear?**; it is also used in the mother's next question, **Am I dreaming?**

23. **réclame**

Use the 3rd-person verb form to match the subject of the verb on the other side of the relative pronoun; *le même, mon fils André*.

24. **essaie** (or **essaye**)

Both spellings of the present indicative are acceptable.

25. **pense**

The subjunctive is required after *il faut que*. It looks just the same as the 1st person indicative here.

Part B

Two Sample Essay Answers

Read the following essays to see how a student might have answered this question. You will note different ability levels in the two responses. Try to critique the essays yourself and then read the evaluations that follow to get a feel for how they would be graded.

Sample Essay 1

Aujourd'hui, la technologie est présente partout. Que ce soit à l'école, au travail ou dans sa propre maison, il est impossible d'éviter d'y être exposé. De plus en plus jeune, on apprend à se servir des différents outils de la technologie. Cela a bien sur un effet sur l'art. D'abord, il y a l'apparition d'un nouvel art : celui du cinéma. Ensuite, il y a les changements dans les arts qui existent déjà : la musique électronique, le dessin à l'ordinateur, les trucages et effets de lumière au théâtre, etc. . . . Je crois que, d'une certaine manière, la technologie a rendu l'art accessible à tous. Ce qui aurait pris des années d'études et des heures à accomplir il y a deux cents ans peut aujourd'hui se faire rapidement et simplement avec un ordinateur. Personnellement, je suis particulièrement intéressée par la musique. Elle m'aide à m'évader du monde stressant et sans trêve de tous les jours. Lorsque je compose, je préfère rester aussi loin que possible de mon ordinateur pour pouvoir conserver la vieille tradition du papier et du vrai piano. Je pense qu'il est important pour chacun de trouver au moins une forme d'art qui l'aide à se distraire dans un monde ou le travail et la productivité semblent être mis en valeur plus que la créativité.

Sample Essay 2

Aujourd'hui, il y a de plus en plus de technologie et de moins en moins de vrai art. Il n'y a plus de gens qui font des peintures comme avant ou de la sculpture par exemple.

Dans ma vie, l'art, c'est important pour m'exprimer. J'aime bien aussi regarder l'art. Parfois, je joue de la musique ou je fais des dessins. J'aime bien aussi écouter la musique. J'aime aller au cinéma. Le cinéma est un art que j'aime beaucoup. Je vais au cinéma souvent. Les peintures et les sculptures, on ne les trouve plus que dans les musées. Les gens ne font plus de l'art comme ça. J'aime bien écouter la musique parce que ça me calme ou alors pour les fêtes. J'aime bien danser aussi.

La technologie, ça donne de l'importance aux jeux vidéo par exemple, et de nouvelles façons de s'amuser que l'art. Mais aussi ça a créé le cinéma. Alors l'art existe toujours avec la technologie. J'aime beaucoup le cinéma, donc je m'intéresse toujours à l'art même si c'est à travers la technologie. Puisque j'aime la danse et la musique aussi, l'art joue un rôle important dans ma vie.

Evaluation of Sample Essay 1

This is an excellent essay. It is very well written and shows good mastery of sentence structure and a broad range of vocabulary. The student expresses her original ideas clearly and well. She makes good observations about the world around her and draws from her own personal experience. The essay is organized and flows nicely from one point to the next. It reads smoothly and would earn a very good score.

Evaluation of Sample Essay 2

The second essay is extremely disorganized. This detracts greatly and makes following difficult. The sentences are not that poorly written, but the overall effect is not successful. This essay would not score well.

Part C: Sample Answers to Speaking Questions

Les Bonbons

Here is how a student might have answered the questions that accompany the sketches:

(1) On voit une petite fille devant une boîte de bonbons. L'emballage a la forme d'un cœur comme les cadeaux pour la fête de la Saint Valentin. La boîte est ouverte.

Elle adore les bonbons à la cerise. On ne voit pas de couvercle ayant le guide qui explique ce qu'il y a à l'intérieur de tous les bonbons. Comment savoir où est la cerise ?

Elle aura essayé plusieurs bonbons sans succès. Elle les a laissés à moitié mangés.

Du succès ! Elle a trouvé la cerise qu'elle cherchait. Elle la savoure.

Sa sœur aînée la découvre en même temps qu'elle consomme la cerise. Sa sœur voit tous les bonbons goûtés, son cadeau massacré. Elle n'a pas l'air content.

(2) Je crois quil s'agit d'un cadeau qui appartenait à sa sœur. Elle l'ouvrait quand quelqu'un ou quelque chose l'a interrompue. Peut-être que c'était le téléphone. Elle aura pris le couvercle avec elle.

(3) La grande sœur n'est pas contente mais je ne crois pas que la petite mérite d'être punie. Une boîte entière de bonbons sur laquelle personne ne veille, c'est une trop forte tentation pour une petite fille. Elle est animée par la curiosité, pas par la méchanceté. J'espère que sa sœur pourra la pardonner.

La Croissance

Here is how a student might have answered the questions that accompany the sketches:

(1) Une jeune mère et son fils viennent de planter un jeune arbre dans leur jardin. Ils ont creusé un trou, et ancré la plante. Ils ont l'air satisfait. Maintenant il faudra veiller sur le petit arbre pour qu'il pousse et devienne grand.

Les années passent vite dans la vie des jeunes. Maintenant on voit que l'arbre a vraiment grandi. Il est tout droit et répand ses branches feuilletées. C'est un bel arbre fort et costaud. Le petit garçon, lui aussi, a beaucoup grandi. Il est aussi grand que l'arbre à cette époque et il est beaucoup plus grand que sa mère. Celle-ci semble petite devant l'arbre et à côté de lui. C'est un beau fils. Comme l'arbre, il est fort, bien bâti et en pleine forme.

(2) La mère devient de moins en moins gardienne. Un fils sain et fort commence peu à peu à jouer ce rôle lui-même. Quand il y a quelque chose de lourd, c'est lui qui s'en occupe. Quand il y a des tas de neige ou de feuilles à enlever, c'est vers lui qu'elle se tournera. Elle est toujours jeune mais quand elle sera affaiblie par les années, c'est son fils qui veillera sur elle.

(3) La mère a bien veillé sur les deux. Elle a sans doute arrosé fidèlement son petit arbre. Quand il gelait l'hiver, elle l'emballait de toile. Elle a nourri son sol de vitamines. L'arbre poussait et fleurissait en même temps que le petit garçon. Celui-là s'épanouit pareillement au bons soins de sa mère. Le grand garçon et le bel arbre témoignent l'amour maternel de cette femme. Ils ont grandi ensemble, comme des frères élevés dans la même famille.

APPENDIX
Audio CD Transcripts

AP French

Pre-Exam Transcript

SECTION I

Part A: Listening

Exchanges

Get ready for the listening part of the Advanced Placement
French Language Pre-Exam practice.

Directions: Listen to the following brief exchanges between two people. You
will hear each exchange twice. Then, based on what you have just heard,
choose the most likely rejoinder from the four choices you are given. Blacken
the corresponding oval on your answer sheet.

Now listen to the first exchange.

Exchange 1

M: Il y a avait quelqu'un au téléphone mais il a raccroché avant que je ne
réponde.

W: Il n'a pas laissé de message sur le répondeur?

Listen to exchange 2.

Exchange 2

M: Ce matin je vais sauvegarder tous mes fichiers récents à l'ordinateur.

W: Mieux vaut prévenir que guérir! Je devrais le faire aussi mais je ne
prends jamais le temps.

Listen to exchange 3.

Exchange 3

M: Tu veux goûter cette glace à l'eau ? C'est la marque Esquimau.
W: Quels sont les parfums ?

Listen to exchange 4.

Exchange 4

M: J'ai passé une nuit blanche hier soir.
W: C'est pour ça que tu as l'air crevé !

Listen to exchange 5.

Exchange 5

M: J'ai mal au dos, j'ai trop fait aujourd'hui.
W: Je conseille une douche longue et chaude.

Listen to exchange 6.

Exchange 6

W: Le courrier n'est pas encore arrivé ?
M: Non, c'est un nouveau facteur, il prend son temps.

Listen to exchange 7.

Exchange 7

M: Tu veux m'aider à laver la voiture ce matin ?
W: Oui, il fait du soleil, je mettrai d'abord mon maillot de bain.

Listen to exchange 8.

Exchange 8

M: On est rentré ce soir entre chien et loup.
W: Je ne comprends pas. Qu'est-ce que cela veut dire *entre chien et loup* ?

Listen to exchange 9.

Exchange 9

W: Didier devient commandant au mois d'avril ! Gisèle nous invite à la cérémonie aux Invalides ! Elle est si fière de son fils !

M: Elle devrait l'être, sa carrière militaire s'est envolée d'emblée. Il a beaucoup de succès dans l'Armée française. Devenir commandant si jeune, c'est un accomplissement rare !

Listen to exchange 10.

Exchange 10

W: Où est ta serviette de plage mouillée ?

M: Je l'ai jetée sur la chaise en bois dans la cuisine.

Listen to exchange 11.

Exchange 11

M: J'ai rendu mon thème en retard.

W: Ton prof l'a-t-il accepté ? Je sais qu'il est très sévère. Qu'est-ce qu'il a dit ?

Listen to exchange 12.

Exchange 12

M: Qui a pris mon marteau sans le remettre ?

W: C'est moi qui suis coupable. Je ne sais pas où je l'ai laissé.

Listen to exchange 13.

Exchange 13

M: Le climatiseur est en panne. J'étouffe.

W: Allons au centre commercial, il fera frais et confortable là-bas.

Listen to exchange 14.

Exchange 14

M: Je t'ai envoyé un e-mail et on me l'a rendu, pas livrable.
W: Je crois que ma boîte à lettres est remplie au maximum.

Listen to exchange 15.

Exchange 15

M: Mais non ! Ne jette pas mes pantoufles !
W: Elles sont affreuses, toutes en lambeaux et elles ne sont pas euh . . . fraîches !

Dialogues

Directions: Listen to the following dialogues. Afterwards, listen to the questions based on the dialogue you have just heard and choose the best answer from the choices that follow. You will hear each question twice. Blacken the corresponding oval on your answer sheet.

Now get ready for the first dialogue.

Dialogue 1: La Placomusophilie

M: Ce champagne est mousseux, tu l'aimes ?
W: J'adore ! Ah, . . . frais, froid et léger ! Archimousseux !
M: À propos, savais-tu que je suis devenu placomusophiliste ?
W: Pardon ? Placo . . . quoi ?
M: Placomusophiliste . . . cela veut dire que je collectionne les petites capsules en métal que l'on trouve sur les bouchons de champagne. On les appelle *plaques de muselet*.
W: Plaques de muselet ? Un chien méchant porte un muselet . . .
M: La petite cage en fil qui retient le bouchon dans la bouteille s'appelle un muselet aussi. Quand tu l'enlèves tu trouves la plaque en dessous; elle protège le bouchon. Voici celle dont nous venons de boire le champagne.
W: Hein ! Pas vilaine du tout. Fond argenté, petite grappe de raisin pourprée en relief, de petites feuilles vertes, les initiales de la maison entrelacées. C'est charmant. Je l'aurais jetée sans même regarder. Moi aussi, je voudrais les collectionner.

M: D'accord, celle-ci, je te la donne pour commencer. Elle est à toi ! Je possède environs 100 capsules à présent. Il y a beaucoup de sites sur l'Internet où on peut acheter, vendre et échanger.

W: Je ne savais même pas que ce placo-monde existait ! J'aimerais bien voir comment tu les exposes.

M: Il y a des répertoires, des plaques qui s'accrochent au mur, des albums, des vitrines. C'est une petite manie surtout en France. Tu verras, presque tous les sites ont une adresse française.

W: J'aime beaucoup l'idée d'avoir un dada français. On a un petit souvenir de ce que l'on a bu, et puis, à part l'achat de la bouteille, ça ne coûte rien !

16. Pourquoi les gens aiment-ils collectionner les plaques de muselet ?

17. Est-ce que ce passe-temps est répandu ?

18. Comment peut-on devenir collectionneur ?

19. Y a-t-il des sites où l'on peut se renseigner ?

Now get ready for the next dialogue.

Dialogue 2: Le Placard

W: Ton placard est rempli à ras ! Il est si bourré que si tu ouvres la porte toutes tes affaires tombent par terre en avalanche. Il est temps de trier et de ranger !

M: Franchement c'est un tel fatras que je ne sais où commencer.

W: Je t'aiderai. Vidons-le d'abord. Puis tu en feras quatre tas: jeter, vendre, donner, retenir . . . et le dernier tas ne peut pas trop dépasser les autres, d'accord ?

M: Bonne idée. Ça ira vite !

W: Pendant que tu fais le triage je nettoierai l'intérieur du placard. Je passerai l'aspirateur, j'essuierai les étagères, et je jetterai tous les cintres déformés.

M: La besogne est plus réalisable à deux. Merci de m'aider !

W: De rien ! Tu sais l'organisation c'est un peu mon rayon !

20. Pourquoi le dernier tas ne doit-il pas trop dépasser les autres ?

21. Est-ce que la femme trouve cette tâche odieuse ?

22. Que veut dire *trier*?

23. Il paraît que le problème n'est pas seulement un manque d'organisation mais aussi que les choses sont . . .

24. Vont-ils tout ôter au commencement?

Now get ready for the next dialogue.

Dialogue 3: L'Ordinateur

W: Je meurs !

M: Oh là, c'est sérieux !

W: Je viens de perdre tout ce que j'avais rédigé hier soir. J'ai travaillé jusqu'à une heure du matin sur ma thèse !

M: Comment cela est arrivé? Il a planté,* ton ordinateur?

W: Non. J'ai ouvert le fichier ce matin pour continuer mon travail. J'ai effacé par inadvertance à peu près trois quarts de mon texte et je l'ai fermé sans faire trop attention. Quand le petit panneau jaune est apparu, me demandant si je voulais retenir les changements, j'ai répondu . . . oui.

M: Je sais comment tu peux le repêcher.

W: T'es sérieux? Ça se fait?

M: Bien sûr, tu n'es pas la seule personne à perdre quelque chose d'important dans le vide de l'autre côté de l'écran !

W: Comment fait-on alors?

M: L'ordinateur tient des dossiers provisoires. Ils sont datés. On ne les voit pas normalement parce qu'ils sont cachés, mais on peut les faire venir, et tu reconnaîtras ton dossier numéroté par la date.

W: Quel soulagement ! Tu es top !

* Il a planté = *Did it freeze?* (*This expression means that the computer has frozen, and is now no more animated than a potted plant.*)

25. Est-ce que cette sorte de perte de document est rare?

26. La jeune femme a-t-elle sauvegardé son travail?

27. Comment pourront-ils revoir le document perdu?

28. Comment la jeune femme a-t-elle perdu son document?

Now get ready for the next dialogue.

Dialogue 4: Le Violon d'Ingrès

W: Devine quoi ! Je craque de bonheur !

M: Ça va, je mords. Raconte.

W: Tu sais que chaque fois que je vais à Paris je fais la visite de la boutique qui s'appelle Pain d'Épices, dans le Passage Jouffroy. C'est un monde féerique de poupées, de jouets, et ce qui m'attire le plus, de miniatures.

M: Tu as fait des achats ?

W: Bien sûr ! Une pelle de jardin aussi grande que l'index, une salade aux crevettes sur une assiette de porcelaine moins grande qu'une pièce d'un euro, un petit tapis turc, un service à thé, des pains et des carrés de fromage, une lampe . . .

M: Acheter c'est le plaisir des femmes, en voilà la preuve . . .

W: Mais ce n'est pas tout. Tu sais que je crée moi-même de petits plats miniaturisés pour m'amuser. Je les modèle en argile et puis je les passe au four. Tu les a déjà vus, je confectionne de petites pizzas, des tranches de Bûche de Noël, des tartes, des fromages à l'italienne sur corde, même des spaghettis.

M: Oui je m'en souviens, tu as vraiment les doigts de fée. Tes créations sont très vraisemblables.

W: J'ai montré quelques exemplaires de mon travail à la propriétaire et elle veut les mettre en vente dans sa boutique ! C'est le clou de ma carrière !

29. Est-ce que la jeune femme est miniaturiste professionnel ?

30. Quelle sorte de magasin est *Pain d'Épices* ?

31. Quel genre de miniatures la jeune femme confectionne-t-elle ?

32. Avoir *les doigts de fée*, est-ce un compliment ?

Section II

Part C: Speaking

Get ready for the speaking part of the Advanced Placement French Language pre-examination practice.

You have one minute and 30 seconds to look at the following series of five pictures and to answer the questions that accompany them. You will have 60 seconds to respond to each question. Read the questions carefully and listen attentively. You must answer each question.

Your score on this section will be based on how well you understand the question asked, as well as your answer. Your response to each question will be scored on its appropriateness, its grammatical correctness, and your pronunciation. The purpose of this part of the test is to get a full sample of your speaking capability. Answer each question to the best of your ability. Your answers should be long enough to use all of the time allotted for each response.

In the event that you are still answering the question when you hear the speaker say, "Listen to the next question," end your response so that you will not miss the next question. Don't worry if your response to the question isn't finished. If you catch yourself making an error while you are speaking, simply correct it. You will hear a tone that signals for you to begin speaking.

You may now turn the page and begin to study the first series of pictures. You have one minute and 30 seconds.

Now get ready to listen to the questions. You will have 60 seconds to answer each one. Speak after the tone.

Pre-Exam Speaking, CD 1, Track 3 (Le Chat)

1. Racontez l'histoire présentée dans ces images.

   Listen to the next question.

2. Qui a plus peur selon vous ? Le chat ou la fillette ? Pourquoi ?

   Listen to the next question.

3. La vie des jeunes est pleine de petits périls quotidiens. Même si la crise est banale, elle nous enseigne sur la vie. La fillette, qu'est-ce qu'elle aurait appris ?

Now get ready to listen to the questions. You will have 60 seconds to answer each one.

Pre-Exam Speaking, CD 1, Track 4 (Samedi Matin)

4. Racontez les événements présentés dans ces images.

   Listen to the next question.

5. Comment les taches ménagères sont-elles partagées chez vous ?

   Listen to the next question.

6. D'après vous, les enfants, doivent-ils recevoir de l'argent pour les besognes accomplies ?

Now get ready to listen to the questions. You will have 60 seconds to answer each one.

Pre-Exam Speaking, CD 1, Track 5 (Le Grand Bal)

7.   Racontez l'histoire qui se déroule.

Listen to the next question.

8.   Croyez-vous que le jeune homme est nerveux d'habitude ?

Listen to the next question.

9.   Discutez la tradition américaine du bal lycéen à la fin de l'année scolaire.

Now get ready to listen to the questions. You will have 60 seconds to answer each one.

Pre-Exam Speaking, CD 1, Track 6 (Le Professeur)

10.   Racontez l'histoire qui se déroule.

Listen to the next question.

11.   Pourquoi le jeune homme ne s'est-il pas réveillé ? Donnez des raisons vraisemblables.

Listen to the next question.

12.   Commentez la conduite des élèves pendant l'absence de leur professeur.

Now get ready to listen to the questions. You will have 60 seconds to answer each one.

Pre-Exam Speaking, CD 1, Track 7 (Les Vacances Européenes)

13. Décrivez ce qui se déroule dans cette série de dessins.

Listen to the next question.

14. Avez-vous jamais été en France? Si oui, comment l'avez vous trouvée? Si vous n'avez jamais été en France, que voudriez-vous voir si vous y alliez?

Listen to the next question.

15. Vaut-il la peine de faire la queue pour voir quelque chose de vraiment célèbre?

Now get ready to listen to the questions. You will have 60 seconds to answer each one.

Pre-Exam Speaking, CD 1, Track 8 (Le Chien Errant)

16. Décrivez ce qui se passe dans cette série d'images.

Listen to the next question.

17. Quelles promesses les enfants auront-ils dû faire à leur mère pour pouvoir garder le chien errant?

Listen to the next question.

18. Quel rôle les animaux domestiques peuvent-ils jouer dans la vie familiale?

Now get ready to listen to the questions. You will have 60 seconds to answer each one.

Pre-Exam Speaking, CD 1, Track 9 (Les Escargots)

19. Décrivez ce qui se passe dans ces scènes.

Listen to the next question.

20. Avez-vous jamais essayé les escargots ? Si oui, comment les avez-vous trouvés ? Si non, comptez-vous les goûter un jour ?

Listen to the next question.

21. Devrait-on manger quelque chose que l'on n'aime pas, pour plaire aux autres ?

Now get ready to listen to the questions. You will have 60 seconds to answer each one.

Pre-Exam Speaking, CD 1, Track 10 (Le Coup de Soleil)

22. Dites ce qui se passe dans cette série de dessins.

Listen to the next question.

23. Comment le garçon aurait-il pu éviter ce coup de soleil ?

Listen to the next question.

24. Expliquez pourquoi ce n'est pas une bonne idée d'aller à la plage tout seul.

Now get ready to listen to the questions. You will have 60 seconds to answer each one.

Pre-Exam Speaking, CD 1, Track 11 (La Pizza)

25. Racontez l'histoire qui se déroule.

Listen to the next question.

26. Donnez quelques raisons pour lesquelles le troisième garçon ne voudrait pas de saucisse.

Listen to the next question.

27. Commentez brièvement le vieux dicton *chacun son goût*.

Now get ready to listen to the questions. You will have 60 seconds to answer each one.

Pre-Exam Speaking, CD 1, Track 12 (L'Équipe)

28. Comparez et contrastez les deux situations.

Listen to the next question.

29. Comment l'acte de perdre peut-il nous enseigner?

Listen to the next question.

30. Pourquoi est-il difficile de perdre en public?

Now get ready to listen to the questions. You will have 60 seconds to answer each one.

Pre-Exam Speaking, CD 1, Track 13 (Le Dîner)

31. Maman doit servir à manger chaque soir. Dégagez les différences évidentes dans la préparation de ces deux repas.

Listen to the next question.

32. Selon vous est-ce que sa famille sera décue de ne pas avoir un repas préparé à partir de zéro ?

Listen to the next question.

33. Croyez-vous que nous, Américains, perdions la tradition du dîner familial ?

Now get ready to listen to the questions. You will have 60 seconds to answer each one.

Pre-Exam Speaking, CD 2, Track 1 (Les Choristes)

34. Dites ce que vous penseriez si vous voyiez le premier dessin sans voir le suivant.

Listen to the next question.

35. Contrastez l'apparence publique et la réalité.

Listen to the next question.

36. Est-ce que toutes les vedettes de l'écran et du théâtre sont vraiment aussi parfaites qu'il le semble ? Et les mannequins qui apparaissent sur les photos et dans les défilés de mode ?

Now get ready to listen to the questions. You will have 60 seconds to answer each one.

Pre-Exam Speaking, CD 2, Track 2 (Le Message)

37. Comparez et contrastez les deux scènes.

Listen to the next question.

38. Discutez les progrès qui permettent l'échange immédiat des messages aujourd'hui.

Listen to the next question.

39. Imaginez les progrès futurs en ce qui concerne la communication.

Now get ready to listen to the questions. You will have 60 seconds to answer each one.

Pre-Exam Speaking, CD 2, Track 3 (Le Mangeoir)

40. Comparez et contrastez les deux scènes.

Listen to the next question.

41. D'après vous, a-t-on pendu ce mangeoir pour attirer les écureuils ?

Listen to the next question.

42. Les choses finissent souvent à servir de manière non voulue dans la vie. Quelquefois c'est gênant mais cela peut aussi mener au bon. En pouvez-vous signaler un exemple de la vie actuelle ?

Now get ready to listen to the questions. You will have 60 seconds to answer each one.

Pre-Exam Speaking, CD 2, Track 4 (La Bagarre)

43. Comparez et contrastez les deux scènes.

    Listen to the next question.

44. Comment est-il possible de faire la paix après une dispute ?

    Listen to the next question.

45. Est-ce que les garçons se disputeront de nouveau ?

Now get ready to listen to the questions. You will have 60 seconds to answer each one.

Pre-Exam Speaking, CD 2, Track 5 (Le Téléphone)

46. Décrivez ce qui arrive.

    Listen to the next question.

47. Quand on est impatient chaque seconde semble durer une éternité. Commentez cet aspect de la vie.

    Listen to the next question.

48. Avez-vous jamais renoncé à une idée longtemps contemplée, pour la trouver tout d'un coup possible ?

Now get ready to listen to the questions. You will have 60 seconds to answer each one.

Pre-Exam Speaking, CD 2, Track 6 (Le Loisir)

49. Comparez et contrastez les deux scènes.

Listen to the next question.

50. Tout le monde apprécie et recherche un moment pour se détendre. Le loisir joue-t-il un rôle important dans votre vie ?

Listen to the next question.

51. Comment aimez-vous passer votre temps libre ?

AP French
Test 1 Transcript

SECTION I

Part A: Listening

Exchanges

Get ready for the listening part of the Advanced Placement
French Language Practice Test 1.

> **Directions:** Listen to the following brief exchanges between two people. You
> will hear each exchange twice. Then, based on what you have just heard,
> choose the most likely rejoinder from the four choices you are given. Blacken
> the corresponding oval on your answer sheet.

Now listen to the first exchange.

Exchange 1

W: Mes parents vont partir en croisière et veulent que je les accompagne,
toutefois, je m'inquiète un peu.

M: Pourquoi, veinarde ! Tu as de la chance. Ne t'en fais pas !

Listen to exchange 2.

Exchange 2

W: Sophie veut emprunter mon tailleur rose, tu sais, celui que tu
préfères ?

M: Ah bon ? Il est très seyant. Si elle te le rend je ne vois pas de problème.

Listen to exchange 3.

Exchange 3

M: Qu'est-ce qu'on va manger ce soir?

W: Puisqu'il fait si chaud je préparerai quelque chose de léger.

Listen to exchange 4.

Exchange 4

M: Si on allait à la plage ce week-end?

W: Ne pourrait-on pas faire autre chose? J'ai déjà eu un coup de soleil cet été et je dois faire attention à ma peau.

Listen to exchange 5.

Exchange 5

M: Je crève de faim et j'ai mal au cou. Essayons de trouver une aire.

W: Bonne idée. Arrêtons-nous.

Listen to exchange 6.

Exchange 6

W: Papa, tu as ta carte bleue; il me faut 30 euros.

M: Mais dis donc, le distributeur de billets n'est pas un puits magique, ma chérie!

Listen to exchange 7.

Exchange 7

M: J'ai visité le Parc Astérix, hors de Paris. C'était génial!

W: Quelle attraction as-tu aimée le plus?

Listen to exchange 8.

Exchange 8

W: Regarde mes photos, elles sont sensationnelles!

M: Mais comment as-tu pu les développer si vite?

Listen to exchange 9.

Exchange 9

W: J'ai envie de faire un riz au lait cet après-midi.

M: Chouette ! Mais n'y mets pas de raisins secs, s'il te plaît, je le préfère nature.

Listen to exchange 10.

Exchange 10

W: Je constate que l'alliance de Mme Saulnier est la plus belle que j'aie jamais vue. J'aimerais bien féliciter son mari sur son choix exquis.

M: Ce n'est pas possible. Elle est veuve.

Listen to exchange 11.

Exchange 11

M: Mais quelle mine tu as ! Qu'est-ce qui ne va pas ?

W: J'ai le cafard, et en plus la teinturerie a perdu mon pull préféré.

Listen to exchange 12.

Exchange 12

M: J'ai toujours voulu voler au bord du Concorde.

W: Tu as raté ton coup ! Le Concorde n'est plus en service.

Listen to exchange 13.

Exchange 13

W: Mince, mon séchoir ne marche plus et je viens de me laver les cheveux !

M: Ne peux-tu pas les laisser sécher naturellement ?

Listen to exchange 14.

Exchange 14

M: C'est la canicule ! Il fait trop chaud pour respirer ! Je meurs de chaleur !

W: Tu exagères ! Viens t'asseoir sous la banne et je t'apporterai une boisson froide.

Listen to exchange 15.

Exchange 15

M: Auriez-vous vu mes clés quelque part, Mademoiselle ?

W: Lesquelles Monsieur, celles du bureau ou vos clés domestiques ?

Dialogues

> **Directions:** Listen to the following dialogues. Afterward, listen to the questions based on the dialogue you have just heard and choose the best answer from the choices that follow. You will hear each question twice. Blacken the corresponding oval on your answer sheet.

Now get ready for the first dialogue.

Dialogue 1: Le Départ

M: À quelle heure devons-nous compter être à l'aéroport demain matin ?

W: Tu sais qu'il est préférable d'arriver bien avant le départ.

M: Au juste, si le décollage est pour 10 heures, essayons d'y arriver avant 8 heures.

W: Ça ne va pas suffire ! Avec les bagages et les contrôles, il vaudrait mieux compter sur trois heures d'avance.

M: Alors, il faudrait quitter la maison à 5 heures du petit matin !

W: Et si tu veux être sûr d'éviter les embouteillages, même plus tôt !

M: Après tout, ce sera un soulagement d'y être bien avant l'heure. C'est décidé, on s'en ira à 4 heures et demie.

W: Les bagages sont déjà faits, nous pouvons les descendre tout à l'heure et les mettre aussitôt dans le coffre.

M: Tu vas étaler nos passeports, les billets, les clés et nos portefeuilles, comme d'habitude, avant de te coucher ?

W: Absolument, avec nos habits de voyage et tes lunettes. Tu seras responsable de l'appareil photo et du Guide Michelin.

M: Ça y est, j'irai faire le plein maintenant.

16. Finissez cette phrase: "Il est evident que . . ."

17. N'auront-ils pas faim s'ils partent si tôt?

18. Comment savons-nous que leur départ sera tranquille et pas pressé?

19. Partagent-ils la responsabilité également?

Now get ready for the next dialogue.

Dialogue 2: La Poupée

W: Gérard, viens voir cette poupée qui bronze! Elle est adorable!

M: Comment ça se fait? C'est inouï!

W: Je ne sais pas, mais elle arrive munie de lunettes de soleil, un bikini, et sa propre petite serviette.

M: Fais voir. Mmm, il paraît que toutes les parties du corps exposées au soleil prendront couleur si elles sont en contact avec la serviette! Tiens, il y a même une petite ombrelle.

W: Je suis sûre que Chantal s'en raffolera. Qu'en penses-tu?

M: Tu as raison, elle est vraiment mignonne et Chantal pourra l'amener avec nous en vacances.

W: Cadeau de Noël ou d'anniversaire?

M: Attendons jusqu'à sa fête au mois de juin; ce sera parfait.

W: D'accord, mais j'ai hâte de la lui offrir.

M: Pourquoi ne pas en prendre deux, puisque sa petite copine Christiane nous accompagne en vacances cette année.

W: J'aurai dû penser à cela. Tu es un ange. Quelle idée sympathique!

20. Dans quel rayon se trouve ce couple?

21. Combien de petites filles ont-ils selon vous?

22. Est-ce qu'ils sont d'accord sur cet achat?

23. Quelles sortes de vacances vont-il faire?

24. C'est une nouveauté, cette poupée?

Now get ready for the next dialogue.

Dialogue 3: Les Voisins

W: Nos nouveaux voisins sont si gentils !

M: Je les aime bien aussi, ils sont très sympa. Ah, la jeunesse, que de choses les attendent !

W: Tu parles ! Elle est enceinte de quatre mois.

M: Formidable ! Tu te souviens de la naissance de Martine ? Nous étions si jeunes !

W: Ouais ! Comme c'était hier ! Mais nous avions nos parents pour nous guider et nous aider. Ces jeunes n'ont personne au monde.

M: Ils vont se débrouiller . . . tu sais, je pourrais repeindre le vieux berceau.

W: Et moi . . . tricoter quelques petits chaussons . . .

M: Je téléphonerai à Claude. Il est bricoleur . . .

W: Qu'est-ce que nous allons nous amuser . . .

M: Tous les voisins voudront aider !

W: Qu'est-ce que tu penses de Claudine, comme nom de fille ?

M: Et si c'est un garçon ?

25. Croyez-vous que ces gens aient aimé être parents ?

26. Qu'est-ce qu'ils ressentent à part la bonne volonté ?

27. Comment le jeune couple va-t-il recevoir l'amitié de leurs voisins ?

28. Les jeunes parents, comment savent-ils élever un enfant ?

Now get ready for the next dialogue.

Dialogue 4: Au revoir au franc

M: Étant collectionneur de monnaie assez fana, j'avais le cœur brisé pendant l'hiver de 2001 quand il a fallu abandonner le franc français.

W: Comme nous tous, dire au revoir à la Marianne et son bonnet phrygien . . . c'était pénible pour tous les Français.

M: Oui, plus on était âgé, plus c'était triste.

W: Vous vous y êtes habitué finalement ?

M: En 2000, l'an durant, je faisais un petit triage sur place chaque fois que je recevais de la monnaie, après mon café, après un achat quelconque, et cela pour mettre de côté les plus belles pièces.

W: Moi aussi, j'ai conservé quelques pièces qui allaient disparaître.

M: J'ai même commandé une collection belle épreuve des derniers francs pour me consoler de leur perte éventuelle.

W: C'était la fin d'une époque.

M: Eh oui, mais peu à peu mon âme de collectionneur s'est remise. Il fallait que je ramasse les nouveaux euros !

29. Presque tout le monde a gardé quelques francs. Pourquoi ?

30. En fin de compte l'euro réjouit le cœur du numismate. Comment ?

31. Le changement monétaire était le plus dur pour qui ?

32. Où peut-on commander une collection belle épreuve,* selon vous ?

* une collection belle épreuve = *a proof set of coins*

Section II

Part C: Speaking

Get ready for the speaking part of the Advanced Placement French Language Practice Test 1.

You have one minute and 30 seconds to look at the following series of five pictures and to answer the questions that accompany them. You will have 60 seconds to respond to each question. Read the questions carefully and listen attentively. You must answer each question.

Your score on this section will be based on how well you understand the question asked, as well as your answer. Your response to each question will be scored on its appropriateness, its grammatical correctness, and your pronunciation. The purpose of this part of the test is to get a full sample of your speaking capability. Answer each question to the best of your ability. Your answers should be long enough to use all of the time allotted for each response.

In the event that you are still answering the question when you hear the speaker say, "Listen to the next question," end your response so that you will not miss the next question. Don't worry if your response to the question isn't finished. If you catch yourself making an error while you are speaking, simply correct it. You will hear a tone that signals for you to begin speaking.

You may now turn the page and begin to study the first series of pictures. You have one minute and 30 seconds.

Now get ready to listen to the questions. You will have 60 seconds to answer each one. Speak after the tone.

Speaking A (Perdre du poids)

1.   Racontez l'histoire présentée dans cette série d'images.

2.   Expliquez pourquoi beaucoup de gens ont de la difficulté à suivre un régime.

3.   Selon vous, quels sont les attributs nécessaires pour réussir à son but, quel qu'il soit ?

Now get ready to listen to the questions. You will have 60 seconds to answer each one.

Speaking B (Au Volant)

4.   Contrastez comment ces deux personnes se comportent au volant.

5.   Qui est le meilleur conducteur selon vous ?

6.   Est-il possible de bien faire attention à la route en tenant un portable ou une boisson à la main ?

AP French

Test 2 Transcript

SECTION I

Part A: Listening

Exchanges

Get ready for the listening part of the Advanced Placement French Language Practice Test 2.

Directions: Listen to the following brief exchanges between two people. You will hear each exchange twice. Then, based on what you have just heard, choose the most likely rejoinder from the four choices you are given. Blacken the corresponding oval on your answer sheet.

Now listen to the first exchange.

Exchange 1

W: Qu'est-ce qu'il y a à la télé ce soir?

M: France Deux a ton feuilleton "Sous le Soleil" à dix-huit heures suivi du "Maillon faible" et puis la pub et les informations.

Listen to exchange 2.

Exchange 2

W: Je viens d'acheter une nouvelle voiture. Elle est si petite et facile à garer. Regarde par la fenêtre . . . j'en suis si contente!

M: Dis donc, c'est la Smart Car de Mercedes! J'ai lu qu'elle était très solide et consommait peu, et . . . tu as choisi la décapotable? C'est archichouette!

Listen to exchange 3.

Exchange 3

M: Mon frère s'est cassé le nez hier.

W: Oh non, le pauvre ! Comment va-t-il ?

Listen to exchange 4.

Exchange 4

M: Tu veux jouer aux dames ou aux échecs ?

W: Tu gagnes toujours et aux dames et aux échecs ! Jouons aux cartes !
Belote ?

Listen to exchange 5.

Exchange 5

M: Tiens ! La souris ne répond plus. Regarde, la flèche ne bouge même
pas. Comment me brancher pour lire mon courrier électronique ?

W: Ce n'est que la poussière. Ouvre la souris et sors la boule. Tu verras
des moutons à l'intérieur. Voici une tige mouillée d'alcool. Quelquefois je les retire avec des pincettes.

Listen to exchange 6.

Exchange 6

W: Papa, tu sais quoi ? J'ai vu sur l'Internet un bouquin Fantômas exactement comme celui de Pépé. Il valait presque 200 euros !

M: Dis donc ! Dommage que ce soit le seul qui me reste. J'ai dû jeter les
autres à cause de la moisissure.

Listen to exchange 7.

Exchange 7

W: Mémère m'a offert cette drôle de poupée qu'elle avait quand elle était
toute petite. Je n'en ai jamais vu de pareille.

M: Mais c'est Bécassine ! Tu ne la connais pas ? Je ne me suis jamais
senti si . . .

Listen to exchange 8.

Exchange 8

W: Les voisins nous invitent à leur mas en Provence !

M: C'est gentil mais tu sais que je supporte très mal la chaleur du Midi.

Listen to exchange 9.

Exchange 9

W: Tante Mireille veut savoir si nous pouvons accueillir la famille cette année pour le Réveillon. J'aimerais bien le faire. Crois-tu qu'on puisse finir les travaux à temps ?

M: Franchement pas. Pour la Saint Sylvestre peut-être.

Listen to exchange 10.

Exchange 10

M: Veux-tu bien te dépêcher un peu ! Je ne veux pas être en retard ce soir. Allez, pousse ta viande !

W: Tu pourrais quand même me laisser faire ma toilette en paix. Après tout, tu as failli rater ton train ce matin, et si ce n'était pas pour moi, tu serais toujours au lit !

Listen to exchange 11.

Exchange 11

M: J'ai envie de donner un petit lapin aux enfants. Ça leur ferait plaisir et ils pourraient apprendre à être responsables.

W: Ah non, Thierry, c'est une mauvaise idée ! Je te prie de trouver un autre cadeau. Après quelques semaines toute cette responsabilité tombera sur moi ! Je le sais !

Listen to exchange 12.

Exchange 12

M: J'ai remarqué que l'essuie-glace côté volant grince.

W: Oui, j'ai oublié de te le mentionner, mais c'est vraiment irritant. Pouvons-nous le réparer ?

Listen to exchange 13.

Exchange 13

W: Sylvie veut suivre des leçons de karaté. Je préférerais qu'elle choi-
sisse un instrument de musique comme ses frères.

M: On a assez de musiciens. Qu'elle fasse ce qu'elle veut. D'ailleurs c'est
une très bonne idée !

Listen to exchange 14.

Exchange 14

W: Papa, je voudrais me faire percer le nombril.

M: Jamais de la vie, et surtout pas tant que je marche sur terre !

Listen to exchange 15.

Exchange 15

W: Chéri, tu ronfles !

M: Tu exagères ! Je respire à fond, c'est tout !

Dialogues

Directions: Listen to the following dialogues. Afterward, listen to the questions
based on the dialogue you have just heard and choose the best answer
from the choices that follow. You will hear each question twice. Blacken the
corresponding oval on your answer sheet.

Now get ready for the first dialogue.

Dialogue 1: Le Portefeuille

W: Zut et rezut ! Mon portefeuille, où il est ? Il n'est pas dans mon sac, je
. . . je l'avais pourtant tout à l'heure !

M: J'irai regarder dans la voiture. Tu l'auras laissé sur le tableau de bord,
ou bien sur le siège avant.

W: D'accord. Entre-temps je déballe mes achats et je cherche le ticket de
caisse. Il doit y avoir le numéro de Carrefour là-dessus.

M: Rien dans la bagnole. Tu as téléphoné ?

W: C'est ce que j'allais faire mais je n'ai pas encore trouvé le sacré
ticket !

M: Calme-toi ! Le voilà, vas-y. S'ils l'ont trouvé j'irai le récupérer tout de suite.

W: Ah ! Je l'ai laissé à la caisse ! Oh, que je suis bête. Quel embarras ! Ma carte bleue, mon permis de conduire, presque trois cents euros en argent liquide . . . Ce n'est pas possible !

M: Arrête ! Tu vas craquer, Je . . . oh là . . . ton portable sonne . . . Oui . . . ben oui . . . oui, merci ! C'était Carrefour. Ils ont trouvé ton portefeuille, comme tu disais, à la caisse.

W: Oh ciel ! Quel soulagement ! Tu vas me le chercher ?

M: Il faut que tu viennes le chercher en personne, chérie ! Allez, en route !

16.   Où la dame avait-elle laissé son portefeuille ?

17.   Qu'est-ce qu'elle venait de faire ?

18.   Son mari, va-t-il récupérer le portefeuille à sa place ?

19.   Pourquoi son mari cherche-t-il dans la voiture ?

Now get ready for the next dialogue.

Dialogue 2: Le Bleu

W: D'où vient ce bleu sur ton front ? Il est affreux !

M: Tu ne trouves pas qu'il met en valeur le bleu de mes yeux ?

W: Sois sérieux. Raconte. Il est au beau milieu des yeux . . . ça te fait loufoque comme ça !

M: Je n'ose pas te dire comment je l'ai fait. Tu vas t'amuser en te moquant de moi.

W: Je te jure, pas un mot moqueur ! Vraiment, tu peux me croire. Moi, taquinerais-je ?

M: Bon, ben, je ratissais les feuilles mortes. Je les avais mises en tas ici et là. Il y en avait autant . . . des feuilles jusqu'aux mollets partout . . . et j'étais en train de les ramasser quand . . .

W: Ne dis plus un mot ! Je craque déjà. Ah c'est trop beau !

M: . . . et ta promesse de ne pas me taquiner . . .

W: Tu as laissé le râteau par terre, les pointes en l'air . . .

M: C'est ça. Je ne pouvais pas le voir . . .

W: Et tu as marché là-dessus en te cognant la tête . . . du manche . . . comme dans les dessins animés . . .

M: . . . Voilà, c'est un peu ridicule, quoi . . .

W: Un peu ridicule ? C'est le comble !

20. Selon vous, est-ce que cette fille taquine souvent ?

21. Où était ce bleu ?

22. Pourquoi ne pouvait-il pas voir le râteau ?

23. Où travaillait-il ?

24. Est-il sérieux en demandant si le bleu fait ressortir la couleur de ses yeux ?

Now get ready for the next dialogue.

Dialogue 3: Le Prêt

W: Alors tu vas à la banque pour finaliser ton prêt ce matin ?

M: Oui. Mon dossier est en ordre et mon avocat y sera aussi.

W: N'oublie pas de mettre ta nouvelle cravate !

M: Celle-ci ? D'accord. Oui, Tu as raison . . . (*il met la cravate*). Me connaissez-vous, Madame ? Permettez-moi de me présenter, Gabriel-André Gautier, homme d'affaires !

W: Un jour ce ne sera pas si marrant. Alors bonne chance, mon pote. Tu as ta serviette . . .

M: Quand je rentrerai, je serai déjà propriétaire de mon propre studio . . . C'est mon rêve, tu sais . . .

W: Oui, chéri, c'est le mien aussi.

M: Alors je m'en vais . . .

W: Oui, vas-y et courage ! Tout ira bien, je le sens.

M: Au revoir ! On va faire sauter les bouchons à mon retour !

W: Au revoir, mon PDG !

25. Quel est le ton de la femme ?

26. Que veut dire *PDG* ?

27. Qu'est-ce qu'il devra faire, ce Monsieur, après l'ouverture de son studio ?

28. Est-ce que sa femme partage ses idées pour l'avenir ?

Now get ready for the next dialogue.

Dialogue 4: Au Restaurant

W: Qu'est-ce qu'il y a de bon? J'ai faim!

M: Pour moi, ce serait l'entrecôte grillée, pommes de terre dauphines et une salade verte.

W: Tu ne devrais pas prendre de bœuf, tu sais . . . il y a des risques . . .

M: Quels risques? Tu ne veux pas dire la vache folle. Écoute, c'est du Charolais; il n'y a rien de mieux* au monde!

W: Je renonce à la viande, moi.

M: Comment, la petite végétarienne californienne! Depuis quand, ça?

W: Depuis que mon cholestérol est trop élevé! Et c'est . . . c'est plus naturel, les fruits, les légumes . . .

M: Naturel! C'est la goutte qui fait déborder le vase! Figure-toi que l'homme chasse et consomme la viande depuis qu'il a mis les pieds sur terre. Il n'y a rien de plus naturel! Je parie qu'il n'y avait pas de végétariens cro-magnons!

W: Je prendrais des artichauts au four, des carottes râpées et du céleri rave! Qu'est-ce qu'on va boire, mon homme des cavernes?

* Rien de mieux *is grammatically incorrect but people persist in saying it anyway.*

29. La femme se laisse-t-elle convaincre par les propos de son mari?

30. Pourquoi ne doit-elle pas prendre de viande?

31. Qu'est-ce que c'est que le Charolais?

32. Qu'est-ce qu'elle commande?

Section II

Part C: Speaking

Get ready for the speaking part of the Advanced Placement French Language Practice Test 2.

You have one minute and 30 seconds to look at the following series of five pictures and to answer the questions that accompany them. You will have 60 seconds to respond to each question. Read the questions carefully and listen attentively. You must answer each question.

Your score on this section will be based on how well you understand the question asked, as well as your answer. Your response to each question will be scored on its appropriateness, its grammatical correctness, and your pronunciation. The purpose of this part of the test is to get a full sample of your speaking capability. Answer each question to the best of your ability. Your answers should be long enough to use all of the time allotted for each response.

In the event that you are still answering the question when you hear the speaker say, "Listen to the next question," end your response so that you will not miss the next question. Don't worry if your response to the question isn't finished. If you catch yourself making an error while you are speaking, simply correct it. You will hear a tone that signals for you to begin speaking.

You may now turn the page and begin to study the first series of pictures. You have one minute and 30 seconds.

Now get ready to listen to the questions. You will have 60 seconds to answer each one. Speak after the tone.

Speaking A (La Glace)

1. Racontez ce qui arrive dans cette série de dessins.

2. Bien que les rapports entre frères et sœurs ne soient pas toujours harmonieux d'un jour à l'autre, comment la sœur aînée réagit-elle ?

3. D'après vous, quelles sont les responsabilités des aînés envers leurs cadets ?

Now get ready to listen to the questions. You will have 60 seconds to answer each one.

Speaking B (Les Oignons)

4. Comparez et contrastez ce que vous penseriez si vous voyiez le premier dessin sans voir le suivant.

5. Les apparences sont souvent trompeuses. Commentez l'idée de ne pas trop vite tirer une conclusion.

6. Avez-vous jamais pleuré de joie ? Pourquoi pleure-t-on si on est heureux ?

AP French
Test 3 Transcript

SECTION I

Part A: Listening

Exchanges

Get ready for the listening part of the Advanced Placement French Language Practice Test 3.

Directions: Listen to the following brief exchanges between two people. You will hear each exchange twice. Then, based on what you have just heard, choose the most likely rejoinder from the four choices you are given. Blacken the corresponding oval on your answer sheet.

Now listen to the first exchange.

Exchange 1

W: Mathieu, peux-tu me prêter 50 balles?
M: Et tu me rembourseras à la Saint Glinglin! Je ne crois pas!

Listen to exchange 2.

Exchange 2

W: Ma sœur va se marier!
M: Encore? On dit qu'à chaque femme il faut un mari intermédiaire!

Listen to exchange 3.

Exchange 3

W: J'ai les cuisses trop fortes !

M: Mais non, tu es belle, je n'aime pas ces mannequins maigrichons ! Toi, t'es une vraie femme !

Listen to exchange 4.

Exchange 4

M: Dépêchons-nous, toute la bande nous attend au cinéma.

W: Pas besoin de nous presser, ils nous tiendront des places et il y aura la pub d'abord, tu sais.

Listen to exchange 5.

Exchange 5

M: J'ai démissionné ce matin !

W: Comment cela, tu as quitté ton boulot ? Pourquoi ?

Listen to exchange 6.

Exchange 6

W: Je contemple la chirurgie pour améliorer ma vision. Je suis nulle sans lunettes et j'en ai assez de les mettre.

M: Dis donc ! Ça ne se défait pas ! Il faut que tu réfléchisses bien avant de le faire.

Listen to exchange 7.

Exchange 7

W: Je trouve que le maître-nageur est mignon !

M: Tu trouves que tous les maîtres-nageurs sont mignons !

Listen to exchange 8.

Exchange 8

W: Voici mes chaussons de bébé ! Maman les gardait dans une boîte avec du papier de soie. Je trouve ça touchant.

M: Ce n'est rien, elle a nos dents de lait quelque part dans une enveloppe.

Listen to exchange 9.

Exchange 9

W: Je vais au centre commercial avec Mado. On mangera sur le pouce là-bas. Pourrais-tu donner à manger aux enfants . . . et bien sûr à Mic-Mac ?

M: Pas de problème pour le dîner, mais ne dépense pas trop !

Listen to exchange 10.

Exchange 10

W: Quelle journée noire et morne. C'est agaçant ! Le mois de février est interminable !

M: Bof ! Et moi . . . qui le croyais le plus court !

Listen to exchange 11.

Exchange 11

M: Je vais aider Benoît et Gaston avec leurs collections de timbres cet après-midi après l'école. On va tout organiser.

W: Excellente idée ! Je débarrasserai la table dans la salle à manger pour que vous puissiez y travailler.

Listen to exchange 12.

Exchange 12

M: Tu sais, je crois que je commence à perdre des cheveux. Ne crois-tu pas que mon front se dégarnit un peu?

W: Ce n'est pas vraiment remarquable, chéri, et d'ailleurs, tu peux toujours laisser pousser la barbe! . . . De toute façon, je t'aimerai n'importe comment.

Listen to exchange 13.

Exchange 13

W: J'ai échoué à mon examen de chimie, et je n'ose pas le dire à Maman et Papa! Ma vie est terminée!

M: J'ai eu un 18, moi. On a deux semaines avant le prochain. Je t'aiderai chaque soir et tu l'auras cette fois, pas besoin d'inquiéter les parents.

Listen to exchange 14.

Exchange 14

W: Si nous sortions prendre l'air?

M: J'allais mettre mes pantoufles!

Listen to exchange 15.

Exchange 15

W: Je viens de faire 3 kilomètres à pied. Ah, ça fait du bien!

M: Tu n'es pas à bout de souffle?

Dialogues

Now get ready for the first dialogue.

Dialogue 1: Les Étoiles

W: Viens t'asseoir à côté de moi sur la terrasse. Les étoiles sont éblouissantes !

M: Tu veux à boire ?

W: Un blanc frais serait plaisant, merci bien !

M: Voilà ton vin, oh là, tu avais raison, quel spectacle !

W: Oui, pas de nuages, on voit si clair.

M: Santé, chérie !

W: Ah ! Santé. Tu sais, quand tu es loin de nous, je regarde les étoiles et je pense que les mêmes étoiles que je vois ici sont visibles là, où tu es, et qu'elles veillent sur nous deux ! Et je me sens moins seule.

M: Je n'ai jamais pensé à cela, mais tu as raison. Choisissons une étoile !

W: Comment ? Qu'est-ce que tu veux dire ?

M: Alors tu vois par exemple, celle-là. La cheville gauche du chasseur ? C'est Rigel. Quand on n'est pas ensemble on regardera la même étoile en même temps, et on sentira un peu la présence de l'autre.

W: J'adore cette idée ! La nôtre sera Sirius, là-haut, l'étoile *chien*, parce que c'est la plus brillante de toutes et on ne manquera pas à la trouver. D'accord, c'est la nôtre, mais ne le dis pas à Mic-Mac !

16. Si les étoiles sont éblouissantes, comment sont-elles ?

17. Que fera le couple après avoir prononcé *santè* ?

18. Quand son époux lui manque, que fait la femme ?

19. Décrivez le ciel cette nuit-là.

Now get ready for the next dialogue.

Dialogue 2: L'Au Pair

W: Papa, Mme Wilson, tu sais, la gentille Anglaise dans la rue de la Mé-
sange, elle m'invite à voyager en tant que jeune fille au pair avec son
mari et leurs deux enfants, c'est-à-dire si tu donnes ta permission,
bien sûr.

M: Où ça et quand ?

W: Ils vont partir pour trois mois en Italie et en Grèce. Oh Papa, j'aimerais
tant y aller, tu sais, j'aurais mon logement, ma nourriture, un petit
salaire à la semaine, je pourrais améliorer mon anglais, apprendre
l'italien . . .

M: Je connais M. Wilson, je l'aime bien . . . euh . . . il faudra demander à
ta mère aussi.

W: Maman est déjà d'accord et elle craque pour leurs enfants, ils sont
adorables avec leur petits accents, et pas gâtés . . .

M: Je vais réfléchir un peu . . .

W: Oh Papa, ils nous invitent tous pour expliquer leur itinéraire et répondre à tes questions. Dis oui . . .

M: Trois mois c'est long . . .

W: Je vais te manquer, c'est ça ? Ça va passer comme un clin d'œil . . . je
t'assure, et on a le courrier, le téléphone . . .

M: Tu promets de nous contacter chaque jour . . .

W: Je le jure, et deux fois le dimanche . . .

M: . . . Voilà, d'accord, tu embrasses ton vieux Papa ?

W: Oh merci, Papa, tu es top !

20. Est-ce que ce couple va rentrer en Angleterre ?

21. Pourquoi la jeune fille veut-elle devenir au pair ?

22. Comment sont les enfants de ce couple ?

23. Est-ce que la fille finit par convaincre son père ?

24. Quels progrès personnels la fille envisage-t-elle ?

Now get ready for the next dialogue.

Dialogue 3: Le Manuel de Latin

W: Viens vite Papa, Aubain a jeté son manuel de latin et il ne peut pas le repêcher !

M: Il l'a *jeté* ? Qu'est-ce que cela veut dire ? *Il l'a jeté* ?

W: Euh, il paraît qu'il en avait marre d'étudier, il s'est levé d'un bond et l'a jeté en l'air . . . juste comme ça . . . très haut. Il a poussé un cri de fou en même temps, je ne sais pas ce qui lui est arrivé . . .

M: Et ce manuel, où il est ?

W: . . . sur le toit, Papa.

M: Sur le toit, bien sûr, sur le toit . . . et pourquoi n'est-il pas venu me le dire lui-même ?

W: Je crois qu'il cherche l'échelle, Papa, mais elle est trop lourde pour un garçon de quinze ans, et j'ai peur qu'il ne se fasse mal. Oh viens Papa, avant qu'il n'essaie de la monter tout seul . . .

M: Oh, là (*à haute voix*) Aubain, attends, j'arrive . . .

25. Comment expliqueriez-vous le geste d'Aubain ?

26. Pourquoi ne peut-il pas récupérer son manuel ?

27. Aurait-il jeté son manuel de manière préconçue ?

28. Que dira le père à son fils à propos de cet acte, selon vous.

Now get ready for the next dialogue.

Dialogue 4: La Caravane

M: Où veux-tu aller en camping cet été ?

W: Cela m'est égal, chéri, on s'amuse toujours quand c'est toi qui fais l'itinéraire . . . mais à propos . . . je crois qu'on devrait acheter une caravane cette année, tu sais, avec une véritable petite cuisine, des lits, l'eau courante, un véritable abri roulant . . .

M: Mais ce n'est pas du camping, ça ! Dormir sous les étoiles, ça c'est du camping.

W: Quel âge tu as ?

M: Tu sais bien qu'on a tous les deux quarante-trois ans !

W: Pile ! Tu pourras mettre ton sac de couchage sous les étoiles si tu veux, mais on n'a plus l'âge de se réveiller dans la boue et de monter et défaire la tente à chaque escale.

M: Hmm, j'admets que j'avais un peu mal au dos l'an dernier, et . . . ce soir-là quand il pleuvait des hallebardes, on s'est vraiment trempé jusqu'aux os . . .

W: Tu vois, si nous avions une caravane nous pourrions tout faire et tout voir, même quand on sera plus âgé . . . je pense à l'avenir, quoi . . .

M: On pourrait aller les regarder si tu veux . . .

29. Quel est l'essentiel, selon la femme ?

30. Qu'est qu'elle entend, en disant *pile* ?

31. D'après vous, vont-ils éventuellement s'acheter une caravane ?

32. Pourquoi devraient-ils considérer l'achat d'une caravane selon le raisonnement féminin ?

Section II

Part C: Speaking

Get ready for the speaking part of the Advanced Placement French Language Practice Test 3.

You have one minute and 30 seconds to look at the following series of five pictures and to answer the questions that accompany them. You will have 60 seconds to respond to each question. Read the questions carefully and listen attentively. You must answer each question.

Your score on this section will be based on how well you understand the question asked, as well as your answer. Your response to each question will be scored on its appropriateness, its grammatical correctness, and your pronunciation. The purpose of this part of the test is to get a full sample of your speaking capability. Answer each question to the best of your ability. Your answers should be long enough to use all of the time allotted for each response.

In the event that you are still answering the question when you hear the speaker say, "Listen to the next question," end your response so that you will not miss the next question. Don't worry if your response to the question isn't finished. If you catch yourself making an error while you are speaking, simply correct it. You will hear a tone that signals for you to begin speaking.

You may now turn the page and begin to study the first series of pictures. You have one minute and 30 seconds.

Now get ready to listen to the questions. You will have 60 seconds to answer each one. Speak after the tone.

Speaking A (Les Bonbons)

1.   Racontez ce qui se déroule dans ces images.

2.   Croyez-vous que ces bonbons soient à la fillette ? Si non, à qui ?

3.   La fillette devrait-elle être punie parce qu'elle a chipé des bonbons qui ne lui appartenaient ?

Now get ready to listen to the questions. You will have 60 seconds to answer each one.

Speaking B (La Croissance)

4.   Comparez et contrastez les deux dessins.

5.   Discutez les rôles changeants de mère et de fils avec le passage du temps.

6.   Développez un lien entre le jeune arbre et le jeune homme, tous les deux nourris par la même mère.